ASTONISH ME!

ASTONISH ME!

First Nights That Changed the World

DOMINIC DROMGOOLE

P

PROFILE BOOKS

First published in Great Britain in 2022 by

Profile Books

29 Cloth Fair, Barbican, London EC1A 7JQ.

www.profilebooks.com

1 3 5 7 9 10 8 6 4 2

Typeset in Minion Pro and Blinker

to a design by Henry Iles.

A CIP catalogue record for this book is available from the British Library.

ISBN 978-1788166805

eISBN 978-1782837930

Printed and bound in Great Britain by Clays Ltd, Elcograf S.p.A.

For Siofra, Grainne and Cara,
with all my love

Contents

Introduction

ASTONISH ME!

In the film ***Shakespeare in Love***, its writer, Tom Stoppard, presents an abiding truth about human endeavour, and a particular one for the arts. It is always darkest before the dawn. It is only when the barriers are mountainous, the impossibilities annihilating, and the spirit broken, only when all hope has gone, that the miraculous occurs. The essence is gathered into a short scene and a pungent phrase. Fennyman, an aggrieved investor, has cornered Henslowe, the manager of the Rose Theatre, and is demanding when he will see a return on his investment. Henslowe rattles out his explanation:

> 'Let me explain to you about the theatre. The natural condition is
> one of insurmountable obstacles on the road to imminent disaster.'
> 'What do we do?' quizzes Fennyman.
> 'Nothing. Strangely enough it all turns out well.'
> 'How?'
> 'I don't know. It's a mystery.'

The final phrase makes all sorts of sense to anyone who has worked in any form of cultural endeavour, and has been astonished by how phoenixes, small and large, can arise from the ashes of burnt dreams. At the instant that all seems lost, words can be spoken, paint daubed or music played, and everything starts to make new sense. From the midst of panic and confusion, thoughts, tunes or feelings previously felt but unexpressed find a new voice. The skies start to clear. In the instant of its first expression, both the artists involved and those who give witness feel the air shift.

This book focuses, chapter by chapter, on a series of seismic first nights, ranging across different public art forms, across history and the globe. It is a celebration of the artistic achievements that overcame the odds to change the story of culture, and whose effects rippled out to change the world. Our opinions can be swayed by politicians, our understanding can be refreshed by philosophers, but, for our perception of the world and each other to be realigned, nothing can touch art.

The more we look into the origins of our artistic impulse, the more we see its public nature. Early theories that rock art was the expression of lonely primitive artists wandering away from the tribe to record inner feelings have given way to collaborative understandings. These spaces were used for shamanistic hoolies. Groups came together with music and dance, working in response to the art on the walls, to celebrate life, to summon spirits and to effect soul-swerves in the participants. The etched bison, the stencilled hands, the scratched boars, the horses in flight ghosting round the walls, were all part of a wider work which included bodies morphing in and out of smoke and firelight, with music driving the shindig along from horns, pipes and whirring strings. Acousticians have discovered that images are clustered at points of maximum resonance within the caves, where music could be amplified, as it later would be by the vaults of cathedrals.

Wagner coined the term *Gesamtkunstwerk* to describe the 'total work of art' he aspired to. For him it meant a synthesis of music, image, lighting and performance in the immersive experiences he desired. In this he believed himself an original. In fact he was within an old and unceasing tradition. Each of the events in this book creates an aura which envelops not only the elements of presentation, but brings into the circle the buildings that house them, and those who give witness. The earliest cave rituals – the painted bodies, their expressive movement, the art and the music – were *Gesamtkunstwerk*. When Thespis broke free from the chorus in the theatre of Dionysia, he was part of a unity which included the theatre, the Acropolis behind, and the sun-drenched hills in the distance. When a group of Parisian snobs crowded into a room in the Salon des Refusés to bark with laughter at Manet's *Le Déjeuner sur l'herbe*, they were part of a pattern of confrontation and reaction which defined the total work. When Fela Kuti danced, prophesied and sacrificed at his Shrine in Lagos, he and the crowd pushing through to dawn were part of a single dynamic entity.

An exhibition of iconoclastic art like *Sensation*, Stravinsky's ballet *The Rite of Spring*, the unveiling of a sculpture as bold as Michelangelo's *David* – all are accelerated in their subversion of the collective reality of their era by the presence of a crowd. The public bring shared time with them to an event, the scars and prejudices of history and the present. They also bring a future. A crowd can be an ugly or a static beast; it can also be wise and optimistic. Populism is much besmirched, but in its capacity for a jump towards something brighter, it can startle. The mob is often more tolerant, more radical and more progressive than the academy or the elite. All artists want to share their new reality, and the presence of a throng helps usher that along.

Each of these extraordinary events involved a vibrant dynamic between artist and audience. Scutty venues were crammed for the Sex Pistols, theatres packed for Oscar Wilde and Tennessee Williams, exhibition spaces crushed with people for Damien Hirst, festival fields overflowed for Ravi Shankar, queues reached around the block for Hitchcock's *Psycho*. Each artist knew how to create a story to pull in the punters. Whether Japan in the seventeenth century, or Lagos in the 1970s, a work of art is not itself alone, it is an aggregate of the attention of those looking.

Monteverdi's *L'Orfeo* is both the work itself and an accumulated impression within those who love the work. An experiment like *L'Orfeo* – a work which invented opera as a form – needs permission to exist. Just as we collaborate to invent fictions like money and religion, so new forms of art need collective assent. Miraculously, it can happen in an instant, when a group react with passion to something new. An old rhythm is disrupted by a new, and a door is opened when no-one knew the door was there.

When the isolation of lockdown eased, it felt rejuvenating to witness the glee with which we discovered afresh the joys of congregating. To be in a theatre again, to sense the palpable thrill of collective imagination, was like discovering storytelling for the first time. To hear music and dance in a group reawakened the sickly thrill of one's first disco. To look at art beside others was to recall how we open each other's eyes wider. It took a dearth to remind us how gathering together squeezes extra life and meaning into art.

The best art is not made for audiences, it is made with them.

This is a canon based on 'and' rather than 'or'. It is absurd to exclude someone because they are a portly, bewigged Hanoverian, just as it is daft to exclude an elegant young Black woman from Texas. Beyoncé and Handel, Arthur Miller and Lorraine Hansberry – each pushed at what was possible. The intricacy of Fela Kuti's music is celebrated with the same enthusiasm as Stravinsky's. The shock value of Sarah Kane's new theatre is measured against the new aesthetics of Nefertiti. There are artists here – Okuni in seventeenth-century Japan, or Xiao Lu in modern China – who have not been given the same weight of consideration. They are here, like all the rest, because their art had a seismic effect.

I have also tried to widen the net of those who contribute. The audience has an underrated role in allowing art, but so do a pool of collaborators in making it. When writing about Manet, I try to give an impression of the role played by his greatest model, Victorine Meurent. Hitchcock's film *Psycho*, and its signature shower sequence, would never have been achieved, without the commitment and the fatalistic imagination of its star, Janet Leigh. Handel could never have had the resounding effect of his first *Messiah* without Susannah Cibber. And where would Beyoncé be without Jay-Z? In several cases – the Sex Pistols, and the Young British Artists – it is the collective who were the art, the movement the milestone.

The narrative is not chronological since there is no desire to imply progress. The episodes dance from continent to continent and back and forwards across time. Now we have so much culture available, all alive in virtual simultaneity – imagery from all epochs in graphic detail on the internet, music from all ages at the touch of a button – any idea of progress has been thrown into confusion. When we listen to Tallis in a fine recording, or study Michelangelo's *David* online, the idea that either were rungs on some upward ladder of achievement is rendered absurd. Just as it is by time spent reading *Hamlet*, or staring upwards in the Pantheon.

Artists work within an understanding of the past, aware of their peers in the present, and enlivening the conversation for the future. Many make work in a state of flow – what the Welsh call *hwyl*. In that state they are not asserting their primacy over other artists (or not entirely); they are partaking in a simultaneity with other such actions in history. Stravinsky enjoyed the Russian folk-singing practice of overlaying different rhythms; cultural history is not dissimilar. Generations of makers fold their work into a present moment that encompasses the past, the fleeting present and the future, where all dissolve into a shining, still moment. A series of chakra points whence light illuminates the landscape. The map of those chakras is not a timeline, nor one of geography.

Courage and boldness are threads which enliven the fabric of each story. Excitement and adrenaline are stitched in alongside. Each moment of delivery is preceded by differing degrees of trauma. Fela Kuti had the Nigerian army set murderously against him; Okuni had the patriarchal rigidity of seventeenth-century Japan; Oscar Wilde, a society rigidly set against his preferred sexuality; Xiao Lu, the weight of the Chinese state. Breaking a mould is never easy. Artists know that, and somehow the audience sense the same.

When genuinely new work is being attempted, one can feel the static charge which electrifies a public space. Just as before a great party, the collective fear of failure creates a charged vacuum which everyone must respond to; so before a momentous first night, there is both emptiness and possibility. Only the bravest enter with confidence and start telling their story. To tell these tales from the past is not to celebrate conservatism and stasis, it is to celebrate revolt and disruption. Remembering these artists within their own context, rather than through the prism of our own moral codes, is the only way to see the width of the abysses they dared to leap.

Art thrives, too, on an enlargement of perspective. Beasts were drawn on walls in caves in part to understand them; animal headdresses were worn in shamanistic gatherings to see the world through their eyes.

Millenia later, Tolstoy, in *Anna Karenina*, whirls the reader from one character's standpoint to another, eliding invisibly from Anna to Levin to Vronsky to Karenin. In one's dizziness one falls from character to character, and world view to world view, until, out on a hunt, one finds oneself empathising with the grumbling of an overworked hunting dog. Through an act of centrifugal empathy, Tolstoy inveigles himself and his reader wholly into the canine perspective.

At the Bush Theatre, as a young producer, I was involved in mounting the quietly miraculous plays of Billy Roche, including one called *Belfry*. At its heart is a scene where a group of five people we have come to know and love gather for a birthday party. Played with a flitting lightness, the panicked rituals of creating the do, the quick and hysterical pleasures within it, and the identification earned for each character, whisk the audience into a state like ecstasy. The human truth comes to life, quick and transient, and we sense something beyond. When we see things from multiple perspectives, and are turned fast, we suddenly glimpse something outside each individuals viewpoint. Something clearer and more spacious. Call it truth or dharma or life, or what you will. On a nightly basis, it was there with Billy's play.

All the sensibilities collide and ignite access to something else floating alongside. Tennessee Williams articulated this idea: 'We see from the outside what we could not see within – a perception that could only occur through the detached eye of art. As if a ghost sat over the affairs of men and made a true record.' Chekhov, too – the master juggler of multiple perspectives – was always able to read the webs of reality in individual viewpoints, and to perceive the web of truth beyond.

In collaborative art, each of many perspectives are engaged. There is often a single artist at the centre, but alongside them are their subjects, their collaborators, and the audience that witnesses. At a certain point, within this divine tangle of prospects, the veil of each personality and the fog of each sensibility is whisked away by the scattering whizz of small particles of truth. Then the larger generosity of life sparkles.

Observation – acute observation – is close to the heart of love. Whether it is gazing on the glories of nature enabled by the bonanza of the sun, or of the art we make to understand our universe, the act of looking together has helped us to advance, and with joy. Our ability to observe and to connect together, to celebrate the 'is-ness' of the world we can see, and the world we cannot, is close to the best thing about us. This book is about the charged moments when we look as one, and when what we see washes our eyes bright and clean.

It is not hard to imagine a first night. Write a poem, make a sketch, or compose a tune. Let it express sincere feelings. Determine to say your poem to a parent, display your sketch to a lover, or sing your tune to good friends around a table. Before you unveil your creation, you will feel a quickening of the breath, a drumbeat of palpitation and a sharpening of focus. As you do, the air will seem to thicken, and the walls to bulge inward.

Imagine the same process when someone has something passionate to say, when they have spent careers finding the the tools to say it, when they have gathered an army of collaborators to make it happen, and when a crowded room is there to give witness. Take your own imagined first night and multiply the thickening of the air, and the closing of the walls by a thousand. Maximise your pounding heartbeat by the same, as the crowd's adrenaline produces a communal sharpness of terrifying lucidity. Envision that and you have any of the world's myriad first nights taking place as you read this.

Beyond such regular occurrences, conjure up the rarest. The moments when not just an individual's passions are to be exposed, but when the life of a whole community, the story of a tribe, or the concerns of humanity itself, are brought into a shared light. When a crowd come together to witness a creation which encapsulates their history and points them in a fresh direction. Moments of cultural singularity, as in physics, magnetic points in space and time, that suck in past and present and hurl out a reconfigured future. Moments that compel matter beyond to bend inwards, and torque it into new shapes.

Such charismatic events are the theme of this book.

• • •

1

Push On Out and Do Something Bigger

A TALE OF
LORRAINE HANSBERRY

8 PM, 10 MARCH 1959, BARRYMORE THEATRE, NEW YORK

The first and only Broadway preview of *A Raisin in the Sun* was about
to begin. Philip Rose, the show's producer, shuffled his way towards his
seat. For the preceding half hour he had been hiding in a cubicle in the
men's room. Short of breath, nauseous, his vision swirling with anxiety,
he looked through the gathering for the one person who could offer an
exit route from his panic.

The crowd were made up largely of theatre folk, mostly white. They
were drawn by the young Sidney Poitier, who enjoyed the fizzing aura
of an actor on the cusp of stardom, but not by much else. The advance
bookings were horrendous. The subject of the play, the determination
of a Black family to move to a white neighbourhood, was not a seller.
The producer, director and playwright had never worked on Broadway
before, so they weren't going to shift tickets. The fact that the director,
Lloyd Richards, was the first Black man to helm a Broadway show, and
the playwright the first woman of colour to write for the Great White

Way, should have ignited curiosity. But New York's radical audience would at best fill a third of the stalls for a single show. The other 99.99 per cent were not after an experiment; they wanted some razzle-dazzle.

Rose pushed through to the back of the stalls. His destination was the face that smiled towards him, a face with eyes steady, and lips wrinkled with a twist of humour: the playwright, only twenty-nine years old, and the wisest head in the room. She exuded calm and a mischievous sense of her destiny. She knew why she was there. In her presence, no matter the difficulties, everyone felt the angels were onside. They held hands, squeezing each other's fingers too tight.

This was the culmination of several years of mould-breaking, and taboo-busting. Everything depended on the next two nights. The play began. And was a bit dull. The production had played seven weeks out of town, and somehow it slouched. Everything was slow – the entrances, the movements, the words. Soon enough, the audience began that ancient ritual of disapproval, the communal cough. What, the coughs rumbled, was this play doing here?

At the first interval, an air of panic hovered over the polite applause, and a number of punters left. At the second, the press agent grabbed Rose, and said, 'We need to talk.' He dragged him off to a nearby bar, bought him a drink and talked tough. 'You can open tomorrow and post closing notices immediately. It'll get slaughtered. Or you can delay the opening for two weeks. I'll call Elia Kazan. He's a friend. He can redirect and do some rewriting. Maybe, just maybe, it can be fixed.'

This PR guy was a senior New York player: Philip Rose was a sweet newcomer. 'Why are you telling me this? There is nothing I can do.'

'This is New York. Look at this audience. You think they're enthusiastic?'

Rose stood up, winded. This was all his nightmares bunching together. 'Let me go and watch the end of the play. I can't accept those options. But I'll think about getting drunk.'

The applause at the end was polite, but a long way from celebratory. Rose, with some colleagues, fulfilled his pledge to get smashed. Soon, worse news arrived. They were up late enough to see the next day's papers. *Sweet Bird of Youth* by Tennessee Williams had just premiered and all seven major journals were full of praise for its wonders. Any theatre person knows the critics have a limited budget of goodwill, and you don't want them spending it before they visit your shop. For the Williams play, they had used up their superlatives not only for the week, but for the whole year.

During some light rehearsal the next day, the atmosphere was glum. Everyone acted brave, though the polite response of the night before had killed optimism. At six o'clock, flowers and gifts started arriving, and people began the roundelay from dressing room to dressing room, with rictus smiles, messages of hope and eyes of terror. The playwright spent the afternoon setting and styling her hair, and climbed into a chic black dress, set off by dazzling earrings. She walked up to the theatre with her husband from their apartment in West Village. An enclave formed around her in the fourth row of family and friends .

Lorraine Hansberry was about to arrive in history.

MAY 24 1963, 24 CENTRAL PARK SOUTH, MANHATTAN

In a flat belonging to his family, an extraordinary meeting is convened by the Attorney General, Robert Kennedy, brother to the President. In the southern states, a febrile state of tension, pressure cooking for over a century, is poised to explode. The long sickness of segregation and exclusion, and the institutionalised racism which underpins it, has been focused in street battles in Birmingham, Alabama. The crisis has crystallised in a single image – a Black woman pushed to the ground by policemen and held down by an officer pressing his knee into her neck.

The meeting – of political and cultural leaders – is to discuss what can be done. The NAACP is there, and the lieutenants of Martin Luther King, together with Harry Belafonte and Lena Horne. So too is Lorraine Hansberry and her great friend, James Baldwin. There is a perception that Kennedy is flattering those present by inviting them into his home, allowing them an influence congruent with their exceptional status. Many are seduced by this. Some aren't.

One of those present, Jerome Smith, is neither celebrity nor political leader. He is a Freedom Rider from the South, one of those who boarded buses crossing the countryside and sat in areas designated 'Whites Only'. His reward has been frequent beatings by the police; he is in New York to have surgery on his jaw after one such beating. Smith does not know sophisticated New York manners, nor high-status deference and poise. He is from the streets. Before Kennedy can set an agenda, he goes off like a blunderbuss. He lambasts the lawmakers and law-keepers of the South, talking of his own brutalised experience in volcanic eruptions.

Robert Kennedy makes a clumsy play. He turns to the rest of the room with a 'who-is-this-guy?' look. He attempts to exclude Smith as an uncouth southerner and to guide the discussion back to political niceties. Many are prepared to allow this, overwhelmed by Kennedy's charisma. But not Lorraine. There are many reasons to love her, but few greater than for what she does next. James Baldwin said she had a capacity to tower over the room, even when sitting down. This is one such moment.

She interrupts Kennedy while he is talking, greatly to his surprise, and says: 'You have a great many very accomplished people in this room, Mr Attorney General; but the only man you should be listening to is that man over there [pointing at Smith]. That is the voice of twenty-two million people.' Kennedy stares flabbergasted, stopped in his tracks. What was supposed to be a Manhattan salon is proving more turbulent and less easy to accommodate than expected. Lorraine goes on: 'We are not remotely interested in the insulting concept of the exceptional negro, we are not remotely interested in tea at the White House ... We are one people and as far as we are concerned we are represented by the negroes on the streets of Birmingham ... We would like from you a moral commitment!'

Kennedy looks insulted. He and his family believe they own America's moral positions. As Smith continues, and Kennedy persists in ignoring him, Lorraine stands up again and sums up: 'What I am very worried about ... is the state of the civilisation which produced that photograph of the white cop standing on that Negro woman's neck in Birmingham.' With a thin smile at Kennedy, she walks out. Most follow.

Much about the meeting was repugnant to Lorraine, but mainly it was the invitation to become part of some exclusive club. For her, the cause wasn't to be represented by leaders and celebrities, it was being led by the Black working class. They were living the difficult lives and fighting the hardest battles. Their only representative in the room was

Jerome Lewis, and, if he didn't have the manners or the articulacy of Third Avenue, all the more reason to listen. The problem wasn't only racism, it was also top-tableism. It was not good enough to invite certain people to sit on a dais; the dais had to be levelled.

Some of the emotional overspill of this meeting can be seen in the interview Baldwin did straight after with a New York psychologist, Dr Kenneth Clark. He looks shocked and in the process of absorbing fresh truths. In this legendary piece of television, he picks up the words of his friend Lorraine, of the need for the US government to make 'a moral commitment'. Though Robert Kennedy thought the meeting had been useless, a month later his brother Jack proposed the legislation that would become the Civil Rights Act. When he did, he spoke of more than a political movement; he spoke of '*a moral commitment*'.

In the five years since her play opened, Lorraine Hansberry had come a long way. Even further than from her beginnings on Chicago's South Side.

THEY FOUGHT BACK!

Lorraine Hansberry was born on 19 May 1930, into a family set-up full of contradictions. She learnt early that fighting each day with grace and humour was the only way to avoid being crushed by them.

Her family lived in a working-class Black neighbourhood on the South Side of Chicago, yet their wealth and connections isolated them. Her father Carl was known as the 'Kitchenette King' and was a real estate entrepreneur among the Black community. His balancing act was a firm belief in both civil rights and capitalism. For him progression was getting ahead. Lorraine's uncle Leo was a pioneering scholar of African studies, a pupil of W.E.B. Du Bois, who himself taught both Kwame Nkrumah, the first Prime Minister of Ghana, and Nnamdi Azikiwe, the first President of Nigeria. Many of the tensions which played through Lorraine's life and art – assimilation vs opposition, communitarianism vs getting ahead, and how to balance the international and the local – were written into her story early.

As was the need to fight. As a child she remembered 'skinny little South Side bodies panting the hours away – with kids who fought – Blacks and whites'. Walking home from school, she would be a target for white kids because she was Black, and for Black kids because of her class. As she said of the South Side, 'Each piece of our living is a protest.' She never forgot the moment she saw a group of Black youths turning up with baseball bats to chase off a crowd of white racists: '*THEY FOUGHT BACK!!!*' Throughout her life, she would never shy from a scrap.

Her father fought one of the defining battles of the time. In 1937, real estate was the borderland of race relations in the northern states. Carl Hansberry had set his sights on living at 6140 Rhodes Avenue, Chicago, a building whose access was limited by a racially restrictive covenant. Enlisting the help of the NAACP, Carl went to war through the courts. Soon his family were under siege, a mob of angry whites patrolling outside. They were cursed and spat on when they went out. Lorraine's mother wandered their home at night with a Luger pistol. One evening a bladed block of cement was hurled through their window and lodged itself in plaster near the head of the seven-year-old Lorraine. After three years, they won their case in the Supreme Court.

These traumas Lorraine later chose to turn into art, in a play about people, their homes and communities. Given the freight of pain, it is astonishing how light and human her work is. The anguish was felt, but it was never allowed to conceal the messy comedy of life. Accuracy was what mattered. As she said over and over, the path to universality is through the specific. The family in her play, the Youngers, were not 'a general family, not a general Black family, not a US Black family, they were a Black family from the South Side of Chicago'.

Lorraine attended the University of Wisconsin. Her passion for drama ignited when she went to see Sean O'Casey's *Juno and the Paycock*. 'I remember sitting there consumed as that wail rose and hummed through the tenement, through Dublin, through Ireland itself, and then mingled with seas to become something of the Irish wail that was all of us ... ' She fell for both O'Casey and his earlier compatriot, J.M. Synge. She loved the honesty of their realism and its critical edge. They were not writing characters who were 'a credit to the race'; they loved the flaws of their Irishmen and Irish-women alongside their glories. They were using 'the most obvious instrument of Shakespeare: the human personality in its totality'. Their concern was not to judge, but to remove judgement, and allow life to flourish. Lorraine quoted the poet Weldon

Johnson's aspiration to follow the Irish: 'What the coloured poet in the US needs to do is something like Synge did for the Irish; he needs to find a form that will express the racial spirit by symbols from within rather than symbols from without'.

Lorraine had a rich collection of linguistic seams to mine, the blues and gospel rhythms of Chicago, street patois, the new ideological language of university graduates, old phrases from the South, and the precision of her own poetry. O'Casey and Synge demonstrated how these languages could come alive in the mouths of ebullient and independent people.

FREEDOM IN NEW YORK

The world was shifting as Lorraine Hansberry was a student. Colonialism was coming to an end, the Cold War falling into rigid place, and America fissuring on ideological lines. Leaving Wisconsin, she headed for New York and to Greenwich Village, learning its manners and its arrogances, and it was not long before she was agitating. Hansberry was born to exemplify Joe Hill's exhortation to organise. She joined any leftist society which passed her eye, and soon grew to lead them. An eager debater, she honed her skills at Speakers' Corner in Harlem, coming to the attention of W.E.B. DuBois and the icon of radicalism, Paul Robeson.

She moved uptown to Harlem, and joined the tiny editorial staff of the journal *Freedom*, founded by Robeson. Here she resourced, received and edited articles, and began to write her own. *Freedom* was pitched well to the left of the NAACP, aiming to conjoin civil rights with revolutionary socialism. Lorraine was soon knocking out essays on anti-colonialism, civil rights and feminism. Argument has raged over whether she was a socialist first and a Black nationalist second, or vice versa. Or maybe for her they were dynamic and provocative companions pushing each other further. What she knew was that it was dangerous to settle on a single right, and that morality was always moving forward. Her instincts also told her the most dangerous people were those without humour. All the while, she fed her curiosity in theatre, enjoying evenings on and off Broadway. Friends recall her reciting chunks of Shakespeare, Chekhov, Synge, Arthur Miller and more. And they remembered her desire to talk theatre at any opportunity, besting them all with her knowledge.

Along the way she married Robert Nemiroff, a Jewish New Yorker. It is a relationship which defies diagnosis, and seems to have been born of shared political beliefs as much as passion. Nemiroff could be controlling after her death in management of her estate, but it is hard not to admire the depth of his commitment to her talent. Lorraine's passions were reserved for her own sex. Typical of her, as soon as she was assured of her sexuality, she joined the appropriate society, a group called the Daughters of Bilitis, and started writing for their journal, *The Ladder*. Lorraine was intersectional long before the word was coined; happy to fight on behalf of her sexuality, her gender, her race, and all.

By a lucky break, though Nemiroff might not have been able to offer much love, he allowed her financial independence. He and a friend co-wrote the song 'Cindy, Oh Cindy', a piece of harmless pap which was such a number 1 smash hit it bought Hansberry the freedom and time to write. Now she could fight with art as well as activism. At a time when few Black writers had ever been produced on Broadway – and no Black woman ever – the very commitment to write was a challenge to the status quo.

BANANA CREAM PIE

One Saturday evening in 1957, Lorraine invited her friend Philip Rose to dinner at her apartment in Greenwich Village at 337 Bleecker Street. They were theatregoing companions and she wanted to read him sections from a play she was working on. She served spaghetti and banana cream pie, then read her scenes. A fire was lit in her friend's imagination.

When he went home, the characters he had met in Lorraine's play were still alive and chatty in his head. So much so that he couldn't sleep. He had to meet this family again. At six-thirty in the morning, he rang Lorraine.

'I want to produce your play.'

'Are you nuts? It's the middle of the night..

'I want to – I can't sleep..

'I'm sorry you can't sleep. It's probably my cooking. Call me when it's daylight. And take a Tums.'

They spoke the next day. Rose's passion was persuasive enough to bypass the fact that his producing experience amounted to zero. They started bold, and continued so, hiring a Black director, Lloyd Richards, another first for Broadway. Lorraine carried on finishing her play, while Rose read books and manuals on how to produce, then started looking for money, a Sisyphean task which would consume the next two years. As they defined it, all looked hopeful apart from two obstacles; no-one would invest in the play and no-one would give them a theatre.

Regular backers did not believe an audience would come out to watch Black characters *emoting*. Some producers flirted with the project but demanded changes which undermined the play's integrity; or they wanted a new director; or to downgrade the enterprise by hiding the production in a small theatre. One general manager told them to delay. 'How long?' they asked. 'Ten, twenty years. The world may be ready by then'. Though the play is quiet and domestic, to these theatre owners it seemed to endanger the fabric of their buildings.

Yet miracles started occurring. A surprise cheque from here, an unforeseen commitment from there. The courage and the goodness were there, though lagging way behind what they needed. Securing a star would be the key.

TALK TO MY AGENT

Sidney Poitier had just filmed *The Defiant Ones* and *Porgy and Bess* and his star was in the ascendant. He had the special charisma of an energy about to break. Lorraine and Rose knew him from the Village scene, and invited him round to hear a mysterious new play, telling him Lorraine was going to read all the parts, though not that she was the author. After drinks and chat, Lorraine started. Soon, they were transported from Central Park West to a small apartment in Chicago. Poitier laughed and leant forward into the story.

At the end of the second act, he insisted on knowing the writer. They told him to guess. They laughed as he went through a list of big names, and they shook their heads. His last shot was the biggest name in town, the poet Langston Hughes, which delighted them all the more. Then, in shared recognition, they all shouted together, 'Lorraine Hansberry!' Poitier was fulsome in praise, then, rightly suspecting he had been set up, said he had to rush, and left. This was a relief to Lorraine, since her third act was still a shambles. But, once it was complete, it was sent to the star.

By this time Rose was in hospital, partly from exhaustion at the efforts to raise money. He was lying in bed, when he was told that Poitier had come to visit.

'I've read your play. How sick are you?'

'Sick enough that it won't matter what you think. Take your best shot.'

'Well, I have to tell you that I've decided, regretfully – to play the part.'

Rose shrieked and fell out of his bed, as Poitier ran off down the corridor throwing over his shoulder, 'Talk to my agent'.

With a star on board, everything started to make sense. Money trickled in, though still way short of what was needed, and other casting fell into place. When the Black acting community found out there was a play with an ensemble of truthful Black characters, a thousand actors turned up to the open call. There was a history of Black characters in comedies, musicals and slapstick, the 'dose, dese and dem' kind of roles, but little that looked hard into their lives. Rose's team secured Ruby Dee, who was something of a name, and found premium players for other parts.

Their struggle was with the central role of Mama, the family's totem of steadiness, and their strongest link with their past. Late in the day, Claudia McNeil came in. Primarily known as a singer, she had recently played a small part in Arthur Miller's *The Crucible* and made a strong impression. For the team, she captured the essence of the role, even if she lacked experience. It was a gamble, but they went with her, and had a cast.

REHEARSALS

Rehearsals began on 27 December 1958 in the New Amsterdam Roof Garden Theatre on Times Square. This had once been a great theatre, but was now unused, as 42nd Street had become a no-go area. At the meet and greet, the reading flew. Lorraine charmed and Rose bustled around with a manic smile, a smile that concealed the fact he didn't have a New York theatre to play in, nor the money to get to the end of rehearsals. He had secured one week in New Haven, and two in Philadelphia, but that was it. The objections were consistent. No white New York audience would pay to see a non-musical about Blacks, and there was no Black audience. Nonetheless, speeches of passion were made, and the reading flew.

While Rose charged around, Lorraine oversaw rehearsals. Her notes for the director survive. Giving notes is a delicate business: they must mix praise and sharpness, and have to define, through practical solutions, the aesthetic of a show. Hansberry's are unimprovable. They encourage truth, wit, passion and dignity. Towards the end of rehearsals she saw a run which pleased everyone, but whose emotionalism alarmed her. She cautioned: 'I like chocolate milk – yet there is nothing quite so nauseous as allowing all that chocolate syrup to fall in a mere one glass of milk. I feel precisely the same about excessive emotionality in a deeply emotional play. There are too many goddamned people on their knees at the end of that scene.' Elsewhere, she defined her instructions in emphatic capitals: 'PLAY WITH IMMENSE EMOTION AND UNBEARABLE RESTRAINT.' She knew her range and wanted the actors in key. She sums up her argument with a beautiful metaphor: 'I consider it a mistake to ever put the wail of TRAGEDY into a mere drama. It makes the pot look so very much larger than the broth, that one can lose one's appetite from hunger.'

At the end of rehearsals, there was a small run-through for friends. It was met with generous laughter, and a liberal use of tissues. The cast headed off on tour, though still without a New York run in place.

ON THE ROAD

Before the first performance in New Haven, Lorraine wrote to her mother: 'Mama, it is a play that tells the truth about people, Negroes and life. And I think it will help a lot of people to understand how we are just as complicated as they are – and just as mixed up – but above all we have, among our miserable and downtrodden ranks, people who are the very essence of human dignity.'

The show had an electrifying first night and its producers stayed up all night discussing it. Rose continued smiling manically, charming investors asking where the New York party was going to be, when he still didn't have a theatre. When they moved to Philadelphia, the excitement grew. To everyone's surprise, the audience was changing, and the proportion of Black attendees soaring. As the director remembered: 'This woman in Philadelphia got to the window and asked for a ticket. It was, I think, $4.80. She started into the theatre and was surprised to be told she couldn't go in until eight o'clock. So I asked her, "Why are you paying $4.80 to come to this play?" She said, "The word's going around my neighborhood that there's something here that has to do with me."'

This was a time when Lorraine and James Baldwin grew from acquaintances to the firmest of friends. He was smitten by her: 'a small, shy, determined person, with that strength dictated by impersonal ambition: she was not trying to make it – she was trying to keep the faith'. He was even more smitten by the experience of her play: 'I had never in my life seen so many Black people in the theatre. And the reason was that never in the history of the American theatre had so much of the truth of Black people's lives been seen on stage. Black people ignored the theatre because the theatre had always ignored them.'

Thankfully, some of the excitement from Philadelphia had filtered back to New York. John Shubert from the all-powerful Shubert Theatre chain came down to watch a matinee. It was a make-or-break moment. His approach was strange. He didn't watch much of the play, but he did watch the audience – before and during the play and as they left. Their commitment was more important to him than anything on stage, and their commitment impressed. He spoke to Rose: 'I guess I'll have to give you a theatre. You can have the Barrymore in five weeks.'

'What do I do with my show for five weeks?'

'Go to Chicago – we have the Blackstone Theatre there – you can play there. Then the Barrymore.'

After two years of begging and politicking, all was settled in minutes.

THE G-MEN TAKE NOTE

It was not only the critics and the New York theatre scene keeping an eye on Lorraine. She had long been a subject of interest for the FBI. As the popularity of the play grew, and its effect on Black audiences sharpened their sense of themselves, the interest grew to alarm.

Seven years before, in March 1952, an invitation had come to Paul Robeson to attend an Inter-American peace conference in Montevideo, Uruguay. Robeson's passport had been revoked by the government, so he had asked Lorraine to attend as his representative. She was to be one of five US delegates, amongst a group of 280. The conference had been planned for Argentina, then Brazil, then Chile. Each in turn banned it. In Uruguay, everyone attended in disguise, pretending they were convening for a huge party. At the conference, they played loud music and danced merrily outside, before retiring within to deliver earnest papers about the future of Marxism. At one point, while Lorraine was delivering a paper on feminism, word came in that the police were entering. Everyone hid notepads and pens in handbags, and pretended they were at a ladies' tea party. The police glowered and left.

Outside there were mass demonstrations to legitimise the conference. Eventually these succeeded, so they were able to move outside, where the attendees grew to about 5,000. Lorraine spoke to the crowd – articulate and self-possessed – and played them a speech of Robeson's. They went wild for this beautiful, unclouded twenty-two year old. She, too, was thrilled: 'We began to walk, I shall never know where so many young people came from ... they linked my arms with theirs and walked four abreast through the streets of Montevideo.'

A month after her return from Uruguay, the state department came to her mother's home and took her passport away. The FBI began surveillance of her movements. Lorraine took a pseudonym for her socialist articles, John Henry, and another, Emily Jones, for her gay writing. But, as the tour progressed and gathered in popularity, the FBI collected reviews and playbills, and J. Edgar Hoover sent special agents along to see if the play was Communist. One reported back, quite astutely,:

> *The play contains no comments of any nature about Communism as such but deals essentially with negro aspirations, the problems inherent in their efforts to advance themselves, and varied attempts at arriving at solutions ... The quality of some of the acting was applauded, some of the lines drew applause primarily on a racial basis, others appeared to be applauded not only by negroes in the audience but by a substantial number of whites.*

The FBI resolved to continue to monitor the play and bring Lorraine in after it had opened in New York. The pressure on a first night is intense in any circumstances. For Hansberry, given all the communities whose hopes and aspirations she had to match, it was extreme. To have the FBI breathing over her shoulder can't have lightened the burden.

11 MARCH 1959, BARRYMORE THEATRE, NEW YORK

On the first night in New York, two hours after the lights had lowered in the auditorium, and Lorraine and her friends had held hands and breath, Sidney Poitier –Walter Younger – stepped forward on stage. He took time to find his words. The audience sat rigid with tension. By this stage, his choice was their choice, his need their need, his pain their pain, so entire was their engagement. His character's task was to explain, with a concrete directness, why his family wished to occupy their new home, and why they would not be bought out by a neighbourhood representative alarmed by the idea of interracial communities.

The reticence and restrained emotion in his speech, as he recounted the history of his family, choked the audience. This wasn't the cheap aspirin of manufactured catharsis, this was the live crackle of history on the move, impelled by the actions of the humble and defiant. Civil Rights progress might still be decades away, yet no-one could say that change had not occurred in that moment, as a rusted window on the future pushed open. *A Raisin in the Sun* had arrived. The performance had been note-perfect. The energy which had gone AWOL the night before had surged into the room. Everything was fierce and exact, with theatrical precision – life in a state of poetry. Poitier was in a zone of fiery grace as he and McNeil blazed at each other and the rest of the cast shone. As the curtain closed, the audience went crazy, as call after call returned. The critics stopped in their shuffling exit at the back of the stalls to watch the unprecedented ovation.

Soon enough, the chant of 'Author! Author!' went up. Lorraine shrank into her seat, reluctant to take credit. Poitier was as reluctant to give credit away, until he noticed that his arm was being repeatedly punched. He turned to see his co-star, Ruby Dee, pounding him, hissing in a stage whisper, 'Go get her, you son of a bitch. Go get her.' Realising his responsibility, he leapt off stage, ran up the aisle as if flying, and practically carried her back. When Lorraine hit the light and bowed, an almighty roar went up.

Later, Rose and Hansberry made their way to Sardi's, New York's time-honoured post-show hang-out. Before entering, Lorraine said that, like Chekhov after his *Seagull* premiere, she wanted to run home and pull the covers over her head. But the doorman opened the door for her for the third time, and she was nudged forward. Once in the room, silhouetted at the top of the stairs, the whole room stood; everyone was clapping, even the waiters and busboys. Neither Hansberry nor Rose had realised just how many had wanted them to succeed. In his words, 'A beautiful twenty-nine-year-old Black woman stood there – the face of change'.

There are few rushes of sweetly addictive energy more intoxicating than the sensation you are sitting on a Broadway hit. It is a brief mainline of pure adrenalised bliss. Less nutritious than crack, it is hard not to relish. We presented two Shakespeare shows from the Globe in the Belasco in 2013. The happy hour from when a circle of producers and press agents sat in the lobby of a hotel with their smartphones out, all shouting out the rave reviews simultaneously dropping online, through to the entrance at the grand party, where we took the leading players aside, and told them it was a major win, that hour was one of the most unhealthily happy of my life. On an earlier and more glorious journey, Lorraine and Rose went from Sardi's to the Plaza Hotel, where everyone was gathered. Rose was told the reviews were raves, and announced the fact to the crowd. Mayhem ensued.

A few nights later the duo returned to Sardi's for another party. There are a series of photos from that night, taken by the great Gordon Parks. They capture an impossible mix of 1950s hep cool and volcanic joy. Poitier, Harry Belafonte and James Baldwin all exhibit the difficulty of containing those two contradictory states. In some they exemplify effortless chill, sharply poised for the camera. In others, they are just busting with happiness. The crowd squeezed into this space ignite en masse with the same mix of hipster entitlement and exuberance. The walls are plastered with caricature portraits of old famous clientele. Their faces are white. The faces at the party, claiming this space for their own, are largely Black. One face stands out, making no attempt at self-possession, or self-presentation, just unfiltered joy. It is Lorraine. Her hair tousled, skin glistening, eyes alight, she is arriving in the annals of the great, and doing it with grace. There is none of the angry 'Now! This is my moment!'; simply the relief of someone knowing she has done what she was meant to do. In one haunting shot, taken from behind a guitarist, Hansberry's face has an erupting smile. The neck of the guitar crosses her at the neck, and her ecstatic face seems to float free from the rest of her body.

The tragedy is that Hansberry did not know many more nights like this. She would be dead within six years, from pancreatic cancer, at the age of thirty-four.

Somewhere in a less celebratory part of town, a man filed a report. Had the play flopped, the FBI would have brought Lorraine in. But 'in reconsidering an interview with the subject, it is to be noted that the subject and her play have received considerable notoriety almost daily in the New York press – in view of this it is felt that an interview with her would be inadvisable'. No-one can argue with success, not even the G-men.

REBUILD THIS HOUSE

When James Baldwin was quizzed about the civil rights issues of the 1960s, he talked about a question of reality. That the dominant White culture had created an artificial reality which would not, and could not, admit the true nature of Black experience. It would neither recognise their alternate reality, nor help to forge a new inclusive one. Lorraine's achievement was to show Black life as it was, to show it to a large audience, and shift their idea of the world around them. The way to fight is not only to attack the existing state of affairs, or to torch it; another way to fight a wrong world is to birth a new one.

In *A Raisin in the Sun*, after two acts of seething tension in the Younger apartment, Mama returns to the flat with the surprise that she has spent the insurance money they are fighting over. She has bought a new house in a white area. Everyone is astonished. This is not the answer to their antagonisms, this is an entirely new idea. 'I just seen my family falling apart today ... just falling to piece in front of my eyes ... When it gets like that in life – you just got to do something different, push on out and do something bigger.'

The play's action has been criticised by some, at the time and since, as assimilation, or bourgeois ambition. This is an injustice; the writing is too wise to say that aspiration is the answer. What Hansberry proposes is stepping forwards. Whether to a new address or to peace, justice, love and beauty, the first step has to be taken, no matter the confusions and compromises down the line. In a radio discussion, Baldwin and Hansberry concurred: 'It's not a matter of acceptance or tolerance. We've got to sit down and rebuild this house.' 'Yes, and quickly.'

Nonetheless, the critics must have hurt. Norman Mailer patronised her and called her work 'a play about insurance money'. Black radicals attacked her for instilling a middle-class sensibility into working-class life. The Left was suspicious of her success, and had ample evidence to lampoon her, primarily in the cringingly patronising coverage of Lorraine in the press. The apogee of this was a critic who wrote of his pleasure at seeing how 'our dusky brethren [could] come up with a song, and hum their troubles away'. Lorraine felt these attacks, recorded them, and did her best to answer them. She believed in a theatre strangled by neither commercialism nor the self-congratulation of the avant-garde. Fighting for this space exhausted her.

Theatre encourages difference and debate, and nowhere more so than in *A Raisin in the Sun*, which brings so many contrary viewpoints on stage. What lifts it above disputation is that it does not just bring ideas, it brings people. Walter, Ruth, Beneatha, Mama, George – their lively, actual existence denies critiquing. They are individuals – ill-fitting blends of need and wisdom and devilment – and do not represent anyone but themselves. It is that *lively action*, in the Elizabethan phrase for actors, that makes them recognisable and identifiable.

This universality is achieved through the specificity of life lived, of people heard. In the play's third act, Mama warns her daughter Beneatha not to presume she knows her brother: 'When you starts measuring somebody, measure him right ... make sure you done take into account what hills and valleys he come through before he got wherever he is.' Lorraine measured her characters right; those who attacked her, less so.

Exhausted with others' interpretations, she wrote a piece for *Village Voice* that demonstrates the modesty and yet enormity of her ambition:

The symbolism of moving into a new house is quite as small as it seems and quite as significant. For if there are no waving flags and marching songs at the barricades as Walter marches out with his little battalion, it is not because the battle lacks nobility. On the contrary, he has picked up in his way, still imperfect and wobbly in his view of human destiny, what I believe Arthur Miller called 'the golden thread of history'. He becomes, in spite of those too intrigued with despair and hatred of man to see it, King Oedipus refusing to tear out his eyes, but attacking the oracle instead. He is that last Jewish patriot manning his rifle in the burning ghetto at Warsaw; he is Anne Frank still believing in people; he is Michelangelo creating David, and Beethoven bursting forth with the Ninth Symphony. He is all those things because he has finally reached out in his tiny moment and caught that sweet essence that is human dignity, and it shines like the old star-touched dream that it is in his eyes.

A DETERMINED ALONENESS

Lorraine died on 12 January 1965. At her funeral Paul Robeson sang, in his last public appearance. In the congregation sat Malcolm X, who risked his life to attend; he was facing a cascade of death threats and his story ended three weeks later. He and Lorraine had befriended each other and spoken with a quiet honesty as both sat under the shadow of imminent death – Lorraine from cancer, Malcolm X from violence.

In the early-1950s, Lorraine had thought of herself as lost in the 'swirl and dash of the Sartre-Camus debate', paused like many of her generation before the commitment of involvement. In later years, she sharpened her radicalism and grew closest to the Malcolm X creed – 'by any means necessary'. Her community, she believed:

> *... must concern themselves with every single means of struggle. They must harass, debate, petition, give money to court struggles, sit in, lie down, strike, boycott, sing hymns, pray on steps and shoot from their windows when the racists come cruising through their communities. The acceptance of our present condition is the only form of extremism which discredits us before our children.*

Fame had bought Lorraine its habitual mixed bag of crazed comforts and cutting loneliness. Baldwin remained an ally to the end, and she enjoyed a passionate friendship on the barricades with Nina Simone, who celebrated her in the song 'Young, Gifted and Black'. These three formed a trinity, who argued and drank and laughed and argued again. Neither that pleasure, nor two further great plays, settled her spirit. She drank too much, lived too fierce, laughed too hard, loved too keenly and died too fast, with a determined aloneness. As she wrote, 'The thing that makes you exceptional, if you are at all, is inevitably that which must also make you lonely.'

When the world lost Lorraine Hansberry, it lost a great playwright and a woman who could have helped steer American culture and politics for decades to come. It is impossible to overestimate what she could have done and meant. Small compensation is provided in those pictures of her beautiful, swinging glee on the night of her great success. A glee not for herself, but in the knowledge that on that one occasion the world's endlessly imprisoned goodness had been allowed to step out footloose and free, and dance for a brief but gilded moment.

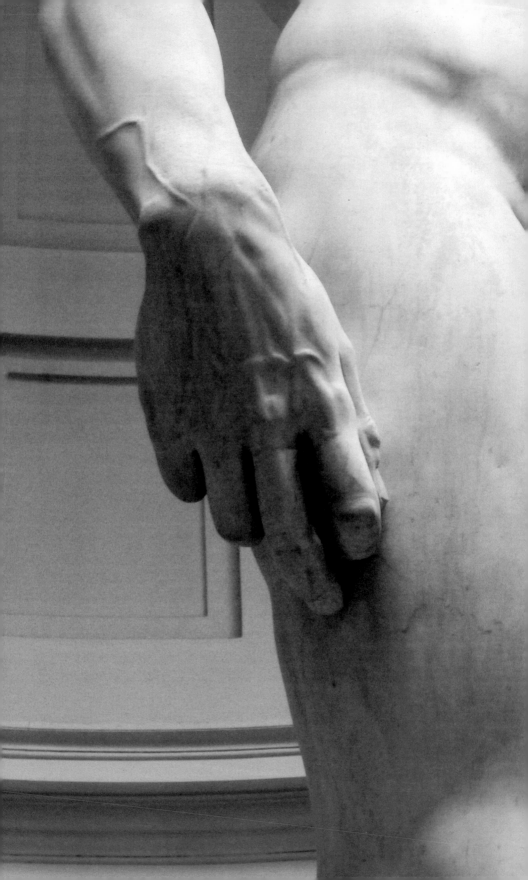

2

Giant

A TALE OF *DAVID*

The white marble dust was still packed thick under his fingernails. Traces of it stuck in the grooves of his frown's wrinkles. For two years he had worked like a baker in a thick cloud: no amount of scrubbing would clean that away. His face creased with its habitual anxiety, as forty men began manoeuvring his Giant towards the carriage built to convey it. One false move, one small chip, and its smoothed perfection would be blemished. Forty men shouted and screamed, squabbling with Tuscan brio, frantic to get this right. They were holding something as precious as a god, as delicate as a newborn baby. Tugging and turning winches, they inched the Giant towards its chariot. Beyond them a crowd of dignitaries, passers-by and street scallies watched.

Six weeks before, the authorities had instructed that Michelangelo's statue of *David* should be moved from the workshop to its new home. The Wool Guild had chosen Simone del Pallaiuolo to oversee the transport. Everyone wanted to be involved. Weighing in at 12,473 pounds of Carrara marble, and 17 feet high, moving it with the requisite care was a task almost as rarefied as making it. The marble was refined, and its surface eggshell fragile. Engineering was a skill on

39

a par with sculpture, and Del Pallaiuolo had come up with the perfect contraption. The hulk would be inserted upright into a huge wooden cradle, its feet suspended above the ground, its head floating above the walls, and held in place by a web of ropes. They were fastened with a new slipknot, which tightened as it stretched.

Sliding forward over greased wooden beams, the carriage was designed so the marble could sway minimally in response to jolts, but would not bump on the floor, nor its sides. Once trussed up, everyone drew breath before starting the pull to the Piazza. A five-minute walk away, it would take days of slow progress. The first pressure was applied, wood creaked, marble and ropes stirred, and the whole edifice nudged forwards. *David* began his megalithic shuffle across the Tuscan earth.

All knew they were handling a sacred object. Florence had recently been turned topsy-turvy by the firebrand puritanism of Savanarola, whose idea of a New Jerusalem included destroying secular culture. His was the passion of a man swimming against the tide. As humanist art displaced religious, and the artist edged out the prophet, Florence was the centre of the revolutionary wheel, and this object its focus.

As the carriage inched forward, Michelangelo's dusty, furrowed brow may have relaxed a millimetre. For him to complete this task was astonishing. His long creative life was a complex dance of projects dreamt of, half-done, almost finished, or walked away from. Many of his works survive in a midway place between conception and creation, their poetry in the suspension between the two. This one was finished, and a miracle of achievement.

By around eight o'clock, the carriage had reached the edge of the yard, and there it ground to a halt. Forty men stood around looking grumpily at Del Pallaiuolo. The gate wasn't big enough, and the statue couldn't get out.

They were going to have to knock the wall down.

A BLOCK OF CARRARA MARBLE

In December 1466, thirty-eight years earlier, and nine years before Michelangelo was born, the block of marble from which *David* was hewn had arrived in Florence. Its appearance was a sensation – the largest block cut from the Carrara hills since the time of the Caesars, a thousand years before. People marvelled at its potential, wrote poems to it and schemed; then, with the flitting hunger for sensation of the age, forgot all about it. A colossal *David* had long been intended as part of the decorative scheme for Florence's stupendous Duomo, whose dome had recently been completed by Brunelleschi. A group of men, the Operai, had been appointed to oversee embellishments. Their plan was to commission twelve outsized Old Testament figures, one for each buttress. A mammoth Joshua was created by Donatello out of terra-cotta. As a balance to this, they contracted one Agostino di Duccio to make a *David* on the same scale, from marble. This *David* was dubbed the Giant. No-one had fashioned a figure this size from a single block since antiquity.

Di Duccio travelled to Carrara in Northern Tuscany, as sculptors had for millennia. He commissioned artisans to chisel from the mountain a single block nine brachia – nearly eight metres – tall. This was skilled, physical and dangerous work. The stony hills were too hazardous for oxen to help with sheer horsepower, so the hard graft was all human. As was the artist's eye which helped divine the best stone. These high-altitude quarrymen were geologists and engineers, guided by instinct and feel. They could tell good stone from sight and touch, from sound when struck, from smell when the sulphur impurities were released, and from taste in licking the rock to gauge lime content. They had to avoid fissures and bad veins or there could be problems later.

Before the block was moved, an approximation of the human form was hewn from the stone to lighten the load of carriage, and simplify later working. These initial steps were crucial, since they determined the top and bottom, back and front of the eventual figure, and the direction of the grain. They had to be done with care. In this case, they weren't. Di Duccio bungled it. In Michelangelo's words, he did it 'in such a way that neither he nor anyone else ever had the courage to lay a hand to it'.

Nonetheless, the block was lowered down the hill, put on a cart and pulled by seven or eight teams of oxen through the Tuscan landscape to Averna, from where it sailed to Pisa. There it was transferred to a river barge to Florence. For a piece this large they had to wait for the rainy season to ensure there was sufficient depth in the Arno to float it.

At Signa, seven miles from Florence, it was transferred back to a cart, since the rapids were too risky. At the end of the adventure, the hero block was brought with fanfares into the heart of the city.

The strain of this endeavour ate up the energy required to go further. Agostino di Duccio's protector, the great Donatello, died, and with him went the city's enthusiasm for his protégé. This, and his mismanagement of the blocking out, meant his departure. It left a sense of pessimism around the marble, which remained neglected for the next three decades. Over time, it was weathered down by wind and rain. As it aged, it became harder to work, for marble is most pliable when just quarried, due to its moisture content. The fame of the block, though, was undiminished. Artists from Florence and further afield would look in on it, as if on a tethered dinosaur, an ageing dragon in its cage, and imagine how it could be set free. The municipal will stalled until 1501, when the Operai decided to raise the Giant to its feet.

DAY TWO OF THE JOURNEY – AND A FLORENTINE RIVALRY

The barrier of the wall was swiftly resolved, with permission and some sledgehammers. The Giant resumed its torturous progress, through the wide streets, standing upright, as fourteen beams were forever circulated, a team of men retrieving the one at the back and passing it from hands to hands to the front.

On its first night, a gang of youths stole up, and hurled stones at the Giant, until beaten off. They did no major damage but this terrified the artist and the Operai. Thereafter the statue was kept permanently under watch. The stoning could have been an act of yobbery; it could have been a protest against idolatry from the remnant of Savanarola's zealots; most probably, though, since the young men were from pro-Medici families, it was a gesture of factional disgruntlement. Whichever, they were locked up in the Stinche, the city prison, and fined.

One conspiracy theory held that the stoning was ordered by Michelangelo's greatest rival, someone who would have been there to witness the beginning of the journey and have kept an eye on it as it lumbered along. There is as little evidence for this as for most conspiracy theories, but they tend to proliferate around Leonardo da Vinci.

For five years the older man was at work in the same city as Michel-angelo, fighting for ascendancy in the same smaller community. Their Olympian ambitions and Empyrean insights stoked each others fires. It also promoted behaviour of playground infantilism. Once, when Michelangelo joined a group discussing Dante's *Inferno* that included Leonardo, the older artist asked him to clarify a knotty passage of verse. Michelangelo replied, 'You explain it: you who designed a bronze cast for a big horse, but who couldn't cast it!' and strode off. This crude allu-sion to a public embarrassment of Da Vinci's in Milan has all the wit of a primary school child blowing a raspberry.

Leonardo's wit was more elegant. In a contemptuous discourse, he contrasts the sculptor and the painter. The former he thought the lesser artist, a slave to his primary material and, crucially, dirtier. There are no prizes for guessing who he was referring to when he wrote, 'The sculptor uses the force of his arm ... a highly mechanical operation, accompanied by much sweat which mingles with dust and converts into mud. His face becomes plastered all over which makes him resem-ble a baker'. The painter, on the other hand, 'sits before his work at the greatest of ease, applying delicate colours with a light brush. He enjoys the accompaniment of music ... heard with pleasure without the crash-ing of hammers.' This is elegantly put, but its essential argument that the sculptor – Michelangelo – is a muscly Doughboy and the artist – Leonardo – a luxury item – is not a big evolutionary step forward from his rival's raspberry-blowing.

Clothing mattered to Leonardo: in Florence he favoured a rose-pink tunic, and processed about, peacocked and perfumed, with a glam-orous entourage. Michelangelo, with his bruiser's broken nose and surly manner, favoured the plain dress of a worker or hermit. Their differences extended in all ways: in their homosexual desire, which in Leonardo was expressed and at ease, and in Michelangelo tortured and repressed; in their style of painting, which in Leonardo is misted with the smoky atmospherics of *sfumato*, and in Michelangelo is clean-lined and crisp; and in their public persona, where Leonardo played urbane dandy, and Michelangelo was neurotically awkward.

The city promoted the rivalry, at one point commissioning both to make frescoes in the same building. Both began their projects, and then – competitive in diffidence as all else – both dropped them. But not before Leonardo, on seeing the troop of naked figures writhing in his rival's cartoon, expressed his opinion that he should not make his figures too gnarled with muscles, lest they look like a 'sack of walnuts'.

The two may have once been close. Neither was incapable of realising the technical brilliance of the other. Their respect would have been all the keener when they were competing to sculpt the Giant.

COMPETING FOR THE COMMISSION

The new power broker in the city was Piero Soderini, soon to be elected *Gonfaloniere* for life. This was Florence's attempt to restore order after a decade of mayhem. Preaching an end to gangster capitalism and the exploitation of the poor, the zealot Savonarola had booted out the Medici family to establish a 'popular' republic. His grim, fundamentalist heaven on earth had lasted about three years, before being brutally expunged and its leader executed. Soderini seemed the man to fill the vacuum. Once in place, bread and circuses were required, and preferably pious ones. The resurrection of the Giant was ideal.

At the beginning of 1501, Michelangelo was in Rome, and had just secured a triumph with his Pietà for St Peter's. In the spring of that year, he was tipped off that the legendary marble had been raised, and there were moves afoot for a commission. He hurried home to Florence.

Soderini was known to support Leonardo, who had himself recently returned to Florence, from Milan, possibly encouraged by the same signs. Though not renowned as a sculptor, Da Vinci bore the aura of genius, and not without flourish.

Another competitor, Andrea Sansovino, pitched hard and public. He demanded the right to make the Giant. Because of the mistakes made in the blocking out, Sansovino argued it could not be transformed into a human figure, and would need further lumps added. This was a resignation of the highest art since the supreme skill was to carve *ex uno lapide* – from a single stone. Michelangelo contended this could be done. His solution was radical. His *David* would be naked, thus requiring less volume of stone. In justification of this choice, he argued that *David* would be clothed not in robes but in his faith. Necessity created a new interpretation.

This was the biggest commission of a generation and the Operai would have been cautious. Michelangelo was a relatively unknown quantity, the fame of his success with his Rome Pietà not having swept Florence yet, and still a young man. He was known not to finish work, and the naked idea was a red rag to those who would burn idolaters, and those who saw sodomites around every corner. The fact that they were, then as through history, around every corner, made everyone all the more nervous. Sasovino was the safe bet, Leonardo was the heavy hitter, so why should they place their faith in this taciturn young man with the heavy-browed intensity?

To clinch the deal, Michelangelo made a model in wax, fashioning a young David with sling in hand. For the contemporary chronicler Vasari, this figurine sounded a call to civic responsibility. Having weathered the different tyrannies of mad monks and the Medici, the city would be personified by this David, as the defender of civil liberties. It would exemplify *fortezza* and *ira*, strength and anger, and the capacity of the human to shape their own life. This political pitch towards the republican camp was a sophisticated manoeuvre. Tellingly, it was also sincere. Michelangelo won the commission. Insult was added to injury for Leonardo, when he was invited to join the committee to decide the placement of the work. For his own reasons, he accepted.

DAY THREE – AND GRAVEN IMAGES

On the monster shuffled, its fame growing ever greater. It's elephantine journey became a spectator sport, electrifying the city. Crowds positioned themselves for the best views, and for the chance of eye contact with the figure floating inside.

Several years ago, I witnessed the carriage of the young Kumari, the living goddess of Nepal, around Durbar Square in Kathmandu. A slowly swelling crowd of worshippers and visitors awaited her arrival for an hour and a half. Many began with a weary diffidence, yet waiting created anticipation, and anticipation stirred hunger. Just before her arrival, a pulse of alertness and potential rippled through the group. A very young woman, she was carried by priests so her feet could not touch the ground, and placed in a box on a palanquin. Eight priests then carried her forwards. Under instructions not to show any emotion, nor to make eye contact, she would not move her gaze from straight ahead. What began as a desultory ceremony became a thrilling street ritual. Middle-aged men became like Beatles fans, rushing ahead of the moving cortège to try and catch a better glimpse of the numinous child. A crackle of charisma and aura surrounded the goddess, as if robbed from the attendant crowd, and pulled into herself. Whether supplied or inherent made no odds. It was there.

The same charisma attached to *David* on his stately picaresque. Rarely before had an artwork garnered this amount of pre-publicity. The journey was a rebuke to the monopoly on the sacrosanct that the religious had held for the preceding millennium. It was explicitly a passage away from a cathedral, the place for which it was originally intended, towards the Piazza della Signoria, the home of state power. Art was stealing the numinous from the church.

As they hove into view of the Piazza, the spiritual boldness of what was being attempted would have chimed loudly for Michelangelo. In the same open space, six years before, he had seen the bonfires of the vanities organised by Savanarola. Among the books and icons cast into the flames went a pile 'of nude statues, and many other vain things'. The artist and the preacher had spent their youth together in the Medici household, before the preacher had turned his rage on his protectors, and helped to expel them from the city. Michelangelo himself was susceptible to the mystic's vision of purity and asceticism. He would himself have struggled with Savanarola's passionate adherence to the second commandment, 'Thou shalt not make unto thee any graven image'.

A sense of shame about his gift pervades Michelangelo's resistance to his own talent. He was an artist who wrestled with the purpose of every action, large and small. From the moment he began obsessively drawing as a young man, he lived with a distrust of his own brilliance, a fear his gift may descend into the cheapness of facility. A piece of art should come to life against the will of its maker. When he went on to paint the Sistine Chapel, the act of creation is forever a torment to his God, just as it was to him.

This sense of gravity would have been enhanced by the memory of what followed the bonfire of the vanities. Once Savanorola's power had ebbed away, he himself was hung and burnt, his flesh roasting in the same square where he had revelled in the torching of human effigies.

The same piazza they inched towards.

SCULPTING DAVID

In the margin of Michelangelo's contract for the *David*, it is recorded 'on the 9th, he gave it one or two blows with his hammer, to strike off a node it had in its breast'. This blow, an attempt to undo the bungled blocking of Di Duccio, signified two things. First, there was no going back. Michelangelo was trapped in the stone and its destiny. Second, the statue's eventual state would have to be nude. The node he demolished was for a belt buckle, without which there was no room left for clothing. From his first stroke, whatever he would do with the weathered chunk, it would be his, and radical.

The note continues: 'on the said day he began to work with determination and strength'. Michelangelo was a supreme artist, but he was a physical worker as well, and knew how to put in a shift. The romantic cliché of the sculptor liberating shape from stone makes the process sound mystic and yielding. It isn't. It was hard athletic work, the sculptor stripped to the waist, with the sirocco, a blasting wind, sharking through the city. On a scrap of paper, decorated with preliminary sketches, Michelangelo wrote: 'Daviete cholla Fromba/e io chollarco' ('David with his sling/And I with my bow'). The 'bow' is a sculptor's drill and the identification with his subject couldn't be more explicit. Michelangelo was now the underdog in an epic battle with this colossal block, the warrior who must defeat stone with art.

After a month of work, in order to protect himself from the wind, Michelangelo ordered an enclosure of planks and trestles to be erected around the space. He wanted the piece brought to perfection in isolation. It was a private matter between him, the stone and God. Two months later, on 20 December, he asked for a roof to protect him from the rain. Now not even God could get a look-in. Enclosed, and enveloped in his cloud of white dust, not eating or sleeping for days on end, he chipped away.

The wax model he had created to win the commission was mapped in exact proportion onto the stone. The model was submerged in water, and as the water was drained away, millimetre by millimetre, he chiselled out what emerged. We can see this process in figures which Michelangelo left half-finished, notably his *Saint Matthew*, who is left pulling himself free from the stone, as Kenneth Clark described, 'like the early premonitory rumblings in Beethoven's Ninth'. Caught for eternity halfway between liberation and incarceration, the artist left him suspended in struggle. This was not the intention for *David*. He was meant to be free.

Michelangelo worked with six different chisels, slowly tapering down from coarse to fine: from a *subbia*, a pointed chisel used to cut chunks, down to the minuscule *ferro staccato* for refining muscles and folds. The process is a balance of caress and force. If you dab at the stone forever, no progress is made; if you hit it too hard, one slip can wipe out a year's work, and destroy the dreams of a city. Michelangelo, as far as we know, was celibate throughout his life, yet he seems to have sublimated a lover's tenderness and vigour into the stone. He was attached to these tasks from birth. His wetnurse had been the daughter and wife of stonemasons: he said of her, 'I drew in from her milk the chisels and hammers with which I make figures'.

The final stage was marked by a laborious refinement and sanding, described by Vasari: 'Lastly they rub the figure with points of pumice stone to give it a flesh-like appearance. Tripoli earth is used to make it lustrous. Finally it is rubbed over with bunches of straw, till shining and finished, it appears to us.'

And there it stood. Heart-hurting in its grace.

An object constructed with stone, wax models, chisels, earth and straw. Mechanisation and technology are capable of achievements of infinite complexity and sophistication. Nature and the human hand make beauty.

THE RIGHT HOME

Shortly before Michelangelo made the final touches to his masterpiece, a committee convened in the courtyard to decide where it should be placed. As committees go, this must be one of history's most distinguished. Its cast of politicians and artists included Soderini, Botticelli, Perugino, Filippino Lippi, Piero di Cosimo and

Leonardo da Vinci. Machiavelli was possibly there, too, steering discussions. It was 25 January 1504, and they met in the freezing cold
to look at the sculpture in the courtyard, then adjourned indoors to
discuss by the fire.

Certain decisions were made instantaneously, before the commission had left the courtyard. They knew they had a masterpiece on
their hands and realised that putting it atop a cathedral buttress, high
above the city, made no sense. Lifting six tons of marble one hundred
metres in the air was not a challenge anyone relished. It was clear that
the precision in this work, and its depth of detail, would be lost at a
distance.

As the committee walked around it, another reason may have
occurred, though I doubt anyone mentioned it. Whatever one's sexual
orientation, gay or straight or both, it is impossible not to be struck
by the fact that *David* has a posterior of spectacular perfection. In a
recent museum competition of the world's best buttocks, *David* came
in only fourth, which calls for an immediate stewards' inquiry. The
thought of this extraordinary feature, not only far away up in the sky,
but only visible to the occasional chap sent up to clean the Dome, may
have broken their hearts. When someone first suggested the statue
should be closer to eye-level, one can imagine a vigorous chorus of
'Oh, yes', 'Absolutely' and 'I agree' erupting with poorly concealed
enthusiasm.

Soderini – and Machiavelli, if present – would have quickly assessed
the usefulness of the *David* as a symbol. Here was a new emblem of
their potency as a state, an elegant statement of courageous heroism.
Whether he was facing north to the Sforzas in Milan, or south to the
Borgias in Rome, here was a figure which could face any Goliath and
throw down a gauntlet with a light authority. If it was to show off the
achievements of Florence, there was only one destination, the prime
place of social life and the seat of civic government: Piazza della
Signoria. So, after forty years of waiting to go up on the cathedral, it
was decided the stone should go elsewhere.

Precisely where in the square went under discussion in a minuted
meeting. There was a move to have it placed within the Palazzo del
Vecchio. Another faction moved for a pedestal outside the Palazzo,

presently occupied by Judith slaying Holofernes, and upsetting many by its condoning of female violence. A third faction proposed the loggia on one side of the square, which offered defence from the weather, and from yobbery. Leonardo came out for this, but stated that it shouldn't be in too central a position. He worried it might upstage political or religious ceremonies. 'Maybe it should be tucked away close to a distant wall', he argued, in an inglorious attempt to throw shade.

Not satisfied with trying to hide the statue, Leonardo also wanted changes. 'Certain areas', he asserted, should be covered up, and only shown 'with decent ornaments'. A tiny doodle he did on the spot shows the statue with its offending member neatly hidden by 'a bronze leaf'. It is hard to credit the seriousness of this for Da Vinci, an artist whose notebooks contain a section titled 'On the Penis', in which he argues against 'covering something that deserves to be displayed with ceremony'.

Rivalry knows few bounds.

DAY FOUR – ARRIVAL AND DELAYED GRATIFICATION

On 18 May, at eight in the morning, the creaking caravan, attended by a crowd like the effigy of an ancient god, passed into the piazza. It had taken nearly four days to travel a few hundred metres. By the time it arrived, statue and artist had both become celebrities. Michelangelo, the outsider from the small town of Caprese, ever gruff and self-effacing, had moved to the centre of Florentine life.

This should have been the moment for a grand unveiling. Not in Italy, the spiritual home of delayed gratification. I opened a play once in a Renaissance palazzo in Florence. It was scheduled to start at 8.30. I went backstage to wish the actors good luck at 8.15. They looked at me as if I was mad. The audience started arriving at about nine. By 9.30, the foyer was packed, with everyone sneaking up to each other and whispering '*In bocca di lupo*' in each other's ears ('Into the mouth of the wolf'). I suggested to the venue that we might consider going ahead. They looked at me as if I was simple, and told me we had to wait until the audience were properly warmed up. Driving people mad with waiting is part of the art. The show finally began at almost eleven. The Italians don't race.

With *David*, it became a matter of weeks. Ten days after its arrival in the square, it was decided to place *David* at the entrance to the palazzo, displacing Judith, who was relegated to the loggia, in punishment for depressing the patriarchy. Then, on 8 June, with the Giant in his new home and all ready to go, it was concluded that the plinth was a bit dreary. Such a masterpiece needed something fancier. A new plinth was commissioned and took several weeks. When that was ready, everyone stood expectant ... and it was decided to press the pause button again. *Il Gigante* needed to be garlanded with gilded leaves to cover up his modestly proportioned genitalia, as Leonardo had proposed. Three separate artisans fashioned a brass-wire support, onto which were soldered twenty-eight copper leaves.

The delays were symptomatic of the Italian desire to hold on, but also testament to the scale of the occasion. In its radical perfection, the *David* was too big for the city, too big for the stakeholders, too big for understanding. The delays were a pushing-away of the problem of what this unknowable step forward in human capacity might unleash. Finally the Operai ran out of excuses and had to show it in its totality. It was revealed on its pedestal outside the palazzo, where it stood for another 369 years, until moved indoors to the Accademia.

The audience stilled and drew its breath, inhaling with it beauty and the divine, and exhaling air infected with a new understanding of grace.

The Italians may not race, but when they arrive they really do.

DAVID ITSELF

When unveiled at last, what did people see? The *David* was the first free-standing colossal nude made since antiquity. The massy freight of the ancient world had been presented with the nimble lightness of the modern spirit. There is nothing radically original in an outsized naked figure. The template was set by the Doryphoros of Polykelites, the figure of a spear-bearer cast in bronze in about 440 BCE, and much copied in marble by the Romans. In this depiction of human beauty, we see a naked man, standing in the *contrapposto* pose, where one straight leg takes most of the weight, while the other leg kinks and drifts. Michelangelo did not ignore this tradition: he took it on and bettered it.

In *David*, the form is perfected with new detailing. We are knocked back by the beauty of the figure, and there is added drama. Alongside the grace, there is tension and readiness. The left leg is nudging forward, the heel off the ground, and the neck twisted to the left. The body is alert, the brave underdog and selfless soldier ready to fight for his people. The enlarged head and the outsized right hand speak of power in action. They show the physical and moral strength of the hero, and the artist – the furrowed scowl feels akin to the intensity of Michelangelo. The Greek spear-bearer is a remarkable exercise in form, but emotionally stolid by comparison.

Nor is this just a push in the direction of realism from an obsessive knowledge of anatomy. Each element is scientifically observed, not to create photographic verisimilitude, but to make a piece of perfection in life. The aliveness of *David* is proven by its protean variety, depending on the angle from which it is seen. Straight on, he is epically heroic; from one side slender and fragile; from another, fearful and vulnerable; close up, intense and determined.

Here we see stone made into flesh; the flesh of a body made into a dream of perfection; and all made into music. Art and nature not in opposition, but in a double helix dance. Somehow in two years of near continuous hammering and chiselling and buffing, Michelangelo caught the briefest instance of alive time, one drop, and held it so perfectly in its stone flesh, that it would stay in its own sharp and fragile present instant forever, while human flesh grew and decayed, and history rose and fell around it.

Ars longa, vita brevis.

BEFORE

The principal innovation in Michelangelo's depiction was in the narrative. Every previous depiction had shown the hero after the battle, David standing with the severed head of Goliath in his hand or at his feet. This was less possible here because of the bad blocking out. Yet Michelangelo chose – he was not forced – to depict the moment before the fight. David is looking at the problem, his hand on his sling, concealing his fear, sizing up the task, and arranging body and spirit for the the leap into action. The poised and alert moment of fullest life.

Every actor, every artist, before a first night. Michelangelo knew that victory is morally inert, and triumphalism vain glory. Preparation is everything. Pushing forward, as Orpheus always must, staying in the before. As the man from Duluth says, 'He not busy being born is busy dying.' Great hope in before.

3

I, An Actor

A TALE OF THESPIS

A GOAT AND A BASKET OF FIGS

*I am Thespis, who first created the form of tragic song, inventing a
new entertainment for the country people. We performed at the season when Bacchus led the chorus into the theatre. At that time, the
prize was a goat and a basket of Attic figs. Now my juniors reinvent all
this. Countless ages will beget new innovations, but my own is mine.*

So speaks the first actor, making the very first thespian boast. Tonally,
it is a poor start for the profession. As with much involving Thespis, the
quote is of dubious provenance. His life has to be rebuilt from fragments
of reference and slivers of recollection. However dubious, there is
something authentic about the voice. The bombast rings true, as does the
beady-eyed, and begrudging, detail about the prize. This attitude seems
ungrateful – who wouldn't swap an Oscar for a goat and a basket of Attic
figs? What is familiar is the disgruntled attitude towards the youth. Here
they are, these young ones, stealing my tricks, then changing them and
claiming it's all new.

The present eye praises the present object is a line crafted by Shakespeare
two thousand years after Thespis, and put into the mouth of someone

from a thousand years before, Ulysses (*Troilus and Cressida*, Act III). It echoes through history. In the eyes of the old, the young are forever pulling their focus, and blithely taking credit for their inventions. In case anyone is confused, Thespis is unequivocal about his achievement, *My own is mine.*

His own was what we came to know as theatre. Other currents, secular and holy, streamed into its making, but one morning, under a spring Mediterranean sun, Thespis added a catalytic element. At a time when a confluence of factors brought Greece its greatest power, a capacity for innovation; a time when they were reshaping the cosmos, the state and the human psyche in new directions; at that moment, one man, Thespis, said to himself, *I've had enough of this ensemble malarkey, I want some attention for myself.* He stepped out from the choric group who had previously worked so effectively together. Having had enough of complex harmonies, he fancied singing a melody. Alone.

Whether this was led by innovation, vanity or a search for truth is an open space anyone can fill as they wish. But this movement of individuation, of claiming the space for the single voice, is one of the great *I am* moments in cultural history.

LOSING ONESELF IN A CROWD

We often hear that public art – theatre, opera, dance, music – emerged from religious ritual. We hear this truism and nod, with little idea of what it implies. There is shame in the nodding, as if we are being told off for the shallowness of modernity. Religious ritual evokes images of lines of solemn men, carrying long candlesticks towards an altar, under a rainy sky. The basis for our public art, we guess, must concern pain, and ceremonies with drawn-out pauses, where you sit on bad chairs.

Nothing could be less true. The rituals at the basis of our culture are crazed cocktails of Ayahuasca tripping and dance marathons, with a pronounced orgiastic element. The accent is very little on good behaviour, and very much on losing your shit. Public art is based on good times.

The Egyptians kicked off with pageantry on a gargantuan scale. In Herodotus's account, the rite to celebrate Bast, Egyptian precursor of

Artemis, involved thousands of men and women sailing down the Nile in a fleet:

> *Women have rattles and clatter them, while men play the flute. The rest sing and clap their hands. As they come to a city they bring the boat to land. Some women continue rattling, others shout abuse and jeer at the locals. Some dance, and others stand tall and pull up their garments. This they do at every city along the river-bank. When they come to Bubastis, more wine is consumed than during the whole of the rest of the year.*

This is a long way from solemnity. Thousands of revellers make a huge noise on a river, rock up somewhere and abuse the locals, dance a bit and flash their whatsits, before moving on to an epic piss-up. In a ceremony for Anhur, Egyptian ancestor of Ares, one group of priests try to block a second from returning a portable wooden shrine to a temple. Each group numbers around a thousand, and they all have wooden staves.

> *A hard fight with staves ignites, and they break one another's heads. I believe that many die of the wounds they receive.*

There is a strong element of hooliganism here, and the unbeatable element of fun. Whether a rave, a riot, a football crowd or a religious frenzy, there is little to match the dangerous and cleansing pleasure of losing oneself in the derangement of a crowd.

THE TELESTERION AND THE BIRTH OF THEATRE

As with many cultural influences, the carnival approach to religion migrated across the Mediterranean to Greece. As the Axial Age – 'a historical deep breath bringing the most lucid consciousness' – waxed across the belt of the world between 800 and 400 BCE, a desire grew to leave behind the shackles of the body. In the East people sought to escape the flesh through contemplation and interiority, in Greece they aimed for ecstasy (*ek-stasis* – 'beyond the body') through dissolving the self in the throng. One centre of this movement was the cult of Eleusis. An old agrarian religion founded to help comprehend the passage of the seasons, this cult rapidly advanced. A hall was built in Eleusis, a long walk from Athens, where it was believed the goddess Demeter had stayed while searching for her lost daughter, Persephone. This mystery sect became a central cog of religious life for Athenians.

The creed required a transformation of the self, using hallucinogens. Those seeking initiation fasted for two days, stood in the sea and sacrificed a piglet, then set off en masse for Eleusis. Hungry and fearful, they were surrounded by those already initiated, who screamed abuse at them. As a defence they swung branches called *bacchoi* and chanted themselves into a trance in honour of Dionysus, the god of shape-shifting. This odd form of mental torture –walking in a hot sun suffering communal abuse – lasted about eight hours.

By the time they reached Eleusis, the pilgrims were shattered, weak and susceptible to elation or despair. At this vulnerable juncture, they were given a special drink – *kykeon* – brewed from barley and penny-royal, and infused with psychotropic effects from the ergot fungi. As the sun set and torches were lit, the tripping crowd were hustled around the streets of a city they didn't know, through shadows and alleyways and past peering strangers, and then pitched into the darkness of the initiation hall, the *telesterion*.

What exactly went on in this space, the first great indoor theatre, is little known. Whatever occurred, it was the template-setter for all subsequent theatrical attempts to mess with the brains of disoriented audiences. We know: that things were done (*dromena*), most probably an immersive re-enactment of the myth of Demeter and Persephone; that things were said (*legomena*) in spoken or sung commentaries on the actions; and that things were shown (*deiknumena*), including the revelation of something concealed in a sacred basket. Exactly what was in the *kiste*, or holy chest, was a secret so well kept in antiquity we have no idea what it was. The penalty for telling these secrets was death. Along the way animals were sacrificed, and there was an 'unspeakable' event which terrified every nerve ending not already scorched. The derangement concluded in bliss with the reunion of Demeter and Persephone, mother and daughter, in rhapsodic scenes and tableaux.

What is most remarkable about this first step in the evolution of theatre is that it was largely staffed, and entirely run, by women priests. This is not surprising given that the central story of a mother and a lost daughter is female, but it runs counter to the exclusively male narrative we have been handed down of Greek drama. There were six categories of priests, descending from the *hierophantes*, the high priestess, and only one, the *dadouchos*, was male, and they were good only for carrying torches. Given that the lowest rung were called *melissae*, 'bees', one might compare the hierarchy to a hive. The high priestess, queen bee or star, took on the leading roles of Demeter and/or Persephone.

No tidy message or packaged meaning was presented here; this was experiential. The audience did not identify with characters, they became them. They were plunged into the heart of the most painful story imaginable, a mother searching for a lost daughter, torn away afresh each year. Through partaking in that pain, and in the joy of their reunion, many found that having looked death square in the eye it held less fear for them thereafter. A shard of that insight – of the fluidity between death and life – spiked their consciousness, and bolstered it for the remainder of their days. Plutarch compared the initiation to the human response to oncoming death:

> *Wandering astray at first, tiresome walking in circles, some terrifying paths in darkness that lead nowhere; then just before the end, all the terrors – panic and shivering, sweat and amazement. Then some wonderful light comes to meet you, pure regions and meadows are there to greet you, with sounds and dances and sacred words and holy views.*

Aristotle quoted an initiate, 'I came out of the hall a stranger to myself.' What better definition of art?

EASTER WITHOUT THE AGONY

The god Dionysus featured in the the Eleusinian Mysteries and in Athens he had his own festival. Though tamer than the hallucinatory intensity of Eleusis, it was not short on transgression. Dionysus was a chameleon of a god, the offspring of Zeus with, according to differing accounts, either Demeter, Persephone or Semele. He was known as 'twice-born', to account for some of the confusion, and was variously human, semi-divine and finally immortal. Like Demeter and Persephone, he was closely allied with the cycle of each turning year, with death and rebirth.

The Dionysia originated as a rural festival and the god himself began life in the pantheon as a foreigner, from Thrace, northeast of Greece. Once people came to realise the fun they could have with him in this life, and the solace he offered for the next, room was swiftly made on Olympus. Closely associated with wine, his rural festival was held across the winter solstice, at the moment of least fertility and the greatest need for it: the same moment as, and precursor of, our Christmas. It featured feasting, singing and dancing, a parade around the village and liberal drinking. This rural shindig spread quickly across the demes, and attracted the attention of the principal city state.

In 534 BCE, the Athenian leader Peisistratos established a Dionysia, building a small temple to the god on the south slope of the Acropolis, with a theatre cut out of the rocky hillside. Each year for four days, across the vernal equinox (late March), the shrine became the focal point of Athenian life. This was the moment to celebrate the end of winter, the return of Persephone from the underworld, the many reincarnations of Dionysus and the rebirth of life after death. Easter without the agony.

The day before the festival, the wooden cult image of the god was moved from its sanctuary to outside the city walls. On the first morning, the effigy was carried back in ceremonial procession. The city's other festivals were stately, hierarchical affairs, where everyone knew their precise status and enjoyed the formality. The Dionysia was a more improvised do. Buckets of wine were quaffed, amid music and dancing. Maenads, the female devotees of the god, hurtled through the streets clad in ivy crowns and waving their *thyrsus* – a sort of leaf-clad magic wand – at one and all.

Women would boss men; men would wear women's clothes; slaves would walk side by side with aristocrats. All would mingle together, and the hint of upstart rebellion within the cult would satisfy the democratic hunger of the city state. The most distinctive element of the procession was a profusion of colossal cocks. A large proportion of the participants would be carrying huge *phalloi* – wooden, bronze or occasionally gold. One group pulled a prized cart bearing a monster phallus. Primarily this was a fertility symbol, though it had an admonitory backstory. When the cult of Dionysus had first come to Athens, the city had rejected it. Shortly after, a plague afflicted male genitalia. Athenians weren't going to mess with the god again: all waved their sculpted cocks with zeal.

Burlesque encouraged wild fun and the heightened freedom drew the crowd to the cusp of a mystic state. Like on a night of drugged-up raving, when a dance track hits a coincidence with a communal high, when a oneness sweeps through every nervous system, and smiles and souls and waving arms and gaping pupils interlink, so in Athens during a Dionysia, the whole group would intermittently fall into a trance, a brightened state of consciousness, which spread from one celebrant to another. At this moment they believed that Dionysus was amongst them. They experienced *entheos* – 'a god within'.

THEATRE WITHOUT ACTORS

At some point, however improvised, the procession had to arrive at its destination – the amphitheatre beneath the Acropolis. The statue to Dionysus would arrive first and be sat proud in the orchestra. A pig, or goat, or bull, would bite the dust, its bleeding carcass carried around the theatre to purify the space (the correlation between the spilling of blood and the gaining of purity is a troubling one which bedevils tragic narratives to this day). The *strategoi*, a class of military and civic leaders, would pour libations to the gods. The allies of Athens would bring in gifts of tribute. Then, once these rituals had taken place, all settled in for the entertainment.

For three days, the citizens gathered would bathe in the early spring sunshine, the scent of pine on the breeze, and listen to choric recitations of ancient myths. These were purveyed in the form of dithyrambs – delirious narrative hymns in praise of Dionysus. The voices were accompanied by the *aulos*, a mournful wind instrument which can carry plaintive melodies and over long distances. Different choruses would sing these hymns, and dance in a line, sometimes, when in satyr mode, clad in goatskins. The songs began as short and burlesque in tone, then acquired gravity and pathos as the stories were stained with the pain of human life. Whether it was the satyr uniform, the sacrifice or the prize, this form of storytelling took its name from the humble billy goat, *tragos*, and the word for song, *oidos*. Thus goat-song becomes our *tragedy*.

The journey to the theatre, and the performance within it, was all about the subjugation of the individual. Through chanting, singing and dancing, performers and audience became a single entity in praise of the god. With their choreographed movement and their drilled singing, the chorus were the embodiment of a wider group that submerged their identity to give communal witness to stories of trial and pain.

Then Thespis decided to step apart.

THEATRE WITH ACTORS

With evidence scant, there is freedom to imagine how Thespis first said, *Step aside team, leave this to me.* Before he differentiated himself from his colleagues, he may have had an existence as a solo performer. We have a later image of him driving a cart across the country, standing proud at the front, the wagon behind stuffed with the tools of his trade. It is still possible to see performers in the parks of Quito, Ecuador, who continue an ancient tradition, telling stories through a variety of comic and pathetic characters to an audience all around, jumping from persona to persona with a drop of their shoulders and a shift of tone. In the Djemaa-el-Fnaa, the great market-place of Marrakech, one can watch circles of attendees fall spellbound as a hooded man walks to and fro chanting magical tales in a hypnotic monotone. Thespis may have been in this tradition, and most likely, too, in that of the old Homeric bards, wandering from court to court emoting ancient tales. We know from one source he was thought to have invented the mask to denote character. Quite possibly he learnt his trade on the back of his cart, swapping linen masks and identities, as he leapt from epic role to role.

At some point between 538 and 528 BCE, Thespis's ambition grew. Either he was previously part of a chorus and chose to step out, or he came in from outside and grafted himself on. One spring day an audience sat down on the benched seats scored into the hill below the Acropolis. They looked down at the stage, at the city spreading below and the high hills beyond, and saw something brand new. An individual stepped forward from the line of the dithyramb-chanting chorus, and spoke alone. Aristotle tells us Thespis added a prologue to the story, and then interacted in dialogue with the group. He may have begun as a chorus leader, who then chose to don a mask when impersonating a protagonist such as

Odysseus. One of the early words for an actor – *hypokrites* – can mean 'an answerer', and there is evidence the first solo parts were there to respond to the enquiries of the chorus.

On the first occasion, as Thespis strode forward and said with a modest honesty *I am Odysseus*, the thrill must have been gobsmacking. The audacity and the cheek of it. Then the pleasure in joining in the game, when fifteen thousand spectators assented, with a collective imagination, *Alright, you are Odysseus*. Years later, when a second actor stepped forward and announced with the same truthful conviction, *And I am Penelope*, and husband and wife spoke to each other, no-one had seen such audacious imitation before. The audience must have held their breaths with the thrill.

In that instant, tectonic plates of the imagination shifted. Where previously the presentation had been abstract, a musical line of harmony floating on the breeze, and a ripple of bodies in unison on the skyline, invoking little beyond its own beauty, suddenly there stood an individual personifying the character they spoke of. Here was Odysseus or Achilles or Agamemnon. Where previously the narrative had been filled out by the imagination, taking clues from the chanted hymns, to conjure up Mount Olympus or Troy or Thebes, now there was a person claiming to be a live presence in those spaces. Much remained in the mind's eye, in the absence of sets or props, but the long march towards realism had taken its first tentative steps. The excitement of that first transportation created a drug we are still addicted to.

What we know of Thespis is that what he did caught on. When he stepped forward he did not boom or bluster, nor did he whisper or shrink. If he had done the former, he would have alienated his audience, if the latter they would have thought him inept. Neither bullying nor underselling would have served acting. His verse was in the best form to approximate human speech and reflect its cadence; the amphitheatres of antiquity were designed with acoustic genius to allow the voice to glide with minimal force across broad slopes; they were also designed like baseball stadia to give the figure in the centre a focus which would unerringly reveal phoniness or tension. Within that diamond, Thespis would have moved with a limber ease and truth. He occupied the modest human space with a natural grace, and within this frame he birthed a form.

The process evolved, and swiftly. What began as a chorus chanting dithyrambs grew within decades into drama of ever more sophisticated complexity. It furnished us with a canon of many of the greatest plays humanity has made. One actor became two actors with Aeschylus, and two became three with Sophocles and Euripides. The chorus which had once dominated the stage diminished into a backing group for the star performers. Mankind has never loved sitting still in a room for too long; nor has it long tolerated equal billing.

The speed with which individuals raced to forge their path outside the chorus left little time to lament what was lost. There is a generosity of purpose within the group, a dissolution of ego and a shared joy, which is hard to find in the pleasures sought alone. Thespis was the first to fly solo, clearly enjoyed it, and wanted more. Somehow that is not surprising. Soon actors were taking up more and more space within the narrative, trying on multiple characters and masks, and sucking up more of the available oxygen. A festival originally intended as an impersonal tribute to a god was subverted by the hunger for attention of that pesky Promethean, the human.

Actors towards the end of their life often bemoan the neglect of their industry and the theft of their ideas, as Thespis does in the quote where I began his story. They also look back on when they were happiest, when they were young and in companies, sharing energy and enthusiasm, joining evenly in common endeavours, before ambition or jealousy or status stepped in and poisoned the pot. There is a pinch of bogusness in this lament, alongside a large element of truth. It is hard to find greater joy than the shift put in alongside your fellow worker to make something together. The chorus is still the best of us.

ICARUS, HIS FALL

Thespis hailed from the deme Icaria. Not the island named to denote the nearby fall of Icarus, but a mainland region. It acquired its name from a wine-soaked escapade resulting in the death of one Icarius. This scrappy, boozy legend is not a bad place to start the mythology of actors, but Icarus would be yet more apposite. The old myth of the arrogant son who flew too high on the wings his genius father made, only to have the wax that glued them together melt in the sun's blaze and plummet to his death, applies well to actors, artists and all innovators. Their individuation sets them apart, the apartness leads to delusions, the delusions to tragedy.

The warning of the artist father Daedalus that his son should not fly too high is often remembered; what is forgotten is his equal contention that Icarus should not fly too low. He warns that the sea is as dangerous as the sun. If its spray soaks the wings, they will cease to function. Not too high, and not too low: don't soar, and don't dip. Try and achieve what is hardest for any actor, or any artist: know your range and live within it. Tread the difficult path of being human, half god and half animal, and not good enough to be either. All the greatest achievements are in this place of delicate equipoise, successfully balanced between the sea and the sun.

SOLON AND THESPIS

Solon the lawmaker, an early Athenian of renowned austerity and moral rigour, was intrigued by the new developments in the drama. Plutarch tells of his visit to the theatre:

> *Thespis was beginning to develop tragedy. The experiment attracted people because of its novelty. Solon, fond of learning anything new, went to see Thespis act. After the spectacle, he accosted Thespis and asked him if he was not ashamed to tell such lies in the presence of so many people. Thespis answered that there was no harm in talking and acting that way in play. Solon smote the ground with his staff and said: 'Soon, however, if we give play of this sort so much praise and honour, we shall find the same play in our solemn pledges.'*

In a world spiralled into ever greater confusion about the distinctions between actual and virtual realities, it is not difficult to echo the crack of Solon's staff on the ground.

4

The Eye of the Storm

A TALE OF RAVI SHANKAR

Nothing in our world captures the Dionysiac liveness of the first public art ceremonies as closely as the rock festival. There is a direct and unevolved line from shaman-led groups in firelit caves through to tripping kids dancing round flickering flames in Glastonbury fields. The primitive urge to abandon the self in order to mould a new one is still possible in such an arena. Even if the sad truth is often waking up in a dank tent with a headache and an unlikely new friend, it can still happen. When youth scarf down shrooms and flex and flow through the night, dissolving selves in the collective pattern, they revive old customs.

Such festivals may now be commodified into lifestyle parades, but in their earliest manifestations these mud-spattered holidays from hierarchies reignited much of the ancestral fire. Nowhere more so than at the first great trinity of festivals held in 1967, 1969 and 1971 – big events that created templates which have survived the last fifty years. Each of the trinity complemented the other. The first gloried in music at Monterey, a second revelled in anarchy and freedom at Woodstock, the third found a conscience at the Concert for Bangladesh. At each, a generation came together and invented new identities.

A generational shift, a countercultural climate and a political weather map of fear and loathing created the soil which nurtured the movement.

Starry-eyed dreamers, mavericks and exploitative sharks assembled to harness it. One man sat in the middle of all three, arriving as if from another world. He lent his consummate musicianship, his calm grace and (in the case of the third) his political conscience. It was neither a rock star nor a beat poet who provided the *omphalos* for these three world-shifting events. It was a classical musician who sat at the centre of the turning wheel, one from a tradition wholly alien to the audience he played so sweetly to: the Indian sitar player, Ravi Shankar.

Ravi Shankar was about as far from a hippy as one could find. He would often dismount from a plane to be greeted by longhairs in saffron robes and pyjamas, while well turned out in a three-piece suit. His musicianship came from decades of sixteen-hours-a-day discipline, under a guru whose pedagogic methods would now have him locked up. Though never averse to free love, Ravi was strict about steering clear of drink and drugs, keeping body and soul in shape to maintain his marathon playing sessions.

Yet, despite his otherness, or maybe because of it, he was able to sit simply in the middle of this epoch-defining wildness and, through the focus and simplicity of his art, help a jittery generation sit still and hear each other's breath.

MONTEREY, 16–18 JUNE 1967

The flower children wanted their Summer of Love. The hippy movement had found myriad modes of living in fragments. Now it wanted to show how it could come together. Communes were one thing, the crowd another. The conservative wisdom was that a crowd meant a mob, which meant chaos and depravity. The counterculture wanted to demonstrate the opposite: that a gathering could be kind and wise. And, if conservative wisdom was going to double down its fears with policemen, the hippies would festoon them with flowers. As local authorities got nervous, one of Monterey's organisers, John Phillips, wrote the anthem 'San Francisco (Be Sure to Wear Flowers in Your Hair)' to promote the festival, and as a call to calm. No-one expected it to go to Number 1 across the world, and to make this festival the focus of the young world's hopes.

The county fairgrounds in Monterey had long hosted folk, jazz and blues festivals. They lent both a festive air and a seriousness. There was always a groove, as well as a healthy degree of academic nodding. Rock and pop wanted some of the same respect and Ravi was the first brick in the wall. At the time he was held in such high esteem by his peers – pulling together superstar status and genius musicianship – that promoters knew, if he was in, others would join. Whenever choosing an actor for a play or a company for a festival, the first choice is the most crucial, setting a mark others will want to emulate. Once Ravi had agreed, others followed. The occasion was billed as an era-defining celebration of 'Music, Flowers and Love'. A foundation was set up to cover expenses for the artists, who would offer their services for no fee. All except Ravi, who had signed for a handsome sum. No amount of Age of Aquarius blather was going to persuade him to waive it. The first rock festival was Pied-Pipered into existence by a sitar virtuoso and hardened pro.

Bringing Indian music and culture to the West was not a late career swerve for Ravi: it was hardwired into him from childhood. He sailed away as a boy with a dancing troupe run by his elder brother Uday. It was based in Paris and toured Europe and the USA through the 1920s and '30s to sensational effect. Cherry-picking shapes and moves from myriad subcontinent cultures, Uday created a false unity called Indian dance, which he presented to the West. Hailing from a profusion of distinct principalities – cultures defined by widely different histories, creeds and geography – Uday managed to sell an impression of singularity to the outside world. Later, when he returned, he sold the same back to India itself.

Twenty years later, though Ravi was always painstaking to point out the varying provenances of his music, he performed a similar feat with his music. As the first great ambassador for Indian music to the wider world, he brought together a variety of traditions, and forged, if not a unity, then an inclusive conversation. Uday's innovations in dance met the world when India was a nation wanting to be free; Ravi's, in music, when India was young. In both cases, the formation of the national identity was in a dynamic relationship with its ever-changing presentation of itself to the world. Though artists of all forms were part of this conversation, for a nation so huge and a culture so infinite, a surprising amount of this endeavour fell on the two brothers, and the largest proportion on the diminutive but teak-hard frame of Ravi.

The Monterey arena was surrounded by a bazaar of New Age stalls, and as Ravi wandered through he was enveloped in a crowd of 'the gentle people' promised in the San Francisco song, proffering garlands, joints and love. Only seven thousand could fit in the stadium, and tens of thousands more meandered through the fairgrounds beyond, creating one of the first transient townships of the rock festival era. The police who had been sent to crack down on trouble found flowers and friendship. As Ravi recalled to his daughter Anoushka: 'It was 1967, it was all beginning, everyone was really positive, all seeing all the lights in their eyes.'

The sweetness of the energy met music of raw and open passion. Monterey brought together different tribes of American music – soul, rock, protest, experimental – Jefferson Airplane, The Byrds, Jimi Hendrix – who had never presented alongside each other before. It added a new tone of British musician – The Who, The Animals – rougher and looser than the world-conquering Beatles and Stones. And Monterey added international music to the mix, including not just Ravi but the South African trumpeter Hugh Masekela. Such combinations are a commonplace now, but when they happened for the first time, they opened the ears of the audience and the talents of the musicians. Tired acts felt rejuvenated. Amongst a host of career-defining performances, two stood out. Janis Joplin introduced herself to a new audience with a gut-wrenching explosion of song on 'Ball and Chain', and the young Otis Redding poured heart and talent into his first major appearance before a white audience. Joplin was twenty-four and dead within three years, Otis was two years older and dead within six months; both were creating a legacy at high speed.

All knew they were playing for a wider audience than those present. As they made up the story of their generation, the eyes of the world were upon them. A television special was being recorded, albums would follow, and a film made by D.A. Pennebaker. They were playing for the crowd, for the moment and for posterity. The film is a masterpiece of the strange art of capturing the live moment. At their best, concert films can recreate a sense of participation. When this film captures in the frame of a powerful sidelight the silhouette of a sweat-soaked, bent-with-heartache Otis Redding drawing on every fibre of feeling as he sings

'I've Been Loving You Too Long', it privileges us all with being there at a simultaneous moment. Then, now and always.

Amidst the passion and mayhem sat a lacuna of peace. After overnight rain, Sunday afternoon was grey and cold, with a further shower to dampen ardour just before Ravi and his musicians climbed onto the stage at 1.30 pm. Ravi had requested this slot. He wanted clear air between himself and the rock/pop elsewhere. As Anoushka explains, 'He was clear about the presentation of his music and the sanctity of it.'

In a small confected glade of joss sticks and Hawaiian orchids, he tuned up. The informality, the relaxation and the attention to quality settled the air. The neurosis of styling and ego, never far from the rock acts, dissolved in the purity of technique. Ravi was there for the music, and the audience could learn to be as well. Narcissism dissolved into the exchange of playing and listening. 'I love all of you,' Ravi stated, 'What am I doing at a pop festival when my music is classical? This is not pop – but I am glad it is popular.' He knew how to charm and how to calm. The adrenaline rush of a rock crowd was of no use to him: he needed peace and knew how to render it. No bombastics, no desire to dominate, just one human meeting many individual humans. Modesty and might.

He commenced with a meditative *alap*, the gentle reverberant spare notes full of space, which clean the ear for any raga, as the space between the notes creates both a vacuum and small scuds of life within that void. On the evidence of the film, the opening bewitches the audience, who sit nodding as if in a trance. Drugs probably helped. Ravi then interrogates the melody with further density during the *jor*, before accelerating into the virtuosic and pyrotechnic *jhala*. The crowd were silenced, then entranced, then exhilarated. Pennebaker's footage shows the stars of the day – Jimi Hendrix, Jerry Garcia, Brian Jones – sitting in obeisance.

Though other acts were restricted to forty minutes, Ravi played a nearly two-hour set, the delighted bursts of conversation between the sitar and Alla Rakha on the drums drawing rapturous applause. The arena exploded at the end. Michelle Phillips of the Mamas and the Papas said, 'He mesmerised. The result was endless, grateful applause, tears of joy, flowing flower petals, and, if you were looking for it, a religious experience.' 'An extraordinary epiphany,' said Pennebaker, who placed the climax of this session at the end of his film. 'You couldn't follow this with anything, no matter how interesting.'

After reverence and stillness, there had to be compensation. It came from London. Over the last few years, The Who and Jimi Hendrix had got to know each other touring the UK. They tossed a coin to see who would go last on the final evening at Monterey. Hendrix won and put The Who into bat. Determined to leave no speaker unturned, The Who indulged in football terrace violence, with Pete Townshend smashing up his guitar and slamming its neck against the amps, and their wild man drummer Keith Moon kicking over his drum kit as he left the stage. This was a long way from flower power. 'Follow that, Jimi,' was the essence of their gesture.

Hendrix had tricks up his sleeve. Before playing some of the most febrile and inventive electric guitar licks ever, he had concealed a can of lighter fuel behind the amplifier stacks. After a brief but energetic bout of guitar-humping, Hendrix whipped out the lighter fuel, doused his instrument with it, then set it on fire, before smashing it on the stage and hurling it out into the audience. The collision of London violence with West Coast idealism was an electrifying one.

To Ravi, this was sacrilege. He revered music – his sitar was a gift from god. Destroying an instrument with such wantonness was a sign of sickness. Anoushka explains: 'He was really disturbed by Jimi Hendrix because, for him and the culture he came from, the instruments are sacred. Like anything that's a medium of learning you literally worship it, you keep it in the prayer room, you light incense around it. There was a massive culture difference there.' But for all his shock he adored the whole event: 'He loved Monterey, there was a freshness and a sweetness.'

After this engorgement of sacred quiet and then crazed wildness, it was impossible for any act to follow. The weekend finished with a downbeat set from the Mamas and the Papas. At its close, Mama Cass looked out and said; 'You're on your own'.

WOODSTOCK, 15–18 AUGUST 1969.

There are many reasons why Woodstock shouldn't have happened. Dreamt up by inspired oddballs, and executed by madmen, it remains a source of wonder any acts got to the stage at all. The fact that almost half a million people showed up to hear them, that they fed, watered and washed themselves, and listened to mould-breaking music, was a manifestation of the spring of goodwill which swelled up from beneath the event, and flooded the culture around it.

Goodwill was needed. Since Monterey, dark clouds had gathered. If 1967 was the Summer of Love, then 1968 was the year from hell. Martin Luther King and Robert Kennedy were gunned down by assassins of shadowy provenance; the Tet Offensive in Vietnam made graphic the purposeless slaughter of that conflict; the violent repression of the Prague Spring and the *évènements* in Paris; the violence at the Democratic Convention in Chicago: all fractured and fragmented the youth movement. A balm was needed, and what better than a gathering in the Age of Aquarius, another demonstration of how peace and love could flourish en masse. As one producer hoped, 'The world was watching us, and we had a chance to show how it could be if we ran things.'

So it was that, over one weekend in August 1969, the hip and hep from across America clustered on the 600-acre dairy farm of Max Yasgur, in Bethel, New York. Other local farmers were not welcoming. They tried to stop Yasgur from hosting, posting signs proclaiming *Buy No Milk. Stop Max's Hippy Music Festival*. They threatened to shoot hippies who trespassed on their land, and convened a vigilante squad, supposedly to assassinate Yasgur. Even amid the violent politics of the age, it would have been odd if a cow farmer had joined the Kennedys, Malcolm X and Martin Luther King on the roster of martyrs.

The festival sprung from the imagination of Michael Lang, a stupidly handsome and laid-back head-shop owner from Miami. He was very much of the *If we build it, they will come* school of mystic management. In 999 out of a 1,000 cases this approach leads to disaster, but if you catch the right wave, the results can be spectacular. Having come up with the idea, he was content to let it grow organically, and not deny its energies. Whenever his frantic lieutenants attempted to get some steerage from him, they could usually spot him posing on the skyline on a white horse. By happy fluke they landed on Yasgur's farm, a natural bowl of land sloping down to a large pond. It was the perfect amphitheatre.

An army of volunteers arrived, soon hammering together a stage, fences, gates and a rudimentary infrastructure. They dug wells and brought in power for utilities. They mounted lighting towers and sound systems. They built crude roads and optimistic parking space. All scheduled around Max's milking schedule. If that chaos wasn't great enough, that supreme leveller the rain arrived in torrents, turning roads, paths and fields into an endless, sloshing brown. The facilities were not remotely equipped to provide sanitation or first aid for the numbers arriving. A Health Department officer came to inspect the site. He went into the office to start his investigation, but when he came out he discovered that his fifteen-year-old daughter had disappeared amongst the youth. He spent three days looking for her, and never completed his checks. The permit to perform didn't arrive until hours before the show began.

The biggest problem was a simple one – numbers. The intention was for the festival to be ticketed and, given their advance sales, the organisers were expecting around 60,000 to show up. There were already that many present and incorrect two days before it began. Increasingly panicked reports made it clear an exodus was occurring. The cities and towns of America were voiding themselves of youth, all heading for Woodstock. Traffic jams and tailbacks extended for tens of miles. People dumped their cars in ditches on the sides of roads and set off on foot. As David Crosby tells it, 'We thought we were all individual, scattered hippies. When we got there, we said, "Wait a minute, this is a lot bigger than we thought." We flew in by helicopter and saw the New York State Thruway at a dead stop for twenty miles and a gigantic crowd of at least half a million people.'

Before the organisers could finish gates or a box office, the audience simply walked in. What fences they'd constructed were flattened. Originally conceived as a profit-making venture, it was renamed a free concert. If front of house was chaotic, backstage was worse. There was very little assurance when or in what order acts would perform. The traffic jams were so lengthy the organisers got on to Yellow Pages, and started ordering helicopters to ferry musicians from the local Holiday Inn, if they had got that far.

Whoever arrived was swiftly pushed on. If there was no-one there, they improvised. At one point they sent on an Indian guru and told him to do some guru-ing. At other moments, the organisers would go on and preach a new improvised creed: 'The man next to you is your brother, and you'd damn well better treat each other that way, cos if you don't then we blow the whole thing.' Then someone else would come on and warn everyone to 'steer clear of the brown acid'. Richie Havens extended what was supposed to be a couple of songs to over an hour when there was literally no-one to follow. On the spot he improvised a new song, 'Freedom', which became an anthem.

Thanks in part to Havens' epic set, the organisers had a chance to get their house in order. Over the next few days there were epic performances from Janis Joplin (again), Joe Cocker, Creedence Clearwater Revival, Sly and the Family Stone and ,in only their second show together, Crosby, Stills, Nash & Young. 'It was a hectic scene, and we were all kind of winging it,' David Crosby recalled. They winged it together, and somehow, despite the persistent danger of the whole stage being electrocuted by Heath Robinson wiring, they collaborated to effect the 60s' most celebrated manifestation of peace and love. There was nudity, crazed trippy dancing, public sex and some fine music. There were two births and two deaths. On the final morning, as dawn rose, Jimi Hendrix noodled a spacey reset of 'The Star-Spangled Banner' and the remaining stragglers dissolved back into America.

Ravi Shankar, like many of the performers, got stuck in a traffic jam. A helicopter was sent to rescue them, which they shared with Hendrix, who sat in silence. There was little about Woodstock that Ravi relished; he was given a short slot on 'folk night' at ten o'clock. He was worried his sitar would get wet in the downpour and he found it hard to connect with his audience. He looked out on a churned field full of small encampments around fires, and indistinct figures merging. 'It reminded me of the water buffaloes you see in India, submerged in the mud.' Ravi had grown dis-enchanted with the hippy scene which had embraced India with such enthusiasm in 1967, and then passed onto another fashion soon after. As Anoushka remembers, 'By Woodstock he had a sense that it was over, and he was wanting out of it.'

Nonetheless, Ravi was unable to provide anything but his usual magic, with his usual, simple presentation – a carpet and a few people seated together as in a front room. His genius for settling himself and others was sustained. From the beginning of his career, and in all the venues he performed in before a bewildering array of audiences, he always had this capacity to look out and still the air. This is the opposite of rock-star bombast, with banks of silhouetting lights bullying the audience into submission. This is exhaling gently until the audience joins in the same exhalation, and everyone shakes themselves into a calm space, from which they grow together. Then, as usual, he played like the demon of the wind. Though he hated Woodstock, Woodstock loved him. As at Monterey, he provided a centre of gravity.

Woodstock proved itself, too. Against the backdrop of an America veering into violence, they made an environment where neighbourliness and respect flourished. Then, as now, hardliners in opposing corners of certainty may relish antagonism and violence, but the space in between, the nuanced space where most live, is where peace and goodness slumber, until events like Woodstock come to wake them. The hippy movement later lost much of its way in believing every rule was made to be broken, and bequeathed us the miseries of disruption capitalism. But, when it was intent on breaking the wrong rules, it was a glory.

In case all got too sweet and hippy-dippy, there was always The Who to sour the stew with some London sass. They were headlining and, though everyone quickly realised in the chaos that monetary rewards would be skimpy, they refused to go on until they were paid. In cash. A banker in Sullivan County was summoned from his bed at midnight, and flown to his bank by helicopter wearing his pyjamas, to enable cashier cheques to get to relevant parties. Only then would The Who go on. They were happy to risk a riot if not paid. Finally they went on at 5 am, performed a blistering set, then smashed the place up. No excess of peace and love there.

A small community stayed after the festival was over. Some never left. From the dazzling and kaleidoscopic film which recorded the 360-degree craziness of Woodstock, one image lingers. A chap glumly wandering around with a binbag painstakingly picking up all the mess from Max Yasgur's fields. But for his boots, entirely naked.

CONCERT FOR BANGLADESH, 1 AUGUST 1971

There are many reasons why the Concert for Bangladesh had to happen. The connection between popular music and humanitarianism didn't fully manifest until Ravi and George Harrison forged it. News from abroad was 'over there' as far as many rock and pop musicians, and their audiences, were concerned. Tragedy was uncool. That was all about to change.

In November 1970, a cyclone struck the country then known as East Pakistan, killing over 200,000 people. A lack of government aid, along with prolonged disenfranchisement and an attempt to force the Urdu language on Bengali speakers, led to inflammatory resentment between the people and their overseers in West Pakistan. This rage voiced itself democratically in elections of December of that year, and then in armed insurrection after a genocidal crackdown launched by the West Pakistan military. A liberation struggle erupted, led by Mukti Bahini freedom fighters. On 26 March 1971, they declared independence under the name Bangladesh. Millions fled first the natural disaster and later the fighting. Their destination was India, and in particular the streets of Calcutta, which overflowed with refugees, among them relatives of Ravi. For Shankar, the conflict and the rivers of misery forced on the refugee population revived memories of the darkest days of Partition. A catastrophe was destroying hundreds of thousands of lives. When the Indian government asked for help, the world looked the other way.

A passionate friendship, if not a brotherhood, had sprung up between Ravi and George Harrison. It began with the Beatle's fascination with the sitar and its complex music, developed through mutual education and graduated into a fully formed love. Both were genii in their own sphere, inclined to search for spiritual meaning to resolve troubled souls. Both shared a silly sense of humour and lack of pomposity. In the summer of 1971, humour and joy were absent for Ravi. He told his Beatles friend at length of his pain and grief at how things were unfolding in Bangladesh. George was profoundly touched. When Ravi stated his desire to stage a concert to raise money to help, Harrison not only volunteered to play but offered to run the show. As Ravi remembered, 'George saw my anguish and said, "I'll see what I can do."'

George had been affected by his travelling around India and was looking for fresh attachments after the bitter collapse of the Beatles. His own career was riding high on the back of his solo album, *All Things Must Pass*. His drifting through transcendental meditation, the Maharishi and Hare Krishna can appear like spiritual tourism from a later perspective, but at the time he was a pioneer. The risks behind mounting a politically motivated concert were unquantifiable, since no-one had done it before. Creating the form took a freedom from ego and a lightness of imagination which marked Harrison out.

First, he rush-released a charity single, 'Bangladesh', in which he called for recognition of the country, and told how his friend had requested his support. Blending Bengali and Western instruments, the music revolves around the simple incantation of the country's name. As Harrison said, 'The priority was to attract world attention to what was going on.' Suddenly everyone was singing along, and learning of geopolitical events which had been a mystery a week before. This marks the Bangladesh concert out from the later concerts it spawned – Live Aid, Farm Aid, the Free Nelson Mandela Concert and Live 8. Those were inspired by a continuous media noise, which necessitated a response. The Harrison-Shankar project brought the plight of Bangladesh to the attention of the the West, throwing light rather than reflecting it. 'It was a miracle, really,' Ravi said later. 'In one day, the whole world knew the name of Bangladesh.'

To settle on a date, George took advice from a local Indian astrologer who recommended August as propitious. Happily, Madison Square Garden was free on the first day of that month, a Sunday. He jumped boldly in before he had any acts to join him. The advert only announced George and Ravi, but on the strength of that tickets sold out within hours. He then hit the phones to see who he could rustle up. This looks easy fifty years later, when concerts and supergroups are a commonplace, but it was new territory, the first benefit of such a magnitude.

Harrison went after his old friend Bob Dylan, but found it a hard sell, since Dylan was within one of his periodic moments of withdrawal from the public gaze. 'Look, it's not my scene, either,' Harrison argued. 'At least you've played on your own in front of a crowd before. I've never done that.' Dylan hadn't performed for two years; George had not appeared live since the Beatles stopped touring in 1967. He knew the level of expectation he had to live up to and had no desire to trade off the Beatles name. Having asked Ringo to join in, he changed his mind and tried to discourage him. Starr was having none of it. 'Well, I'm coming,' he said.

Many of the acts remained on a promise right up to the soundcheck, some even up to the show itself. At the rehearsal there was Harrison and Starr, Eric Clapton, Billy Preston and a handful of others. They rehearsed, but it was palpable there was much work to do, and that the scale of the event had got to their spectrally thin frontman. Harrison was going to require every ounce of courage in his slender frame to perform again in public, and to do justice to his friend and the cause.

On the day itself, Harrison swallowed his fears, and his concerns about whether the other acts would show up. He stood in front of a packed house of 20,000, and acted as the perfect gentleman-master of ceremonies. His first task was to ask the audience 'to try to get into' the opening section of Indian music. Maybe not the most enthusing words to introduce an act. He then announced Ravi, together with Ali Akbar Khan on sarod, Alla Rakha on tabla and Kamala Chakravarty on tamboura. Both Shankar and Khan had ancestral roots in Bangladesh, and their different Hindu and Muslim heritage comprised a powerful statement for harmony. They learnt their craft together in the humble music room at the Maihar gharana at the feet of Ali Akbar's father, their shared guru, Baba. Here they were thirty years later, on the other side of the world, at one of the concerts of the century.

Throughout their performances in the West, Ravi demanded respect for their music. He took a tradition which began as background entertainment for kings and made it the centre of any event. He insisted on the construction of a low platform for himself or his band, a symbolic gesture in a vast stadium but an important one for him. It raised the status of the music. Anoushka says, 'I remember him saying when we played for Queen Elizabeth when I was a kid, "Everyone will be seated; then I will come on and sit above, because that is what the music deserves."'

At Madison Square Garden, Ravi spoke a few brief words about the plight of the Bangladeshi refugees. The musicians tuned up, followed by the now customary surge of applause. Ravi eased the air with his gentle joke, 'If you appreciate the tuning so much, I hope you will enjoy the playing more' and asked the audience to refrain from smoking during the set. The four musicians then launched into a traditional *dhun* titled 'Bangla Dhun'. Ravi managed his customary magical balance of the spare and meditative with the virtuosic. As Anoushka says:

A key part of the music is the spiritual element. My father kept a
balance – the acrobatics, the flashy and the fiery things had a place –

*a performative element that is meant to be there – you want people
to gasp and you want to have that ecstasy at the end – but it's part
of a bigger process. The alap at the beginning is foundational and
establishes a spiritual space that the fireworks happen within.*

The blend of technique and improvisation, of consummate artfulness
with a nakedness of soul, almost defies imagination. Ravi was still playing in this way for three-hour stretches at the age of ninety-two, weeks
before he died, while connected to an oxygen tank. He was a force.

During the break in the concert, a Dutch TV film was shown, doc-
umenting the catastrophe taking place in Bangladesh and India. Ravi
sensed the stirrings of an empathy and a consciousness that had not been
there before. George Harrison then came on, supported by his super-
band, including Starr and Clapton, and played with the same humility
and strength that Ravi had exhibited. He medleyed his most soulful
songs – 'While My Guitar Gently Weeps', 'All Things Must Pass', 'Here
Comes the Sun'. At that point, he switched to his Fender Stratocaster and
glanced at the set list taped to the body of the guitar. He saw the word
'Bob?'. He had no definite idea what was going to happen next. 'I looked
around, and he was sort of coming on ... It was only at that moment that
I knew for sure he was going to do it.'

Dylan played a masterful set, his joy at returning to playing visible;
Billy Preston lit up the auditorium; Ringo Starr spread his unique brand
of front-parlour merriment; and at the end they all came together to sing
'My Sweet Lord' and 'Bangladesh'. After two more rough years for the
benighted spirit of the sixties, years in which ego and greed had broken
bands and movements, and drugs had taken Brian Jones, Janis Joplin,
Jim Morrison and Jimi Hendrix, this was a rediscovery of faith. Here was
an occasion when the goodness of those lost years could find a home
again. *Life* magazine described it as 'an occasion of almost devotional
intensity'; *Rolling Stone*, as 'a brief incandescent revival of all that was
best about the Sixties'.

Following the two concerts – there were afternoon and evening performances – all the artists and a bevy of others celebrated in a New York
basement club known as Ungano's. Harrison remembered Dylan being
so pleased by life that 'He picked me up and hugged me and he said,

"God! If only we'd done three shows!'" Just for good measure, since no event would be complete without it, the celebrations broke up near dawn when Keith Moon of the ever-reliable Who started smashing up the drum kit.

Raising consciousness was one aim of the concerts, another was raising money. Like Handel's performances of the *Messiah*, more than two hundred years before, there were mouths to feed and distress to alleviate. Initial ticket sales amounted to $250,000, which was passed on to UNICEF. But Harrison had been smart enough to organise both a movie and an album. Both were hugely successful and millions were sent to Bangladesh. The money helped, but not as significantly as the recognition. Two men stepped up and made a difference.

The Western world moved on from its late-sixties craze for Indian music. As George Harrison sang, 'All things must pass'. Musical taste, international curiosity, the peace and love lifestyle, dreams of a universal shift in values, all must pass. The disappointment of so many dreams from the era has been the occasion of much bitterness. But, even if all these fragile aspirations have been swamped by the tawdry corruption of history, even if they were a little daft in the first place, the good they left behind outweighs the bad. If now buried beneath the mud of Woodstock, it is still there waiting to be dug up.

The West never lost its love for Ravi, who in turn never succumbed to bitterness. The culture he emerged from had taught him never to look for simple or solid answers. Transience was all. It may have been why he was always happiest, sitting as the still eye at the centre of a storm, in a stadium of many thousands, all bringing their best human energy to a single space, for a fleeting and passing coming-together. He was a man who could find joy everywhere. He knew to keep looking for it. 'We must turn inward to the deepest of our own roots to find the very best of who we are. It is a constant search, trying to reach something that I can see and feel, that I can almost touch but never hold on to.'

5

Astonish Me!

A TALE OF FOUR IDIOTS

29 MAY 1913: THÉÂTRE DE CHAMPS-ÉLYSÉES, PARIS

Backstage, behind the heavy drape of the curtain, Sergei Diaghilev swept in to say some final words to the corps of the Ballets Russes. This was the moment when he traditionally emboldened their spirits in the cause of advancing the new. It usually involved florid rhetoric and impassioned verbosity. On this night, his message was succinct: 'Whatever happens, the ballet must get to the end.' His instruction to the orchestra was the same: 'No abandoning the ship!' This is not an inspiring message to hear on a first night. It was a prescient warning.

'The entire thing was done by four idiots,' was the judgement on *The Rite of Spring* by one of its key contributors – Enrico Cecchetto, the dance master of the Ballets Russes. It is a blunt summary of the show's creation, and not entirely untrue. One can hear within it the unmistakable tone of the grumpy technician surrounded by a maelstrom of modernists. He went on to list them ...

FIRST M. STRAVINSKY, WHO WROTE THE MUSIC ...

Four years earlier, after the premiere of his *Fireworks* in St Petersburg, Igor Stravinsky received a card from Diaghilev: 'Call tomorrow at 3.00'.

He turned up the next day, and was left to wait for twenty minutes. He could hear laughter from an inner room. Not without pride, he got up and headed for the street. As he gripped the door handle, he was stopped by a voice, 'Stravinsky, come in, come in.' The composer often wondered how his life might have turned out, had that voice come a moment later.

Igor Stravinsky was born to a baritone father in 1882, and bred in the imperial theatre. As a child on his family's country estate, he fell hard for the folk music he heard from local labourers. Country people existing close to the earth, they sang harsh melodies built from a few notes of limited range. There was a wild power to their rural liturgy. When they wanted to make a real noise, they didn't wait for each other to finish, nor did they harmonise; they just piled tunes on top of each other. Layering lines of music like bricks, they built a wall of cacophony. It reverberated in the young composer's head.

Diaghilev's first request was for Stravinsky to arrange the music of Chopin for the ballet *Les Sylphides*. Diaghilev had the producer's instinct that age and experience are meaningless in the face of talent, and shot him quickly up the ranks. A telegram arrived asking him to compose the music for a new ballet, *The Firebird*. Here Stravinsky started to unveil a radical new technique. Forgoing the proportions of propriety, he followed his instinct to experiment. Melody and harmony were no longer the masters, but subservient to rhythm. Rhythms compacted on top of and within each other, like those village songs. Amongst this pile-up of tempos, mini-melodies dash in and out as if in crisis: melodies from the depths of the earth, convulsions of nature. As Jean Cocteau described it, 'Composers vied with each other to find new ways of being misty and melting ... then, suddenly, in the midst of these charming ruins, up sprang the tree Stravinsky!'

Stravinsky was an instant master of tension and release. Gentle, almost mundane, phrases are repeated with little or no variation, as if awaiting an act of violence to disrupt their repetition. They sharpen the appetite for it. If the music sounds familiar today, it is because it resembles the soundtrack to every Hitchcock masterpiece, and is the template for every drama which copies his manipulation of suspense. Hitchcock's great maxim was that any film scene, elevated or banal, can be electrified by the audience's knowledge that there is a bomb under the table. In Stravinsky's music there is always a bomb under the table. He is the dread merchant of anxiety. Though the music was never easy for dancers, *The Firebird* was a hit, and Stravinsky an instant star. His next ballet, *Petrushka*, further liberated music from its patterning, and again had Paris at his feet.

As he was finishing *The Firebird*, Stravinsky claimed, 'I had a fleeting vision. I saw a solemn pagan rite: sage elders, seated in a circle, watching a young girl dance herself to death. They were sacrificing her to propitiate the god of spring.' This was his bid for ownership of the idea for *The Rite of Spring*. After his Paris success, back in Russia in the artist's colony at Talashkino, he and an old friend, Nicholas Roerich, thrashed out their story. With Diaghilev, they decided to entrust this work to the dancer who had become the composer's artistic ally, Nijinsky.

Having written the music for *The Rite of Spring*, Stravinsky sat down to play the score to the conductor, Pierre Monteux. 'Before he got far, I was convinced he was mad,' said Monteux. 'The very walls resounded as Stravinsky pounded away, stamping his feet and jumping up and down. My one desire was to flee the room and find a quiet corner in which to rest my aching head. My only comment was that such music would surely cause a scandal.'

SECOND, M. ROERICH, WHO DESIGNED THE SET ...

In a crowded field of eccentrics, Nicholas Roerich stands out. If certain spade-bearded, nineteenth-century figures seem always destined to end up founding cults in the Himalayas, Roerich was their archetype. Born into wealth, as with most in this story, he shared with Stravinsky a passion for Russian folk traditions. He studied Law in St Petersburg, but was drawn to archaeology and art. Both passions drew him to the artist colony in Talashkino, where seemingly sensible people dressed up in medieval costumes. Idealising their Russian past, they brandished tankards, swung axes and listened to native music. You get the impression they probably said 'thee' and 'thou' a lot (or the Russian equivalent), and burst into hearty laughter at not very funny jokes. In a world of cultural exchange, central Russia has steadfastly resisted assimilation. It is a land that has never been colonised, or sentimentalised. The two things are probably connected. This primal world obsessed Roerich, and floated up in his misty pastels of mystic kitsch.

When Diaghilev brought Roerich and Stravinsky together to discuss a new ballet, Roerich claims to have presented two possible scenarios, one based on a chess game, the other an ancient sacrifice. This runs counter to the composer's claim, and they sparred for decades over whose idea it was. Roerich's claim is stronger, since several scenes are drawn from his paintings. He also gives the most lucid description of the genesis of the idea:

> *The first set should transport us to the foot of a sacred hill in a lush plain, where Slavonic tribes gather to celebrate the spring rites. In this scene an old witch predicts the future, there is a marriage by capture, and round dances. The wisest ancient is brought in to imprint a sacred kiss on the new-flowering earth. The crowd is seized with mystic terror.*

All of the above happens in under fifteen minutes. That is the daytime. Then we move on to the evening:

> *The second act presents a celestial mystery. Young virgins dance on the sacred hill, amid enchanted rocks, then they choose the victim they intend to honour. In a moment she will dance her last dance before the ancient old men wrapped in bear-skins. They dedicate the victim to their God.*

After the marriage by capture in Act i, we now have the sacrifice of a virgin in Act ii. The music may have been modern, but the sexual politics weren't. Roerich adds a baffling postscript to this brief narrative: 'I love antiquity for its sublime happiness and deep thought.'

No matter the strangeness of the source, Roerich and Stravinsky were both in their element colliding the ancient and the modern. They also loved looking at pictures of old folk costumes. This was ominous.

THIRD, M. NIJINSKY, WHO COMPOSED THE DANCES ...

A young English dancer auditioned for the Russian company in Paris. Her name when she did so was Hilda Munnings. Later in life she became the celebrated Lydia Solokova. Once in the company, as an interim measure, she was given the unconvincing soubriquet of Hilda Munnigsova. Whatever the name, she was an acute observer. She said of Nijinsky,

'Like a faun, he was a wild creature who had been trapped by society. When addressed, he turned his head furtively, looking as if he might suddenly butt you in the stomach. He moved on the balls of his feet, and his nervous energy found an outlet in fidgeting.' Not unlike the young John Lydon.

Nijinsky was born in Kiev in 1890, to a dancing family whose parentcraft mixed grace and brutality in toxic measures. He joined the Imperial Ballet School at ten, and at seventeen was a phenomenon, thick-thighed and long-torsoed, and able to dance with both pneumatic power and willowy lightness. This was the age he came under the purview of Diaghilev and he was soon in both his company and bed. In public, Diaghilev and Nijinsky posed as the avatars of the future. In private, they squabbled with venom.

The Ballets Russes had entranced and shocked Paris since their first appearance there in 1909. What Parisian critics loved was the way these 'Northern Savages' played to the fashion for the primitive and untamed. In Nijinsky they had a star whose brute strength and cataclysmic vulnerability bottled this very essence. His acting realism went against the traditional florid vanity, and there was an arrhythmic spontaneity to his moves, as feet and legs and thighs jerked or twisted or stamped as if sparked by electric currents. He had that irreplaceable looseness that made you think his limbs were opting independently to float in patterns together.

At Monte Carlo in 1911, Nijinsky leapt into legend. Coming to the conclusion of an unremarkable ballet called Le Spectre de la rose, he took five running steps from the middle of the stage and leapt through a window at the back on the sixth step. No one in the audience saw him land. Everyone saw him fly out and, in their imagination, he continued, on into their hearts. In fact, behind the set, four men caught him and wrapped him in warm towels.

Success brought little pleasure to the young star. Born and bred in the dancing community, it was by far his most effective language, and he was uncommunicative in others. As Munnigsova put it: 'He seemed always to be alone; he was incapable of mixing ... He would talk shyly and softly, without looking at the person, and move away quickly.' Another witness found him after a performance, curled on the floor like a bird fallen from its nest. His hands were clutched over his heart, which she could hear beating. 'He was like a crumpled rose in pain.' These vulnerabilities needed caution and care. They received neither. He was sweated as an asset.

Once Nijinsky had become a star, his team decided to dump Michel Fokine, the choreographer who had harnessed his talent, and to promote the young man. His desire to tear the tulle and the tiara away from ballet was in sympathy with his colleagues. Nijinsky, the great executant of Fokine's choreography, had begun to distrust its marshmallow centre, its lack of a steely central truth. For him there was too much atmosphere and virtuosity. Stravinsky aimed to strip the shimmering and the trills from music. Nijinsky aimed for a more gravitational, earthed movement. Out went the aspiration of those long-armed stretches and soaring leaps, aiming for a rarefied Olympus. In came the human figure, feet in the clay, falling down and down, and finding hard earth.

His first work, Debussy's *L'Après-midi d'un faune*, in 1912, caused an almighty stir, when his faun appeared to be enjoying a *petite mort* all over the fallen scarf of a nymph. This was too much for his colleagues, who tried to rein him in. But freedom once released, in the hands of the carefree, is hard to regulate. 'I detest nightingale and prose poetry,' Nijinsky said. 'I eat my meat without sauce béarnaise. There have been schools of painting and sculpture that went suaver and suaver until there was no expression but only banality left; then there always came a revolt.'

FOURTH M. DIAGHILEV, WHO WASTED MONEY ON IT ...

'Étonne-moi!', Diaghilev would bark at Jean Cocteau, when he started to write the scenario for his ballet *Parade*, 'Astonish me!'

It was the injunction Diaghilev hurled at all collaborators. Art for him wasn't a realm of meditative insight, it was a grandstanding event intended to spark what the sociologist Émile Durkheim called 'l'effervescence sociale'. Event for Diaghilev was everything. He wasn't interested in long runs, or cashing in. He wanted firework displays of newness, points of intimidating light which defined the future. The artistic elements were only part of this totality. It included the public gasp at the unveiling, the sound of chatter around the theatre, the reams of print columns across European journals, and the earnest discussions in academic treatises. All these excited reactions were part of the work itself, and all emanated from the maxim, 'Etonne-moi!'

What Diaghilev's taste was – indeed, whether he had any – was moot. He was a connoisseur of the creepy art of knowing who was hot and who was not. Over the course of his working life he commissioned designs from Picasso, Matisse, Coco Chanel, Max Ernst, Joan Miró and Braque, so he could always compel the attention of the gifted. He offered no insight or emotional capacity; he just flattered their ego that he judged they were still high-status. But he had the courage of an iconoclast and, with the face of a pug and the sleepy eyes of a killer, he commanded respect, deserved or not. Hilda again: 'He radiated self-assurance like royalty. Tall and heavy with a little moustache and a monocle, he advanced into the room. Everyone who was seated stood up and silence fell. Any male dancer he spoke to would click his heels together and bow.'

He wanted to revive Russian culture, and his boldest stroke was in realising that the best place to achieve that was, perversely, Paris – the capital of the future with a power to intimidate the world far greater than any city on the icy Neva River. In 1907, he presented in Paris a series of concerts of Russian music through the ages, which was a big hit. A year later, Mussorgsky's *Boris Godunov* was equally successful. Diaghilev wanted to follow this with another opera season, but ran out of money, so opted for ballet instead, since it was cheaper. Lacking his own ballet company, he returned to St Petersburg and stole an entire one from the Imperial Theatre, naming it the Ballets Russes. He had already fallen hard for Nijinsky, whom he had discovered dancing in *Le Pavillon d'Armide*. The first season they put together was thought traditional and disappointing. Diaghilev quickly perceived that the West had a voracious maw for the new. Noise and sensation were needed. His impresario's instincts told him that Stravinsky was the man to create it.

As he introduced the composer to the company, he announced, 'Mark him well ... he is a man on the eve of celebrity'. As with many such utterances, from a man with the publicist's instinct for shaping taste, it turned out to be self-fulfilling. *The Firebird* made Stravinsky a celebrity, and Nijinsky more so. In the game of snakes and ladders which Diaghilev orchestrated, Stravinsky became indispensable and Fokine, whose choreography had delivered their success, was dumped. Diaghilev's love for the young Nijinsky may have been genuine, but his promotion of him, and the size of the tasks he entrusted to him, were errors of judgement if his criteria was the nurturing of an artist. It is hard to think they were. He just wanted to drain the young man of his life-spirit until he broke.

THE FIFTH IDIOT

Unknown to Cecchetto, there was a fifth idiot, Gabriel Astruc, the theatre manager. In his own way, Astruc was a dreamer as outlandish as Diaghilev. His ambition was to outstrip the Paris Opera by producing a modern repertoire brimming over with talent. Born in 1864 into a family of Sephardi Jews, Astruc found that doors were always shutting in his face. The Dreyfus affair had blown up in France only a decade before, leaving behind a divided nation, with a host of anti-Semites still on the warpath. So, in the face of closed doors, Astruc decided to build his own set. In 1913 he constructed the Théâtre des Champs-Élysées, an architectural landmark with a first season to match of dazzling promise. Predictably, it attracted anti-Semitic abuse. An anti-Dreyfusard novelist called Leon Daudet, who edited *Action Française*, a Catholic periodical, wrote: 'The Jew behind the Grande Saison de Paris is demolishing the Parisian season. The itinerant camper is a curse on the sedentary population. When Astruc is finished with Paris, he will do the same with Vienna or Berlin. This is the behaviour of the Jewish bank applied to theatre.' This sort of poison passed with little or no comment.

The expenses involved in building the new concert hall left Astruc in a vulnerable financial position and Diaghilev added to the pressures. The Russian charged 25,000 francs for *The Rite of Spring*, double what *Petrushka* had cost the year before. Astruc knew it was madness but was so dazzled by the stars – Diaghilev, Nijinsky and Stravinsky – that he coughed up. It was money he couldn't afford, but as he put it with the sweet and sacrificial devotion of the true fan, 'this folly, which I had not the right *not* to commit to, cost me my management'.

CHANGE AND STASIS

The Rite of Spring, as with many works internally at war with themselves, emerged from an embattled age, one on the brink both of war and of profound cultural change. The advance of technology, and a new understanding of the human and his social space, were pushing against an embattled but determined stronghold of tradition and stasis. The tension between the two was electrifying. Everywhere the boundaries of what is possible or normal in music were being stretched, by Debussy, Mahler and Strauss. Cultures outside the Western tradition were of increasing interest, too. Gauguin had recently sent his Tahitian landscapes back to Paris; Matisse and Picasso had appropriated the jagged angles of African masks. The Russian ballet was seen as part of this celebration of otherness, becoming a new focus of the season, 'a bright moment in Western culture'. Yet there was a conservative clique who were tiring of what they deemed the novelty of the exotic. Their yearning for the past was blended with a xenophobic suspicion of the curiosities of the present. It was a volatile cocktail.

The first stirrings of this distaste began to make themselves clear for Debussy's *Les Jeux*, choreographed by Nijinsky. The initial premise for this show was a three-way gay male encounter and a plane crash. This somehow morphed into a flirtation between a young man and two women, and a game of tennis. Strange are the ways of ballet. Debussy objected to the new scenario, but changed his mind when Diaghilev doubled his fee. The work floundered on Nijinsky and his designer Léon Bakst's lack of sporting knowledge. The youths bounded around with tennis rackets, but never used them to hit the balls. This was a relief, since they were footballs. The mystique of the Ballets Russes was still strong, and the complaints were mutterings rather than storms. They were to follow.

HE LITERALLY HIT THE ROOF

For *The Rite of Spring* to achieve the revolution he required, Nijinsky's corps needed training. He demanded 120 rehearsals to dictate the terms of each tremor. This was not chaos unleashed; even the harshest critics of *The Rite* would not call the dance unorganised. The new style demanded an exacting degree of muscular control.

As ever, Nijinsky first looked for a basic position, an establishing mannerism, which captured the essence of the piece. His starting stance was the arms tightly folded high on the chest, with awkward closed fists half supporting lolling, bent heads. Knees were bent and turned in, and feet also, as if pigeon-toed. Here was not the aspiration to grace of Western ballet. This was a prehistoric species, hunched in automatic self-defence against the land, the weather and their superstitions. From this starting point, they moved in ataxic spasms, as if up a steep incline. The movement so contorted their physical features, it looked as if it might break them. The steps were simple – stamping, trembling, jerking – and held a jolting, crude energy. The dancers had to unlearn a life of classical training in order to enact the awkward motions.

Equally taxing was the demand that they should not emote. Used to looking elegantly intense, they were instructed to detach all emotion from their faces. This gave the movement a detached, almost clinical quality, as if emptied of interior life. Each of their physiques had to dissolve into the primeval purpose of the rite, jerking like puppets controlled by an omnipotent hand. During rehearsals, Nijinsky snapped if the dancers betrayed a smidgen of sentimentality. 'There are no human beings in it,' he wrote to Stravinksy. 'It is the life of stones and trees.'

Nijinsky's demands for an unballetic look, combined with his inability to articulate what he wanted in any other way than through demonstration, took its toll. Used to gliding elegantly to the melodies of Chopin, the corps were not ready for impersonating pneumatic drills to thunderous new music. One remembered, 'he rehearsed like an inexhaustible demon ... With every leap we landed heavily enough to jar every organ. Our heads throbbed with pain, leaving us continually with nerves jangled.' Nijinsky drove rehearsals forward with the implacable intensity of someone who knows that something is terribly wrong. As Hilda put it, 'one day he lost his temper to such an extent he literally hit the roof'.

To ease their pain and confusion, and to try and bridge the gap with Nijinsky, Diaghilev invited in Marie Rambert, a devotee of the new cutting-edge school of eurythmics. She was soon nicknamed 'Rhythmitchka'. She joined an eccentric rehearsal room, which included a giant German pianist known as Kolossal. His moniker was not on account of his large size, but because he frequently used the fashionable expletive 'kolossal!' to express his approval. The room was regularly visited by the reserve conductor, who bore the unimprovable name of Rhené-Baton.

Nijinsky wrote to Stravinsky, 'For an ordinary viewer, it will be a jolting impression and an emotional experience. For some it will open new horizons flooded with rays of sun.' Stravinsky didn't agree when he attended rehearsals. He insisted they had been dancing to the wrong tempo. He pushed Kolossal away from his piano stool, banged the lid, then hammered out the correct tempo. Nijinsky told the composer his pace was impossible to dance to. They had a full Russian tantrum-off. The later judgement of Stravinsky was crushing: '[Nijinsky's] ignorance of the most elementary notions of music was flagrant'.

Things weren't much easier for those who knew their music. The conductor, Monteux, had recovered from his initial hearing of the piece, but never ceased detesting it. Later in life, he claimed he had conducted it over fifty times, and not enjoyed it once. Still, he put together an impressive plan to help the musicians achieve its demanding time switches and its unique orchestration. This involved seventeen full rehearsals, a previously unheard-of number. 'It is hard to describe the astonishment of the orchestra when we started the first rehearsal,' Monteux reported. Almost immediately, the musicians stopped, asking if the parts were correctly printed. This continued for a while until the conductor snapped, 'Stop asking me if you have a mistake. If you have one, I will let you know.' Stravinsky had reinvented the rhythmic system with new time signatures for each bar. There were sudden endings on the third beat of a bar, and dead stops just before a climax. All the traditional language of growth, accumulation and diminuendo were discarded.

The intention of the music to ratchet up tension and jangle the nerves didn't make for a harmonious process. At rehearsals, the musicians started to laugh at the sheer impossibility. This was not the sort of endeavour where tearful speeches were made about fighting through together, and bands of brothers. This was a group of professionals gritting their teeth and pushing on. They had no idea what they were making, but they knew it was their job, and they were being paid.

Little did they know that what they were working on was, in the words of Jean Cocteau, 'a masterpiece: a symphony impregnated with wild pathos, with earth in the throes of birth'. Nor did they have any idea how it would go down with its first audience.

THE MURDER SUSPECTS

Exactly who was responsible for murdering *The Rite Of Spring* on 29 May 1913 has been much debated. If I was to bring all the suspects into a room, and spring a Poirot surprise on the culprit, I would nominate a previously unsuspected agent. None of the 'idiots' above. Rather, I would accuse the hall. Or, if not the hall itself, the newness of it. The Théâtre des Champs-Élysées was and is a splendid edifice, and a beautiful one for music. But it had only opened in April and had played largely concerts in its seven weeks, apart from Debussy's poorly received *Jeux*. Theatres need time and damage for authority. They need bruising and emotion to give them charisma. The new hall was too cold and comfortable for a crowd used to being squeezed together in red plush and gilt. They had not become friends to this space yet. It was a fatal environment in which to attempt anything so bold.

It was also an unseasonably hot day – 85° Fahrenheit (29°C) – as the two different crowds gathered to pack the theatre. One was the wealthy and the fashionable, decked out in evening dress, top hats and gowns; the others, the bohemians in trademark soft caps. Ticket prices ranged from 40 francs for the *loges* down to 2 francs for the gallery. Tickets had long sold out and the audience included a roll call of early modernism – Ravel, Debussy, Delius, Proust, Picasso, Gertrude Stein, Gabriele D'Annunzio, and a host of others.

Crucially, in terms of the creation of mayhem, the two audiences rubbed together in one central section. There was a walking space between one row of *loges* and another behind the dress circle. Here Diaghilev positioned his claque of supportive painters and musicians. A river of long-haired radicals flowed between the ramparts of boxes glinting with diamonds and pearls. This was the high-art equivalent of putting two rival tribes of football fans in the same end. As another attendee, Jean Cocteau, saw it:

All the elements of a scandal were present. The smart audience in tails and tulle, diamonds and ospreys, was interspersed with the suits and bandeaux of the aesthetic crowd. The latter would applaud novelty simply to show their contempt for the people in the boxes. Innumerable shades of snobbery, super-snobbery and inverted snobbery were represented ... The audience played the role that was written for it.

THE BEGINNING OF THE MODERN

There remains some discussion over what happened in the first two minutes, as the solo bassoon began proceedings with its plaintive mournful cry. Some say the sad elegance of this refrain silenced the audience and induced respect; others, that the trouble had already started. The latter is more likely. The first recorded witticism of the night is the composer Saint-Saëns exclaiming, 'If that's a bassoon, then I'm a baboon!' (This, like many of the night's other gags, loses much in translation.) Behind the curtains, the dancers assumed their opening positions, and fear settled in. As Stravinsky remembered, 'Mild protests against the music could be heard from the beginning ... then when the curtain opened, the storm broke.'

At that moment the production revealed a second major culprit: the costumes, and their designer, M. Roerich. Even a crowd eager to bridge the cultural divide might have struggled. For the crowd present, with a predisposition to criticise, they were a red rag to a bull. The men sported brightly coloured tea cosies on their heads, floating above clouds of wiry facial hair; the women wore felt wigs with long plaits that made them look like zombie dolls. The make-up looked like warpaint. The chaps wore cross-gartered socks as if styled by Malvolio at his maddest; the women were belted and strapped into their dresses at the least flattering points. The patterns strain at a Mongolian chic, which has never really caught on outside Mongolia. For an audience that was negatively disposed, and already unsettled by the jangled wires of the music, this gave them their path out – laughter and derision.

Soon after the curtain rose, the smart remarks started coming in. As the dancers adopted Nijinsky's mannerism for the piece, tilting their heads against their hands, cradling their cheeks in distress, one wag called out, 'Doctor, Doctor!' Another replied, 'Dentist!' and then, as the dancers carried on, a third joined in with 'Two Dentists!' It was uproar. A comtesse stood up, tiara askew, and called out, 'I am sixty years old and this is the first time anyone has dared make fun of me.' Soon after this peculiar boast, the audience made a lot more fun of her. A bohemian voice cried out with indignation from the gallery, 'OK, whores of the 16th, are you going to shut up soon!' D'Annunzio and Debussy, seated in Astruc's *loge*, got into a quarrel with a neighbouring *loge*, screaming into their faces. One elegantly dressed lady in an orchestra box stood up and slapped the face of a young man in the next box. Her escort rose, and cards were exchanged between the men. A duel followed the next day.

The noise was soon deafening, and was drowning out the music. Diaghilev climbed into the gallery, shouting, 'I beg you. Let them make their show.' D'Astruc's plea was more practical; 'Listen now. Boo later.'

Stravinsky himself raced out after scarcely five minutes. Sitting in the middle of a row, he had to scuffle his way past people's knees – never a dignified exit. 'I said, "Go to hell!" "Excuse me, messieurs, mesdames," and left the hall in a rage, slamming the door.' He came backstage to find pandemonium. The noise was so loud the dancers couldn't hear the music. For any piece, this would have been tricky; for one as fiendishly complicated in its rhythm, it was fatal. Dancers were running around with little bits of paper in their hands quarrelling over whose count was right. Nijinsky – made up and dressed for the evening's later performance of *Le Spectre de la rose* – his face as white as his crepe de Chine shirt, was quivering with furious emotion and threatening to charge on stage and make a further scandal. Stravinsky grabbed his dressing gown to stop him.

To help his dancers, Nijinsky climbed onto a chair on the edge of the stage, and started bellowing out the beat count. Stravinsky stayed beside him, still gripping his gown. The choreographer beat the rhythm with both fists, and shouted, 'One, two, three.' This Stravinsky understood, though he got confused as Nijinsky continued. 'I wondered what on earth the numbers had to do with the music, for there are no thirteens and seventeens in the metrical scheme.'

The forty-six dancers on stage, deafened by the mass chaos in front of them, had the impossible task of presenting the ballet to the audience, trying to hear the orchestra in the pit and to catch what they could of Nijinsky's random mathematical shrieks from the wings. Proper troopers, they carried on jerking fervently in prehistoric fashion, even as their wigs, their hot flannel costumes, and the sheer number of them packed together, generated a furnace-like heat. By the end of the first half, less than fifteen minutes in, they were all soaking. Many rushed into the wings in tears, and begged for the show to be stopped.

Diaghilev, the smell of a historic scandal flaring his nostrils, insisted on continuing. As a calming measure, he decided to turn the house lights on and off, reasoning that, if people could see how badly they were behaving, they might think better of it. There was a brief lull, but it was more a drawing-in of breath than a cessation of hostilities.

The police arrived in the intermission to remove some of the more boisterous elements and as usual made things worse. The aggro was soon reignited between the posh fops and the bohemian scruffs. One of the double-bass players reported that 'many a gentleman's shiny top hat or soft fedora was pulled down by an opponent over his eyes and ears, and canes were brandished like menacing implements of combat'. Chairs were knocked over and brandished as weapons, sections of the audience stampeded, and fist fights broke out. One woman called Maurice Ravel 'a dirty jew', and another took out her hatpin in order to stab the man next to her, who may or may not have been Jean Cocteau.

In the middle of the chaos, stood one of the many heroes of the night, conductor Pierre Monteux. He didn't like the music, he could hardly hear his own orchestra, missiles were regularly raining down on him and his musicians, but he was determined to get to the end. Come what may. Sometimes finishing is its own achievement. As Stravinsky recalled: 'The image of Monteux is more vivid in my mind today than the picture of the stage. He stood there impervious and nerveless as a crocodile.'

Somehow the dancers hauled the bloodied body of the ballet through to the end alongside the music, though not always in time. 'We could see Diaghilev, walking up and down, holding his head. We must have been a lovely picture for the audience, racing around, jumping, turning, and wondering when the whole thing was going to collapse.' When it did finally finish, and the curtains closed after another fifteen minutes of mayhem, collapse was all they were ready for. The dancers – who had spent long months rehearsing something utterly unfamiliar, who had given their all, and had it rejected with as much hatred as has greeted any work of art – fell to the ground, spent. Diaghilev walked among them, telling them to get up because they had another couple of shows to do that night. The impresario later turned to a friend and said, 'Exactly as I wanted it.'

On the other side of the curtain, the brawling carried on before spilling out into the streets, and then slowly dissipating its frenzied energies into the big quiet of a Parisian night.

WHAT DID THEY MISS?

While the punching and hissing and demonstrating went on, something passed the audience by. A masterpiece. Within its complex but incandescent aliveness, the music stands alongside the other major modernist achievements: Eliot's *The Waste Land*, Joyce's *Ulysses*, the scrambled perspectives of Cubism, and the paranoid cramped visions of Kafka. As Eliot wrote, the music managed to reconfigure 'the rhythm of the steppes into the scream of the motor horn, the rattle of machinery, the roar of the underground railway, and the other barbaric cries of modern life'. While many of the events under discussion in this book invite in the past, absorb it thoughtfully and use it to re-form the new, Stravinsky's work stands as the ultimate example of something invadingly modern, punching a hole in the window that separated past and future.

Alongside the music was a ballet of potential greatness, though never allowed the time to mature (or to ditch the disastrous costumes). Diaghilev ushered it out of the company's repertoire with the ruthless nonchalance with which he ushered Nijinsky out of his company, and his life. It had extraordinary originality. Within the shamanic frenzy, a new language was finding its voice. Much of the ballet tradition was tutus and airy elevation, the dancer as a javelin of flesh stretching up to the empyrean; Nijinsky clad his dancers' feet with clingy sod and curved them down towards the earth. Within this new language he found room for ecstasy, for despair, for joy, and a host of new emotional colours.

Beyond the stature of the piece as music and dance, the audience missed something more important: one of the great instances of art as a canary in the mine. This was the music of terror before the terror arrived, the suspension of musicological rules, as Europe was about to suspend all rules of civilised behaviour. The first throes of *The Rite of Spring* took place on the brink of a war that would plunge Europe into a charnel house of bones and trenches. The suspense at the core of the music was not cheap thrills; it was the heart-frozen terror of many nations pausing before opening a door. They knew there was carnage on the other side. *The Rite of Spring* is the dark side of the European soul giving birth to a death-spreading modernity. For an epoch waltzing blithely to its own end, it is apt that, on the night when art gave its clearest indication of what was coming, the audience should respond by sneering from their fastnesses.

TO BE LOVED ALONE

Nijinsky himself was dismissed from the Ballets Russes in 1919, a death blow to his morale and soon to his sanity. He began scribbling in a notebook in January of the year and, seven weeks later, Swiss doctors studied four notebooks full of his writings, and promptly interned him in a sanitarium. His dancing had already been showing signs of his incipient schizophrenia. He was in and out of European institutions for most of the next thirty years, spending large periods in complete silence. In Vienna in 1945, he chanced across a group of war-weary Russian soldiers, singing old folk songs and playing the balalaika. Inspired by the long-forgotten music and language, he started dancing around the fire they encircled. The soldiers were slack-jawed at his skill as he flickered in the firelight. He died five years later in London.

Diaghilev floated along in his rackety way, ever a millimetre from triumph or disaster, in one cosmopolitan capital or another. At times he behaved abominably to lovers and colleagues; at times, with great kindness. He never lost his talent to surprise, nor dispelled the suspicion that that was his only talent. He died in Venice in 1929. Ten years later, on the brink of another cataclysm, in his poem 'September 1, 1939', W.H. Auden wrote the sharpest analysis of the relationship between the exploited and the exploiter:

What mad Nijinsky wrote
About Diaghilev
Is true of the normal heart
For the error bred in the bone
Of each woman and each man
Craves what it cannot have, Not universal love
But to be loved alone.

Astruc ran up terrible debts on this show and unplayable ones on the theatre. He was hounded to his end by the proto-fascists of Action Françcaise, and forced to give up the directorship of his theatre. Roerich lived a titanic life across many continents, usually guided by his spiritual masters, the mahatmas, in the Himalayas. They communicated telepathically with him through his wife. These same masters told him to create a spiritual Pan-Asian community all worshipping the future Buddha, who may have looked suspiciously like Roerich.

Stravinsky's fame grew and grew, as did his ability to cultivate it. His top-table impulse took him ever further west, from Russia to Paris, to New York, and finally to Los Angeles and Hollywood royalty. His music, and its freeing of rhythm from its subservience to melody and harmony, had a profound influence, not least on jazz genii of improvisation and explorers of the cul-de-sac like Charlie Parker, John Coltrane and Ornette Coleman. He lived a long and lauded life. Not for him the determined fury of Nijinsky, nor his consuming passion for the destructive fire of creative truth.

The artist Valentine Gross described the evening of 29 May 1913, in the Théâtre des Champs-Élysées, thus: 'The theatre seemed to have been struck by an earthquake. It seemed to shake.'

Somehow a contrived event, dreamt up by four eccentric mavericks, two of them touched with genius, taking place two thousand miles from their homes, made the earth shift. Great wonder to have been there when such a night of brawling and beauty could define the age.

DANCE, DANCE, OR WE ARE LOST – PINA BAUSCH

In March 2020, on a beach in Toubab Dialaw, Senegal, before a calm Atlantic Ocean, and under a milky evening sky, thirty-eight dancers from across Africa enacted with unparalleled beauty an ancient rite. Their silky tunics fluttering in the sea breeze, the sand swallowing the noise of their galloping feet, groups of men and women rippled towards and away from each other like the yin and yang of a single organism. Passers-by on bicycles and pulling carts stopped to stare at this wonder. Tannoys blared out music from a different universe, composed in St Petersburg in 1912. However foreign in place or time, its ominous pulse and earthed energy seemed to fit this unending horizon line, and the bodies lurching and lungeing in organic harmonies across it.

Dancers from Pina Bausch's Wuppertal company, still mourning the loss of their etched icon of a leader, travelled to Senegal to train the dancers to perform her masterpiece, *The Rite of Spring*. They were determined to spread the legacy of Pina to new places and new generations. The production was meant to tour, but Covid-19 had put a stop to that, so, with time running out, the company rushed to the beach to film a version. They wanted to record their collective effort, before returning to homelands and new stories. Their last months of rehearsal are clutched tightly in their bodies in thirty minutes of pure expression.

Bausch premiered her work in 1975 in the Opernhaus Wuppertal. In that arena white bodies dressed in monochromatic shifts and trousers stamped their feet into mud and dirt. Though the story is a celebration of spring, here it is transformed into a scratched shifting woodcut of the male and female need for each other's energies, and of their tender mutual repulsion. The choreography is as ancient as bodies on rocks in caves, arms reaching and pleading, backs arching in pain, tribes stamping in frenzy. Stark and raw, it unleashes from within the dancers reservoirs of lust, fear and rage. The dirt beneath rises up to cling to legs and trunks and faces like invading warpaint. In an ancient ritual, the earth is reclaiming the foolish dancing mortals who flit in such elegant panic across it.

In 1975, dirt clings to white skin; in 2020, golden sand cleaves to black skin. In both cases, thanks to the singular genius of Pina Bausch, we are shown the shimmering beauty of human potential, and its resounding futility on earth or sand.

In both cases, one of the greatest pieces of music written for dance is reborn and redeemed. Rhythms piling on rhythms across history.

6

Bowls of Light

A TALE OF NEFERTITI AND AKHENATEN

Late in her short life, Lorraine Hansberry was seized with enthusiasm for a new project. She had been searching for a story from the past which could bundle together her feelings about the present. The resulting notes for the play, and the first scribbled scenes, are scattered on lined yellow paper in her playful and vivid hand. In vain she searches for an idiom for her characters, and falters over Messengers saying, 'News, my Lord', and Lords saying, 'My ears await thy news.' The failure to find an original language meant a swift shelving. But the notes reveal her startled enthusiasm. In her excitement, she was, as usual, ahead of the curve. There was quite possibly identification with a figure she thought to be suffering 'infinite loneliness', who was 'worst of all, happy in his wisdom'.

The title of the play, spelled out in excited capitals, was to be 'AKHNATON THE KING'.

ALL CHANGE

In 1353 BCE, after two thousand years of tradition and evolution in Egypt, and before a thousand more of the same, everything went a little crazy for seventeen years. The old Egyptian goddess of justice and harmony bore the name Ma'at. She was a byword for the way things had always been, an ideal of order and balance which held an empire together longer than any in history. Ma'at was not a concept which interested Nefertiti and Akhenaten.

Artistic and political radicals have often believed it best to go all in. Not for them small nudges, or incremental reform: they favour the Year Zero clear-out. No-one has exemplified this more comprehensively than Nefertiti and Akhenaten. Succeeding his father, Amenhotep III, in 1353 BCE, as Amenhotep IV, the son changed first his name, then the state religion, and then its politics. To cap it all, he and his wife moved the entire body politic to a newly built capital city, Akhetaten, in the middle of the desert, as far from the two megalopolises of Egypt – Memphis in the north, Thebes in the south – as they could manage.

The profundity of these shifts, their velocity and the piecemeal nature of the surviving evidence, have left behind one of history's great mysteries. Akhenaten has been described variously as a proto-fascist, the first monotheist and a hermaphrodite; Nefertiti, as a schemer, a true believer and an artistic innovator; the pair of them, as cult leaders, political radicals, or uxorious spouses. Medical experts have ascribed the king's strange body shape, and stranger behaviour, to both Frohlich's syndrome and Marfan syndrome. Conspiracy theorists have determined they were alien progeny sent to earth. Freud and Jung became so animated in their argument over this pair that Freud fainted and had to be carried by his protégé to his sofa. For Lorraine, he was a pacifist and 'a king obsessed by his own humanist philosophy and its dissemination into the world – a man three, perhaps four, thousand years ahead of his time'. In films, opera and literature, Akhenaten and Nefertiti have become an ongoing cultural hallucination. The concealing sandstorm around them, from which they flit into view and then as swiftly out, ensures their survival.

The speed of their changes and innovations was matched only by the speed of their disappearance. The city of Akhetaten vanished with the same alacrity it was built. When the writer H. Rider Haggard went to visit the sunken remains, he called it 'the very epitome of the vanity of human hopes'. Yet the Egyptian pair somehow managed to cheat oblivion. Most of their radicalism was patent; what was latent, but no less fundamental, was a new understanding of art. Somehow, in the boldness of that vision, they managed to beat both death and time.

A NEW DAWN, A NEW DAY

Surrounding the new city of Akhetaten were a collection of stelae, tablets set into the escarpments which ringed the plain. On these were a message from the king:

> Behold, it is I Pharaoh who has discovered it ... I shall make Akhetaten for the Aten, my father, in this place. I shall not make Akhetaten for him to the south of it, to the north of it, to the west of it, to the east of it. I shall not expand beyond the southern stela of Akhetaten toward the south, nor shall I expand beyond the northern stela of Akhetaten toward the north, in order to make Akhetaten for him there. Nor shall I make it for him on the western side of Akhetaten.

The pharaoh knew how to make a point. The repetition is partly the royal style, but also speaks of the degree to which he was stepping outside the circle. Previously, Aten had been a god among a panoply of gods, but Akhenaten pushed him into unique prominence. All the anthropomorphic gods, half human and half animal, that had dominated the Egyptian religious scene for millennia, were downgraded. Unemployed went their priests, their festivals fell silent and their temples were emptied. Most swiftly toppled was Amun, the previous chief god, whose priests were left whistling in the wind.

All the iconography shifted. Traditionally, religious imagery had human leaders meeting gods eye to eye. Anubis, Iris, Osiris and Horus were all offered gifts and sacrifices by figures standing in the same plane, and at the same height. In the new imagery, Akhenaten and Nefertiti stood below the sun disc of Aten, which radiated light and life towards their suppliant arms. Rather than meeting imperfect deities on the level, they stood beneath the one perfect god and channelled its power to others. This was a new understanding of a luminous oneness in all things. *Amun* means 'he who is hidden', and the old religion put a heavy stress on secrecy and the hieratic power of its priesthood. Aten's full title runs, 'He who rejoices in the horizon, in his Name as the Light which is in the sun disc'. The sensibility was one of bright openness. It was time to take religion out of the temples and into the light of day, to open doors previously shut in the faces of the non-elite. Time to break through the carefully preserved secrecy of the priests, and to tell people not to be afraid to live.

A single new temple in Thebes was never going to suffice, so Akhenaten and Nefertiti opted for a new world. At some point on a journey along the Nile, someone had noticed that as the sun rose it made a pattern with the hills that matched the hieroglyph for Aten. This was a sign, and required a response. Starting in year five of their reign, they began the build. Working with brick and smaller blocks of rock to hasten the process, they threw up roads, buildings and infrastructure at the same delirious speed the Chinese have recently managed in Shanghai. Within four years, they had constructed housing for workers, elegant districts for the ruling class, a collection of palaces for the royal family, multiple temples for Aten and, within the surrounding rockface, a necropolis of new tombs for the mighty. After eleven years of ruling, Akhenaten and Nefertiti could have looked out from one of their 'appearance balconies' over a gleaming new metropolis, and watched the sun sink into the desert and glint in the Nile, below them a crowd of all classes joining in worship of a new god and a new way of life.

YIN AND YANG

Central to the communication of this radical message was a new styling. In the absence of the usual range of gods, Nefertiti was promoted to co-star. There seems to be a genuine partnership intended for Akhenaten and Nefertiti. Raising her to equal or similar status in art and iconography was central to this. Where there was a huge monolith of Akhenaten, there would be a corresponding one of her. In any religious image when the sun disc threw out its long arms of energy and life, ending in the image of the ankh – the cross topped with an oval – it threw its rays equally to both. They share the billing. For Lorraine Hansberry, Akhenaten was more than just a good husband, he was a proto-feminist, refusing to take a new wife, even as Nefertiti produced daughter after daughter.

This ludic novelty with gender played out, too, in the images of Akhenaten. His face is long, fluid and sensual, while touched with a glint of ruthlessness, and his hands tapered and delicate. Slender-shouldered and wide-hipped with a swelling abdomen, he is often portrayed with breasts. Though historians have explained these peculiarities as the result of medical illness, or a form of endocrinal hermaphroditism, it looks more like a determined act of feminising. Aten was a god without form or sex, he/she being referred to as both mother and father. For both Akhenaten and Nefertiti, this looks like a move to bring all aspects of a creator-god into a single figure. They were both/either man/woman. Alongside their claims to have originated monotheism, they have a fair claim on pre-empting the yin and yang crossovers of Daoism. Change has the dynamic of a vortex and, if encouraged to run free, generates more change at a dizzying rate. History moves slow for epochs. Then, when it shifts, it is a whirlwind.

In the new reality, everyone had to be depicted with a common body type. Across households and tombs, where previously men had been depicted bulging with macho muscularity and the women retreating into demure flatness, all now shared bulging tums and wide hips. Alongside the upheaval of the elite, the enfeeblement of the priests, the tax scourging to pay for this phantasm, and the neglect of the empire's outer reaches, everyone now had to be photoshopped in stone towards the same physique. The pharaoh and his queen were asking a lot of their subjects.

Yet, when Akhenaten and Nefertiti stepped up to the altar in their new temple to Aten; when the crowd, chanting the transcendent and radiant words of his Hymn to the Sun, had hypnotised themselves into a monotheistic trance; when they raised their hands to the blazing sun bearing bowls of beaten metal which reflected the sun's rays as if they were holding light; when all were struck with shared togetherness and humility by the glories of creation; and when nobody had done this before, it must have felt like utopia there in the wilderness.

DISASTER

Then something went horribly wrong. It coincides with the unveiling of the city of Akhetaten, which prompts the thought this must have been the most disastrous opening of all time. Precisely what happened remains a tantalising gap in this headlong story. In year twelve of Akhenaten and

Nefertiti's rule, 1341 BCE, they initiated gargantuan festivities in their new capital, inviting embassies and dignitaries from subject states and co-rivals. The whole of the ruling class attended.

The greatest show on earth turned into the greatest calamity. Activity up to that point had been fast and relentless. Then it stops, and stops permanently. No more growth to the city, no more tombs in the hills. No more Akhetaten, no more Akhenaten. The clues are fragmented. Reliefs carved in tombs indicate upheavals; a royal birth had resulted in the death of a mother; a royal child had died; there was a plague epidemic in the Near East. We know the reforms had created enemies. The rest is conjecture.

Whatever went wrong, it cast a shadow over the city, and the self-belief that drove the project. Was the equivalent of an Olympics opening ceremony upended by a sandstorm? Or the accidental injury of a priest? In an age prone to superstition, some surprise, small or large, may have thrown a shadow of inauspiciousness over the endeavour. Or maybe Akhenaten and Nefertiti had moved too far, too fast. Like armies who have conquered without considering how to feed themselves, whirlwinds of change founder on a lack of logistics. And, like armies in retreat, once they start to move backwards, radical movements are helplessly exposed to the sniping of enemies.

Nefertiti disappears from documentation shortly after 1341 BCE, though it is hard to say whether she died, or succeeded her husband prior to the accession of his son, Tutankhamen. Akhenaten died in 1335 BCE, though the date almost goes unrecorded. At that time a tradesman scribbled on a honey jar 'Year Seventeen', then hurriedly replaced it with 'Year One'. Within a few years, the pharaoh fell from the ruler of the world to someone only remembered from the inscription on a honey jar. His successors worked to scrub out his memory. Tutankhamen took the apparatus of power back to Thebes, reinstating the status of the old gods. A successor, Horemheb, smashed all the Aten imagery he could get his hands on, and scraped the name of the pharaoh and his wife from public monuments. This was deliberate erasure, being cancelled from history. The city was stripped of its stone for building elsewhere, deserted of humans, and left to be reclaimed by the desert.

Regimes do not work so effortfully to conceal a non-event. Whatever happened in Akhetaten, its potential terrified the controlling interests of Egypt. They pulled a curtain across it, so history could never again conceive it had taken place.

ART GETS ONE BACK

In 1912, 3,253 years after the opening and closing of the City of Light, a German archeological team led by Ludwig Borchardt was scratching around in the same spot in the desert. They dug in what they had identified as the studio of the court sculptor Thutmose. Aware that he was the chief portrayer of Nefertiti, they proceeded with care. Then they stumbled on something extraordinary. Even covered with sand and dust, its beauty made them gasp.

A picture survives of the group holding their discovery, two North African men, and two Germans in pith helmets. A local man has it securely in his hands, while Borchardt supports *his* hands with his own. The uplifted head, the tensed neck and the upturned eyes of the figure all strain towards the light, as if yearning for long-missed oxygen and sunlight. She looks like an earthquake survivor, miraculously rescued. The men hold her with the tenderness they would show a child, and turn all eyes inward, in obeisance to their rescued deity. Nefertiti is back – alive, or as alive as a stucco bust can be, and still a queen.

Borchardt was rendered speechless: 'Suddenly we had in our hands the most alive Egyptian artwork. You cannot describe it with words.' But he was not guileless. Deliberately undervaluing the worth of his find, he smuggled it out of Egypt in a fruit crate and secured it for Germany. Once he had it there, he kept it under wraps for ten years, whether from a lover's possessiveness or a bombast's showmanship is uncertain. In 1924, it was displayed as part of the Egyptian Museum of Berlin.

If the first major opening in Nefertiti's cultural career was a disaster, her second coming was a triumph. She was a sensation, soon an image of human beauty renowned across the world, as powerful in its allure as the Tutankhamen artefacts simultaneously unveiled in Britain. Stamps, postcards, book covers, film images, all paid respects to this startling image lifted gingerly from the desert.

Its power is undimmed, hypnotising half a million people each year in the Neues Museum (as the Berlin museum is now called). After hours of shuffling through crowds gazing numbly at pots, even in the stifled air of a museum, Nefertiti has the power to brighten the soul and water the heart. Her name means 'the radiant one has come' – a moniker which lifted her to semi-divine status. Both name and status seem unimpacted by time. Grace and sensibility fund the delicate equilibrium of the whole piece; her high cheekbones and swan neck are not ends in themselves, but serve the clarity of her seeing. The symmetry of the figure is perfect apart from the transfixing imbalance of an empty left eye alongside a right one of quartz fixed with beeswax. The effect is regally ancient and wholly modern, divine and informal. For those who prize the human face above a golden mask, she leaves the Tutankhamen artefacts for dead.

We know little of Thutmose, the sculptor, but that he frequently personified his queen. Just as Akhenaten had himself portrayed with his transexual body-shape and his vividly particular face intact, so Nefertiti seems to have encouraged Thutmose to work to the life. This was not humanity idealised, but humanity realised. Previously, Egyptian statuary and relief, though it is often achieved to baroque perfection, seems incapable of shaking off its formulaic genesis. In this collaboration, the artist was not there to denote beauty, but to create it. At the end of time, witnesses would return her gaze, and encounter her for who she was: not a figure from a piece of propaganda, but a rare and extraordinary woman.

Little could either Thutmose or Nefertiti have imagined, sitting in his studio fashioning their image, that 3,500 years later, the greatest star in an interlinked world would become one of their greatest fans. Beyoncé adopted the queen as an icon of high aesthetics and of Afrofuturist inspiration. In her famous portrait, naked and big-bellied with her twins, the head of Nefertiti is posed beside her. At the end of the great reveal at the beginning of her Coachella concert, there she is, fully kitted out as her revered predecessor, headdress precisely in place. Millions of young women across the world gasped (and bought the merchandise). That is quite a resurrection from the desert sands.

DIVINE MODESTY

Beyond the naturalism – a word which can mislead – and the androgyny – an idea which can be misinterpreted – it was another factor which revolutionised the art of the Akhenaten age. The revelation of Nefertiti's bust, in all its breathing delicacy, forced a reassessment of their aesthetic. A rash of terms has been hurled – 'mannerism', 'realism' and the 'baroque' among them – but none seem to capture its freshness. E.M. Forster spoke of its 'exquisite deformities'. From faience inlays with scenes from nature, through to the statuary and reliefs which depict the life of the royal family, a thread runs through. When Hamlet speaks to the players of how he would like his playlet acted, he tells them: 'Suit the action to the word, the word to the action, with this special observance, that you o'erstep not the modesty of nature.' The key word there is modesty. Nature is not bombastic or didactic or majestic; nature is modest. It is itself. That is the spirit of this art. Under the all powerful sun, the life which passes by is just itself.

A painted floor survives from a palace in Akhetaten. With a light exuberance, it celebrates fish swimming, animals leaping, birds rising in flight from clumps of reeds. Elsewhere, there are water tanks with fish, birds and lotus all sharing the composition as if sharing an Edenic garden. Some of the near-contemporary work in Crete echoes this (there may have been dialogue between the two), but not until the modern age can studies of such carefree vitality be found. If a single and simple word has to be found for this representation, it is life. Too lively for truth, too joyful for realism, too fecund for naturalism – life, life, life.

In the human sphere, the same infusing modesty is extended to domestic scenes. The most startling is of Akhenaten and Nefertiti seated, playing with their children. The bodies twist on laps, rest on shoulders, point to each other, lean in for kisses and glance at each other with the playful dynamic of a young family. The body shapes follow the standard androgyny, the perspective is weirdly confused, but the movement and the feelings are instantly recognisable. In other vignettes, we see the royal couple shyly preparing to go to bed; the family dining en famille with a relaxed informality; the queen tentatively adjusting the pharaoh's collar before a public occasion, and in another chucking him under the chin. All with the tangled dynamics of human interaction. It is an eruption of liveliness.

There is a sense of us backstage with the family, getting to know them as individuals behind the public space. It is hard to deny the publicity value in this, and it would be wrong to sentimentalise the pharaoh's political or family life, both of which would make the modern world blanch. Yet there seems to be a consistent sensibility. The sculptor Bak said of his pharaoh that he had 'received the teaching of his person, the chief of sculptors'. The art of this moment was as much part of the project as the new city, the politics and the new faith. Hansberry believed that:

> Out of his love for truth and reality Akhnaton encouraged the regarding of himself as a mortal man. No earlier king had allowed an artist to represent him in poses which did not include divinity or the majesty of power.

It is the legacy which has endured.

Sigmund Freud was long obsessed with Akhenaten. In his last work, *Moses and Monotheism*, about the possible connection between Akhenaten and the founding tenets of the Jewish religion, Freud writes of how 'religions owe their compulsive power to the return of the repressed; they are reawakened memories of very ancient, forgotten, highly emotional episodes of human history'. As with faith, so with art. The gentle ideas and energies which Akhenaten and Nefertiti set free could be hidden, erased and buried, but they could not be destroyed. Even under sand and dust and earth, these modest scenes waited to tell the future their story.

When, almost a thousand years later, a Greek artist chose to present a young warrior on a pot, putting on his armour with a sheepish expression, and with a single foot not in profile but presented foreshortened towards the viewer, he created a revolution in perspective. It is a technical innovation smuggled, not in a presentation of braggadocio or bombast, but in one of gentle intimacy. When, six hundred years later, a Roman painter portrays a woman walking away from us with a light step, and brushing her hand against a flower stem, the back of her soft cheek all that is visible, we are allured in a way that no amount of garish display can achieve. When, fifteen hundred years later, a shy young man on a wooden stage turns to us and says, 'Now I am alone,' before unloading his innermost thoughts to us in verse which follows the fine tracery of his thought, we are beguiled in a way that no amount of shouting can. When Ozu's camera catches the small moments of privacy that his actors offer up, we receive it as far more potent than the crash-bang-wallop of a superhero movie.

Maybe the true revolution of the pharaoh and his queen was in this presentation of privacy and quiet grace. Maybe it is that which terrified the priests, not opposition or aggression, but plain human happiness under the sun. The counterblast against bombast and fakery was spoken with a quiet voice, and in recognisable accents, which did away with the mystery of priests. Maybe it is in off-duty and playful moments that the world moves forwards.

7

Jumping Rocks

A TALE OF OKUNI

1603, KAMO RIVER BED, KYOTO

Art has a perverse resilience. Buried deep under the sand, it leaves a trace memory in the air, the soil and the collective mind. No matter how much silt and concrete piles up above, no matter how far it recedes into oblivion, it winds its way back into the sunlight. No less does it have a mysterious capability to spread across the world, often when there is no apparent means by which it can communicate itself. We don't know who first thought of blowing red ochre dust at a cave wall with one's hand in the way, to leave a sign for the future saying, *I was here*. We don't know who first painted bison on rock walls with such monolithic actuality they seem alive in the stone; who first carved an animal head on a human body; or sculpted miniature figures of women bulbous with breasts and all things fertile. These forms traversed the globe at a speed which still has archaeologists bemused.

In the absence of planes and trains, webs and satellites, we wonder how creative ideas can cross such distances and such inhospitable terrain. Perhaps they are a form of morphic resonance, where cultures give simultaneous expression to a collective subconscious. Or perhaps we underestimate the human capacity to admire, and to communicate that admiration. Our ability to first say 'Wow!' and then 'Can I tell you about this incredible thing?' and our ability to be enthusiastic (from the Greek 'seized by god'), may be one of our signal virtues.

In 1599, the Globe Theatre was erected beside the River Thames in London, just west of the Eurasian land mass, by a company of actors, to produce the dramatic writing of their age. In this theatre, performers and spectators looked at each other in a shared light, and enjoyed a continuous sense of dialogue. In 1603, a smaller theatre was built in the dry river bed of the River Kamo in Kyoto, then the capital city of Japan, an island just east of the Eurasian land mass. In shared light, with open communication between stage and audience, a new form of theatre born of music, dance and song was incubated and birthed. Although six thousand miles separated the two – they were further isolated as islands and Japan was as closed as any country could be – they walked similar paths.

OLD AND NEW

By 1603, Noh theatre, Japan's dominant performing style, was more than two centuries old and showing signs of age. Its dramatic form had become constricted and its pained artistry allowed little freedom for the imagination of the performer. This stiffness was accompanied by an obeisance in performance. Presentation to court nobles, sitting at a distance from the stage or on a higher level, reinforced the subservience codified within it. With spectators sometimes in a separate physical space – a room off a courtyard or behind a screen – the chances for encounter were minimal. It matched, to some degree, the other high-entertainment form of the nobility, *gagaku*, an abstract style of trance music, accompanied by dancing so slow it stilled the pulse, that dated back to the seventh century. Both forms had a refined purity, a frail elegance and a subtlety so extreme they were almost fundamentalist.

They had become the exclusive domain of the nobility and the samurai class, and were unsuited for wider entertainment. The Edo shogunate, the feudal military government which took control of Japan in 1600, stratified the country into four classes, with the ruling samurai at the top, and the merchant class firmly at the bottom. This deprived the merchants of political influence, but no-one benefited more than them from the rapid growth of Japanese cities, and the economic boom. The money they had to spare they sought to spend on a range of pleasures – performance, geisha and the courtesans of the pleasure districts. The trance-like sanctity of Noh and Gugaku were not for them. They wanted something livelier.

In the racier parts of town, amongst the roustabouts and the whores, this bustling new class wanted to assert their identity with new styles of entertainment, those which reflected their own radical change. In Kyoto, in the river bed of the Kamo, there was a freedom and energy in the environment which was fertile ground for innovation. The broad audience were drawn for pleasure, and ripe to be hijacked by artistry.

The new form came from an unlikely source.

OKUNI

Okuni was born in 1571, in a time of civil chaos, known as the period of the Warring States. Her father was a blacksmith at the Izumo Grand Shrine. She grew up to be a *miko*, a shrine maiden who expressed her own worship and channelled that of others in dance. There was a shamanic element to this role and it was here, performing the devout Buddhist prayer dance, that she built up her range of technical skills. It was said she learnt her light and springing step crossing the Hii River as a child, dancing lightly from stone to rock.

She found fame on another river bed. Okuni left to dance in Kyoto around 1587 and there she formed her own company, gathered together from the waifs, strays and misfits of the discarded female population. This ensemble seems to have pitched itself somewhere between a women's refuge and a tough dance school. It turned Japanese culture on its head. In 1608, Okuni returned to Izumo, and retired, and then she slips off the radar. The sum of biographical detail is slight.

In the absence of such information, we can look to the imagery. About Shakespeare we thankfully know more than enough, since if we had to judge him only from his Stratford monument and the woodcut in the First Folio we would think him little more than a stolid bank manager. For Okuni, we are better served pictorially, since we have depictions of her remembered in action. From these fleeting reminiscences her presence is vivid, as is her expertise. We see her on the low kabuki stage, surrounded by a lively and shifting audience, women and men, children and the elderly. Visibly delighted, they sit close, and grip the edge like groundlings at the Globe.

Okuni commands the middle of the space, poised and authoritative. In three pictures, she is playing a samurai. In each she has physically transformed, her body swerved in an 'S' shape, with the arrogant lounging confidence of a self-possessed male. Her boldness is expressed in her main props – two swords, one tucked into her *obi* (sash) at the left hip, the other slung lazily over her shoulder. In another she leans on her sword with nonchalant poise. It is rare to see such precise imitation of the warrior's swagger in a male actor. The weapons are born with a light confidence, with an implicit threat, while her face is light and nimble.

Carrying such swords was a right preserved for the samurai class. For an actor to carry one would be transgressive; for a woman to do so was crossing all sorts of boundaries. She looks happy to do so.

LIBERTIES ON SHIJO STREET

Shijo Street was Kyoto's red-light district – a highly complex set-up. The history and moral shading of courtesans, sex workers and brothel-keepers in Japan encompassed an emotional range from elevated romance to raw brutality. It has few parallels. Some commentators, working on little but prejudice against showfolk, state categorically that Okuni was a prostitute but there is no evidence for this. Indeed, it was illegal for performers to visit brothels, and edicts were proclaimed to prohibit the blurring of boundaries between performing and sex work. But, wherever the sex industry flourished, street entertainment did so, too. Travelling *ronin* (unattached samurai) demonstrated swordsmanship; blind bards chanted the tale of the *Heike*, Japan's martial epic; black bears snarled in cages and monkeys jumped through hoops; and puppet groups and dancers bustled in and out. In the middle of this riotous chaos, on a plank floor, and enclosed within wooden, jerry-built walls, Okuni's company performed.

Travelling groups wandered the country at this time spreading straw mats on grasses and hard earth, and created ad hoc performance spaces. Okuni's company aimed for something more permanent in their river home: a floor of freshly sawn cypress planks, low walls which showed enough to titillate the passing spectator, but not enough to satisfy; large double doors, like a Buddhist temple gate, to convey spurious grandeur; and a covered backstage space, the *gakuya*, where they could concoct theatrical surprises. Brightly coloured cotton hung along the eaves for festive glamour. Street entertainers were not the only rivals for box-office sales; other companies soon imitated Okuni's theatre and sprang up nearby. As in London, theatres clustered near theatres, and all wanted the same shilling. At the Globe, they blasted a trumpet from the bell-tower to alert London to the beginning of a play: in Kyoto, they blew a conch shell.

Showmen, show-women and sex workers of every type gathered beneath the bridge at Shijo Street for one main reason: the dry land between the riverbanks had not been recorded in the recent Land Survey Register. Officially the land didn't exist. An enterprising impresario could build a theatre there without asking for government permission. Even better, there was no land tax. The river bed was a no-man's land in the heart of the capital. A similar freedom was enjoyed within the Southwark liberties outside the city walls of London, where theatres flourished beside brothels. The banks of both rivers attracted scoundrels and scallywags as well as performers, but that did not keep the punters away. Curious folk, in both Japan and England, were drawn to these makeshift festivals of street banditry and high entertainment. The outlaw element added to the magnetism.

In England, unlicensed actors were classified as rogues and vagabonds: in Japan, arising from the beginnings of Okuni's company, they earned the derogatory term *kawaramono*, 'objects of the river bed'. As with the land they worked on, the actors escaped official attention in Japan. Following the Land Survey, which declassified the river bed, there was a Population Census. The purpose was to bind farmers to their land and the rest of the population to its home, so they could be more efficiently surveilled and taxed. There was no category for performers, so they escaped definition and thus restrictions of movement. The legal benefits of running away with the circus have rarely been so clearly mapped out.

Shijo Street created a whole new city space, where commoners, merchants, servants, samurai and nobles mixed together with an ease replicated nowhere else. As in Elizabethan London, Okuni's theatre grew in a space where high and low, rich and poor, gathered together in a new social dynamic. In this environment, part street market, part street theatre, like an Edinburgh Festival with hookers and lethally sharp swords, something extraordinary happened.

A MOMENT OF IGNITION

Somewhere around 1603, Okuni stretched her range – and that of her theatre –with the invention of kabuki. As well as generating the thrill of breaking through boundaries, it is clear that its innovations invoked pleasure. Kabuki travelled all over Japan fast.

The word derived from the verb *kabuku*, meaning 'to be slanted' – literally, 'to lean away from the centre', but here 'to strike out from the norm', to be eccentric, a bit punk. In Izumo, where Okuni was raised, the word had been used to shame a person. In Kyoto, it flattered a trend setter. Its sense of newness was reinforced after the visit of a Jesuit traveller called Alessandro Valignano to Kyoto. His embassy, full of vivid popinjays, dressed to dazzle as only Italians can, had stunned spectators. Soon after, a craze for exotic dress – for sleeveless vests, bloused pantaloons, round hats and Kirishtan crosses and rosaries – swept Kyoto. The new fashion was nicknamed kabuki.

The earliest kabuki dances were based on the *nenbutsu odori*, an improvisational blend of stamping and rhythmic body movement. This foot-pounding had its origin in religious supplication, with a call for rain and fertile land. In Okuni's theatre, as the women danced in unison, the pulse they stamped on the planks became less of a plea and more an expression of joy. The misfits whom Okuni had gathered together celebrated their outlaw unity to a shared rhythm. The delirious spirit of this group dance became a central part of kabuki, just as the closing jig wiped the pain away from a Shakespearean tragedy at the Globe.

The particular vividness of Okuni's new dramatic form seems not to have been one of volume or bombast, however loud the hammering of feet. She seems to have traced patterns on a gentler curve. Trumpets can both blast and whisper; it is often the whispering which has the stronger effect. Kurosawa's cinema is one of sensation and tension and drama; Ozu's is one of empty spaces, unspoken words and still faces. Within a frame of energetic dance and music, we can imagine the simple dramas of Okuni's early theatre as closer to the Ozu mode.

In one kabuki playlet, a pottery maker is on his way home, balancing two baskets on a shoulder pole. He stops at a sweet store; a beautiful waitress serves him biscuits and tea; he is struck by her beauty; she falls in love; they dance together. Presented simply, the audience is engrossed by the humble weight of this gentle drama. In another, a town dandy flirts with a courtesan. The social niceties involved in obtaining a courtesan were complex and required finesse. As the coquette puts the young man through his paces, a clown stumbles between them. The audience witness a comic scene of dalliance from the courtesan world surrounding them. They are stories told with delicacy, presented with the confidence of modesty, that flood the heart and imagination.

The early essence of kabuki was improvisational. Plays were passed on by word of mouth, before they were written down. New variations and new stories were created in performance. The stories could flick and switch to match the randomness of life, a heterogenous mix and match which matched the wellspring generosity of their first pulse. In Okuni's theatre, with music, dance and song as essential ingredients, and with every performer expert in each, the recipe, show by show, was up to the performers. Given their freedom within the liberties of the river bed, they were able to tell stories no-one had before.

These weren't stories of myth – of emperors and empresses – or of political upheaval. They were more akin to *I Love Lucy*. The earliest works were skits, comic-dramatic sketches showing love gone wrong, collisions between unknowing men and prostitutes, or pricking the pomposity of the overweening neighbour. The first standard roles were a man, a woman and a clown, leaving much room for filth and innuendo, which has never gone down badly. As with the perennial virtues of the sitcom, they were stories for an audience watching their own lives. Characters came on in the outfit of their trade: the fish peddler, the wet nurse, the flower vendor. With arched eyebrows, and a dazzling range of kimonos, the company told stories both acute and truthful about the lives of the townsfolk, the watching merchants and their families. Once they had overcome the surprise of recognition, the audience settled into the privileged pleasure of being mirrored in art. (Shakespeare only wrote one play set in London, and only one in his own moment. It too was akin to a sitcom, and possibly the closest correspondent to the early kabuki, *The Merry Wives of Windsor*.)

The biggest revelation was gender. The company featured principally women, and was run by a woman. This was new, though not a revolution. What really turned the tables was a woman portraying a man, and a powerful one. Whether this happened on a whim, by artful design or with radical intent, is unknown. Whichever it was, it must have caused at its first unveiling a sucking in of breath, before that breath was expelled in merriment. Okuni took a risk and got away with it. Her first incarnation as a man, with short hair and a new kimono, marked the moment of change. How she felt, the first time she revealed herself in a man's dress, and the first time she stretched out her limbs, gravelled her voice and entitled her desires, is emancipating to conjecture. The crowd, after it had bypassed its shock, must have gone wild for it, since it became a staple of the rash of kabuki companies which swept the country.

Six thousand miles away, similar transgressions were playing out in London. On the Globe stage in 1603, in the play *As You Like It*, a boy actor would be playing the female character Rosalind, who in the course of the play impersonates the young man Ganymede, who pretends to be a young woman for a love game. The freedom actors and audiences felt as these transformations unfurled would have unleashed and empowered both. Together they read the game-playing within gender, and saw the liberating possibilities of reinvention made manifest through performance. In Kyoto it helped to define the pioneer spirit of this new form.

BOUNDING HIGH

Kabuki was a performer's theatre from its inception. There was little doubt who were the stars, or who sold the tickets. At the heart of the form was dance, and at the heart of the dancing was Okuni. A lifetime working at the Izumo Grand Shrine had ingrained the basics of movement and expression in her bones. She had a wide mastery of different forms, and an acute understanding of the power of a body in space. She knew how to tell a large emotional story with a deft movement. She knew how to direct the focus of the audience wherever she wished within the frame of her body, or within the wider frame of the stage. Her body, her colleagues, the stage, and the space within and without them, were her instruments.

There was a buoyancy within her. Her jumping steps came from a child's carefree steps in the river's sand. Leaping in the air made her happy; her happiness made her want to leap. It is the child's joy in motion writ exquisite and infectious. Her audience shared the happiness that was rivering up through her chest. When it burst out in the switches and stretches of her hands and feet, they felt the same release. They sang and clapped with her. The stooping, crouching and bending of Noh, with its overwhelming servility, was not for them. She was in front of no lords here; there was no subservience, just a shared pleasure in bounding high.

Beyond her gazelle-like leaps, other elements were woven into the new form, and again they correspond to the English theatre. Music was a partner to the action rather than a servant. The musicians sat on a tiered platform in full view of the audience. They comprised a percussionist with gongs, woodblocks and bells of varying timbres, one player of the *nohkan* (flute) and another of the *jabisen*, a Chinese guitar. As with Shakespeare's theatre, with musicians on view, the artificiality of the event was on display. A further element of theatricality was introduced by costume changes. These could be dazzlingly quick, and executed with a magician's *legerdemain*. They enabled actors to perform several dances in quick succession. The ability to shuck off a persona with a flick of the shoulders and the disappearance of a kimono added to the giddying contingence of personality, and the identity-conjuring power of performance.

The form soon moved beyond its birth in skits and simple dramas and grew to take in tragedy. The first of many such plays concerned the courtesan Yugiri and her lover Izaemon, whose star-crossed misfortunes ended with both taking their lives. Tales of *shinju* or double suicide, where frustrated couples jumped this life in the hope of meeting again in the next, prompted so many incidences of the same in real life that the government tried to prohibit them. Not a million miles from a well-known couple from Verona.

One of the most renowned features of the kabuki theatre is the *hanamichi* or 'flower path', a walkway bridge which extends into the audience, via which dramatic exits and entrances can be made. It was a path to and from the stage, but also a space where scenes could be played. Its virtue was its proximity to the audience and the sense it gave that the action was in and amongst them. Gathered closely in a shared light, this was democratic theatre, where all collaborated to magic a story to life. Actors would pause to address the crowd, and the latter responded with praise thrown back, shouting the names of favourite performers in the middle of the scene. Rough, raw and ready.

Too rough and too raw, as it turned out. Kabuki swept the country, both under the banner of Okuni and in other formats. It was seen in similar zones of pleasure in the large and growing cities. Given its portable format, it could crop up anywhere. The authorities noticed its growth, tolerated its popularity for twenty years, and then decided to control it. Several factors frightened them: the proximity between the performances and the sex-work industry; the democratic freedom in the interplay between the stage and the audience; and the improvisational nature of its storytelling. It is hard to know how to censor something which wanders so freely. One element tipped it over the edge into the dangerous: the primacy of women in its creation and its ongoing life. Kabuki could carry on, but only without women.

From 1629, *onna-kabuki*, or 'women's kabuki', was banned for being too erotic. *Wakashū-kabuki*, 'young boy's kabuki', was permitted in its place, for distinctly questionable reasons. Yet, in 1652, that too was shut down for being too erotic. At that point the form was left in the hands of adult male actors, *yaro-kabuki*, presumably on the principle that they weren't remotely erotic. The freedoms of the river bed did not prove durable. The form invented by women, exercising a freedom to invent for a brief interval, was stripped away from them.

THE FLOATING WORLD

As kabuki is a word with multiple meanings, so the word *ukiyo* splits into itself and its opposite. Traditionally it meant something similar to the Buddhist word *samsara*, 'the sorrowful world' of cyclical suffering which we struggle to escape through lives of meditation and virtue. Around this moment, just as kabuki was forming its shape, its homophone *ukiyo* appears with the opposite meaning, 'the floating world' of pleasure and sensation, the feast laid out for us in the here and now.

The merchant class who had been dumped to the bottom of the Edo (modern Tokyo) caste system took their revenge in two forms: in seizing economic power, and in radical pursuit of happiness. The 'fleeting or transient world' of *ukiyo* describes the urban lifestyle of this period and the playgrounds of pleasure within it. This grew fastest in Yoshiwara, the licensed red-light district of Edo, where kabuki was a central part of the happiness provided. History has belittled the *ukiyo* movement as hedonistic; at the time it could be trivialised to mean 'stylish' or 'erotic' as if little more than a fashion, but at its heart was a determined pursuit of contentment taken from the transience of the world's beauties. Asai Ryōi celebrated this spirit in his novel *Ukiyo Monogatari*:

> *Living only for the moment, savouring the moon, the snow, the cherry blossoms, and the maple leaves, singing songs, drinking sake, and diverting oneself just in floating, unconcerned by the prospect of imminent poverty, buoyant and carefree, like a gourd carried along by the river current: this is what we call ukiyo.*

It sounds not a million miles from the flâneur-ing hymned by Baudelaire a couple of centuries later in Paris.

The essence has come down to us in the form of *ukiyo-e*, 'pictures of the floating world'. These woodblock prints and paintings had their beginnings in the theatre districts. They depicted scenes of kabuki actors, dancers and musicians, geishas, sumo wrestlers and prostitutes. They branched out to include scenes from history; stories from folk tales; landscapes garlanded with nature at its most fleetingly choice; and erotica. Their origins were in the revelatory delights found in congregation in the new pleasure gardens. Musicians plucking the *jabisen*, dancers executing a graceful twirl, actors striking a pose, audiences with their faces shining with excitement - all radiate happiness from these evanescent paintings.

The most celebrated of such paintings, known as the Hikone screen, places fourteen male and female figures in a wide expanse of resin-yellow space. A small band of musicians perform in front of a painted screen; a couple play a board game, with flirtation tickling the space between their eyes; nearby, a man reads some poetry behind a woman lounging on a low stool – she is being painted by a young woman with silent fascination; a girl near her points across empty space to a standing group of two women and a samurai, all flirting – him lounging on his sword, the two women twisting away from him; this group is observed by a young girl, her back to us, a sprig of blossom dangling from one hand. The sense of gossamer-fine bliss chimes like a light bell. Music and movement and small human dramas swirl together, offering a clue to the quiet pleasures of early kabuki. A floating world indeed; hard to imagine one better.

The *ukiyo-e* woodprints of this milieu became a factor in the way of life they were depicting. Cheap enough to be enjoyed by the class who inhabited them, the prints were soon decorating their homes. The growth of this art form was at the heart of the growing perception of Japanese art and culture in the west, particularly its later landscape forms exemplified by Hokusai. From the middle of the nineteenth century, Japonisme became an important trend, as the floating world of civilised contentment wafted westward. These scenes of urban, human content had a profound influence on the French Impressionists.

MODERN OSSIFICATION

Modern kabuki has travelled an enormous distance from its beginnings. An event which began as an eruption of playful improvisation has now itself become a rarefied art form, as technically precise as classical ballet or Olympic gymnastics. The witty innovations of how to embody character in the moment are now statuesque tropes which the audience anticipates. The poses, known as *mie*, are catalogued and refined through long training.

There is a trace element left of Okuni, still, in the perfection of the *roppo* manoeuvre, where a performer bounds off down the *hanamichi*, hopping from one leg to the other, building up such momentum that, out of sight of the audience, he will be caught by an assistant in the green room beyond, rather like Nijinsky in *Le Spectre de la rose*. These are enjoyed as an isolated tour de force, like a thrilling octave passage in a piano concerto. The art of the female-role specialists (*onnagata*) is now ironically one of the most celebrated elements. In order to emulate the hover-walk of the female role, young actors spend hours with a sheet of paper between their knees, to achieve the apparent weightlessness.

People now go to see perfection of form, a long way from its original rough charm amongst the roustabouts and the whores. Then they went to see their lives reflected by spontaneous storytelling; now they go to see a statuesque art. Hamlet advises the players: 'The warm clown cannot make a jest unless by chance, as the blind man catches a hare.' It is a perfect description of the fully awake artist's ability to stay alive and in the room, twitching and alert, sensitive to the audience, the play and the air they share. It is how all great theatre and art begins – lawless, wild and fully within a moment.

The kabuki theatre began as a reaction to the hierarchies of the Noh tradition. It was bandit drama, initiated by a troupe of misfit women meeting a middle-class audience eager to find and define the pleasure to be found in life. It shucked off the convention of subservience to the nobles and the samurai. Today in the kabuki theatre, there is a complex etiquette of codes to dictate how the fan base for each star performer should relate to the star. Kabuki performers began as misfits rejecting the obeisance of one form; they have now become the masters in another. As beautiful a phrase as 'the floating world' is hard to reconcile with the results of the pleasure-seeking it let loose. In its infancy, the closeness of this spirit to wood and air and flesh kept it fresh. It drew water from the well of humanity and nature.

Okuni was said to be 'the seed that vanished into the earth and not the full blooming flower'. It is hard to connect her to what became of kabuki. But it is a fully *ukiyo* pleasure to imagine the priestess with her troupe of dancers, who had learnt her light, springing step. To conjure up how they danced on the planks laid on the river bed to the sound of bells and flutes, in gorgeous patterned kimonos and wide hats, to a crowd who thought they were watching an enchanted garden of nodding flowers. And how, one day, in a spirit of boldness and mischief, Okuni cut her hair and changed her make-up, snuck onto the stage before she was recognised, and stepped out from within a black robe as a male character. How the audience held their breath in confusion, then, with the innocent radicalism of the free spectator, let out a warm hearted roar of approval.

Then how Okuni, like the chosen maiden in *The Rite of Spring*, danced until her feet could dance no more, in an ecstasy of discovery of her own potential, and how she was now free to be whoever she wanted to be.

L'ORFEO

FAVOLA IN MVSICA

DA CLAVDIO MONTEVERDI

RAPPRESENTATA IN MANTOVA

l'Anno 1607. & nouamente data in luce.

AL SERENISSIMO SIGNOR

D. FRANCESCO GONZAGA

Prencipe di Mantoua, & di Monferato, &c.

In Venetia Appreſſo Ricciardo Amadino.

MDCIX.

8

Killing Us Softly

A TALE OF ORPHEUS AND MONTEVERDI

The word mystery derives from the Greek *mysterion* – a secret rite, consisting of sacrifices, purification and song. It has carried that meaning – the introduction to a larger, hidden reality in ritual – through history. In England from the Middle Ages on, it carried a double meaning from the word *ministerium*, meaning a craft, so the plays performed by the craft guilds became 'The Mysteries'. These working-class dramas combined the mystery of each guild that provided a play – the carpenters, the coopers, the nailmakers – with the mystery of Christ's Passion, the story they unfolded.

The form began in Egypt, though we know less about the nature of their storytelling. Their most celebrated dramatic myth, the Osiris Passion, told the story of King Osiris, and how he was slaughtered and dismembered by Seth, the god of chaos. Such dismemberment the Greeks picked up and ran with. The king's wife, Isis, collected together the body parts and reburied him, another trope the Greeks relished. Death and resurrection, as we have seen with the Eleusinian Mysteries, were central to the attraction of such cults for a world which was predominantly rural and agricultural, and waited hungrily for the spring. Their purpose was further refined in the most influential of Western mysteries – that celebrating the first artist, the cult of Orphism.

WHITE FROCKS AND NO BEANS

A chain runs between Dionysus and Orpheus that is devilish to unthread. Chronology and causation are so muddled, it is tempting to abandon consistency and make up a new myth, which is all part of its fecund charm. Orpheus was variously a semi-divine figure: the son of Apollo and the muse Calliope; a priest of Dionysus; the founder of a cult; and the first great musician.

The starting point for the Orphic world view was taken from the death of Dionysus (one of several endings for the god). In this version, the Titans, under instruction from Hera, dismembered the god and ate him up. Having saved his heart, Zeus zapped the Titans with lightning and they were incinerated. From their ashes sprang the human race. We were thus forever in large part wicked (the Titan element), and in small part divine (the bits of Dionysus the Titans had eaten). From this we have the dualism of human nature and an explanation of original sin. The Orphics ran with this dualism. They recognised the soul of man as divine, and their priests, kitted out in white frocks, pushed humanity further along that road. Once freed from the burden of the Titans' flesh, the soul of the Orphic initiate could live with the blessed in the afterlife. Much of this runs close to Christian teaching and myth. Which is hardly surprising, given that the Christians stole it wholesale.

The Orphic religion flourished around the sixth century BCE. It was welcomed to Athens at first, but never established a wide sacerdotal presence. Though a minority religion, its influence was extensive, largely through its power over the imagination of tragedians and artists. The genesis and growth of the movement reflected frustrations: a spiritual dissatisfaction with the origin stories of Homer and Hesiod and their amoral mythologies of warring gods and grumpy warriors; a need to make the divine conform to some sort of ethical code; a hunger for personal contact with the supernatural; and a need to tell better news about life after death.

The Orphics, birthing a creed from Dionysus, Eleusis and the itinerant seers of their age, believed the soul could be freed from its titanic inheritance. To achieve this, the *teles*, or initiates, had to undergo purification, and a dramatic reliving of the death and rebirth of the god, much like the Dionysiac ceremony in the Telesterion at Eleusis. But these rites were more portable, and could be brought to a space near you, by itinerant priests. The cult stressed a code of moral conduct, embracing non-violence and vegetarianism. There was an unreadable, but passionate, avoidance of beans. The reward was freedom from metempsychosis, and eternity alongside Orpheus; the uninitiated were doomed, like those in India stuck in *samsara*, to reincarnate indefinitely.

THE FIRST ARTIST

The model for the cult, Orpheus, was a mythical hero from Thrace, the same outlaw, peripheral region which Dionysus hailed from. He left behind him a cache of formidable poetry, and a reputation as a devoted priest, but it was his legend as the first musician which lingers longest. Orpheus's father Apollo taught him to play the lyre and his mother Calliope to sing. His poetry and song were limitless in their capacity for calm. The wild Thracians became gentle on hearing him, beasts were tamed, and trees and rivers swayed in rhythm. When he travelled with Jason and the Argonauts to win the golden fleece, he settled tempests and distracted the crew from the sirens with the superior beauty of his song. Residing in a cave, the grace and order he brought to the countryside created an Eden of nature in harmony.

Love will always tear such placid perfection apart, and so it does when Orpheus falls headlong for Eurydice. She rejects him several times, but finally succumbs to his entreaties. On the day of their wedding, in the excited rapture preceding consummation, Eurydice is bitten by a snake and dies. Orpheus's grief is so great he stops singing. On the few moments when he does, his songs are so unremittingly bleak he casts a pall over the world. Exhausted by his lament, everyone encourages him to go down to the underworld to seek out his beloved.

Following on from heroes in Sumerian and Egyptian myth, he heads to the underworld, to win her back, and to conquer death. As he progresses, he plays his lyre and his refrains are so beautiful the torturers of Tartarus stop their work, Charon and Cerberus are calmed, and all the shades of the underworld hypnotised. His art was so great, Ovid tells us, he could release the guilty from the weight of their sins. His mission, to persuade Hades and Persephone to release Eurydice, is accomplished with a miraculous catch. Their stricture is that, as they return to earth,

Eurydice must walk behind Orpheus, and he cannot turn to look at her. He sets off with eyes fixed ahead. Increasingly insecure about her continuing presence, the closer they get to the light, the greater his anxiety. Like all sinners, he cannot resist temptation. He turns. At that instant Eurydice melts into a mist and evanesces forever.

Inconsolable for his error and the loss, Orpheus wanders the earth bemoaning the cruelty of fate. One day he stumbles on some maenads performing ecstatic rights in honour of Dionysus. Resenting his isolation, they charge him, but are charmed by his lyre's music and drop their weapons. His music is a force field. After a conference, they decide to compete with their own instruments – curved pipes and pounding drums – and their own screams. Their harsh and chaotic racket drowns out the soulful tune of Orpheus. Now deaf to his charms, they are free to resume their frenzy. They tear him to shreds. Thus the followers of Dionysus render to Orpheus, a priest of Dionysus, a death remarkably similar to that of Dionysus. Confusion reigns.

His severed head rolls down the hill of Mount Pangaion to the Aegean Sea, crying out for Eurydice as it tumbles. Washed out on the tide, it floats to the island of Lesbos. There they create an oracle from this still-talking head, ensuring the island will forever inspire great poetry. The muses, the sisters of his mother Calliope, gather up the rest of his fragments and bury them near Mount Olympus. A nightingale sings over his tomb. His lyre is placed among the stars.

Hence runs the legend. What better story, and what better tradition, to launch a new theatrical form, which wished to make a wholly new marriage of words and music?

FALLING INTO A TELEVISION SET

The Bush Theatre was once a small room above a pub, which somehow had arrived at a miraculous shape. Constructed by a carpenter in 1972, with minimal design input, it was made of steep risers in an L shape. With no seats, and with spectators tucking their bodies between the legs of those sat above, it facilitated a physical immediacy which would be anathema in our era of touch terror. Just over a hundred people could cram into a small room, transforming instantaneously from separate individuals into a collective wall of human matter. An instant congregation. Their focus was fierce. The act of watching there, a vertical block of people tipping forward into an imagined world, was described by one designer as 'falling into a television set'. Always presenting new plays, the intensity of the proximity, and the completeness of engagement, elevated the work to a realm it could never have attained in a flatter, duller room.

In 1607, the Duke of Gonzago's son, Francesco, instructed that a theatre should be constructed in a ground-floor room of their family palace in Mantua. The room still exists, a narrow space in their guest apartments, measuring twenty-eight by thirty-nine feet. The exact shape of the theatre constructed is uncertain, though it corresponded to other chamber theatres thrown up in Italy at the time by its designer, Antonio Viani. As with the Bush's steep risers, the banked seating created the same wall of audience. A thrust-stage platform would have met several rows of chairs set out for the socially senior. The few inhabitants of these chairs and the many on the polygonal risers behind them, about two hundred crammed into each other's laps, and all tipping forward, would have faced a curtain. When that rose, it revealed a backdrop painted with such exquisite fineness that its invitation to suspend disbelief would be gratefully accepted. On each side of the stage, sliding panels of painted scenery crowded in as the stage receded, to create vanishing perspectives. The immersion was as extravagant as that at the Bush.

Only a few years earlier, in another London theatre, the Globe, Hamlet declared his imaginative powers so great he could be 'bounded in a nutshell and count myself a king of infinite space'. It was just what Francesco dreamt of for his new room. This was not due to a lack of resource. When the Mantuans wanted to mount a spectacle, they would, with cathedral bells on. Any excuse, whether a wedding or a papal election, would prompt a public festival with fireworks bombasting out of triumphal arches. Once they built a stage-fortress on a lake, and assaulted it with an army of actors and fireworks, for an audience of five thousand. There was no shyness about grandeur. The largeness aimed at in this venture was inverted. For an intimate and select audience, watching in a focused and undistracted setting, they wanted to implode that excess. To take a story of high drama, and storytelling of opulent variety, and compress it in a small room. A spectacle atomic in its leashed power.

RESEARCH AND DEVELOPMENT

At the Bush we were given a substantial chunk of subsidy, in the long-off days when this was normal. The justification for this, and one it earned, was that the theatre was a research and development centre. Our task was to find new stories and voices, which would go on to have a wider impact. The plays we premiered graduated to a more public life in other media, and the writers we showcased went on to write for other theatres, television and film. We were an innovation centre to keep the wider industry fresh. A similar spirit pertained in Mantua.

Francesco Gonzago was presenting a commission by the court for an intellectual academy, a society of experts known as the Invaghiti. There were many such clubs in Renaissance Italy, groups that came together to debate and write tracts on their favourite disciplines. For long hours and with passion they discussed literature, science and art. Thinktanks of poets and theorists, trading and researching ideas, they were the philosophical cutting edge of their culture.

An abiding passion in such clubs was the best way of relating music and speech in drama. The Invaghiti of Mantua were competitively aware of the innovations which had emerged from another club, the Camerata of Florence. This humanistic society believed that the music of their age was corrupt, swamped by excessively decorated and sugared polyphony. The old honest relation between music and the word was drowning in trills and frills. Their ideal was ancient Greek drama, which they believed had a monolithic power to influence human character and nature. The essence of its force, they believed, was that it was sung rather than spoken, and in tunes of plain monody to a simple accompaniment. For them, this lent the words an expressive emotional and moral strength, which had gone missing in contemporary song. They wanted a revival.

The theoretical leader of the Florentine school was Vincenzo Galilei, father of the more famous Galileo. Its practical leader was Jacopo Peri, who took these theories and converted them into the first two full music dramas. One of these was *Dafne*, which we have lost, presented in 1598, and the second, *Eurydice*, which survives from 1600. These two experiments in how to blend music and speech had all the credentials required for the creation of a new form, bar one. The presence of genius. They were like those early flying machines. They had worked out what a flying machine should be and do, but their attempts spluttered and bumped, lurched and crashed. It was the harmonic simplicity of the Wright brothers' aesthetic sense which created a beautiful and functioning aeroplane.

For this music drama to ascend to the empyrean, a unique ability was needed. Theory had to be transformed into something so beautiful it birthed itself fully alive, and answered all questions with its own outrageous grace. The Florentines had the theorists; the Mantuans had Claudio Monteverdi. Together with his librettist, Alessandro Striggio, a member of the Invaghiti, they took the form invented in Florence, stole one of their stories and breathed inspiration across it.

L'Orfeo was about to arrive and set opera free into the world.

MONTEVERDI AND MADRIGALS

When Claudio Monteverdi was asked by Francesco Gonzago to write a 'fable in music' for the local academy, his first response may have been a discreet sigh. As principal court composer, he led a group of brilliant musicians, and their talent meant an endless series of requests. As he complained in a letter; 'his highness the prince ... very much likes not only to hear a variety of wind instruments, he also likes to have the said musicians play in private, in church, in procession, and atop city walls; now madrigals, now French songs, now airs, and now dance-songs'. Monteverdi and his crew played at the whim of their patrons.

Before he wrote *L'Orfeo*, Monteverdi had already published eight books of vocal music and madrigals: he had churned out reams more for tournaments, plays and ballets. In a competitive field, he was the master of the madrigal, the dominant form of the age. These through-composed, polyphonic hymns and songs had grown in complexity of harmony, and detail of flourish, as the Renaissance progressed. By 1600, they were in danger of becoming a stultified form. A cappella arrangements for singers of virtuoso skill, they had deteriorated into a determined prettiness of word painting, with baroque ascends and descends for appropriate words. Technical display, to show off the skill of singers and composers, was obscuring emotional truth.

Vincenzo Galileo declared open season on counterpoint and madrigals in his essay, *Della musica antica et della moderna*. He declared that the Greeks had used a single melody line, and a single voice could best express the emotions within and beneath the words. His stipulations were that the text must be clear, and the words sung as though spoken. Vincenzo was a great lutenist and a mathematician; one of his sons Michelagnolo inherited the former, Galileo the latter.

MUSICAL MANTUA

This walled city of Mantua, surrounded by three artificial lakes, was a paradise of Renaissance civility. The Gonzagos' palace of five hundred rooms, set across eight and a half acres, was busy with musicians at all times: brass heralding the arrival of an envoy here; lutes serenading young lovers there; scales being practised in one corner and new works being composed in another; a chamber band entertaining a feast in one stone hall and a mighty organ accompanying religious services in another. The apparatus of the state was held up by music. In the war for supremacy between the duchies and principalities of Renaissance Italy, artists were often the weapon of choice.

This wasn't a top-down imposition of culture but communal delight in the pleasures of music-making. Just as with drawing and sketching in the Florence of Michelangelo's youth, or piano-playing in Beethoven's time in Vienna, they were consuming crazes. Anyone educated – male or female – was expected to have a base level of musical skill: singing or playing the lute were required for human achievement as much as reading or writing. Castiglione wrote in his *Book of the Courtier*: 'I am not satisfied with our courtier unless he be also a musician, and unless, besides understanding and being able to read music, he can play various instruments.' The expertise of the Invaghiti was the high point of a pyramid of enthusiasm. Most of the audience knew the forms which Monteverdi played with in *L'Orfeo*. They relished his daring crossovers and combinations. Indeed, much in *L'Orfeo* was accessible at a level its audience could have sung and played.

However, from the base of that skill, the work builds to passages of vertiginous virtuosity and tonal richness, beyond everyone but the best. To achieve that, Monteverdi was blessed with a corps of strength and depth. Mantua was celebrated for its singers, as Giustiniani, a contemporary, noted:

> *They moderated their voices, loud or soft, heavy or light, according to the demands of the piece ... they made the words clear in such a way that one could hear the last syllable of every word, never interrupted or suppressed by embellishments.*

Naturalness and modesty, knowing one's range and expressing it truly, were the key. The Buddha was once praised for his preaching thus:

> *The sound that comes from his mouth has eight qualities: it is distinct and intelligible, sweet and audible, fluent and clear, deep and resonant. His voice does not extend beyond the assembly.*

Neither bluster nor shyness: the middle path.

SWEET ACCENTS AND SONOROUS HARMONY

Attendees at the first full night of opera passed armed guards as they walked into the main piazza of the Gonzagos' palace. Entering a spacious courtyard, the members of the Invaghiti jagged left away from the grand wooden staircase, which led up to the principal receiving rooms. Excited, they passed into a small antechamber, before moving on to the 'theatre', climbing up and along the risers, and squeezing their bodies into a mass of elegantly decked-out flesh. The room's three windows had been blocked out, so the light in the room all emanated from the dusky musk of candles and reflectors. A significant section of the orchestra sat in front of the decorated proscenium stage, which was concealed by a curtain. Nine singers hovered behind it, dressed as the Renaissance ideal of shepherds and nymphs. Amongst them were a couple of star warblers from the worlds of madrigals, including a guest *castrato* from Florence. Their *continuo* accompanists, playing lutes and cittaroni, were positioned in the corners. Further musicians were placed behind the stage – *dentro* – to provide underscore as if from the air itself.

Once the audience settled, the on-stage candles were lit and a trumpet fanfare compelled their attention; a second announced the arrival of the Duke, as he and his entourage glided to their seats in the centre of the cauldron; and a third announced the beginning of the play. As it did, the curtain sped upwards with a silent conjuror's flick which immersed the Invaghiti into the world of the play before they had time to think. A painted backdrop summoned a pastoral scene of trees and rocks like the receding landscapes of a Poussin. This announced the setting of the play amongst the idealised shepherds of old, summoning an Arcadian world.

An allegorical figure enters. As befits an endeavour so profoundly meta, she is music herself – La Musica. It is strange how many revolutionary moments are self-reflexive, yet what better subject for an opera than music. This pivotal moment will not concern a king or an emperor; it is about the first great singer, Orpheus himself. La Musica announces the theme of the work, and the size of its ambition. Cannily she disclaims her own ability to ascend to such a mythic height, thus excusing failure before the show begins. For good measure, she ends her prologue with an invocation for the audience to quieten down:

> Now while I alternate my songs, now happy, now sad,
> let no small bird stir among these trees,
> no noisy wave be heard on these river-banks.

In keeping with her earlier description of Orpheus's power to mollify with the gentleness of his voice, this is an invitation to a new sort of drama. Not one of bombast and force, where the action overwhelms the audience, but one of 'sweet accents' and 'sonorous harmony', of 'calm entreaties'. Lean in, La Musica says, be focused and thoughtful, I need your attention.

On the exit of La Musica, the small stage fills with nymphs and shepherds, who hymn a chorus in praise of the sun, 'the rose of the sky', and Apollo, the god of both sun and music. This Edenic world expresses the Renaissance conviction that in the ancient past the natural world was not just filled with music: in an essential sense, nature *was* music, and speech was poetry. Into the unclouded world which celebrates the betrothal of Orpheus and Eurydice, Monteverdi hurls the whole shebang – madrigals, choruses, *scherzi musicali* and *balli* – to create a carnival of song and dance. Together with the extravagant beauty of set and costumes, all brought to ravishing life in the flickering seductions of candlelight, *L'Orfeo* was the first operatic expression of Wagner's *Gesamtkunstwerk*, where all elements gather within a dominant aesthetic.

Plus – and it was the plus that made the difference – there was a new tool which birthed the form – the recitative. Just as Thespis stepped out from the chorus and carved an individual destiny for the actor beyond the chorus, so with recitative Monteverdi enshrined the solo singer's ability to take control of the narrative. The messenger, who brings the tragic news of Eurydice's death, stretches the muscles of this form. It is Orpheus's heart-broken response that lurches it into new life. An infinitely soft and painful whisper of exclamation is followed by long expressive intervals which sound like the spasms of sobs. Jagged, pitching and rolling speech rhythms and bitter harmonies sharpen the knife of grief and give it a cutting plangency. One of the most articulate expressions of the fractured rage of sudden loss ever created, the ferocity of feeling helped the form to find its voice.

This was not an aria; that device would come later and serve a different purpose, stopping time and action for emotional indulgence and reflection. Nor was it a song, lacking the contortions which melodies exert on language, unnaturally lengthening vowels and decorating syllables with coloratura. Recitative, sung to the simplest *continuo* support from a lute, moves the action forward as decisions are made, helping the plot to maintain its rush forwards. Unlike song, it is expressed at a speed more akin to speech.

The confidence and eloquence of this new voice would have shocked the audience. They would have gawped at this revolutionary technique, glanced at each other transported, and sneaked a look through the murky candlelight at the Duke, hoping it was not too radical for their ruler's tastes. In the room's compressed intensity, they were wrapped in a web of feeling, and shared in the birth of a deeply empathetic mode of expression. At the beginning of the show, only fifteen minutes before, La Musica had sung of the power of music to 'calm each troubled heart ... and to kindle a flame in the most chilly souls'. With a tender voice, *L'Orfeo* demonstrated how.

In keeping with the continuing life of operas, the climaxes rarely come at the end, but pop up all over the shop. They are scattered over the arc of the story, wherever the composer happens upon a banging tune, and can't resist indulging it. These come fast and furious at the top of *L'Orfeo*, though there are still treasures to come. Once Orpheus has passed down into the infernal regions accompanied by Speranza, the god of hope, he encounters Caronte, the obdurately glum bass of a ferryman, who refuses to take him further. He tries various ruses before pulling out his superpower, his ability to kill everyone softly with his song. In a passage called 'Possente spirto', Orfeo's plaintive lines are echoed in *ritornelli* by first violins, then cornets, then a harp, in an ascending scale of ethereal delicacy. Each echo reinforces his desperation, into an ever more airy thinness. Though Caronte is unmoved, the music lulls him to sleep. The special capacity of Orpheus is not to stir passion, but to still.

After Orpheus has persuaded Hades and Persephone to allow him to return with Eurydice, he sets off for the overworld, under the stricture that his beloved walk behind and he cannot look back. As he climbs upwards, his doubts and confusion are expressed in halting and nervous recitative. Shortly before he reaches the light, a loud noise from *dentro* startles him and he turns, breaking his covenant to Hades. After a short and wrenching farewell, Eurydice is drawn back down to the depths, and Orpheus pushed up to hateful light.

He wanders the earth in mourning. Monteverdi contrives a kinder conclusion than the myth. Before the maenads are able to shred him, Apollo descends from heaven in a cloud, courtesy of some ingenious stage-machinery. He picks up his son Orpheus and swoops him off to the heavens, promising to turn him into a constellation. This god in a rickety machine delivers a sublime resolution, but does not reverse the raw pain of the lovers' eternal parting. The chorus concludes with a preachy sermon declaring that 'worthy of eternal glory is only he who conquers himself'. The curtain descends.

The crammed audience, having been squeezed through the emotional wringer for ninety minutes, applauded wildly.

THE INDIVIDUAL VOICE

Francesco wrote to his brother immediately after the premiere of *L'Orfeo*, describing the deep satisfaction of all who heard it. The Duke ordered it should play again and for a wider audience. Having heard it frequently in rehearsal, he could not get enough of it. After the applause died down, a sense of reflection may have descended, and of quiet triumph. This was the experiment half of Italy had been attempting, like competing engineers trying to launch a rocket, or scientists to discover a vaccine. Mantua had got there first.

The triumph would have been tempered, however, since the narrative required to achieve it was tragic. The Mantuans won their prize with a tale of how the passions of the lower world are at war with the lucidity of the celestial sphere, and how humans are trapped in the in-between. Orpheus, habitually a balancer, a bringer of order to chaos, throws himself out of kilter. Apollo rebalances him. Orpheus loses his self-control in the risk of his journey, just as the composer did in the risk of a new form. Both had to look beyond themselves to find a way back to stability. The perfect subject for the first opera, Monteverdi wrote from the marrow of his bones to do it justice.

Greek antiquity held that music had a mystic quality which had an influence over the soul, and purified it of evil. As with music therapy today, it had the capacity to cure a wounded psyche. It was even thought capable of resurrecting those at the point of death. Throughout the tales of Dionysus, Orpheus, Demeter and Persephone, and their attendant mysteries, there is a liminal flirtation on the borderline of mortality. All of these figures move between realms of life and not-life, and bring back lessons from the journey to illuminate aspects of our selves which remain half-lit. Music is the key to the door between the two.

In many ancient cults, music is used to reach ecstasy, to soar to the state where the god can be received in excited elation, and the self dissolved in group hysteria. The ambition of Orpheus was distinct. Rather than deranging nature with the thrill of madness, he wanted to hush the world with a beautiful sorrow. His work was to entrance with the rational rhythm of Apollo's light, and thereby create empathy and illumination. Whether the harrowing of hell, the taming of beasts or the conquest of death, he spoke gently. The early ambition of opera, as expressed in its first masterwork, was to gift such serene beauty to the human voice.

As with the isolation of Thespis, the gift of Monteverdi was for the individual voice, the solo singer. Tectonic plates were shifting in Europe. Just as Vincenzo Galileo pushed for this innovation, his son was poised to create a more lonely universe for the individual to find themselves lost in.

The madrigal was an encompassing ensemble, a gathering of harmonic voices to praise God or summon nature. It was a musical church of ritual like the Catholic one. The Protestant ethos separated the individual from the crowd, and downgraded ritual. Freedom was given to each self, and each conscience, to work out its own relation to the larger reality. We claim such freedom greedily and moreishly, determinedly pushing ourselves away from the crowd, without considering the loss. Much was gained, much was abandoned, or, as W.H. Auden later put it,

> *Accurate scholarship can*
> *Unearth the whole offence*
> *From Luther until now*
> *That has driven a culture mad.*

GUILTY CREATURES

Why does Orpheus turn back? It is one of those questions which haunt us from the first moment we hear this story. The answers morph as we grow older and as certainties become confusions. The chorus at the end of *L'Orfeo* is censorious, blaming it on his inability to check himself. Other critics pile in and accuse him of vanity. They say he is desperate for approval – as with every artist before or since who has played a tune, or daubed a picture, and looked up nervously for a nod. It may be simply he is worried Eurydice is not there, and cannot bear not to check. Maybe he cares too much. Maybe he knows it is wrong to go against nature and bring the dead back. Maybe he doesn't like her in that instant, and loves her in all others.

It is a failure and, as such, a just conclusion for a true human story. The work of an artist, as with their life, has to encompass what we are to be meaningful, and failure is a larger truth than triumph. With our greed and our clumsiness and our cruelties, we remain guilty creatures sitting at a play, and our proper conclusion is decline and fall. One day, we may merit more, one day we may paint, write or sing and *deserve* a myth where Orpheus does not fail. One day, we may have the right to bring Eurydice back into the light, and merit a freedom of movement between life and no-life. One day we might have the strength and calm not to look back.

THE GRAND THEATRE OF THE UNIVERSE

If his tale was one of sorrow, Monteverdi's night was a triumph. *L'Orfeo* was repeated immediately (though it was later dormant in the repertoire for several centuries). Most significantly, the score was published a year later, and would prove a huge creative influence for warriors in the same cause.

Musicians and composers scrutinised the work and must have marvelled at the brilliance of its modernity and experiment – one that was to go on to alter the world of music and drama. Transformed from an academic exercise to sublime art by Monteverdi's ear for the song of the heart, it gave rise to an operatic energy that survives to this day. But, on that night, only two hundred witnesses from a courtly elite, piled on top of each other in a small room, bore witness. Monteverdi himself certainly knew its significance, writing in his dedicatory letter to the Duke of Mantua:

> *The fable of Orpheus was once marginally staged in the Academy of the Invaghiti on a narrow stage, and now is about to appear in the great theatre of the Universe.*

9

Before

A TALE OF JOHN LYDON

10 DECEMBER 1896, PARIS

At around 8pm, in the Théâtre de l'Oeuvre, a distinguished palace of Parisian plush, the curtain went up on a world premiere. As the tasselled fabric rose, an actor named Firmin Gémier strode down to the front of the stage, looked out over the refined Parisian crowd, and shouted 'Merdre!' – the extra r twisting the word to the abstract.

Cue uproar!

Gémier was playing the lead in *Ubu Roi*, a new play by a young malcontent from Normandy called Alfred Jarry. Ten years before, Jarry sat in a classroom in a Rennes lycée, under the tutelage of a Monsieur Hebert. It is hard to think of another physics teacher who has had such cultural effect. Jarry delighted in inventing playlets for marionettes. These puppet shows starred his physics teacher redubbed 'Le Père Ébé. His avatar was furnished with a retractable ear, a distended belly and three teeth, of wood, stone and iron. In such a guise he suffered protracted agonies as king of a make-believe Poland. It is a standard schoolboy tactic – take an authority figure, make him behave in the most degrading manner and drench him in shame and shit. *Ubu* is one of the first examples of a student prank translated into art.

Jarry incubated the project over years, adding episodes and imposing on it a quasi-Shakespearean structure. He begged theatres to put it on, and once he succeeded, he got the reaction he craved. The show lasted just that one night. The audience jeered and screamed at the play and each other. Fist fights broke out, later transcribed into print as critics fought over whether the play was an ordered work of art or a work of arty ordure. Cultural historians have carried the fight on since. Was this shouty juvenilia? Or the precursor of modernism, Dadaism, situationism or a host of other 'isms'? No matter its effect on posterity, Jarry had the *succès de scandale* that only the French can cook up. He spent the rest of his short life as a *fin-de-siècle* wild boy, carrying out interventions on reality, until absinthe rotted his internal organs away.

Tucked away within the audience at the Théâtre de l'Oeuvre on its one and only night was a shy, monocled and excited Irishman – William Butler Yeats. He writes of the night:

> *The audience shake their fists at one another, and the Rhymer whispers to me, 'There are often duels after these performances.' I can see for myself that the chief personage, who is some kind of King, carries for his Sceptre a brush of the kind we use to clean a toilet. Feeling bound to support the most spirited party, we have shouted for the play, but that night I am very sad. I say, 'What more is possible? After us, the Savage God.*

It was a prophetic quote. Eighty years later, the Savage God showed up.

4 JUNE 1976, LESSER FREE TRADE HALL, MANCHESTER

Standing at a rickety box office in Manchester, Pete McNeish heard the cry from a demented hawker outside: 'Roll up, roll up! Come on in! There's this great band from London. They're going to be really famous. They're fantastic! Roll up, roll up!' The outfit of this hawker was not perfectly pitched for mid-1970s Manchester. His assembly of fur coat, leather Stetson and tight leather suit may have suited his own dreams of rock manager chic, but wasn't standard wear in the north-west. As one attendee observed, the hawker was 'definitely a very odd person'.

Still, McNeish, and his promoter partner, Howard Trafford, would have been grateful for the help. Having read about this band in the *NME*, hared down to London to witness them and begged their manager to bring them north, they had been trying anything and everything to get an audience. Their dreams of rock promotion had not included wandering Manchester's studenty Oxford Road in the middle of the night, with a roll of posters and a bucket of wallpaper paste. Their efforts weren't helped by the manager sending posters covered in terrible reviews.

This was a big night for the band as well. It was their first major venue and their first big foray outside London. Unable to secure several halls due to sudden notoriety, the promoters had landed on the Lesser Free Trade Hall, the upstairs studio of the more substantial Free Trade Hall. The larger venue had a history of dissent and revolt. Built on the site of the Peterloo Massacre, it had hosted radical gatherings and trade union meetings as well as leading bands. It was here in 1965 that a member of the audience accused Bob Dylan of being 'Judas' for going electric, and here that Dylan gave the only necessary response, turning to his band and saying, 'Play fucking loud.' In 1886, Oscar Wilde had delivered one of his aesthetic lectures there to a huge crowd, and received the princely sum of £24 3s 6d. Which was more than McNeish and Trafford managed to raise eighty years later.

Argument over who and how many attended this concert still rages. In Manchester estimates vary from seven to seven hundred. Entry was 50p, and takings were the far from princely £14, which would suggest only twenty-eight tickets were sold. But, given a fair amount of scamming, and hangers-on, and crashers, it is probable that there were fifty or so scattered souls in the seats as the concert began.

McNeish and Trafford – soon to be better known as Pete Shelley and Howard Devoto – had planned the night to introduce their own group, Buzzcocks. But their debut was delayed by two sticking points: no rehearsals and nobody else in the band. So, although Buzzcocks were printed as support on the tickets, they decided not to embarrass themselves and went in search of another band. With time running out, they managed to find Solstice – Bolton's third biggest rock band.

Solstice were perhaps the least suitable act imaginable and there had been much aggro between them and the main act during soundchecks. The London band refused to let the Bolton lads use their sound system without paying fifty quid, and, being inveterate thieves, one of the

Londoners had pinched a Solstice guitar strap. Violence was threatened. Relations weren't made more cordial by their leather-clad manager, still outside raising an audience, shouting, 'Don't come in yet. The support band are on first. They're crap. Come back in half an hour'. The audience had been promised something new. This wasn't furnished by Solstice. Unflatteringly described by an attendee as 'the arse end of prog rock', they did an extended version of 'Nantucket Sleighride', a hymn to the hunting of sperm whales. One schoolboy sitting alone at the back was called Steven Morrissey. Later better known without his first name, he remembered that 'the audience were very slim. It was a front parlour affair. Solstice's hair swept off the edge of the stage.' The audience were lulled into a sense of dulled security, a numbed disappointment at life, a feeling all too familiar in the mid-seventies. Yet there was a strange tickling sense that something was about to occur.

Someone announced the main act and, as the future third member of Buzzcocks described it, 'the punk-rock atom split'.

The Sex Pistols ambled on.

THAT SUMMER WAS VERY HOT

1976 was the hottest English summer since 1940, and the fierce sun fired up a crucible of change. In England heat changes everything. When the sun comes out in May, it exposes our awkwardness. When it goes on through the summer, the change accelerates. Super-hot summers boil out the nation's damp and lift the lid of repression.

The year rolled along on a series of slow-moving social changes. The freshly liberated gay scene, turbocharged by the polyamorous declarations of David Bowie and others, was happy to take its shirt off and flaunt its nipples and its Bullworker-buffed chests. The West Indies cricket team arrived and were told by the English captain, a statuesque white South African called Tony Greig, that he was going to make them grovel. They proceeded over a long summer to batter the England players into a pulp. One Saturday evening two old batsmen, Brian Close and John Edrich, came out to bat in a failing light against the four fastest bowlers in the world. Stiff and antiquated emblems of Empire, they were target practice for the lethal West Indians. Black Britain walked taller. At the same time, the gathering forces of second wave feminism were momentarily proud and then soon less so at the presence of the first woman to run a major political party, Margaret Thatcher. Through the summer, everyone tuned in on TV to watch Kojak collaring a criminal, chanting, 'You dirty punk.'

A feeling of decline was almost tangible. Industrial England saw its role in the world flickering out as production fled overseas, and the economy tanked. Unemployment bloomed and left a generation crisscrossing the landscape aimlessly. Our political leaders wandered the world with begging bowls asking for money to bail us out, while fathers and grandfathers hymned the Empire. Recent revisionist history has told the story of how the 1970s were a time of parity and prosperity. There may be some truth there, but at the time, as a young person, it felt dismal, like the future was a long tunnel of hopelessness.

Nihilism was no longer the reserve of sophisticated intellectuals, either. It was the currency of the streets. *We hate everything* was the graffiti of choice. The hippy movement had moved beyond its first stage of benevolent innovation into a state of self-parody which was painful to behold. It had always been a middle-class enclave anyway. The working-class movements of style and sharpness – the Teds, the Mods and the Skinheads – had lost their founding impulse. Their shared exhaustion was only refreshed when they got the chance to thump each other. Or to come together and thump hippies. The drugs of national choice – glue and speed – were accompaniments to frenzy and violence.

The music to serenade this moment was woeful – a blancmange of blandness, with pre-packaged hits from an outfit called K-tel, the nondescript outcrop of television talent shows. Localism, particularity and difference were bled out for a washed and bleached hygienic blankness. No offence to ABBA, who can write a tune, but when the whole world aspires to be ABBA, something is up. Breaking that wall – communicating, confronting, demanding a reaction – felt far away. In the US, Dylan had just launched his Rolling Thunder Revue, a playful troubadour roadshow, which attempted to break down this distancing. The English mode of breaking the wall came from a different direction.

SEX

With spiky peroxide hair, monochrome make-up and some crude metallic adornments, Jordan would board the suburban commuter train as it trundled towards London. She would slot herself in amongst city gents sleeping their life away in grey suits and bowler hats. They might have been alright with the facial accoutrements, had it not been for what she was wearing. All she had on was stockings and suspenders and a rubber top.

Her destination was her workplace, a shop called SEX, which occupied a small space on the King's Road. Run by the Svengali Malcolm McLaren and his partner, the iconoclastic genius of couture, Vivienne Westwood, the shop had searched for an identity until settling on a style set by rubber, leather, chains and synthetics. It was a combination of sado-masochism and determined trashiness. Plastic, junk food, B-movies, advertising, cigarettes and speed were in; arts and crafts and yoghurt and self-demonstrating empathy were out. Jordan, the assistant, was the essence of the shop; she treated her body as a painting. Her whole life was a 'pas de deux with outrage'. With her sculpted hair, haughty attitude and not-so-faint hint of depravity, she was a transgressive mirror image of the new Conservative leader herself. Margaret Thatcher and punk were fertilised by the same soil.

Many an ostentatious flâneur perambulated up and down the King's Road at the time, most exhibiting traditional forms of machismo or femininity. One small gang were different, and they always ended up shambling into SEX. The gang were the Four Johns, so called since there were four of them and they were all called John. Lost boys, magpieing gobbets of wisdom and style from here and there, their most charismatic member looked like a cross between Rimbaud and Uriah Heep. His name was John Lydon. As an eight-year-old boy he had suffered meningitis, which took him out of the world into self-isolation for a year. Over a decade later, he still hadn't fully re-entered. His movements were twitching efforts to avoid attention while simultaneously craving it. His head hunched forwards, it would shift and twist, and then pierce the onlooker with a bullet gaze. He sniggered and shrank from verbal engagement, then shot out volcanic bursts of sarcasm and hostility. Beneath the violence lurked a hidden vulnerability, sure to make both boys and girls fall hopelessly in love. Malcolm McLaren was a mass of inadequacies, but he could spot originality and star quality. Lydon had magnetism and moral force and McLaren needed both. He wanted to launch a band.

He had gathered together three West London thieves and waifs, who had something about them and helped them towards a base level of musical competence. They had attitude to spare, and the smell of the new, but no leader. Various singers were tried; none measured up. Having separated Lydon from the other three Johns, McLaren forced him together with the others. They hated each other immediately; 'We knew Lydon was a cunt on sight', one noted. But they recognised each other's force, and some sense of a future clicked among them. McLaren and Lydon despised each other even more, and with the special fury of those who come from different tribes, one Jewish and one Catholic; those who look far too like each other and those who both know their own minds and never waver. All these tensions bubbled as the Sex Pistols emerged.

Their first gig was at Saint Martin's School of Art on 6 November 1975. It was one among many crashing noises being made by garage bands. They toured tiny rooms around London and further afield for nine months. These were not glamorous events. At one in Whitby, the venue manager came on stage after fifteen minutes and said, 'It's no good lads, you're going to have to stop, they can't hear the bingo next door.' Wherever they played, many would hate them, many would ignore them, but at each the Pied Piper would pick up two or three lost children. These leaderless souls would see a flashing strobe light, hear the electric noise, and join the hard-core cult any movement needs. The music attracted a following, but their desire for chaos satisfied a deeper hunger.

If the band wasn't creating enough electricity on its own, Lydon, renamed Johnny Rotten, would smash up his equipment or hurl chairs into the audience. If that didn't create enough mess, then Jordan or McLaren would act as agents of chaos, and start hurling punches and blows at others, or each other. The master of misrule was another of the Four Johns, an etiolated line of confusion and pain who had renamed himself Sid Vicious. He could always be relied on to start a rampage. This itch for chaos became their calling card. As Neil Tennant, later of the Pet Shop Boys, wrote in the *NME*, 'So how do the Pistols create their atmosphere when their music has failed? By beating up a member of their audience. How else?'

Once initiated, everyone would get pulled into this vortex of mayhem. But the music would carry on. On one memorable night in

High Wycombe (something of an oxymoron), during a rendition of 'No Fun', everybody kicked off. Rotten dived from the stage into the crowd, microphone in hand, and was thrown to the floor. A throng of thrashing people piled on top, all flailing and punching. Somehow Rotten emerged from the throng, microphone in hand. Still singing. They don't teach that at the BRIT School.

Amid the mayhem, the music was getting better. They were starting to get a reputation, and other bands on the circuit didn't want to play with them. Not because of the violence. Because they wiped them out.

PARIS 1896, AND UBU AGAIN

The sharpest review of *Ubu Roi* came from the poet W.B. Yeats dubbed 'Rhymer', a man at the edge of the avant-garde called Arthur Symons. Despite his experimental credentials, *Ubu* was too much for Symons. The quote demonstrates the groovy being outgrooved, and is a note-perfect description of the rough beast who would slouch his way towards Manchester ninety years later:

> *The play has the crudity of the schoolboy or savage: what is most remarkable is the insolence with which a young writer mocks at civilization itself, sweeping all art, along with all humanity, into the same inglorious slop-pail ... In our search for sensation, we have exhausted sensation.*

THE PISTOLS IN MANCHESTER

On that hot night in the Lesser Free Trade Hall, out ambled the four young Londoners, only just out of their teens, slender like reeds and vibrating with attitude from Hades. Bass player Glen Matlock wore a plain T-shirt and paint-spattered trousers; guitarist Steve Jones, an all-in-one boiler suit; and their lead singer, Johnny Rotten, was in a shredded yellow pullover and T-shirt with a pair of old bloke's Oxfam trousers. The young Morrissey witnessed this assemblage and, with supercilious sneer in place at a tender age, wrote to the music papers, 'I'd love to see the Pistols make it. Maybe then they'll be able to afford some clothes which don't look as though they've been slept in.'

But the power wasn't in the clothes. Now, as always, it was in the gaze. Even for a toughened Manc crowd, Johnny Rotten was 'one of the most frightening people I'd ever seen. This lad with a thousand yard stare, just stood there.' With a handful of gigs behind him, the London-Irish boy had trained himself, eyes wide and leering, to have the transfixing power of a great painting, 'Wherever I went in the room, it was as though he was staring at me.' Orpheus had come into the room, wild and angry, ready to go down to the underworld, to harrow hell with his song, and to pull his own personal Eurydice – the benighted youth of his country – away from numbness, and back to life.

Some local wit shouted, 'You're not very sexy.' Rotten fixed him with his spectral glare and asked, 'Why? Do you want some sex?' Then crash, bang, wallop – and they launched into the first song, a cover of 'Don't Gimme Me No Lip Child'. Fast, frenetic and amphetamine-driven, like filaments of electrocuted energy, they carved their way through song after song. The energy was savage, kinetic and joyously free from vanity. In 1976, for old rockers, glam-rockers and public-school prog-rockers, vanity was the order of the day. Being admired was the default position of the music scene. This lot, manically and clownishly tumbling here and there, were the opposite. Their movement wasn't calculated to impress, it was the extension of the fervid delirium of their music.

Not everyone loved the Pistols, and heckling and abuse were liberally sprinkled over the show. People caught on quickly that this was confrontational, and demanded an aggressive response. But Rotten handled himself like the battered old music hall act he aspired to be, and gave back sharply whatever he was given. The acid wit and frothing rage and oh-so-discreet vulnerability were capturing hearts.

They thrashed their way on through their anthemic hymns for alienated youth, 'No Feelings', 'Pretty Vacant' and 'Submission'. Somewhere in the middle of their set they covered the Monkees classic 'Stepping Stone'. It was during the opening chords that a significant proportion of the audience lost their hearts and their adrenaline glands completely. They were lovers for life, hooked on the rush of this whirling berserker energy.

Gawping from the stalls were Peter Hook and Bernard Sumner. The next day Hook went into a shop and bought an electric guitar, 'You just thought, "God we could do that." I still to this day can't imagine why, 'cause

I'd never played a musical instrument.' The road to Joy Division, and then New Order, had begun. Along with them, in the tiny crowd, were other future members of The Smiths and The Fall. The cultural life of any town always owes a debt to its maddest. They all heard the defiant shriek of the future. The band's manager who had been hawking outside, Malcolm McLaren now stood at the back, smirking broadly. He looked 'like a dad at a school pantomime watching his kids perform'.

It was a magic night, primarily because it was always becoming so. Nothing had arrived. If the magic had to be encapsulated into a single word, it would be that elegant little word *before*. This was before the uniform of punkhood had arrived, before anyone had written about it or defined it or explained it, before anyone had gone to war against it or on behalf of it. This was a small group of shabbily and oddly dressed people – some old hippies, some scruffs, some people wearing all they could afford to wear – a small group improvising a new identity together. This was the group present as it became. Before is always more exciting than when or after; before a night out, before a party, before a first kiss, before a play begins, before a new movement shifts the air, just before a wave falls. Great virtue in before.

UBU IN PARIS ENCORE

Another stirred and shaken observer of the first night of *Ubu* was the poet Catulle Mendès. His reminiscence again serves well for the brainchild of Lydon and McLaren:

> *A new type has been put before us. Père Ubu exists ... You will not be able to get rid of him; he will haunt you and perpetually force you to remember not only that he passed this way, but that he has arrived and is here.*

WHAT THE PISTOLS OFFERED

Much of the attraction of the Pistols was their defiance, the claiming of a right to stand there and say, as one Mancunian commentator put it, 'we don't give a toss what you think, this is what we like to play, and this is the way we're gonna play it.' That demand for freedom liberated others. In a world of deadening stereotypes, the Pistols offered something inventive and unjudgemental. As Lydon said, 'People who'd had no self-respect started to consider themselves as beautiful in not being beautiful. Women started to appreciate themselves as not second-class citizens. Punk made that clear.'

Musically the band had the right elements, even if its members were headlocked in mutual loathing. There was an immediate tension between the suburban Matlock with his taste for melody and the further shores of Lydon's imagination. Steve Jones began his career as little more than an accomplished burglar of famous rock stars' homes, but completed it a real musician. Paul Cook swallowed his charisma into himself and channelled it through his drums. Lydon at the front rasped and reported like a young Rimbaud – thoughtful, angry and beautiful. The Pistols were always the first to declare their own musical incompetence, but a steady regime of gig after gig in ghastly spaces made them effective. And the songwriting is classic rock and roll – short declamatory openings carried by guitar riffs, staccato drumming, classic shapes of alternating verse and chorus, simple solos and crashing endings.

As with the Rolling Stones, the scene they emerged from found its way into their DNA. As McLaren described one of their early venues, 'The place smelled like a shithole, a few fucking seats, and a stage the size of a Punch and Judy show.' The grubbiness keeps you honest, but the crucial factor is the diminutive size. Keith Richards writes in his biography of Mick Jagger's unique ability to work a square metre. How he could fill it with energy, shape and surprise. It was a skill learnt in tiny pubs and clubs. A skill handed down to Jagger and Lydon by two hundred years of music hall comedians trained to work the shallow yard in front of the curtain during a front-cloth routine. I worked with the legendary Roy Hudd, and his ability to tell a complex and rich story in as much space as a cupboard, and fill an audience with sympathy and delight, was a wonder. John Lydon, who described himself as 'a mystery figure they could hide in a cupboard and spring out like a Jack in the Box', shared that skill.

The Pistols' debt to music hall wasn't only in stagecraft; there was also the comedy. Lydon's persona was designed to disarm with an unsettling humour whose depth of lunacy was hard to read. Music hall figures were closer to the world of Samuel Beckett and the Theatre of the Absurd than the comforting normality of television comedians. Tommy Cooper and Max Wall moved like creatures from the depths of the audience's subconscious, not like the pub bore who knows a lot of jokes. There is a strain of violence that percolates up within their humour. John Lydon knew and loved them.

Music hall was also a place where performers and audience could look at their communal concerns, and the hard facts of their life. Details of working-class life could be turned over and laughed at. The Pistols had the same facility. Their songs may have bemused the middle-class, but what they were discussing – abortions, atomic bombs, boredom, extreme right-wing prejudice, factories, television – was what their audience were bothered about. And music hall acts were sharp. They had native intelligence. From Marie Lloyd on, these performers quietened their unruly crowds with charm and wit – yes, but also with a threat, the threat of their ferocious intelligence. John Lydon learnt that. Not for him what Mick Jagger has described as the 'central dumbness' of pop.

The biggest offer, though, for punk rock was contact and collision. The mosh pit – swirling, tumbling, out of control – was joyous for its anarchy, but more than anything for the simple virtue of touch. The audience would grab each other, ride each other, punch each other, spit at each other or the band; the band would spit back, then dive off the stage and join in the carnival of contact. The violence wasn't playful, it was cruel and real; as the music journalist Nick Kent could testify, having been slashed by a bicycle chain by Sid Vicious.

The Sex Pistols wasn't really a sexual thing, though, despite the name of both shop and band. There is a sexual disgust throughout the band's lyrics, and in their act. John Lydon himself said of sex, 'by the time you're twenty you think – yawn – just another squelch session'. Sweat and bouncing and bodies and touch and collision should really be a definition of sex, but it wasn't. It was something more communal, more religious, more weirdly innocent, a search for *Fight Club* authenticity, a need for Dionysiac pain and pleasure to ratify aliveness. It was back to the Telesterion. In a time when the rock scene had got operatic and grandiose, this group served up the opposite, a festival of levelling where everyone bit, scratched and rubbed each other – act and audience.

As another Mancunian witness of that concert said, 'Whether they were good or not was irrelevant – I wanted to be excited and they filled the spot.'

UBU ROI IN 2016

At the end of 2016 – a truly miserable year, with a vote for Brexit followed by the election of Trump – I went to watch my daughter in a student drama production. The audience were all feeling at sea, having witnessed the global un-mooring of those events (both enthusiastically endorsed by an aged John Lydon – still goading the liberals). The noxious brew of calculated lying and manufactured tribalism by all sides had spawned the two most cynical political moments of my lifetime. The world seemed in a dank state. Attending student shows is not always the ideal way to dispel such feelings, especially not *Ubu Roi*.

Nonetheless, an aura of excited buzz emanated from the sports hall where the show was on. Together with our ticket, we had a spurting phallus drawn on our hands before entering. The director, an androgynous young man, kitted out in high heels and a frock, stood on a table and told us to go fuck ourselves. He seemed in an enhanced frame of mind. We were led down a corridor into a room split by plastic sheeting as screaming white-metal rock clanged from the other side. Pushing our way through the sheeting, there were a group of people dancing to a band of statuesque young men, playing electric guitars, deadpan, wearing nothing but tight underpants. It was clear that the staging was going to be promenade, at which I balked, not wanting to stand up for an hour and a quarter. A young person kindly steered me to a raised section with a few seats on it. The area was blazoned with an unflattering poster – *Help the Aged*.

After more music, the show blazed into life. It was screamed rather than spoken. Screamed in terrible French accents to further mask all comprehension. The rudiments of the plot – a king, a queen, a Russian invasion – lurked somewhere behind the screaming and the charging about. At one point we processed into an adjacent room to witness a pile of slaughtered bodies. My daughter fellated a courgette, and then, in a complex piece of choreography, had sex with a shopping trolley. Towards the end, a lot of youth lay on the floor, and a couple of young chaps took their clothes off and started rubbing their arses into the faces of (you had to hope) stooges in the audience. Another character – it was hard to work out who – then spent about three minutes strangling my daughter. This was done with sufficient realism that I dismounted from my platform, and went and hovered close by, muttering that he had probably gone far enough.

The show was performed with verve and attack. At the end, the audience went bananas. The director became yet more enhanced by the adulation, and climbed onto the *Help the Aged* platform, where he took off his clothes and started vigorously masturbating. Unable to get much going there, he turned and lifted all the metal chairs over his head, and threw them with great force at the audience. We dodged them. After the year we'd had, with its confining matrix of disappointments and imprisoning dogma, cowed into submission by the poisonous bogusness of creeps various, here were young people prepared to make a good old holy mess. In a ghastly world of bullying accountants and doctrinaire artists and post-truth mobs, this glorious display of self-indulgent punk violence was the ideal tonic. It felt great.

THE FALLING-AWAY

The numbers may have been small, but the electricity from the Sex Pistols' first Manchester gig was of sufficient wattage that there was a demand for a swift return. It happened six weeks later and, on another night of comedy and drama, the group sent a packed house into ecstasy again. They unleashed their signature tune, 'Anarchy in the UK', on the waiting world. Soon after, the same rough beast was unfurled for their first live television performance, on a local Granada TV show supervised by the Ron Burgundy of the Madchester scene, Tony Wilson.

'Anarchy' and 'the Antichrist' were released in small homeopathic doses into English society to loosen it up. By the second performance people were starting to catch on to what punk was, starting to formulate a uniform style and attitude. The trousers were narrower, the hair shorter, and pogoing up and down had become the dance of choice. John Lydon quickly learnt to hate his own disciples: 'The punks ruined it – they adopted a uniform image and attitude. The whole thing was supposed to be about being yourself.'

What had begun as a saving energy – not nihilism but a hostile response to it, when fists flew and icons were destroyed with jubilation – became shrouded within its own violence and found nothing positive beyond it. The cynicism of the music industry, the vanity of its performers, and the emptiness of its shock tactics, left it nowhere to go. The Pistols combusted spectacularly in San Francisco within two years, the mutual loathing too great a combustible energy to contain.

John Lydon, who had aimed as the *Ubu* Orpheus to save the youth of the nation, ended up unable to save his own fellow John and schoolfriend, Sid Vicious, from a squalid descent into murder and suicide. Or himself from the self-consuming allure of televisual panto, butter adverts and *I'm a Celebrity ... Get Me Out of Here!*

But no-one should have the last word but him:

All I want is for future generations to go ...

Fuck it.

Had enough.

Here's the truth.

10

The Female Gaze

A TALE OF VICTORINE MEURENT
AND ÉDOUARD MANET

THE SHRIMP

Paris was proud of its new tram – the first powered by steam – which rolled slowly down lush miles of new boulevards laid out by Baron Haussman. France was proud of all its technological change and the pace it was setting. Science and industry had moved the country ahead of its rivals, and by 1863 some 6,000 miles of railway tracks and 55,000 miles of telegraph wire cross-hatched the nation. Paris was the capital of the world, birthplace of the new. But with change comes inequity, and one of the city's principal agents of change came from the wrong end of town, from the other side of the tram tracks.

Victorine Meurent was born in 1844 to a laundress mother and an engraver father, and at seventeen began modelling for the art teacher Thomas Couture. By this stage she was living away from her parents in a small flat in the Latin Quarter. Modelling was not an easy life and her pay would have been no more than 25 francs a month, earnings that had to be supplemented. Strangely enough, many of the male models, sitting for classical paintings of Hercules or Julius Caesar at one moment, earnt their crust by driving buses. This line of work wasn't available for women. Victorine upped her earnings by singing in cafes, and teaching guitar and violin. Such sketchy details might imply a flame-haired bohemian. But the impression given in paintings of her – and impression is everything in this context – is of privacy, containment and muted precision. Nicknamed La Crevette ('the Shrimp') because of her shortness, she was nothing like the erotic beauties of the Académie, all rolling flesh and flirtatiousness. You could walk past her, and her petite ordinariness would leave you untouched.

Except for one thing. Her gaze. In Victorine's eyes there sat a touch of insolence, a sliver of curiosity, a shiver of warmth. Strong, indifferent and defiant, her gaze suggests a bottomless calm. *Come hell or high water*, it says, *I have no needs*. If you locked eyes with her, you were lost. Your every waking moment would be left trying to work out where that strength came from, what her eyes told you about her, and what they revealed about you. She forced you to engage with how she was seeing the world. You would wake up in the middle of the night, and see that face, and feel challenged to be as fully yourself.

Baudelaire defined a beauty that lay 'in the coldness of the stare, the outward expression of an unshakeable resolution not to be moved ... A dormant fire whose existence we can only guess at, for it refuses to burst into flame'. Victorine exemplified that, and took it further. When Manet first met her, it is easy to imagine his synapses pulsing. He found not so much a muse as a teacher. There was a novelty and a wisdom in that look which he could not control; if he could, his art would be the lesser. He knew he must translate it to the world.

THE FLÂNEURS

At the onset of the 1860s, as change tickled the atoms in the air, Paris was home to a dazzling gang of flâneurs. Among their number was Émile Zola, who recorded their exhibitionist charisma in *The Masterpiece*:

> *As the four of them strolled along they appeared to take up the whole breadth of the Boulevard des Invalides. The gang usually spread them-selves out like that, as friends tacked themselves on, until it looked like a horde on the warpath. As they squared their broad young shoulders, these twenty-year-olds took possession of the pavement ... They picked up Paris calmly in one hand and put it in their pocket.*

These vagabond show-offs were an ever-changing and ever-dazzling cast of painters and writers, among them Zola himself, Cézanne, Pissarro, Fantin-Latour, Baudelaire, Whistler, Berthe Morisot and Édouard Manet. Though fashionably threadbare, they had a sense of clothing that went beyond vanity. Manet was an unapologetic dandy, always to be seen in a long black coat with an extended fur collar, yellow suede gloves, a walking stick and 'intentionally gaudy trousers' – a description which could cover a variety of sins. Baudelaire called for a painter who could mythologise this dress; 'who will make us see how grand we are in our neckties and our varnished boots', so at odds with the sombre colours and frock coats of the Second Empire gentleman.

In 1863, in *Le Figaro*, Charles Baudelaire served up the first definition of the *flâneur*:

> *The crowd is his element, as the air is that of birds, and water of fishes.*
> *His passion and his profession are to become one flesh with the crowd.*
> *For the perfect flâneur, it is an immense joy to set up house in the heart*
> *of the multitude, amid the ebb and flow of movement, in the midst of*
> *the fugitive and the infinite. The lover of universal life enters into the*
> *crowd as though it were an immense reservoir of electrical energy.*

Wandering the streets of Paris, dreaming of their artists' utopia, this gang watched their city morphing around them. The city was itself like an outsized artwork, creating and recreating itself. Scutty streets led into expansive squares which flowed onto bridges opening the eye out wider like ever-changing frescoes. Everything had to be caught within the net of their look: the working, the idle; the rich, the poor; the clean, the filthy; the animate, the inanimate. They were determined to reinvent the rules about what was or wasn't allowed within the purview of art. No more hierarchies or entrance exams; the universal was what mattered.

As Zola put it:

> *Wouldn't it be wonderful to devote the whole of one's life to one work*
> *and put everything into it, men, animals, everything under the sun!?*
> *Not according to the idiotic hierarchy so dear to our personal pride,*
> *but into the mighty universal flow of life ... the mighty All, in a word,*
> *in working order, just as it is.*

In the middle of these streets, the *flâneurs* would halt to have a blazing row about the nature of realism, or to shout acclaim as they stumbled on a circus poster in three glaring colours. The pavements were their battlefield where they went to war with the leaden hand of normality. The Café de Bade was their HQ. There they would flirt with the working girls at rest, drink novel liquors, and give themselves over to a surprisingly suburban craze for an English card game, *le whist*. At the end of a day of hard flirting, drinking and whisting, when the spirit was high, one might exclaim, 'Life! Life! Life! What it is to put life into things, and put life into men! That's the only way to be a God!' The heady badinage of the Café de Bade is glamorised by Zola, but even so, great bliss it must have been to be there.

MANET

Though celebrated in the demi-monde, Manet had been battering on the door of acceptance as an artist for years. He was quick to abuse the Académie des Beaux-Arts, with its elitism and finicky standards, but hungered with an equal passion for its approval. He yearned for the comfort of *bien-pensant* regard, yet was incapable of painting any other way than his own.

Born to a wealthy and well-connected family in Paris, Manet had eschewed the École des Beaux-Arts, a school which taught anatomy and geometry with a grim certainty but devoted surprisingly scant attention to painting. Instead, he went to study with Thomas Couture, which was a halfway house between the strictures of the Académie and the modern. He spent six years there, failing to be impressed by, or impress, his master. By 1863 had moved to his own studio in Rue Guyot. Here he grew a style, both unique and an affront to the meticulous Académie artists. The contemporary fashion for high burnish and the invisible paintbrush was not for him. Impressed by the two-dimensional harmony of imported Japanese art, and by the irreal gestures of Spanish art, he forged a new way. He applied paint thickly with rough and crude brushstrokes.

The most immediate sense of his art was its bursting immediacy. His painted life often seems to be tipping out of its own frame and towards you. The front-lit flatness pushes everything forward, including the backgrounds, primed in a startling white rather than traditional gravy brown. In a gallery of passive prettiness, receding within gold frames,

Manet's grenades of life shout out their presence. The effect is rude and invigorating, like a burst of filthy language bawled out from the steps of a gin shop. The accepted practice was to plan a conceit, make a detailed drawing, and then consider carefully before applying the merest smidgen of paint, but Manet worked the other way round. He started with paint, with colour and contrast, rather than lines and contours. The subject emerged organically from within the kaleidoscope of life. In an early painting, peonies in a vase, the flowers seem to punch their way out of the canvas. *Impressionism* was yet to be coined as a term, and it was here that its purpose was being defined – literally, as something that makes an impression, that touches and changes, just as the city, the crowd and nature do. Manet's work was about bustling energy in space and time, not frozen objects in frozen time. Matter in transition, not stasis.

Manet's other achievement was to reject not only the idea of finish, but also finishing. In several of his works – much as with Michelangelo and his forms that struggled to appear from marble – Manet left them aggressively half-formed, with unfinished space within them. This is most notable in another early work, his panorama of hectic life, *Music in the Tuileries Gardens*. This was a direct response to Baudelaire's call for art that reflected modernity, with its bourgeois bustles and its fandango of fashions (blazing colours, rampant top hats, monocles and moustaches). But its greatest novelty is to leave in its architectural centre – where the eye is led by the movement of the whole – an indistinct grey smudge of paint. This punkish statement is a great declaration about the nature of the eye. How, when we observe a busy scene, the eye chaotically picks a chair here, notes a fan there, takes in an umbrella in the corner. It doesn't organise each detail into a carefully composed whole. It dots around. Manet is true to that, and in the process subverts much that was thought axiomatic. Traditional painting was meant for close and careful inspection; Manet didn't want that, he wanted you to turn and be struck.

His hope was that this painting would storm the barricades. It didn't. It was knocked back at him with scorn and derision. Manet's hurt on rejection was capacious, but his determination to carry on in the same vein undimmed. *Music in the Tuileries* is a wild statement, as are many other early works, but they lack a centre of gravity. And somehow a heart and soul. That would be found in the blank stare of Victorine Meurent.

CALM, STILL AND QUIET

Direct information about the artist and model's working relationship is minimal. Manet said Victorine was 'a model sitter – calm, still and quiet'. And that is all. The indirect information is copious, since it is held in the paintings, as eloquent as novels. Once Manet had found Victorine, he brought her back to his studio, and began to sketch out intuitions in response to her. Something in the engagement, in the way she stared at him, as he stared back at her, brush in hand, took both to a new place. Victorine's remorseless, affectless gaze was the perfect match for that of Manet. He had found a mirror, and more. It feels as if she is the instructor – the larger artist – and he her interpreter. The stillness she brings is the antithesis of his previous work, indeed of much of his work without her. It is a stillness he did not know until she walked into his frame. One can imagine his discomfort under the intensity of her inspection.

Two of the most famous Leonardo portraits – the *Mona Lisa* and *Portrait of Ginevra de' Benci* – capture the spine-tingling sensation of their sitter at the end of a long out-breath. In both there is a serenity, the expression of something finished, of something let go. Most artists manufacture tension in their portraits, characters on the verge, in dread or desire, gulping in air in tension. It is exciting, but melodramatic. It takes mastery to have the confidence to eschew such histrionics, and show characters on the out-breath. Leonardo had this capacity – to be simultaneously flat and full of life. Manet was nowhere near it until, to his great good fortune, Victorine Meurent walked through the door.

Artist and model achieved the effect almost immediately, with a painting that he called *Street Singer*. It shows Victorine in a big frock, emerging through cafe doors, guitar held loosely in one hand, cherries held by the other to her lips. Her dully absent but curious gaze is already in place, while the cherries lend a coquettish slant. Her arched eyebrows have a Japanese formality that can't occlude the penetration of her look.

The *Portrait of Victorine Meurent* – from the same year, 1862 – and reproduced at the start of this chapter – has a more traditional depth and relief. It is as if Manet wanted to see how the model looked in the eyes of the old school. He paints Meurent in a sidelight and with orthodox chiaroscuro, the graduated light and shade giving the illusion of three-dimensionality. Here we have the tones and half-tones of the École des

Beaux-Arts, rather than Manet's experimental harsh front light. In this traditional frame, there is a chance for a rich feeling of love to express itself between them – the empathy of two sad souls.

A third Meurent portrait from this time – *Mademoiselle V. in the Costume of an Espada* – returns to experimentation. It is a playfully daft picture of Victorine got up in a Spanish toreador costume. Some bullfighting is going on in the perspective-free background but it is Victorine, floating at the front, that matters. What is delightful is the unabashed theatricality of her pose. She is the least convincing toreador ever, holding sword and cape like the cheap props they are, and her eyes are filled with the humour of the moment. Again she looks straight at us, with a smirking glance. She blushes at the silliness of it, and at the amount of lipstick she has chosen to wear. Even within all this self-awareness, her expressionless eyes still startle. Somehow they are more real.

Shortly before this painting, Manet had been out walking with his friend Antonin Proust (no relation) when they came upon a group of nude bathers. Manet turned to his friend and said, 'It seems that I must paint a nude. Very well, I shall paint one.' Though the Impressionist movement came to be known for its *plein-air* experimentation, Manet had not been a part of that movement. The city might have artists sat at their easels along riverbanks, parks and boulevards, but Manet liked his studio. He took what he had seen in the world and then found structures for those impressions within old masters. Two pictures funded his imagination. Titian's *Jupiter and Antiope* provided an attitude and Raphael's *The Judgement of Paris* provided the shape for his primary figures.

The painting featured three figures at the front of its composition. They are interwoven, legs close and intertwined, with the ease of those who care little for vanity and much for tactile contact. One man, modelled by Manet's brother Gustave, is reclining on his left elbow, his head in profile looking across the picture capped by a bohemian tasselled hat. His right hand is held up in what can only be described, given its trajectory towards the area between the woman's legs, as a very naughty position. His gaze is away from us, and towards neither of his companions. The second male figure, Manet's brother-in law, off-centre, has a moonish Goya-like face. The trajectory of his gaze is coming out of the picture, but to the specta-tor's right, as if in slight evasion.

The third figure – Victorine – is entirely naked, her body painted without flattery or vanity in profile. The physical mass and the unglamorous colouring of her body are shocking in their abrupt suddenness. Her head and eyes turn around to point straight at us and to transfix. Her head is held on her chin, a small smile crinkles her lips as if from her pleasure at being there, and her eyes have the relaxed ease of a sunny Sunday afternoon. The speech bubble above her head seems unequivocal, *I'm naked, so what? Get over it.* Her clothes are strewn about her to give a naturalistic backstory, as are the scattered fragments of a picnic. In the background, at the focal point of the painting, yet set apart from the narrative, a partially-clothed woman bathes.

Amid this perverse perspective, the four figures each seem to come from different universes. The bather is from the Romantic tradition, the reclining figure seems naturalistic, the moon-faced man statuesque, and then there is Victorine, appearing out of a private lexicon of art drawn up between her and Manet. Such contrasting realities jostling together in the same flat plane seem appropriate to the confusion of life. There are no half-tones here, just excitedly executed blocks of colour. The chaps are decked out in the uniform of modernity – black frock coats, fob chains, dazzling cravats, and a bohemian hat. Appearing within a framework previously used for river gods and goddesses is an act of aggrandisement.

It is a deliberate attempt to bring out the epic in the everyday, Manet's achievement of Baudelaire's desire. But the heroism of modern life is not just found in the modern clothing. In this – as in Manet's other portraits of the time – it was crystallised and focused in Victorine's eyes. Her gaze teaches us how to look.

THE SALON

Every other year, the Paris art world would witness frenetic activity in the run-up to April 1st, the submissions deadline for the biennial Salon. Many paintings arrived at the Palais de Champs-Élysées with their paint still wet. One Swiss artist, James Pradier, was seen accompanying his sculpture with a hammer and chisel, chipping away as it floated through the city.

The Salon was founded in 1667 as the official exhibition of the Académie des Beaux-Arts. By 1863 it had become the world's greatest display of contemporary art. In 1855, it moved from the Louvre to the Grand Palais in order to accommodate the number of submissions. For most of the year, this 250-yard-long, cast-iron exhibition hall had a very different purpose, packed with pigs and cows, as home to agricultural trade fairs. The original aim of the Salon had been to create a new proletariat of artists and the widest public for their art. The pricing retained this aspiration, with a ticket costing only a franc, which made it accessible to all. And it was fabulously well attended, with one in eight of all Parisians squeezing in through the course of its six weeks.

However, the openness didn't extend to the administration, which, under Emperor Napoleon III, had fallen under the sway of two European blue-bloods: Count Alfred Émilien O'Hara van Nieuwerkerke and Charles-Philippe, marquis de Chennevières-Pointel. Whatever your view of history, it is hard to imagine two men with names like that ending up on the right side of it. Neither did much to advance their cause. Chennevières was not a man who loved the crowd ('Democracy has always horrified me and I see in it only principles that are corrosive and destructive'), while Nieuwerkerke was blunt in his disapproval of contemporary realism ('This is the painting of democrats, of men who don't change their underwear'), preferring his art to draw on Classical and Biblical themes, or national history. In an age of steam and electricity, artists were being instructed to serve up pictures of Pontius Pilate, Bacchus and Napoleon.

In 1863, Nieuwerkerke did all he could to discourage submissions, but more than 5,000 works negotiated their way on swaying carts and trolleys through the streets of Paris. The paintings were laid out on every inch of floor and wall, as the jury, a carefully selected group of entirely prejudiced individuals, tramped around to inspect them. The rate of inspection was about eighty an hour. To describe such scrutiny as cursory would be to flatter its rigour. Works of art which artists had slaved and wept over, lost sleep and loved ones over, were dismissed with a glance and a sneer.

If the work was approved, it would receive a number 1 rating and achieve entry, plus a favourable hanging spot. Those that did not win approval were carried away like corpses after a battle by attendants in white coats. They had a humiliating red 'R' (*rejeté*) stamped on the back and their creators were instructed to remove them as swiftly as possible. The same artists who days before had pushed their work towards the

Palais with an excited gleam in their eye had to carry the rejected work back along the same path, and bear the scorn of passers-by.

The aristocratic peremptoriness of the Salon's dismissals caused increasing resentment, and in 1859 a group of artists gathered under Nieuwerkerke's drawing-room window, during one of his soirées, and chanted abuse. Then in 1863 the ongoing battle between modernity and tradition came to a head, as the Count and the Marquis accepted just 2,127 works of art from the 5,000 submitted. This was an unprecedented rate of rejection. Manet, who had entered three paintings, received a letter from the Ministry of State telling him to remove his paintings without delay, as did Cézanne, Pissarro and Degas and hundreds of others. Many crammed in to the Café de Bade to fulminate at the injustice, to cry out against conspiracies, and to plot a response. Friendly journalists were exhorted to write jeremiads and private exhibitions were planned. The noise rippled out across the city, and became a scandal that reached the top of French government.

ENTER THE EMPEROR

Emperor Napoleon III was a short man, with a waxed moustache, of which he was very proud. He had enjoyed absolute rule since his coup d'état of 1851, yet never felt entirely secure. It would not take an enormous knowledge of recent French history to keep a ruler on edge. The behaviour of his wife Eugenie would not have settled such nerves. It was said that she sprinkled 200 francs worth of gold into her hair every morning. It would be hard to describe her as salt of the earth. Her recent enthusiasm for Marie Antoinette, whose furniture and baubles she collected, and whose image she kept above her bed, was not going to avert sleepless nights for her husband.

Napoleon was a great believer in the bread and circuses maxim, especially the latter. His Second Empire was a constant carnival of fireworks, military displays, sumptuous balls and the building of extravagant new boulevards and public spaces. When a war was threatened in Algeria, he sent the celebrated conjuror Robert-Houdin on a 'magic mission' to confront rebel leaders with his celebrated 'bullet-trick'. Amazingly it worked. As he declared, 'One of the first duties of a sovereign is to amuse his subjects.' So, in the face of the Salon scandal, Napoleon decided that he was going to inspect the rejected paintings himself.

One can imagine the nervousness of Nieuwerkerke and Chennevières as the Emperor perused the acres of canvas. Their palms may have been particularly sweaty, as one of the rejected works was a portrait of the Emperor's wife. If the opinions of their jury were discredited, it would be the end of them. But the Emperor and his advisers came up with a ruse. They would not overturn the opinion of the jury. Instead, in a phoney democratic gesture, they would leave the exercising of taste to the public themselves. They dreamt up the idea for a complementary Salon des Refusés, which would open two weeks after the Salon at the nearby Palais de l'Industrie, which had been erected for the 1855 World Fair.

The news was greeted at the Café de Bade with an initial wave of delight, though this soon gave way to qualms about whether it was a good thing to be involved in a gathering of rejected work. Who would want to participate in such a show? But uneasiness was pushed aside by the artists' fervour for their work and ideals. They began planning how to trump the main event.

THE ACCEPTED

In Paris in 1863, women were not allowed onto the upper floor of buses, for fear that, while climbing the stairs, they might reveal a brief glimpse of calf or ankle on the way. By the same measure, they were not allowed to bathe in the company of the opposite gender, unless outfitted in a full-body bathing suit. (A nice irony for a country that, a century and a half later, got into such a lather over Muslim 'burquinis'.) Even at the time, the hypocrisy of this, in a city which gave a large amount of its economy over to sex workers, was patent. And nowhere more so than at the Salon, whose walls were given over to hectares of heroic naked flesh, female and male.

The official Salon of 1863 took this further than before. So much, in fact, that it instantly became known as the 'Salon de Venus', because of the large numbers of such Classical depictions, and because of its signature success, Cabanel's *Birth of Venus*, a painting of unbridled erotic titillation. Five rather sinister cherubs float above an exquisitely gorgeous Venus, who lies on her own golden tresses, on a cresting wave of the sea. All that is most noxious about objectification is exemplified within this work, which is both physically absurd and successfully erotic. Dismissed by the high-minded as pornographic gratification for stockbrokers and bankers, the general public went crazy for it, and it defined the event. The Emperor liked it so much he bought it for 15,000 francs.

The official Salon was thus deemed a triumph. Nieuwerkerke and Chennevières basked in their achievement: the clearing out of all the animal poo, the hanging of more than 2,000 pictures, the galas held for the great and good and the pop-up restaurants for the crowds, not to mention more medal ceremonies than an Olympic Games. The Académie painters loved their medals. The biggest nightmare for the organisers was the day before opening, known as 'Varnishing Day'. The artists were allowed in to give a final polish to their work, while select patrons wandered around. This was when artists learnt where they had been hung and the Marquis would become the focal point of hysterical complaint and lobbying. Since every millimetre was covered with art, it was perfectly possible to be above, beside or below something comically inappropriate. The worst fate was to be 'skyed', which meant one's work was hung at the top of a wall, where no eye ever strayed.

But the medallists were happy and the Salon was praised by all but the dissident artists. To their eyes, as Zola recalled: 'Every picture oozed unfailing mediocrity; every one showed the same dingy, muddy quality typical of anaemic degenerate art doing its best to put on a good face. They hurried ahead, ran almost to escape, condemning everything whole-sale and swearing there was nothing worth while in the place.'

How would their own work fare?

THE REFUSED

Friday 15 May was a crisp Parisian day, with a clear blue sky. Both pavements of the Champs-Élysées were full of people pouring towards the arcade entrance to the Palais de l'Industrie. Once through, they would pass figures collapsed on benches and chairs, overcome by gallery tension. The exhibition was on the first floor and, as visitors climbed the stairs, they became aware of a persistent rumbling noise, like a storm against rocks. The noise of excitement. The space allotted was smaller than for the Salon, but on that opening day it was crammed with 7,000 hyper-ventilating witnesses.

They were here to see 781 works by 430 artists. Many of the artists had dropped out, some of them deterred by the Académie briefing against them. The slurs in the press included the show being dubbed variously the *Salon of the Vanquished, of the Pariahs, of the Heretics* and, most often, the *Salon of the Comics*. There was a desire for it to fail and be laughed out of court. Conditioned by such expectations, the public was boisterous and cruel, packed into rooms as damp and close as a greenhouse in their tight collars and tighter corsets. A hot and fine dust rose from the floor, stirred up by shuffling feet, and the airlessness compounded the hysteria. By the end of the day it was impossible to move through and plot your own way; you could only be swung along by the crowd. Sparrows sought refuge from the mass in the forest of girders above.

The audience had been driven to expect freakish art and they were determined to have their expectations fulfilled. As one report had it, they were 'a tempest of fools, who rain down by the million and scoff at everything in the most outrageous fashion'. People were flocking from outside, but also from the official Salon next door, drawn to mock, but also pulled by the charisma of the event. Once inside, all were pulled to the nuclear core – the final room, with its large canvas placed slap bang in the middle. The Salon Selection Committee had done this partly because of the painting's size, but principally because they knew it would be ripe for ridicule. They wanted it to to be remembered.

The audience lived up to their hopes. As anyone approached this room, the laughter grew louder, and then crescendoed. Women plugged handkerchiefs in their mouths to stop their merriment, while men held their sides and roared. It was a crowd feeding on its own laughter and revelling in it. Faces bulged and expanded with mirth. One woman was seen to have collapsed on a bench, her knees pressed tightly together, gasping. A man threatened the painting with his walking stick. Further hilarity ensued. An assemblage of bulging George Grosz figures squeezed into the frame of the building. The work which drew this climacteric of attention was painting 363, *Le Bain* by Édouard Manet. That title didn't last long, being soon renamed *Le Déjeuner sur l'herbe* by the crowd, a name which began as the height of abuse, but now seems apt in its simplicity.

There was some technical element to this abuse, with Manet's intentionally messy brushstrokes coming under attack. A wag pronounced that it could have been done with a floor mop. But the principal cause for astonishment was moral. It was simply inconceivable to combine in a single picture both a nude figure and people in modern dress. Nudes were fine, and plastered across both exhibitions. People in modern dress smacked of grubby modern realism, but was forgivable, even if the trousers seemed shabby. But both! Within the same frame! *Abominable!* And the frog, which Manet drew beside the picnic basket, made things even worse – a winking reference to prostitution.

There was a school of opinion that it was all a joke, a prank by a rebellious student determined to tweak the nose of his elders. But there was more nervousness in the laughter than humour. Napoleon III continued his show of public engagement by visiting the Salon des Refusés, and pronouncing Manet's picture *indecent.*

THE ACCUMULATING HOOVES OF HORSES

It is hard to imagine a more grisly reception for any work of art, or anything more gruelling for an artist to endure. Manet, for all his careless revolutionary carapace, was sensitive and credulous, and felt criticism. There is no artist who doesn't, whatever they may claim.

And yet, what was most tangible about *Le Déjeuner sur l'herbe* – and indeed the Salon des Refusés – was the sheer excitement, no matter what noise decorated it. On every wall there was a mixture of the excellent and the execrable, but everywhere, whether accomplished or clumsy, was truth and sincerity. In the official Salon, there may have been fewer bad pictures, but there was less originality and much less aspiration. People might have turned out for circus mockery, but others were here for the hope, and that brings its own charge. Manet was amongst colleagues and friends, and the sense of comradeship in such circumstances is inimitable. As James Baldwin said of his friendship with Lorraine Hansberry, 'We had that respect for each other which is perhaps felt only by people on the same side of the barricades, listening to the accumulating hooves of horses.'

The critics were mostly patronising and sneery, but there was a sliver of serious writing and respect for *Le Déjeuner sur l'herbe.* Théophile Thoré-Bürger perceived that, not only in the original content, but also in the deliberate sketchiness, the lack of finish, what was being witnessed was the future of painting. Most crucial of all would have been the respect of fellow artists. Some from the generation of Manet's teachers were warm and respectful, which would gratify deeply. Some from his own generation were sharp and jealous, which would gratify shallowly. He saw several famous painters staring rapt in contemplation.

There is a silent language between fellow artists which is impossible to read or explain. They perceive quickly and penetratingly the quality of attention in the eye of a peer. There is nothing more gratifying than seeing another artist look profoundly at one's work; seeing their curiosity astir, and their impatience calmed for a moment. The words of critics, or the number of tickets sold, don't quite compare. Manet had more than enough of that from artists, and sufficient from the public, to know he was pushing towards a future many wanted to share.

To quote Zola again:

> It was like a window flung open on all the drab concoctions and the stewing juices of tradition, letting the sun pour in till the walls were as gay as a morning in spring, and the clear light of his own picture shone out brighter than all the rest.

STOPPED INSTANTLY, STRUCK WITH AMAZEMENT

How it was for Victorine is harder to know. Writers and novelists have imagined her visiting the Salon on the opening day, suggesting a variety of reactions, often tending towards the rushing-home-and sobbing school. It must have been insufferably painful, having journeyed across Paris in a state of anticipation, to hear the laughter and witness the abuse at a work she was proud of. Much of the abuse was directed at her rather than Manet. One misogynist wit titled her 'the ideal of ugliness'.

There is a different way to imagine this tableau vivant – Victorine standing in the room with Manet, an audience and painting number 363. Her cool and penetrating stare in life meeting the matching gaze from the oil, which transfixes her, and painter, and audience. The British poet and art critic Philip Gilbert Hamerton writes of a moment of stillness before the audience's eruption in mirth, of people who 'stopped instantly, struck with amazement. This for two or three seconds, then they looked at each other and laughed'. In that moment before the cackling began, the interlocking of eyes – depictor, depicted and witnesses – throws up dazzling possibilities. Since art began, the whole conundrum of who is looking at who – artist, painting and audience spiralling in giddy confusion in a hall of mirrors – has afforded many opportunities for philosophical dizziness. In this imagined moment, the depicted Victorine transfixes a whole room including nervous gigglers, her creator/interpreter and her more or less real self.

Everyone's version of history will be different, but I don't see Victorine rushing in tears from the room, her vanity punctured. I see no vanity in her at all. I see her calmly enjoying the moment, relishing the fact that her sensibility claims the painting to the same degree as Manet. When we see Kate Moss in a styled photograph, we do not think of the photographer, we think of Moss. Victorine Meurent will have been staking out the same cultural territory. It is possible to agree with Zola on his interpretation of the moment for Manet – that he was blowing a hole in the wall – yet it is possible to imagine Victorine perceiving the precise opposite. She did not see an absence in that space, she perceived something solid, established and powerful there. Herself expressed.

Her eyes staring out, saying, *Everything is different from today.*

THE ROOM MARKED 'M'

The ramifications from this event were many and long-lasting, but far from instant. There is a myth that the Salon des Refusés occurred and, overnight, Impressionism was born with a capital 'I'. That would be far from the truth. It was another ten years before there was a dedicated exhibition of such work in Paris, and longer before its artists became successful. The battle for recognition remained slow. It was not until American collectors began to make a fuss of their work, and pay top dollar, that Europeans started to bury their prejudices.

Meantime, the group of artists who forged Impressionism – Manet, Monet, Pissarro, Cézanne, Degas, Renoir, Morisot – fell in and out with each other, and sympathy with each other's style. For all their rage and disdain for the Académie, like eager puppies they still submitted their work to the Salon each year, and were still treated with contempt. But, from now on, they knew they had a war to win. As Zola said, 'Here there was a scent of battle in the air, where the bugles sound and you face the foe convinced you will defeat him before nightfall.' Their desire for change was undimmed, and nowhere more completely than in Meurent and Manet.

In one of the greatest *fuck-yous* ever delivered by young artists to old, Manet and Meurent returned for the next Salon with another radical piece of work. This was entitled *Olympia* and referenced two classic nude studies, Titian's *Venus of Urbino* and Goya's *Nude Maya*. In Manet's canvas, Victorine is boldly and frontally naked, her hand placed wickedly, her skin tones deliberately sullied, a black cat placed at her feet (another wink at prostitution), and a black maid bringing her a floral tribute. Her gaze is a concentrated essence of those before. Without raising her voice or retreating, it says on a calm out-breath, *I am the master here.* Unsurprisingly, it doubled the previous outrage.

Manet remained a restless and unsatisfied soul, churning, seeking, renewing. He never settled into the establishment and never in his life-time achieved his due. Meurent's life was full of turbulence and triumph. The emotional effort of this collaboration and the moral courage it took must have exacted a price. She went away to America after these ructions. On her return, she collaborated with Manet again, and on one master-piece in particular, the *Gare Saint-Lazare*, posed against dark railings in front of a cloud of railway steam. In this painting, Victorine's gaze is just as steady, though lambent and soft.

By now her artistic desire had worked itself around to the other side of the canvas. No longer content to dominate proceedings from within the frame, she wanted control of it. Victorine Meurent became a painter of note. Precious little survives of her work, but what there is suggests her art had a boldness and integrity. Late in life, she formed an attachment with another woman, Marie Dufour, and together they lived to a ripe old age in an apartment in Colombes, a suburb outside Paris. To the end, she described herself as an artist.

A self-portrait of 1876, with the gaze again formidably captured, was accepted by the Salon. The same year Manet was refused. Three years later, this pair, the essence of modernity, were both accepted and hung together in the same room marked 'M'.

11

An act of violence

A TALE OF XIAO LU

5 FEBRUARY 1989

Through a long night of sleep, half sleep and dream, Xiao Lu struggled. A mess of thoughts buzzed in her head. Clawing the sheets, she tried to reconcile her confusion in the present with a deep-buried rage from the past. She sweated over questions. Will I find the gun? Should I shoot, or not? She felt a misted certainty, like Hamlet or Macbeth, that the choice was life-changing. A terrorist act, in a public arena, in a police state. Like Brutus on the night before assassinating Caesar.

She wrestled with the whys and the hows and the what nexts. Beyond the personal act ghosted a sense of history shifting, and her own hand in it. Lying alone, the small alarm clock at the head of her bed ticked a quiet ominousness. Seven o'clock floated past. The hour of decision was close. To make something new, to break a mould, requires a metamorphosis. The reinvention does not happen in a single instant; it is a continuum from the moment an idea is formed to the moment it is enacted.

A year before, someone had suggested a gun, and a shooting. From that moment, though the shot hadn't rung out, its actuality was alive in her head. She considered that 'Making art was simply the product of emotional pressures. When the pressure got unbearable, I sought a channel through which to relieve my heart.'

Various pressures – aesthetic, political, familial, personal – were urging her to carry the action through. Representatives of the same pressures – teachers, police, parents, her own history – were forbidding her. A sense of inevitability impelled her, but that made it no simpler. However predestined, she alone had to carry the weight.

An internal dialogue raged in her head.

> 'What do you believe in?'
> 'I believe that art can save a human being's soul.'
> 'What is art, then?'
> 'The traces of martyrdom.'

The clock ticked on.

AN INSTALLATION

Xiao Lu had just graduated from art school – at a moment when a restlessness for change was kicking its way through China, a desire to move on from the prolonged brainwashing of Mao's stranglehold, and its atavistic conservatism. The young, particularly young artists, felt the desire to test freedoms, and the need to push those tests as far as possible. In visual art, it was time to move on from traditional pictorialism, and its Marxist grandchild, socialist realism.

The burden of this was acute for Xiao Lu. Her parents were both acknowledged masters of those forms. When she entered their studio as a child, she saw them slaving in oils over elegant realisations of rivers and lakes. When she arrived in her classroom at art school, there hung her father's work from his time in the Soviet Union being educated in socialist realism. Xiao Lu took one look, and felt an anvil pressure on her chest. Overcome with aesthetic nausea, she dropped her brush and ran out. Everything from the tradition felt familiar, and yet, in its industrial regularity, queasily alien and divorced from life as lived. The separation was symptomatic of a wider unease between tradition and modernity. Such tensions were thickening the air with potential violence.

Her rebellion began with studying Cézanne. His bold crudity was the weapon with which to break open the plastic assurance of the Soviet school. And soon her classmates were talking of bolder experiments from the world beyond. Their ideas were a window opening out her imaginative claustrophobia. The influx of ideas from the West followed an exploded timeline, with innovations from different decades, even centuries, arriving in China all at once, or back to front, with the ancient following the recent as if history had been reversed. Through the 1980s, a jumble of new ideas squeezed their way past the censors, initiating excitement and turbulence.

Xiao Lu put years of oil painting behind her. When it came to her graduation piece, she decided to create an installation. Two phone booths close together – in one, a man, in the other, a woman. Both human-size figures, their backs to us, achieved with black and white photographs. Between them a mirror, with a crucifix of red tape breaking the mirror into four parts, its horizontal line on their eyeline, alerting them both to something foreboding. In the middle of the mirror a dangling phone indicating a broken-off conversation. Yin and Yang, man and woman, stuck in a busted technology, not communicating, full of yearning.

Love under Mao was tainted. Romance was thought to be the vulgar interest of the petty bourgeoisie. Schoolchildren would pass thumb-nailed books of passion from hand to hand. When Xiao Lu got to keep one for a whole night, she and a friend sat up until dawn copying it out, so their handwritten copy could be lingered over. For a host of reasons, primarily the state's toxins being injected into individual hearts, Xiao felt she could not communicate with men. 'Men – to hell with them! It was like falling into a pit, with filthy slurry blocking up my heart ... Coming up against the real thing, I faced off in speechless panic.' Her installation was an attempt to release the pressures of that suffocation.

It was entitled *Dialogue*, and was a long way from China's lakes and mountains, or socialist realism. The Oil Painting Department protested they had never produced anything like this before; a more senior group tried to stop the work from happening. But sympathetic tutors and Xiao Lu's assurance pushed it through. Unknown to her, *Dialogue* was submitted by a friendly tutor to the 1989 China Avant-Garde exhibition, to be held at Beijing's National Art Museum. She knew nothing about the exhibition or its curators, Gao Minglu and Li Xianting, and had already graduated when she received a notice saying her work had been accepted.

Her delight was compromised by a feeling the work was incomplete, that it did not fully express her:

> *Artists are like a roll of film, extremely sensitive. Although my inner self had reacted to something, the exposure time was insufficient. Perhaps a chemical element was missing. The photograph couldn't yet appear. It remained stored in the darkroom. This darkroom was my heart.*

She would find a way to solve this problem. Fortune had delivered her the opportunity to speak with a loud voice.

A BUNDLE OF RAYS OF LIGHT

The Chinese artists of the 1980s emerged during a period of economic and institutional reform, following the implementation of the 'Open Door policies introduced in 1978. Artists are always a lightning rod for change and never more so than in China in that early decade. It was time for something new, and for conventional art and artists to be thrown into a state of flux. As Xiao Lu put it:

> *In the vast territory of China, there was a purely idealistic enterprise which was the rage of that era. Like a bundle of rays of light, it germinated a set of seeds of idealism. They influenced the course of China's historical development.*

Installation and performance art – which questioned the relationship between the viewer and the viewed, and interrogated the role of subject and object – were lent an extra wattage by the nature of the human body within the totalitarian state. A school of art known as *yundong* – a word implying a chain of events or series of linked occurrences – gained a powerful traction. These were events in an imaginary space, or in reality, or in a collision of the two. They emanated from a particular source, had a connective tissue, and together amounted to an artistic statement. They could be an individual moving in space, relating to vacancy or an object, or a mass of people working to a particular pattern. It could be events arranged by a single imagination, or by the shaping hand of history.

Retrospectively, some have named Mao's Cultural Revolution as a vast work of *yundong* art (or another instance of Wagner's *Gesamtkunstwerk*). Given that seven to twenty million people died in the course of Mao's brutal act of reality engineering, this may be taking the importance of aesthetics too far. But, after long decades of the state trying to forge a new reality, it is unsurprising that a form which could challenge such coercions became popular.

The spirit of experimentation came to the boil in 1985, when a ferment of exhibitions, of new practices forged in new spaces, and manifestos pouring hot from the presses, swept China. Among these was a notably bold experiment by the Xiamen Dada group, who at the conclusion of an exhibition burnt all their paintings – 'because it just felt fitting'. In 1986, stultified by a National Oil Painting Conference, an entrepreneur and iconoclast, Gao Minglu, resolved to hold an avant garde show to bring these disparate energies together. Gao and his co-creator Li Xiantiang realised that they needed to take a top-down, Leninist approach to the cultural scene: 'We cannot wait until the populace is ready before presenting it with new concepts. New ideas have always been imposed by a small minority upon the large majority, who then accustom themselves'.

Originally planned for July 1987 at the Beijing Agricultural Exhibition Centre, the exhibition was interrupted by a government-organised campaign entitled 'Against Capitalism Liberalisation'. But the following year the political situation eased and the show looked possible. Not only could it happen, but there was a chance to stage it in the National Art Museum, a socialist-style building next to the Ministry of Culture, hard by Tiananmen Square, in the heart of Beijing. As Gao explains: 'It was very important for the the avant garde to use and modify the symbolic image, putting a heretical show in the sacred art palace that it had never been able to enter.'

Raising the money was a challenge. China's free market economy was only taking babysteps, and it was far from the breeding ground for billionaires of today. Sponsors were sought but many were nervous of an event that carried with it an aura of political risk and a lack of commercial benefits. One company which had agreed to support the event withdrew promised funds with only a couple of months to go. At that point the organising committee had only generated 2,500 yuan, less than two percent of the projected budget. This was not promising. In a last-minute scramble, artists begged their business friends to donate, agreed to contribute 100 yuan each (almost a month's salary) and donated artworks. Even so, when the exhibition opened, they had only raised half the money to cover the costs. Bills were going to go unpaid. Beside the mad extravagant polish of Western avant-garde art, it looked hopelessly crude. But the desperation of its last minute scramble lent it that unquantifiable virtue of excitement. As Gao put it, 'Precisely due to these conditions, the exhibition maintained a certain kind of dynamic energy.'

CURATION

After the exhibition was announced in October 1988, Gao Minglu and Li Xiantiang received slides or originals of 3,000 artworks. Together they picked 250 works by about 100 artists. Once chosen, the artworks were shipped from all over the country to Beijing. Filling three separate spaces in the museum, they tried to sum up the diversity of the new artistic movements. The pamphlet that they printed laid out their ambition: 'This exhibition is the first of its kind to be held on such a large scale in China ... It will gather in one place all the main trends since 1985.'

Under the stringent censorship laws, the organising committee was required to seek approval for all the works. On 4 February 1989, the day before the opening, officers from a variety of capitalised institutions came to examine the art. To legitimise their operation, the committee had invited influential artists and art historians to defend their choices. Many works were criticised for their political and sexual content and after furious rows three pieces were pulled. Much dispute revolved around Wang Guangyi's *Mao Zedong No. 1*, a formal portrait of the dead dictator behind intersecting red lines. The censors believed this put Mao 'in prison'. The organisers argued: 'Mao was one of the most influential figures in Chinese modern history; we should evaluate his historical role using rational analysis and logical thinking. These are represented by the grid.' This dainty bit of sophistry won the day.

Crucially, the organisers managed to skip the question of performance art. They knew the authorities, and the museum, had specifically banned performance art, and works with sexual content. They also knew a large part of what was being attempted would be improvised interactions created on the day. Somehow they managed to slide this past the censors, and to close their eyes to the potential chaos.

Amid the sensationalist output of senior artists was *Dialogue*, the work of a quiet, reserved and little known twenty-eight-year-old woman. No-one would have imagined she was set to steal the show.

OPENING CEREMONY

Xiao Lu gobbled a breakfast cooked by her grandmother and leapt on a bus to take her to the centre of Beijing and the exhibition. Crowds were already jostling around the entrance, eager to see the sensations inside. Xiao had arranged with an old friend, Li Songsong, who had military connections, to pick up a gun. The possession of a firearm, if you were not in the police or the military, was a crime in itself, so their handover had to be clandestine. The crowd gathered around the opening ceremony, while Xiao Lu sat away to one side, on a bench.

A spirit of improvisation swirled even before the doors opened. The great occasion was meant to kick off at nine with a ceremony where black fabric banners would slowly rise, lifted by a multitude of balloons. Due to an absence of balloons (or inflaters), there had to be a swift rethink. Floating the banners morphed into ceremonially laying them out. Performed with solemnity, and adorned with an uncompromising logo which read 'No U-turn', it retained its charge.

As Li Xianting recalls: 'When laying out the black cloth, the atmosphere was intense, and my mind was full of thoughts about the impact this exhibition would have on society.' Gao Minglu concurs: 'The exhibition's opening ceremony was shrouded by a nervous and solemn atmosphere, as if something was bound to happen.' The authorities had attempted to diffuse the event by arranging its opening for the eve of the Chinese New Year, thinking the public would have better things to do. This failed to spoil the party, however, and excited crowds flocked in anticipation. The moment the doors opened, they stormed in.

Xiao Lu did not join the crowd, still waiting for the central prop of her performance. As far as possible she kept her focus on her act. She waited an hour and a half, and was beginning to lose faith in her friend, when he appeared in the corner of her eye. They found a quiet corner and he passed over the firearm. Xiao Lu concealed it in her bra. She reassured Li, when he questioned her ability to put it to use: 'When I started college, I had drills with the army. I've had shooting practice. Calm down. The eyes of an artist see straight.'

Everything was falling into place. So many links in the chain towards this act could have broken, and prevented it, but it was beginning to trace its own pattern in time.

A SMELL OF SHRIMPS

What the crowds witnessed was a jamboree of chaos and fun. This was art unleashed, a collection of nutty modes of free expression meeting an audience whose imaginations had been held underwater for decades. Now they were coming up for air. Wang Deren, an artist who had once contrived a performance piece above the snowline of Mount Everest, was dementedly hurling condoms hither and thither.

His prophylactic munificence shocked many. It enraged another artist, Huang Yong Ping, the founder of the Xiamen Dada group who had famously burnt all their work in 1986. They were sharing the same space and Huang complained that his work was now covered in so many condoms that it was rendered unrecognisable. Wang was unimpressed by the timidity of his rival in the face of creative anarchy, and cried out, 'Huang Yong Ping is a Fake Dadaist!'

The spectator's eye met a riot of strangeness: an inflatable installation not wildly different from a bouncy castle; video and slides melting the solidity of the walls; lumps of twisted plastic replicating human intestines; mildewed surgical gloves preserved under glass; a man clothed all in red washing his feet in a basin lined with photographs of Ronald Reagan. Another man sat in the corner of a gallery hatching eggs, his manifesto hanging across his chest: 'During the incubation period, I will not discuss theoretical questions with anyone, to avoid harming the younger generation'.

Everywhere there was an ugly smell of shrimps. Wu Shanzhuan, an artist distinguished by exceptionally longhair, was exhibiting a piece called *Big Business (Selling Shrimps)*. This involved him selling a lot of shrimps from a makeshift market stand. He had brought in 300kg from a fishing village in Zhoushan, where he worked as an art teacher. Swiftly selling out his shrimp, he told an art critic: 'Before, you made me famous with your reviews of my work. Today, you buy my shrimp!' The ebullience of his exhibitionist salesmanship created a frenzy of raw capitalism around him. It was too much for the police, who stopped him on the grounds that he lacked a shrimp-selling permit.

The atmosphere was crazy and exhilarating, artists and audience thrilled by their charisma in the moment. As one Zhang Peili described it:

> *More than your typical art show, it looked more like a farmer's market ... What mattered that day wasn't the art, or the show itself. Everybody knew we were making history. We were investing in our roles as actors on a stage where anybody could suddenly become a star.*

And then two shots rang out.

COMPASS OF THE MANDATE OF HEAVEN

Xiao Lu had shot her own installation square in its heart. She had got herself into the ideal position, given herself a good look in the mirror, lowered her head for a second of thought, snapped upright, raised her gun and aimed at the the nodal point of the cross of red tape, beyond which was her reflection. She pulled the trigger. The mirror splintered and smashed. Her anxieties of the night before had been sweated out of her, and in the moment – like any great performer, or any great assassin –she knew exactly what she was doing. She shot again. Nothing was going to get in her way:

> *As soon as I have fixed upon something, I have to finish it, and during the process I let whatever happens happen.*

Just before, out of a sweet sense of politeness, she had sought out the curator Li Xianting, to inform him what she was about to do. He hardly listened to this modest young woman – *I'm busy, talk to me about it later* – and swept on. Xiao wandered the halls, the gun concealed in her clothes, feeling no fear. The anticipated gunshot rang out in her head, bursting through multiple folds of oppression. Shortly before she did it, she had run into an old friend, Tang Song, who accompanied and encouraged her. To complete the aesthetic dimension, she had found another old classmate making videos, and asked that he film it. This elevated it from an act of destruction to one of performative art. She arranged herself carefully in shot, before she shot her own work. She breathed easy. Clear and free.

In the instant after, everyone was transfixed in shock. Like a trained hitwoman, Xiao Lu lowered her gun and left the space like a ghost. Tang Song came with her, already claiming space as an accomplice, but a plain clothes security man stepped out of the shadows and detained him. Xiao ditched the gun and looked for a place to hide. She rushed into a work called *Compass of the Mandate of Heaven*, an entirely empty black box, and hid in a corner. After a while, someone approached her, finding her out by a sliver of light, and said: 'I saw the shooting. It was great!' Xiao Lu pleaded for help to escape and the man returned with a group of friends, who clustered around. Scrummed around her, they shuffled her out of the *Mandate of Heaven* and then out of the museum through a rear door. Rushing across the avenue away from the halls, Xiao Lu ducked into a shop called *One Hundred Flowers Art Supplies*. Looking back through the shop's windows, she could see Tang Song being bundled down a flight of stairs and into a police car.

The shots went off at 11.10 am and, after the first moment of stunned fixity, all hell broke loose. Only two hours after the exhibition had opened, the halls were stuffed with visitors, and the excitement at fever pitch. Some, on hearing the shots, thought the inflatable installation had exploded. But the commotion was focused around *Dialogue*. The president of the Beijing Public Security Bureau immediately ordered the exhibition closed, explaining it was a crime scene. Ten plain clothes policeman who had been working the galleries began detaining anyone they could lay their hands on. The atmosphere in the exhibition halls turned on a breath from playful fun to nervous tension. Armed police arrived outside.

To Xiao Lu's horror, as she crouched in the shop across the road, she saw that everyone was being thrown out of the exhibition. Thousands of young artists and art lovers, intoxicated by their two-hour burst of conceptual freedom, spilt into the square. Some lay down on the banners so recently laid out and wrapped themselves in them. Others stood around, watching as the ongoing *yundong* performance, this brute collision of art and state power, provoked by two gunshots, unfurled in excited chaos.

With no plan what to do, Xiao slipped out of the shop and jumped on a passing bus. 'Where to?' the conductor demanded. 'All the way,' she said. She stayed on the bus as it reached its final destination, then sat stock-still as the bus retraced the route to the museum. By the time it got back, the people who came on board were all chattering about the exhibition. In the square, military Jeeps had pulled up and riot squad police were trying to marshall the thrilled crowds. Xiao watched the consequences of her act through the window, stayed glued to her seat as the bus trundled past, and fell into an out-of-body state.

The exhibition was suspended. Participating artists and viewers swarmed the area in front of the museum's iron gates, now firmly shut. Some people on the street, busy with New Year festivities, stopped and joined the tumult. The exhibition committee and officials urgently discussed the situation. Foreign news journalists were crowding around, interviewing people in the plaza. Chinese reporters, tentative at first, caught the spirit of open enquiry and started questioning anyone and everyone. The assembled crowds swirled and shifted, surging toward where news was breaking. Camera shutters clicked and flashes popped. This was a degree of exposure and inquiry which the forces of the state were not used to. When a few vendors turned up with fruit, soda and bread for the artists, now staging a sit-in on the banners, their gestures were greeted with cheers.

For four hours, Xiao Lu went back and forth on her bus, watching the tumult outside the museum slowly subside, and the crowds ebb away, all the while slowly re-entering herself and starting to recognise what she had done. Then, with the same direction and clarity with which she had shot her installation, she got off the bus. She walked up the steps to the front of the museum, and gave herself in.

Something about the gunshots had matched the moment. As Li Xianting frames his memories: 'At that time, I was unaware of the circumstances surrounding the gunfire, but it matched my psychological state. When the gunfire occurred, I became immediately conscious of the sensitive psychology these gunshots embodied. After having been constrained for so long, a new mentality yearned to be set free.'

DIALOGUE

Two years before the exhibition, Xiao Lu had passed a telephone booth by the side of the road. A knot that had twisted her heart and shortened her breath for many months needed to be loosened. She entered the booth without thinking, picked up the receiver, and dialled a number she knew too well. A voice responded, and Xiao blurted out:

'Hello ! I have a boyfriend now, but I cannot feel love. My life is a mess. It's because of you.'

'What's it got to do with me? It's you there's something wrong with.'

'Me? ... It's you who ruined me!'

'What are you on about!?'

He hung up. When she rang again, she got an engaged signal. She dialled again – still engaged. Again, engaged.

He was her godfather, a close friend of her parents, an elderly artist of prominence, and the leading figure in the art of socialist realism. When she was beginning at university, he had been her guardian. During that time, he raped her repeatedly and pursued an abusive relationship.

The tears streamed down her face, and she was unable to stop their flow. The receiver slipped from her hands, and hung from its cord, dangling to and fro, an engaged signal bleakly purring from it. Stuck between hatred and despair, hurt and rage, an image formed.

Two telephone boxes.

380 YEARS BEFORE

Three hundred and eighty years before, in Renaissance Rome, a young painter, Artemisia Gentileschi, was left by her father, a painter himself, in the care of a colleague, Agostino Tassi. Ignored by other members of her household as Artemisia cried out in fear, Tassi raped her. An abusive relationship followed, on the promise that Tassi would marry her, a promise on which he reneged. A seven-month court case followed in the course of which Artemisia had thumbscrews applied to test her honesty. Tassi turned out to be an all-round scumbag and was exiled from Rome, though the sentence was endlessly commuted.

Gentileschi took revenge through her art. It is consistent in much of its subject matter: Jael with hammer in one hand, and chisel in the other, prepares to stove in Sisera's head; Judith slices open Holofernes' throat as blood spurts hither and thither with a volcanic exuberance that her near-contemporary, Caravaggio, might have envied; Salome assesses the severed head of John the Baptist, heavy sword in hand. Rarely is one of her female subjects seen without a sword, a dagger or a knife. Rarely is their expression anything but bold and clear, or their bodies alert and real. There is none of the passive seductive softness shown by other artists of the period.

Artemisia was a revolutionary in her achievement and her content, a great heir to Caravaggio. She was too bold for her age, which found it hard to accommodate the work of a woman, however brilliant.

AND IN VENICE

Some years after the avant-garde exhibition, after her return to productive work in Shanghai, Xiao Lu represented China at the Venice Biennale, She took a large bucket of mud with her from the Grand Canal in Beijing, intending to smear her body with it. Her exhibition space was a church, and the church authorities told her that she wasn't allowed to do this inside. Nervous of her intentions, on the day of her performance, the church stole her mud.

Xiao Lu is always happy to improvise, so she ran up to the church elders and stripped off:

> I was fifty years old and my body was not beautiful, so I felt some pressure. But then I thought to myself, 'It does not matter. Just be yourself. This is my body at my age and it is a unique language.'

While those who would have denied her were still spluttering, she ran out. The church officials shut the door and announced that the place needed to be purged. After she was kicked out, she said to the church officials:

> 'I saw so many naked women in your churches in Italy. Why can you not accept my nudity?' They said, 'The nudity in church paintings is used to tell religious stories and is pure.'

Skewed conversations between people over time and space, which never resolve. The phone left dangling, engaged.

A BALANCED STATEMENT

The exhibition's organising committee, and the artists and critics, unleashed a flood of dammed-up confusion and fury at each other. The committee were oppressors, the critics were conservatives, the artists were not to be trusted. The polite opposition of tradition and modernity, the attempt to create a complementarity between them, was blown wide open. Should artists be free or controlled? Should they acquiesce to tradition or deny it? The top of the bottle had been shot off and the genie was out and about. Passions ran high. For the sake of 'security', the museum was shut down for three days. When they tried to reopen it, 'bomb threats' prevented them. They were fake, but the exhibition had become a free-form playground for subversion. The foreign media were all over the event, which heightened the anxiety of the authorities.

Everyone was keen to hear from the pivot of the event, Xiao Lu. She was held for two days on the charge of possession of a weapon, and then released. By this time, Tang Song, only ever a bystander, had talked himself into the centre of it and claimed space as a co-creator. He wanted a slice of martyrdom for himself, and at this stage she yearned his protection, and in her turmoil had fallen in love with him. Together they produced a carefully phrased statement:

> We consider that, in art, there may be artists with different understandings of society, but as artists we are not interested in politics. We are interested in the values of art and in its social value, and in using the right form with which to create, in order to carry out the process of deepening that understanding.

It was beautifully balanced, as statements in totalitarian states must be.

It took Xiao Lu fifteen years to shuck off the influence of Tang Song, and establish, clearly, her own authorship of the artwork. In that time, they went into exile together in Australia, before returning to China at the dawn of a new liberalisation. It took Xiao the same length of time to come to terms with what she had done, and to walk a little further down the road to full understanding, a destination she doubts she will ever fully reach. Much of this she has set down in her memoir, *Dialogue*.

The feel of the gun in her hand, the pain and the hatred within its power, haunts her. There was nothing glib or easy about what she did, and a sense of sin and shame still beats down on her spirit. One day, she took a pen and, guided by 'ghosts and gods', wrote two sentences:

Did you hear the shots?
Do you know what made me fire that gun?

She put the paper in an envelope, sent it to her godfather, and felt something release from her chest.

THE JOY OF ART

Xiao Lu's two shots, coming on the eve on the Chinese New Year 1989, and heard throughout the centre of Beijing, were later dubbed 'the first shots of Tiananmen Square', the uprising that came four months later. It was an act initiated from within her own history, a personal uprising against her own bloodline. But it had much in common with the revolutionary zeitgeist which led to the June 4 movement.

The exhibition created a carnival of freedom, all the more potent for its brevity. For the thousands there, it gave an adrenalised glimpse of creative and social liberty, which they took into the world around them, alongside a determination to grow it. Its power was its festivity, as Xiao Lu describes:

Art overflows into the atmosphere, makes you drunk, makes you forget yourself, it is the force that makes you tick. The joy of art is the joy of life.

Such festivity posed an impossible problem in totalitarian China. But she had taken the chance to tell a story, to reveal the tensions implicit in the chasm between private and public lives, between tradition and modernity. As she writes:

The conscience of a human being is like the nucleus of an atom. Only you can know the core of your nucleus. It may burn, it may emit light. But it can also explode.

12

Sometimes – there's God – so quickly

A TALE OF ELIA, LAURETTE, ARTHUR AND TENNESSEE

Broadway is often spoken of as sink or swim, but it's less kind than that. To present a show there is to jump off a steep cliff with home-made wings attached. If you've been exceptionally artful with your plumage, and get lucky with the wind current, you can fly and ascend to the empyrean. If you've been clumsy with your appendage, and the air is still, you plunge headlong to a comically exposed shattering on the rocks. The latter is far, far more likely.

To present something crowd-pleasing on Broadway requires nerve and quality. To succeed with real high art takes genius of construction and highly favourable wind patterns. To flourish while presenting work which offers a fiery denunciation of capitalism and the social contract, is virtually inconceivable. Yet, over a handful of years, after the depredations of the Depression and the scourge of world war, American theatre did just that. High radical art in the centre of its circus arena.

At the centre of this achievement were two writers – Arthur Miller and Tennessee Williams – and the director Elia Kazan.

6 JANUARY 1935, CIVIC REPERTORY THEATRE, NEW YORK

A young Elia Kazan sits nervously running his fingers against the cap in his lap, a rabbit's foot tucked under its brim, just as he saw a New York cabby wear it a year before. He is on the aisle in the middle of the stalls, surrounded by an audience in high exhilaration. From the first scene of *Waiting for Lefty*, a rush of tingling recognition has pulsed through them. As director Harold Clurman put it, 'Deep laughter, hot assent, a kind of joyous fervor seemed to sweep the audience toward the stage. The actors no longer performed; they were carried along by an exultancy of communication. Audience and actors had become one.' Remarkably, for it was a world premiere, Kazan looked around and saw people mouthing the lines in sync with the play, as if it was a well-known opera. The precision with which the show articulated its moment was so exact, new-minted words instantly became the soundtrack of their audience's lives.

The setting of Clifford Odets' play is a meeting of the taxi driver's union to discuss whether a strike should be prolonged. Strike plays were the order of the day in 1935, but, however derivative its subject matter, *Waiting for Lefty* felt brand new. Presented by the Group Theatre, the show felt alive with the emotions of its creators – anger, a desire for change and a conviction that change would come. Each actor stood their ground, sure-footed, like some proletarian prophet. The play is confrontational with the audience, acting out the process of a union meeting. *More! More! More!* the audience urge as decisions are made; *Go on! Go on! Go on!'* as choices hang in the balance.

Kazan's nervousness nonetheless grew as the union leader called upon a character to speak. The character quickly revealed himself to be a rat for the bosses, arguing to call off the strike. Kazan took a deep breath, ejected himself from his seat and ran forwards. Previously a technician and jack of all trades, this was his first appearance on any stage. As he denounced the stool pigeon, people thought, for a moment, that he was just an angry guy who had wandered in off the street. When Kazan pointed at the rat and cried out, 'He's my own lousy brother,' they caught up with the fiction and exploded. No-one had heard anything like it. The audience, many of whom had ridden in from Queens and the Bronx, could for the first time on Broadway see their lives expressed, and hear the true vernacular of their streets – knife-sharp, and bleeding with its own poetry.

More scenes followed that were both demonstrative and inflammatory. At the end of the play a character stepped forward. He had lost an eye in an industrial accident, and said – 'These slick slobs stand here telling us the reds is bogeymen. But the man who got me food in 1932, he calls me *Comrade*! The man who picked me up when I bled he called me *Comrade* too. What are we waiting for? Don't wait for Lefty. He might never come ...' Again Kazan, no doubt on fire from his last intervention, ran forward. He told the stage and the audience that their long-waited-for hero, Lefty, had been found dead with a bullet in his head. It was the climax of the play, and the audience went nuts, chanting *Strike! Strike! Strike!* before finally subsiding into long and thunderous applause. When they finished cheering, they didn't leave, sitting in groups and talking furiously. Some clambered onto the stage, keen to stand in the place where the miraculous had occurred and to snatch some of the charisma. Others wandered the aisles, waiting for the actors to appear and explain the magic, as if terrified that departure might kill the experience.

The actors didn't sleep all night. Leaving the theatre, they straggled north through the silent streets of Manhattan, as punch-drunk as they had left their audience. Dressed in their ostentatiously plain workers' clothes – bomber jackets, canvas trousers, plain dresses – they floated through the midnight hours. Happening on an all-night diner, they sat and lingered over untouched suppers, catching eyes and shrugging, unable to credit what had just occurred. When they separated, they walked home rinsed with hope and strength. As Kazan said, 'I felt that strange things mystics talk about, a sudden enlargement of the space around them.' They were where they wanted to be. They had followed their calling and had given the world a push toward the bright.

For Kazan it was a slug of an irresistible drug. It invested him with a charisma to excite others to feed from the same elixir.

ALL THE WINDS STOPPED

On 5 March 1933, the US banks had closed and everyone's savings went up in a puff of smoke. Elia Kazan's father, an Anatolian carpet seller who had brought his family over from Turkey, saw stocks he had bought at $300, which had climbed to $600, sink down to $23. Everything had gone. Kazan rushed to his father's store to find a gathering of Manhattan's carpet sellers – Armenian, Turkish, Greek, Persian – sitting cross-legged and silent like hens roosting. They were in such shock they could neither move nor speak. They could not believe their adopted America, in which they had placed such faith, had wrecked them. A few of them picked up the edges of the carpets and started mechanically clipping with small scissors. Craft was all they had left.

As Arthur Miller describes in his vaudeville, *The American Clock*, a panoramic sweep across the USA of 1929, the Depression caused a nationwide collapse of the spirit, 'like all the winds had stopped'. Every town was suddenly 'full of men sitting on the sidewalks with their backs against the storefronts'. Parts of Manhattan became refugee camps, their occupants grouped around open fires that lit faces and warmed hands. Starving men fainted on the streets. A hundred thousand people applied for jobs in the Soviet Union. Beyond the wound of poverty and unemployment was the relentless falling away of purpose; as Miller wrote, 'a whole generation withered in its prime'.

Among those who saw their parents destroyed, there was a hard clarity about the source of the problem. Kazan wrote in his diary,

> I *know the source of this sickness. The capitalist system. The fascism which keeps the gambler gambling long after he wants to, or has the money – or blood – to play with. My father's neck is marked by the teeth of the (banks). He worked all his life for these men.*

With a clean fury which exemplified his stance towards the world, he wrote: 'I will revenge him ... I will make the revolution. That is all I want.' That passion drove Odets' *Waiting for Lefty*, the sense of good people pressed hard against a wall and fighting back with the desperation of the lost. It was a generation looking to avenge their fathers.

GROUP THEATRE AND KAZAN

On Kazan's first night at a Group Theatre summer camp, shortly after America's economy had gone bust, he heard one of its directors, Harold Clurman, address the assembled actors, sitting before him on the grass, speaking of an 'ideologically cemented collective' and of how art had a responsibility to the public good. When Kazan rang his new wife, Molly, and told her all that had been said, she was dubious: 'He sounds like one of those healer-spielers. I don't want to be cemented to anyone.' All summer Kazan and the Group worked on plays, their techniques and themselves. The aim was to found a new style and to shuck off the mannerisms which revealed ancestral loyalty to British theatre. The Brits could do text and words. The Group wanted to shake off formal gentility and allow in the pungent flavours of the streets – to forge a new, American way, intense and emotional, with access to the subconscious and its unruly fuel. The path would be communal and rehearsals concluded with 'social criticism' sessions, where actors assessed each other's performances and the content of the plays. The dream was that this process would fan out across showbusiness, and revolutionise it from within. From the present perspective it is hard to imagine such Soviet practices in the US of A, but they occurred. It was, more generally, how America saved itself.

To survive the Depression, America tapped into its reservoir of goodness and engendered a spirit of shared endeavour. It was imperfect, it was occasionally venal, it was riddled with hypocrisy (what human moment isn't?), but it had a brightness. Its architect was President Roosevelt with his rallying cry of 'The only thing to fear is fear itself,' but a broad coalition came together to inculcate a spirit of democratic, anti-authoritarian communitarianism. The New Deal was the state-sponsored manifestation of a collective need. The Group Theatre and the many other companies it spawned – the Theatre Collective, Theatre Union, Theatre of Action – all felt the benefit of the Federal Theatre Project, sponsored by the Works Progress Administration (WPA). The Soviet flatness of these names and their preponderance of capital letters tell of a different America. A spirit was abroad, where individuals could discover their strength through joining with others.

The Group Theatre was lucky to have actors of true quality, directors of potential and a writer of genius in Clifford Odets. Through the late 1930s, Odets turned out a series of plays that captured in vivid colours the heartbreak of the American spirit under capitalism. Arthur Miller worshipped at the Group Theatre altar, though they did not take to his early work. And, in 1939, the Group Theatre saved Tennessee Williams from giving up writing by sending him $100, and helped him find an agent.

Over Kazan's seven years with the group, he travelled at speed the rebel arc from ardent disciple, to subversive malcontent, to new leader, and finally to disenchanted cynic. Kazan never did anything slowly, or less than fully. He began as a stagehand: 'I was there, on the spot, eager, energetic, ready for anything, slam-bang, jaunty, never down.' Those are the people you build a company on. Soon he took small parts, then large ones, then he was directing, then running the company. He was ever grateful to the Group, but his lifelong belief in competition, his unholy rage for himself, and his loathing for meetings, were always going to create friction. A member of the Communist Party, he attended a gathering which was hijacked by a Party member brought in from Detroit to preach a crushing critique of Kazan's ideological purity. He decided there and then the party wasn't for him, and walked away.

He had learnt a simple lesson – he didn't like seeing the same people every day. Ideologically he was also looking for plays less certain than the Group's, more accepting of the absurdities and sudden terrors of a way of life changing day by day. He wanted plays to stretch beyond realism, to reach out on the one hand towards the poetic and on the other to the commercial. He wanted a cocktail rather than plain water.

As a director, Kazan began as the great fixer – hence his nickname 'Gadg' – bringing his backstage problem-solving mentality to on-stage dilemmas. He admired old professionals as much as the new methods. His dream was a balancing of the two traditions, the clear, precise and eloquent gesture of the old theatre; with the emotional truth of the new. Though never claiming to be a visionary, he was capable of investing actors and plays with a moment-to-moment weight and charisma. Without fuss, he helped actors present human life on stage, to 'plant their feet and tell the truth'.

A CHANCE MEETING

In autumn 1938, Kazan was on the road with the Group in Chicago, having taken over the lead role in *The Golden Boy*, another Odets drama. An early riser, he was going in to warm up his voice for a two-show day. The theatre next door to his was presenting a play led by the faded star

Laurette Taylor. As he approached the stage door, he noticed a crumpled and dishevelled figure lying below the fire stairs of the adjacent theatre, curled up asleep on the concrete. He took a closer look, and saw it was the star herself, Miss Taylor. Kazan knew drunks and drunken actors, and knew that when they go on a tear in an unknown town, however blind they may get, they have a homing instinct that gets them back to a stage door. Ever the fixer, Kazan picked her up in his arms like a child, carried her through her stage door, and lay her down on a sofa in her green room. She never knew.

The kindness of strangers.

31 MARCH 1945, THE PLAYHOUSE THEATER, BROADWAY

Late afternoon of a warm spring day, and a torrential monsoon was drenching Manhattan. It was the opening night of Tennessee Williams' *The Glass Menagerie*, and its director, along with its leading man, Eddie Dowling, and his wife, ran through the rain towards the Playhouse Theatre, at the unfashionable end of Broadway. Just as the rain eased, they turned into the alley leading to the stage door. It was an hour and a half to curtain-up, and there on the steps, wringing wet, was the play's leading lady, Laurette Taylor, smashed out of her mind on martinis. 'Hel-lo', she greeted them with unconvincing cheeriness. 'It's the rain. Nothing wrong with me. Just the rain'.

With little time on their side, the crowd buzzing its way towards the theatre, and producers flapping about which celebrities were in, Dowling and his wife went into panic mode. They picked Taylor up, carried her to her dressing room and gave her a cold shower. They walked her up and down backstage corridors, forcing her to drink black coffee and eat stewed tomatoes from a can. Somehow they got her down to the curtain only ten minutes late. Whether she was going to be able to carry off the part of Amanda, one of the most exacting roles ever written for an actress, nobody knew.

Laurette Taylor was not popular with Broadway producers. Her last husband had died in 1928 and, as a true Irishwoman, she was said to have held a seventeen-year wake. A master alcoholic in a competitive field, she had previously been banished by Equity for acting while drunk and closing several shows on opening night. Yet there was something about her, and people kept knocking on her door. When Dowling first went to her home with the script of *The Glass Menagerie*, she came to her door scraggly haired, barefoot and in a jaded kimono, and sent him away with a feeling of despair. She read it overnight. Somewhere in the recessed folds of her sodden mind, she heard a clear and clean song. The next day, when the director was summoned back, she had tidied herself up and committed herself to the project. But she asked him, astutely, if 'Broadway, this bastardly place, will buy this lovely, delicate fragile little thing'.

Rehearsals in Chicago saw the cast rehearsing the play as a unit, while Laurette Taylor sat in their midst in a solipsistic bubble, her hat pulled low so her large eyes just peeped out from under. If it was her turn to move, she would give a running commentary, 'Now I get up and walk over there' – waving her hand to a distant point – 'when I get there' – pausing to increase the suspense – 'I open my pocketbook and take out a handkerchief and sniff a little' – she would look pleased with herself – 'No, I don't' – she would suddenly adjust, and then carry on. In the middle of these babbles of consciousness, she would look up and see a circle of faces, looking like they all wanted to cry.

When she had to speak, she seemed to have difficulty forming words. If anything came out, it was a vague muttering – often some cliché that had nothing to do with the play. 'My god, what corn!' Williams screamed from the stalls. Taylor screamed back. Confusion reigned, but at every session some tiny word or phrase or moment would click into place. When it did a small light would flash within her, before she hurried a veil of chaos back into the air around her.

Tennessee Williams himself was anything but a sure thing in 1945. His only previous outing had been an all-time disaster called *Battle of Angels*. This closed in Boston in 1940 before it even made it to Broadway, with its first night a bizarre race for the company to complete the play before the audience left. A fiery conflagration required for the finale had spluttered in the dress rehearsal, and stage management had overcompensated for the premiere. Billowing clouds of smoke and flares poured towards the audience as they bolted for the exit. At the end there was almost no-one left to applaud. Williams was suicidal.

The Glass Menagerie, this wispy and personal play turning a spot on the detail of Williams' tragic family, hardly seemed the confident statement to herald a comeback. Opening night in Chicago got a respectful response, and nice reviews kept it ticking along, but the producers were losing money week on week. Arguments flared between the cast and Williams, and the cast and Williams and the producer. When it became clear they might not get to New York, their temporarily abstinent star, Miss Taylor, started consoling herself with the occasional martini. By the time that they had landed at the Playhouse, a far from fashionable theatre, she had reacquired a habit.

On the opening night in New York, Tennessee Williams sat besuited like 'a farm boy in his Sunday best', in an aisle seat on the left side of the sixth row. The dress rehearsal had been calamitous, and his jitters would not have been settled by the play's opening minutes. As the lights came up on Miss Taylor, she was greeted by a prolonged ovation, celebrating her return to Broadway after a prolonged absence. To stay in character during the applause, she flicked her hair and jabbered nonsense into the phone. Williams tightened his grip on his chair. Then, when Dowling came in with his line, 'Ma I've got some news for you', Taylor jumped straight into the second act. Williams went into cardiac arrest. Somehow they juggled their way back to the correct moment and proceeded on course. Owing to her pre-show entertainment, there was a bucket provided for Taylor in the wings, and every time she exited she would lean over it and retch. As one colleague remembered, 'There was nothing left inside of her, poor thing, but on stage – good god.' On stage, something happened.

Never deemed any sort of beauty, Taylor had within her the capacity for a radiant human-ness, fine and large, which surpasses good looks. Dame Edith Evans would sit in the wings and chant 'I Am Beautiful' to herself before going on. Judi Dench, through an act of imagination, became the most stunning Cleopatra any of us will see. Taylor did that and something more. She had what Williams dubbed 'a supernatural quality on stage'. There was an inexplicable rightness in all she did. It combined an exemplary observation of humanity with an illuminated soft grace. It made the audience pray from moment to moment that its fragile perfection would be preserved. The grounding for the world around it was the realism of the 1930s and the Group. That was the launchpad, but the place Taylor went to was beyond. She employed technique and perception and imagination, held together by a vulnerable will, all alive in the tenderness of a newborn story. The authority of soft truth, and of making in the moment.

At the end, everyone knew theatre history had been made. The cast took twenty-four curtain calls, the cry of 'Author, author!' went up, and the pudgy Williams climbed on stage and bowed to the actors, inadvertently showing the audience his backside. Everyone was sobbing backstage, and so many of the audience came round they had to lift the safety curtain to accommodate them. Arthur Miller called it 'a revolution'. As Easter Sunday and the end of the Second World War approached, America was ready for a release from years of anxiety. How perverse that the voice it cherished at that moment was a hymn to the individual soul, and the radical tenderness of Tennessee Williams.

At the end of a long evening of hoopla, hysterical approval and shrieked praise, Laurette Taylor turned and asked, 'I can't remember anything. Does it look like a success?' She went on to play the part in New York for almost eighteen months, pouring her soul every night into the graceful curves of the patterns she traced. She left little or nothing behind. She died in December 1946, a couple of months after she had left the show.

At her death, Williams wrote, 'There was a rightness about her you could not see beyond. Once in a while, only once in a while and not long, the confusion and dimness about us so thickly is penetrated by a clarity, an illumination of this kind, which makes it still possible to believe that the tunnel in which we move is not closed at both ends.'

29 JANUARY 1947, THE CORONET THEATRE, NEW YORK

The Depression was a formative experience for Kazan and Williams – and equally so for Arthur Miller. His father, Isidore, an illiterate man who arrived in America with a luggage label around his neck, had over the course of his life built up a substantial fortune. The young Arthur grew up surrounded by luxury and staff –and then everything was lost in the crash of 1929. Tennessee Willliams' father, an itinerant salesman of wayward charm and strange habits, led a precarious existence, hustling his way through the mayhem. He lost his ear in an argument over a poker game. These were tough times, and the generation that emerged knew they lived on thin ice.

In awe at the energy and drive of their fathers, Miller, Williams and Kazan had all seen them destroyed by history. The central figure of Miller's first great success, *All My Sons*, is a father in this mould. A successful industrialist, floating on the guilt of a bitter secret, and waiting for justice to catch up; a man blindly committed to building something for his son, and destroyed by the intensity of that ambition. Miller chose Kazan to direct the play over more established figures because he felt an affinity with a man who 'came from a close-knit community of intense feelings, people who knew that no feeling is alien to man'. He was also a little bit in love with Kazan's dynamic charisma:

> *Kazan was eating fire in those days, working with certainty and discretion ... A small compact man, who walked on the balls of his feet, he had the devil's energy ... Life in a Kazan production had a hushed air of conspiracy ... not only against the existing theatre, but society, capitalism – in fact, everybody who was not part of the production.*

Miller loved the freedom within the family of the company, how everyone seemed collaboratively to bring themselves to the just choices. The old Group collectivism was still there, if a little reframed. In return, Kazan saw immediately that Miller had a muscularity in his writing not found in any other dramatist of the time.

There was little pain in the creation of *All My Sons*. Miller and Kazan gelled as warriors for truth and art. The play opened in New Haven, and was a moderate success, and the team kept refining as it toured. It came into New York to a mixed reception; many critics were confused by the disturbingly normal suburban setting, and the bitterness of the truths it enclosed. But Brooks Atkinson of the *New York Times* took up its cause and pushed hard and audiences followed. The play settled into the Coronet for a long run, and made the reputations of Kazan and Miller. The author declared that 'a theatrical production is, or should be, a slice through the thickness of the culture from which it emerges.'

All My Sons passed that test. It was part of the Group mission to expand the franchise of drama and tragedy. The classicists believed that tragedy was the preserve of the European repertory company of dramatis personae – kings, queens, industrialists, mythical figures, historical heroes. As Gore Vidal described it, for Tennessee Williams, his family – a footloose father, a ferociously prim mother, and a psychologically damaged sister – were his 'basic repertory company'. For Miller, it was the middle and working classes of America. The same people as the audience.

A couple of weeks after its opening, Miller went to a factory in Long Island City and signed up to stand all day assembling beer box dividers for the minimum wage.

3 DECEMBER 1947, ETHEL BARRYMORE THEATER, NEW YORK

Tennessee Williams and his guests were holed up in a small shack by the shore in Provincetown. The electricity had gone kaput, so they were living by candlelight. The plumbing was a lost cause too, so they were wading through effluent. Not the best place to relax while *A Streetcar Named Desire* was being cast. Elia Kazan phoned the playwright and asked Williams what he thought of the actor he had sent up to read. 'What actor?' Williams replied. 'No-one has shown up'. Kazan thought 'There goes twenty bucks', and went back to the drawing board. At dusk, the actor showed up at the shack with a girlfriend. He had blown the twenty dollars on much-needed food, and hitchhiked to Provincetown. He took one look at the flooded floor, blown fuses, and the hapless literati and set to work fixing the plumbing and the wiring. The author marvelled: 'You'd think he had spent his entire antecedent life repairing drains'.

Then the actor sat down and read the part of Stanley Kowalski, while the author read Blanche DuBois. After ten minutes, Williams and his guests leapt out of their chairs, and the playwright wired his agent: 'Please use all your influence to oppose any move on the part of the producer's office to reconsider or delay signing this boy'. The actor stayed the night. The next morning he insisted that he and Williams went for a walk along the shore, still unsure whether he wanted to do it. The writer assented, and they walked a long distance beside the surf, without a word. Then they turned and walked back. In silence. The actor nodded and the compact was sealed. Marlon Brando was playing the part.

Brando had appeared in minor roles in a few Broadway plays; he scared some, thrilled others. He worked with Kazan in a play called *Truckline Cafe* and stole the show with a five-minute monologue. His brooding beauty stole the eye, and his androgynous mix and match of tenderness and violence sweated texture into even the blandest text. Kazan knew that, with language like that of Tennessee Williams, this unique man-child could be electric. He had a relationship with his parents as troubled as any, and his rebellion was professional, too – he wanted to make a new theatre. For Kazan, he was the ideal avatar for his own hurt and rage at middle-class gentility. They both felt the same outsider's edge. Though Brando would be no-one's avatar for long. He kept his director in a state of confusion: 'You never knew where the hell he was going to sleep, you didn't know who he was angry with, or what he was angry about. Every day there was a drama.' Brando was the random genius the Group had always sought to exemplify their ideals and nudge them into fresh fields. Tennessee was as enamoured, scenting the future.

Kazan and Tennessee Williams had fallen for each other, too. Williams had seen *All My Sons* and, though iffy about the writing, thinking it a 'message-play', he could perceive the vitality the director brought. He insisted Kazan take on *Streetcar*. Although on first sight an odd couple – Williams fragile, and unable to catch another's eye without blushing beetroot, Kazan brash and all heavy eye contact – they shared a human intelligence. In Kazan's term, they were both 'disappearers'. His favourite phrase at a party was 'I've got to go'; and Williams was always quick to recede into a fastidiously covert gay world. Kazan was so curious about these goings-on that he arranged a double date with a mistress, and both couples shared beds in the same room. His curiosity was satisfied.

Both men wanted to change the shape of the American theatre, and to 'burst the soul's sleep'. In the midst of negotiations over the director's involvement, Williams wrote Kazan a letter about *Streetcar*, which sets out both their stalls:

> *I think its best quality is its authenticity or its fidelity to life. There are no 'good' or 'bad' people. Nobody sees anyone truly, but all*

*through the flaws of their own egos. That is the way we all see
each other in life ... However in creative fiction or drama, if the
aim is fidelity, people are never shown as we see them in life, but
as they are ...*

Rehearsals began on 6 October on the roof of the New Amsterdam
Theatre. Everyone was patient with Brando's method and mannerisms.
He didn't look at whoever spoke, hardly acknowledged what was said,
would fall silent when spoken to, and played with the rhythms of his
own lines, leaving other actors hanging. He was a jazzer, intent on the
looping surprises of bebop. At other times, he would mumble incom-
prehensibly. The gracious and gifted Jessica Tandy, who had landed the
role of Blanche, let it go, and concentrated on her own thing. 'There was
nothing you could do with Brando that touched what he could do with
himself,' wrote Kazan later. 'In those days he was a genius.'

Kazan kept things taut and alert, and the cast on a curve of surprise.
Herein lay his special ability, to convey the greatness of a masterpiece,
but to avoid it ever feeling great or stately. He kept each moment full
of the snap, crackle and pop of life, even as the audience perceived the
majesty. For all that, towards the end of rehearsals it was becoming clear
that Tandy's graciousness was undermining her own character's story
and Brando was running away with the show. He asked Williams for
advice, but the writer was speechless in adoration of Brando. As Kazan
said, 'the son of a bitch is riding a crush'.

Streetcar opened on the road on 30 October at the Shubert Theatre
in New Haven. It had now become severely unbalanced, with Brando
lopsiding the show and provoking laughter at Tandy's expense. Kazan
became exasperated by Williams' refusal to help him address the
problem, and by the anarchic violence with which Brando was subverting
the play. When Kazan asked what to do, Williams' advice was to leave
well alone, 'Don't take sides or try to present a moral. The fidelity to life
will suffer. Go on as you are. Marlon is a genius. She's a worker and will
get better.' As Kazan later understood the whole play, 'We go on with
life, he was saying, the best way we can. People get hurt, but you can't get
through life without hurting people. The animal survives – at all costs.'

The playwright was proved right. Jessica Tandy rose up through
hard graft to meet her co-star. There is one path to glory for American

actors through alcohol, self-destruction, risk and saving grace. There is an alternative route, through putting in a shift. Tandy favoured the latter. It worked, and by the time they had toured Philadelphia she was meeting Brando on the level. The play came to the front, rather than any one actor. The greatest danger for the move to New York was over-confidence. Kazan kept them on their mettle by talking down their chances: 'What we've got here is oysters. Not everyone has a taste for oysters.' Williams sent a pithily elegant telegram to Brando: 'Ride out boy and send it solid'.

They had little need to worry. The opening night was a sensation. As Williams recorded in unapologetic, self-delight: 'Never witnessed such an exciting evening ... Slow warm-up for the first act, and comments like "Well, of course, it isn't a play", the second act sent the audience zoning to mad heights, and the final one left them – and me – wilted, gasping, weak, befoozled, drained and then an uproar which went on and on'. Williams came on stage for his curtain call with what Kazan described as a 'campy shuffle' and someone else as a 'beautifully bewildered bow'. One suspects its bewilderment may have been practised.

Arthur Miller, who attended, was fulsome in praise, announcing that 'Streetcar planted the flag of beauty on the shores of commercial theatre'. To the charge that the play is apolitical, he riposted acutely, 'There is a radical politics of the soul as well as of the ballot box.' Gore Vidal later had an insight about the production's most seismic effect: 'In 1947, when Marlon Brando appeared on stage in a torn sweaty T shirt, there was an earthquake. Before him no male was considered erotic. Some were handsomer than others, some had charm. A man was essentially a suit. He wasn't a body.' Kazan had a less decorous way of saying the same thing: 'Marlon played with his cock and that excited people.'

Stanley Kowalski was an icon of unbridled male sexuality such as mass culture hadn't yet witnessed. In his distaste for rules of duty and deference, and his constant reminder that he was the king around here, he was the emblem of an ardent new individualism. Something new was being unleashed – attractive, seductive and potentially ruinous. People wept tears of mourning for the demise of Blanche and her world, but their desires ran excitedly alongside Stanley towards the future.

It was a triumph for Kazan, who was also on a comet-like career in Hollywood. That autumn he was to release a film, *Gentlemen's Agreement*, which won him his first Best Director Oscar. *Streetcar* was the start of many collaborations with Williams. The Mississipian offered him a new territory, with its feet in the streets, but adorned with a language that dropped fruit from a rich literary tree and let primal truths come out to play.

Williams was reckless in his enjoyment of success. When *Summer of Smoke* followed *Streetcar*, and opened disastrously, he held a bad-notices party. He even had the cheek to invite the critics who had trashed him. Ever the disappearer, he snuck out of his own party with Brando, clambered onto the actor's motorcycle and took off, helmetless, into the Manhattan night; 'I enjoyed the ride, clamping his buttocks between my knees as we flew across the East River and along the river drive with the cold wind whistling, and a moon'. As Blanche says when taken by surprise by an act of human decency, 'Sometimes – there's God – so quickly'.

10 FEBRUARY 1949, MOROSCO THEATRE, NEW YORK

At an early matinee of *All My Sons*, during its tryout run in New Haven, Arthur Miller bumped into his uncle in the foyer. Manny Newman, a short and dapper man, comical in his ceaseless competition, had travelled up from New York. Miller greeted him effusively. Uncle Manny didn't acknowledge the greeting, and shot straight back with 'Buddy is doing very well', talking of his own son. Immediately, his face creased with embarrassment at his own transparency, and he shuffled quickly away. This fleeting encounter planted a seed. Something about the dynamic inspired the dramatist, the thrust of Manny's need to win, the retreat into shame afterwards, and the swiftness of the shift – all the hope and pain packed into a couple of sentences. Miller sensed a story in it, but also a new form, where zigzag, abrupt transitions reflect scattered minds.

A couple of months later, after the successful opening of *All My Sons*, the egg of a play grew to a mere two lines, which haunted Miller: a woman calls out, 'Willy?' and her husband responds, 'It's alright. I came back.' Pregnant with that haiku of dialogue, Miller walked Manhattan and brewed. Watching *Streetcar* had 'printed a license for him to speak at full throat' and the unabashed lyricism of Williams had opened a door for a less embarrassed voice, blending non-realistic elements with heard life. In April of 1948, Miller set out to write the new play. He had acquired a new home in Connecticut, and on a knoll in the woods nearby planned the construction of a writer's studio. One day he took off for the country, and set to. Those two phrases chimed in his head, as he nailed the rafters into the frame and raised it, and tacked a roof on top. Once the studio was established in rudimentary form, a home-made desk followed. Then, with tools still scattered, the wood still smelling raw, and the April sun shining on apple buds in the trees, he sat down and wrote. He wrote till the sun had crossed the sky and sunk, had dinner, and then wrote more. Around three in the morning he stopped, his eyes red sore from weeping, and his throat rough from shouting and laughter. He had written the first half of his play. All from those two lines: 'Willy!' 'It's alright. I came back.' The second half took six weeks.

He sent it to Kazan, who read it immediately. He called Miller, who had been waiting two days by the phone.

'I've read your play' – his tone was that of someone about to report a death. 'My God, Art. It's so sad.'

'It's supposed to be.'

'I don't know what to say. It killed me. My father ... ' and Kazan broke off.

Silence, and a ripple of understanding.

'It's a great play, Artie. I want to do it in the fall or winter'.

That was the conversation. Not a trace of celebration. Miller was overjoyed. Heartbreak is what the play was born for.

All My Sons had become 'all our fathers'. Miller, Kazan and Williams all had fathers who were salesmen. Kazan remembered his father flogging carpets: 'Feel it!' he would shout at a buyer, 'Go on, feel it!' Their fathers dreamt long and hard, coerced their mothers into a shared deception, and were desperate for the success of their sons. All the same energy and dysfunction that was bottled in Willy Loman. It was their tale, but also that of their generation. The play works as an elegy for fathers, but also as a continuing examination of the self, of everyone's hunger for affirmation, and the perilous act of maintaining self-belief on America's thin ice. Kazan saw his father in it; he also had the honesty to see himself.

Lee J. Cobb, an old colleague of Kazan's from the Group, flew across the country in his two-engine plane to demand the part of Willy Loman. 'This is my part, Nobody else can play this part. I know this man.' He was the opposite of the physical type Miller imagined, but in his large and ungainly frame he could carry the weight and sorrow of the world. He was upfront with his praise: 'This play is a watershed. The American theatre will never be the same.'

As with *Streetcar*, the rehearsals were held in the New Amsterdam. Cobb, having pumped himself and the play relentlessly to get the part, started rehearsals doing his best impression of Laurette Taylor. He wandered the room mumbling lines and looking as if a heavyweight boxer had punched him. Kazan feigned a lack of concern, then dropped the act and got as terrified as the author. They dubbed Cobb 'the Walrus' and started to wonder how they had fallen for his self-selling act. Miller despaired. He had written something important, and was watching it disappear. But, on the twelfth day of rehearsal, suddenly Cobb stood up and bellowed to his wife: 'No, there's more people now ... there's more people.' With an indefinite gesture of his hand, he summoned up a world more vivid, more true, than anything Miller had imagined. He continued with the scene from a place of such total encompassing reality no-one in the room could draw breath. In Miller's words, he performed 'with such ominous reality my chest felt pressed down by an immense weight'. Miller turned to look at everyone, some had their heads in their hands weeping, some were slack-jawed, some terrified. Kazan grinned like a fiend. Miller, not a naturally demonstrative man, ran on stage and kissed Cobb, who looked at him and said, 'But what did you expect, Arthur?' Miller had needed his time of circumnavigation before going to Connecticut: Cobb needed to look away from the truth before he looked directly at it.

Before the evening premiere of *Salesman* in Philadelphia, there was a matinee performance of Beethoven's Seventh Symphony across the street. Kazan and Miller decided to take Cobb to see the concert. They wanted to 'prime the great hulk on whom all their hopes depended'.

They hoped the surge and swell of the music might inspire his performance. As Miller put it, 'Lee was showing signs of wearying. We sat on either side of him, inviting him to drink of the heroism of that music, to fling himself into his role without holding back. We thought of ourselves, still, as a kind of continuation of a long and undying past.'

Cobb did just that. At the end of that first show was a profound silence. No applause, and nobody spoke. Then odd things started to happen. Some people got up and put their coats on, then sat back down. Some buried heads in hands. People moved around to talk to each other. Then, after three minutes of dazed incomprehension, someone started to clap. Then 'the roof fell in'. There was no end to it. The applause, once detonated, carried on and on, as all wept, and newly understood their own country and moment.

The effect carried on to New York. At the opening-night party, Miller was dragged over to a phone, where an inside dopester from the *New York Times* read aloud to the author the review, as it came out of the typewriter of Brooks Atkinson, the superlatives underscored by the excited clickety-clack of the type. The achievement was so great everyone celebrated together. An intention that had begun with the Group Theatre's idealism seventeen years before had borne its richest fruit, and everyone wanted to join in. Arthur Miller got a taxi home with his wife, and listened to a radio show which read out the reviews. They competed to outglow each other. He felt a disassociation – and the emptying sense of loss which accompanies any victory.

ICARUS IN MIDTOWN

There is something about Manhattan at night which can stir the flattest of imaginations into romantic life. Mid-century Manhattan was swoonsome. Swelled with confidence by the materialist boom, not yet so rich as to be vulgar, its streets buzzing with bundles of dazzle like Holly Golightly, and swaying with beatniks riding a counterculture groove, it had a dreamful hope. America had beaten the Depression, beaten the Axis powers, and now they had beaten the squares as well. Kazan went out with Marilyn Monroe, who then fell in love with Miller. Picturing those five, Kazan, Monroe, Miller, Williams and Brando – striding out roughhouse style, dressed like stevedores, through pre-dawn Manhattan, is to imagine an America of such beautiful potential, it makes one heart-sad to think of the lurid Trump-Towered gruel that capitalism later served up.

They were five Icarus models, and society was never going to let them fly too high. Each of these five fell away precipitately. When Brando asked Kazan what he thought Stanley Kowalski would be like in later life, the director said, 'Fat as fuck.' He had no idea how prophetic that would prove, as Brando grew old and large, buffering his hypersensitivity within tyres of icecream and butter and lard. The great beauty of the 1940s became a grotesque. Monroe burnt out most of Miller's originality and talent in her consuming flame; he himself became a moral voice of authority, and an analyst of genius, but creatively for the rest of his life he was on a dry slope. Williams kept writing at a height, until the apparatchiks of the newly liberated told him off for not being gay enough, and left him flailing trying to appease a generation he didn't understand.

Kazan's was the saddest and the furthest fall of all. An ex-Communist from the Group Theatre, he named names of old comrades to the House of Un-American Activities Committee. He rehearsed his reasons for decades, providing a catalogue of apologias, without ever delivering an apology. His denunciations of Communism are righteous and reasoned, but they never sound like the whole story. He was always overinflected with machismo, and to confess to one of the many reasons – that he was just plain scared – may have been too diminishing a truth.

He told a funny story of a designer friend who, like him, was an inveterate shagger. The designer was caught by his wife in flagrante with another woman. He leapt naked out of bed and shouted, 'It's not me! It's not me! It's not me!' Kazan detected a truth in this, that the libertine compartmentalises his self and doles out different parts in different environments. Some of that cry reveals his understanding of his own behaviour before the committee - 'It's not me!'. But the libertine is someone who has lost their bearings, however cleverly they justify their behaviour to themselves. The people he betrayed were people he had broken bread with. There is no arguing that away. Above all else, the Group Theatre was a celebration of friendship. This made Kazan's betrayal the more acute.

Yet the Group's faith in communality achieved much. A cadre of actors taught Broadway, Hollywood and the world how to ally truth and spontaneity in new harmonies. Their remorseless focus on ethics sometimes precluded the art. There is a difference between the theatre and the church. But all new art relies on the change achieved by its predecessors. As a rocket sheds the structures which power its gravity-defying first slouch upwards, so art relies on the revolutionary battles of forefathers. The applause at the conclusion of *Death of a Salesman* was in no small measure for work that began on a summer's evening fifteen years before, as the bright shining faces of the Group Theatre company committed to dreaming together of a better future.

13

An Idea of Heaven

A TALE OF GEORGE HANDEL
AND SUSANNAH CIBBER

DUBLIN, 1739

Eighteenth-century Dublin was was a city of 110,000 souls and two utterly distinct cultures. The Anglo-Irish colonial elite lived an expansive life of elegant new architecture, exuberant theatre presentations and astounding gluttony. The menus for their feasts defy imagination: one boasted an opening course of thirty-four dishes, including *Lambs Ears Ragou'd; Badger Flambé with Colleflower; and Fricassée of Frogs*. A travelling Englishwoman, Mary Pendarves, observed of the rich 'I have not seen less than fourteen dishes of meat for dinner, and seven for supper, during my peregrination', and of the poor; 'the poverty of the people has made my heart ache – I never saw greater appearance of misery'. She concluded, unsurprisingly, 'they live in great extremes, either profusely or wretchedly'.

While the enfranchised Protestant elite thrived, the Catholic poor shrunk into destitution. The most grotesque disparity occurred on the nominated 'largesse days'. After the gluttons had had their fill of a feast in Dublin Castle, the doors would be flung open, and a gentleman would cry out, 'Largesse, largesse, largesse.' At this point, poor women would rush in to fight over the scraps. The posh, bloated like true Augustans, watched with pleasure.

In the winter of 1739, arctic weather gripped northern Europe. It was the coldest winter in modern history and its worst impact was felt in Europe's most westerly island. Fish washed up dead and freshly frozen; men were arrested for felling trees in Phoenix Park; and the lamplighters with their last remaining oil fought in vain as their flames guttered and died, plunging Dublin into darkness. Germany, France and England were struck by the same weather, but the effects were less severe. Each had benefited from preceding years of bounty, whereas Ireland had suffered from successive years of meagre harvests. The cold, on top of the scarcity, hit the country hard, especially in the potato-cropping south. The straw covering the stored crops was no protection against the temperatures, and potatoes turned to a blighted pulp. The lack of seed crops meant an inevitable famine would follow.

The following year became known as *bliadhain an air*, the 'year of slaughter'. Tens of thousands died, as the British government enacted measures to protect the market price of crops rather than attend to the starving. As famine hollowed out the country, soldiers killed rioters who looted shops in Dublin, and hung the leaders of a mob in Drogheda, which had dismembered a ship full of corn. Famine was soon followed by its ghoulish twin, fever. From a national population of 2.4 million, over 400,000 died, a higher proportion in a single year than died in the five years of the Great Famine a century later.

As the famine had taken hold, thousands were arrested and locked up for theft of food, or being unable to avoid debt in the effort to support their families. In the absence of government relief, and pricked because the disaster was now biting into the welfare even of the Anglo-Irish population, the burghers of Dublin came together to do what they could. A number of institutions were formed, including the Charitable Musical Society, which set out to raise funds to assist in the liberation of incarcerated debtors. To achieve their aims they needed a venue, and the Society engaged the architect Richard Cassels to build the Great Musick Hall in Fishamble Street. Finished swiftly in 1741, it was Ireland's largest music hall, seating 700 in a horseshoe shape. Two rows of boxes enclosed a sloping parterre, at the end of which a thin wall separated the orchestra from the stalls. It was the sort of venue which these days would seat about 300. Three centuries ago, 700 extravagantly dressed folk squidged in within its fresh wooden walls, creating an excited clatter of flesh and wood.

Once the society had the venue, they needed to fill it. Various charitable institutions came together with a notion. They would invite a giant of European music to come and enjoy a residency in their capital. He would give a defining character to their new venue and help raise funds. They enlisted their viceroy, the affable Duke of Devonshire, a man who sailed through life as if on a calm sea of claret, to invite the figure they had in their sights. They had no conception at the time of what music the man might bring. Nor that his career was on a precipitous slide. Nor did they know about the collection of scriptural fragments which had recently been sent to him, by his occasional librettist.

MR CHARLES JENNENS, ESQ

The musical star who the burghers of Dublin hoped to entice, was also a fixed point in the firmament of Charles Jennens. Born to an iron magnate, this oddly eruptive, stubborn, yet endearing country gentleman came into a fortune of 700 acres in Gopsall, Leicestershire. What might have been a life of leisure was rendered less easy by his dogged principles. In an age tumbling fast towards modernity, Jennens was determined to live centuries earlier. Stubbornly adhering to a belief in the divine right of kings, he could not bring himself to accept the legitimacy of the Hanovers who had recently taken over the British throne. He had a point. George I was 56th in line for the throne when the British establishment invited him to come and run the country. Refusing to swear an oath to the new royals, Jennens disqualified himself from public office.

He was as stubborn in his faith as in his politics. Jennens abhorred the scepticism which was sweeping Europe and the newly fashionable deism gaining ground in Britain which tried to incorporate the mechanics of Newton's clockwork universe into Christianity. The deists saw reason as the centre of nature itself, and believed it was reason that could reveal the truth of God's existence. Their key text, *Christianity Not Mysterious* by John Toland, argued that the acts and miracles of the Bible were intelligible to human reason, unaided by divine revelation. Jennens was having none of this, and was determined to return prophets and the supernatural to the centre of religious experience.

The need to establish the truth of salvation was personal. Charles's no less intense younger brother, Robert, had been studying for the law at the Inns of Court, when he had fallen into a correspondence with a friend given over to scepticism. The correspondent filled young Robert's mind with so many confusions and doubts about Christian orthodoxy that he cut his own throat with a knife, and threw himself from the window of his rooms in Middle Temple.

Charles determined to revenge himself on the rationalists by means of a new oratorio, the *Messiah*, in which mystery and blind faith would be reinfused into religion. As a man of leisure, he had time to meditate at length on his lodestar, the Bible, of whose literal truth he had no doubt. Drawing on this, he created a libretto – or, more exactly, a 'Scripture Collection', as he called it. This patchwork of themes recounted the story of the birth of Christ, his life of miracle and torment, his death, resurrection and intercession at the Last Judgment. Its final section, hymning the littleness of death in the face of the life eternal, would reaffirm the truth of Jesus the Redeemer, and silence the doubters.

Jennens' method of recounting the story was oblique and meditative. There was no desire to present Christ as a character, so all the action was to be reported. There was no desire to tell a story – his presumption would be that a churchgoing public would know the stages of Christ's passion. The libretto was to be a space for private expression, rather than stuck within the suspense of a narrative.

He needed a composer, and knew exactly who he wanted. He had collaborated and been in correspondence with the man for several years, though there is no record of them ever meeting. Countless letters of praise had issued from him, and others of cruel attack when he felt his idol failed to achieve the highest standards. Crucially, Jennens knew how to shape a phrase to excite his idol's compositional skill, how to enable his natural taste for contrast, for passion, surprise and the full-throated roar. When he finished his libretto for the *Messiah* in 1740, he wrote at the base of his title page *majora canamus* ('we sing of big things'). He then packaged his script up, and sent it to a house in Brook Street, London.

Its recipient celebrated its arrival by putting it in a drawer, and there it remained for over a year. Jennens' words could have remained in obscurity for eternity. But, with the composer's fortunes declining, he received an invite to spend a season in Dublin. Something about the difficulty of his present moment, about the promise of new air across the sea, and about a new music he heard inside his bones, prompted him to take out the manuscript.

He found the ideal words.

HANDEL IN LONDON

Georg Frideric Handel arrived in London in 1710 with a splash, befitting both his outsized talent and his considerable frame. His first act was to premiere his opera *Rinaldo*, performed with a spectacular firework display of overpaid star *castrati*, exorbitant costuming, fire-breathing dragons, trundling mountains and flitting birds. It set new standards for theatrical excess and kickstarted a turbulent forty-year love affair between the British public and this outsized German showman. The London audience were renowned for their capriciousness: they rarely stopped their chattering or card-playing in the course of a show, unless a renowned *castrato* started warbling. Handel, with his remarkable capacity to employ the contrasting firepower of thunderous boom and feather-frail vulnerability, was able to secure their attention. Over three decades, Handel and his audience taught each other how to listen to music and how to grow the form.

Handel came to England when Queen Anne was on the throne. When his compatriot the elector of Hanover took over as George I, it seemed improper to leave. His theatricality demanded ever grander stages: his *Water Music* floated along the Thames accompanying the new king, and coronation spectaculars filled Westminster Abbey for his successor, George II. In a London crazy for epic entertainments, his future seemed secure. But London has always taken a pleasure in kicking out the heels from under anyone who might consider themselves safe. Fashion turned against Italian opera, the Puritans ranting against it as a sinister emanation of Popish effeminacy. The John Bull vigour of John Gay's *Beggar's Opera* was held up as a counterblast of Britishness (which today seems perverse, given its own promotion of criminality).

Musical society split into factions, with a clique forming under Frederic, Prince of Wales known as the anti-Handelists. In an odd moment of sense from a British monarch, George II opined that 'he did not think setting oneself at the head of a faction of fiddlers was a very honourable occupation for people of quality'. However, the anti-Handelists turned up at presentations to whistle and jeer. The split in the audience between the two cliques thinned out the money available to both sides, to everyone's detriment, as star castrati and fire-breathing dragons didn't come cheap. Handel slowly slipped from his perch. His last opera, *Deidamia*, opened in the spring of 1741, and played for a miserable three performances.

One response from Handel was to midwife a new form, the English oratorio – a full-length musical setting of a sacred text. The origins for this can be traced back to the medieval mystery plays and the playing of sacred stories in dramatic form. Handel's delight in switching between the ethereally light and the crushingly loud could be played out here in the age-old conversation between soloists and the chorus. Many enjoyed this new form, but others were disturbed by its elemental power. One Puritan critic wrote that, 'Musick is almost as dangerous as 'tis useful, it has the force of gunpowder, and should be as carefully looked after, that no unhallow'd Fire give it the power of destroying.' Others were worried by the presence of sacred language in playhouses. The Bishop of London forced the halt of a performance of Handel's *Esther*, stating that a biblical story should not be played in 'houses which entertained sodomitical clubs'.

With his opera career forestalled, his oratorios controversial and only fitfully successful, a clique of the aristocracy trying to wreck his career, and with money draining out of his account, this was a dark-clouded hour for Handel. His health was far from strong and, in 1740, he suffered a minor stroke and went off to recuperate in a German spa. Soon after, at a dinner, he had a further stroke. At this low ebb, out of the blue came a formal invitation from an Irish musical society to come to Dublin and present his work. There was a world elsewhere. He took out of his drawer some musty pages – a collection of fragments from the Bible.

SOLO DIE GLORIA

On Saturday 22 August 1741, at the age of 56, Handel sat down to write the *Messiah*. He had it finished – solos, recitative, massed choruses, complex orchestration and all – on 14 September. The whole thing had taken just twenty-four days. Almost a quarter of a million notes, or around thirty notes a minute. On finishing, he wrote on his autograph score, *SDG – Solo Die Gloria* (To God Alone the Glory). It is a score pockmarked with blots, smudges and corrections – the evidence of focused activity – but within its 259 pages are precious few errors. It arrived complete.

The words Jennens had chosen struck bells in Handel's heart and the chimes resonated throughout his creative sense. Bold declarative statements – *Behold! Rejoice!* – tender expressions of weakness – *He was despised and rejected* – and joyous affirmations of the sublime – *For unto us a child is given* – were framed by the Englishman to help the German express his soul. There was no collaboration; the words simply arrived in the post and the composer responded. But an expression of feeling in the words provokes a similar or distinct feeling in the composer and, in the transaction between the two, something starts to fly.

Handel's linguistic difficulties must be a factor. Though his English was at times fluent and easy (less so when in a temper, when he combusted in multilingual obscenity), it remained a foreign language. His handling of words when sung is thus deliberate, sculptural, self-enclosed. Less about the sense than the musicality of each word. No word excited the composer more than the old Hebrew word *Hallelujah* – 'Praise You, God'. This event of a word is repeated over sixty times within the one chorus. It excited Handel as it has many artists, right down to Leonard Cohen. The velvety liquid texture of its soft aspirants and the delivering 'y' sound of the *j* has a gentle soulfulness. The four big open-vowel sounds allow force and energy to flow through them. For Handel, the word served as a mantra to entrance himself, an inspiration to service and a vehicle to express his heart. The *Hallelujah Chorus*, as Handel's first biographer said, 'fills the ear with the bow of harmony as it leaves the mind in heavenly ecstasy'.

Freed from narrative and character by Jennens' fragments, Handel was able to look straight and true into the pain of living, the fact of death and the largesse of redemption, and find music to match. Freed to meditate around these iconic words – *Hallelujah, Amen, Peace* – and to pack them with a freight of feeling, Handel was 'liberated from all restraints but those of his art'.

George Frederic set off for Dublin in early November 1741, his score in his luggage. The Irish Sea was more than choppy, so he was stalled in Chester for ten days, compounding his impatience. Eager to test his score, he asked the local organist to assemble a scratch choir, who could sing at sight. A printer by the name of Janson was recommended to carry the tenor solos. The choir assembled in the Golden Falcon pub in Chester, which thus became the first place to hear the *Messiah*. It was a disaster. The story is told by Charles Burney, the contemporary music historian:

> *A time was fixed for this rehearsal; but on the trial of the chorus, And with his stripes we are healed, Poor Janson, after repeated attempts, failed so egregiously, that Handel let loose his great bear upon him; and after swearing in four languages, cried out in broken English: 'You shackuntrel! Tit not you dell me dat you could sing at site?' 'Yes sir,' says the printer, 'and so I can; but not at first sight'.*

On arrival in Dublin, Handel said nothing about the *Messiah*. He kept it packed away as he got to know the town. The warmth and inclusiveness with which he was welcomed made him confident to chance his arm on presentation of this intensely personal work. The still-quick despair from the famine must have maximised its urgency. His problem was finding a singer to achieve the emotional heart of the piece, his account of the rejection and torture of Christ at the end of his life by the community around him – *He was despised and rejected*. Without this capstone, the arch around it would collapse.

By chance, an old colleague of Handel's was in Dublin and she, too, was on the run from London. But, while Handel was leaving a career on the slide, this singer was in disgrace.

SUSANNAH CIBBER

The tale of Susannah Cibber would stretch the imagination of the most fantastical eighteenth-century author. She had been pimped out, spied on, kidnapped, held hostage, rescued, taken to court, eloped and finally banished in disgrace. That she survived all this, and transcended her trials through her generosity and art, is testament to a remarkable woman and artist.

Susannah Arne had become an instant star when, as a young woman, she was forced on stage by her father. Cultivating an image of piety and purity, she became a renowned actress and singer, essaying tragic roles which garnered her a wide following. Her private tragedy was her husband, Theophilus Cibber (son of the poet, Colley Cibber), an actor and authentic Augustan scumbag. Shortly after their nuptials, he was living off her substantial earnings, while merrily carrying on elsewhere, and bringing home nothing but venereal disease. Soon after that he was forcing his wife on another man, William Sloper. The three shared rooms in Kingston and Cibber would knock on their bedroom door and call them down to breakfast.

Susannah and William tired of the company of Theophilus and moved to the country. At which the husband pretended outrage and, together with two hired thugs, stole out to the country and kidnapped his wife. Locking her in a room near Clare Market in London, he left as her guard a Mr Stint, a candle-snuffer from the theatre armed with a case of pistols. Candle-snuffing and keeping guard were clearly incompatible. When Sloper and a host of others came searching for Susannah nearby, Mr Stint was unable to stop her shouting 'Murder!' or to hinder the rescue posse from smashing open a door and taking the hostage away. For good measure, as Stint later attested, 'they beat me severely'. Theophilus ran away over rooftops, then on to Calais.

Returning later, he saw that Susannah was still a star and earning her just rewards in the theatre: so he brought an action against her of what was termed 'criminal conversation'. Theophilus outlined to the court how he had bored a hole in the wainscot of a room that Susannah and her lover shared, and spied on them. In his account, Sloper 'took her on his knees, lifted up her clothes and took down his breeches and took his proven member and put it between her legs'. 'Enough!' shouted the judge, 'There is no occasion to be more particular!' The jury found for him but gave him a derisory £10 in damages.

It was not hard to see where virtue rested in the story and where vice. But the court case and attendant publicity was a disaster for Susannah, who had presented herself as a devout Catholic, and an actress of spiritual purity. Still worse, Theophilus refused to allow her to work on the stage, as he was entitled to do. Help came in the form of a Falstaffian bear of an

225

actor named John Quinn. First, he dragged Theophilus out of the Bedford Tavern, and forced him to fight a duel in the street, where he gave him a sound thrashing. (Cibber got off lightly – Quinn had killed two actors in duels.) Then he invited Susannah to come and work in Dublin, where he was gaining a reputation, and where many talents from the London stage were finding a second home. She still had a hunger to express, to interpret. So she packed her bags and sailed for Ireland.

Susannah and Handel had collaborated before. It was an exceptional combination, since she was musically gauche and technically limited, which usually enraged the German. He had once threatened to hurl an Italian soprano from a window, so dismayed was he by her lack of musicianship. She was an actor rather than a vocalist, but, as Charles Burney said, 'something about her voice and manner softened Handel's severity at her want of musicianship'. She lacked the basic requirement of being able to read music, but Handel chose to overlook this and to coach her. He played the part to her in painstaking detail. She was a fast learner.

Handel was a shrewd producer, and in Susannah he saw a quality he knew could fit his music and carry the event to a more generous place. She had a special capacity for including and compelling people. Charles Burney again: 'her voice was a thread, and her knowledge of music very inconsiderable [but] by a natural pathos, and perfect conception of the words, she often penetrated the heart when others, with infinitely greater voice and skill, could only reach the ear'. The risk was great, through Susannah's lack of technique, but Handel knew it was a gamble which could magnify as well as destroy.

Another threat beyond technique stood in the path of Susannah's success. Her shame in London had trailed her to Dublin as sure-footedly as rumour always tracks the undeserving. All of Dublin was talking about the *criminal conversation* trial. Dread Theophilus followed as well, ever on her path like a sleazy hound of hell.

DR DELANEY

We have one more character to thank for the *Messiah*: Dr Delaney, an inspirational preacher who was the rector of St Warburgh's, a small church between Dublin's two mighty cathedrals. The dean of one of those cathedrals, the mighty Jonathan Swift, said of Delaney that he was 'a man of the easiest and best conversation I ever met with in this island, a very good listener, a right reasoner; neither too silent, nor talkative'.

Had Dr Delaney not been in such good credit with Swift, the *Messiah* might never have taken place in Dublin. To achieve a complete choir, and to have singers who would not sabotage the event, like the unfortunate Mr Jenson of Chester, Handel could only perform it with the help of the choristers from the cathedral choir of St Patrick's, whose dean was Swift. The satirist's opinion of music could not be described as enthusiastic ('I would not give a farthing for all the music in the universe'). Swift's slipping mind and poor health, and his friendlessness following the loss of his beloved Stella, had led to misanthropy and melancholy. No-one knew which way his judgements would fall. When a deputation from the musical society went to him with a request for choristers, they were nervous. They were right to be. Swift refused to give 'a licence ... to assist a club of fiddlers in Fishamble Street'. He would not permit his singers to perform anywhere but in a church. Thankfully, Dr Delaney, as well as a man of the easiest and best conversation, was a great fan of Handel. He got to work on Swift and the increasingly erratic dean changed his mind.

The approval of Delaney himself was far from assured. He was only reluctantly persuaded that the *Messiah* should be performed in a secular playhouse. As opposed to the sceptics and deists as Charles Jennens, he was possessive of the words of the Bible, and enraged by the thought of their potential misuse. As another cleric expressed it, 'An oratorio is either an Act of religion or it is not; if it is, I ask if the Playhouse is a fit Temple to perform it in, or a company of Players fit Ministers of God's Word.'

Delaney was in an emotionally quick state, having recently buried his much-loved wife. Still dressed in mourning, he felt it his duty to attend the performance, since he had secured the involvement of the choristers. With his emotional volatility and his famous principles, there was every possibility that he would not condone it at all. His companion for the show was Thomas Sheridan, the manager of Smock Alley, and a renowned gossip, so little about Susannah Cibber's past would have been spared him. How would this man of faith respond to the performance of sacred text by a shamed woman? Would he echo the English priest who complained that the sacred name of God was about to be sung 'by a set of people very unfit to perform so solemn a service. David said, "How can we sing the Lord's song in a strange Land"; but sure he would have thought it much stranger to have heard it sung in a playhouse.'

As Dr Delaney and Sheridan made their way from the Liffey up Fishamble Street, at around eleven in the morning, they would have seen quite the crowd.

MIDDAY, 13 APRIL 1742

Fishamble Street was a tight and crooked street, and the Music Hall was tucked in a corner. This led to acute sedan congestion. A coach and horses could not be manoeuvred up the street, so for the many who arrived in sedan chairs – a box carried by porters fore and aft – it proved impossible for these cumbersome vehicles to share space. And, once they were in, for them to turn around. Foul-mouthed Dublin porters and steerers flung commands, demands and insults at each other, as these travelling thrones jockeyed to pass each other without scratching their buffed surfaces. Flouncy chaps stared grumpily from their elevated chairs, and encouraged their porters to shove forwards for a better position. All were uncertainly afloat in an angry squall of vanity and fashion.

The advertisement had gone out a week before, in suitably marbled prose, inviting any who wished to pay half a guinea to attend Fishamble Street Music Hall to hear the premiere of the *Messiah*. Tickets flew out and more had to be made. A further advertisement requested it as 'a favour that the Ladies who honour this performance with their presence would be pleased to come without hoops, as it will greatly increase the charity'. A lady without hoops took up half the space of a lady with, so the ladies trooped in hoopless. A similar request went to the chaps, who were 'desired to come without their swords'.

The attendees found it difficult to steer through the crush, or to find room once in. The show was set to begin at midday, so it could be all done by four, the most popular dinner time. Heating the hall in the evening was adjudged too expensive. The cram of bodies must have heated the room, and rendered it airless. For a later performance, it was advertised that, 'In order to keep the room as cool as possible, a Pane of Glass will be removed from the top of each of the Windows', which seems a bluntly efficient form of air conditioning.

Once sat, they would have seen Handel installed at his keyboard, from where he would direct the orchestra, a smaller and tighter ensemble than a modern one, with no harp or lute, and only one trumpet. There were eight soloists, and a chorus who were arrayed beside and to the rear of the orchestra on the shallow stage. A contemporary cartoon of a chorus by Hogarth depicts a more dynamic and chaotic grouping of individuals than the bland uniformity of the present day.

Handel liked to sport an enormous white wig on these occasions, and when the playing went well, as Burney describes, 'it had a certain nod, or vibration which manifested his pleasure. At the close of an air, the voice with which he used to cry out, *Chorus!* was extremely formidable.' Handel was a gargantuan man and his corpulence made his playing almost invisible. Burney again:

> *His hand was so fat, that the knuckles, which usually appear convex, were like those of a child, dinted or dimpled in, so as to be rendered concave; however his touch was so smooth, that his fingers seemed to grow to the keys. When he played, no motion and scarcely the fingers themselves could be discovered ... Handel's general look was somewhat heavy and sour; but when he did smile, it was his sire the sun, burst out of a black cloud.*

He had every reason to smile as the playing progressed, though he and everyone involved knew the performance hinged emotionally on one section. The tension amongst the performers and the crowd would have been palpable when Susannah Cibber stood up to sing.

Most artists live in the floodplain between the twin rivers of self-pity and self-congratulation. Handel was no different. What is surprising is the agility with which he moved between the two tributaries. Alongside a full-hearted capacity for emphatic and commanding joy – *Rejoice! Rejoice!* instructed with Teutonic bombast – was its counter, a tremulous and gentle vulnerability. In his *Messiah*, this rises to a pitch of sacred self-pity in the aria 'He was despised and rejected', where he depicts the torment of Christ, abhorred by the world. The text which Jennens had set played to this capacity with words adapted from Isaiah:

> *He was despised and rejected of men,*
> *a man of sorrows and acquainted with grief.*

He gave His back to the smiters,
and His cheeks to them that plucked off His hair:
He hid not His face from shame and spitting.

Each phrase or half-phrase is wrung out as a gentle sob, before halting nervously as it is responded to with a flutter of strings, which seem to float on the thermals of emotion released by the voice. It is heart-hurting, as though the singer has to break off after each thought, since she doesn't have the strength to go on, and needs to calm her palpitations.

It is the personification of the pain of Christ, but in Fishamble Street, at the beginning of the second movement, other currents crisscrossed through the instant, and maximised its charge. Jennens was not there, but his shared pain with his brother Robert, shut out of the world by the torment in his head, breathed through his words; Handel's music made manifest the isolation of genius in the face of the cruel fashions of the world; and Susannah was facing up to her husband, the daft laws that stopped her performing and the many who judged her by ridiculous standards. She would have known well what many thought as she stood before them and sang. Her courage and her artistry were all she had.

There are performers in every generation who have an ability to convey their feelings, and to do it with a modest grace. There is nothing worse than those hungry to demonstrate the obese size of their emotional capacity; there is nothing better than those who do it with honesty and naturalness. Such performers have an ability to include every person in a room, to invite them without bullying to share heart and hurt, and for all to partake in the delicate torture of a communal pain expressed with fineness. Cibber had that capacity. Garrick said of her when she died, 'the tragedy expired with her'.

Having already been steered through the giddy joys of the earlier Nativity section, the audience had been massaged into state of emotional openness, and the effect created by Cibber was a sensation. Amongst those affected was Dr Delaney, bearing inside him the grief of his recently departed wife. In his friend Sheridan's account, Delaney was so overwhelmed by Cibber's rendition that, full of compassion for this frail lost sinner, he felt compelled to join in. He rose to his feet and cried out: 'Woman, for this, be all thy sins forgiven.'

THE TRUMPET SHALL SOUND

Dublin was a triumph, and the city took the music and the man to their heart for eternity. They claimed the music for their own and still do. The Irish wrote poems of praise, and long paeans in their papers. London was more reluctant, and initially pooh-poohed it. But once it was again linked with charitable giving, and the Foundling Hospital, it became the draw it has remained. Soon after, it swept the world, and become the most popular piece of classical music ever. Horace Walpole said of the piece, that it 'gave me an idea of heaven, where everybody is to sing whether they have voices or not'.

Jennens, with his customary irritability, never forgave Handel for opening the piece in Dublin, and managed to persuade his tin ear that the music was lacklustre. Susannah returned to greater success in London, which was now red-faced with shame at its outbreak of mob morality. Delaney married again. Most important of all, by the close of 1742, the Charitable Music Society had raised £1,225, which secured the release of 143 debtor prisoners. As Burney said, 'This great work has fed the hungry, clothed the naked and fostered the orphan.'

It is hard not to be cynical about the charitable efforts of these societies, when the systemic problems in a colonial country remained in place. Hard for cynicism not to grow to anger when such unreformed problems led to the same famine and dispossession a hundred years later. It would be plausible to say that charity changes little, and art less. Yet, in a good recording of the *Messiah* – one with no pomp, no decoration, and no excess of honeyed beauty; where there is urgency and drive and passion – then one air towards the end emerges with force:

> *The trumpet shall sound, and the dead shall be*
> *raised incorruptible, and we shall be changed.*
> *For this corruptible must put on incorruption and*
> *this mortal must put on immortality.*

One phrase here booms out with the pile-driving force of a deep bass voice. Repeated over and over, it hammers the consciousness, and seems to sum up the heart and desires of its creator – *we shall be changed.*

14

A Day of Reckoning

A TALE OF FELA KUTI

THE SHRINE, LAGOS, 1971 ...

A classic night at The Shrine in Lagos had no beginning, middle or end. It began around eleven with 'an intermission', started a second time at around one – with the first notes of its lead performer, Fela Kuti – and then kicked off a third time around three, following the stop for a ritual. The finale came as dawn was pinking the Lagos sky, when Fela would speak of taking a 'short break'. No-one would dare mention a conclusion. It was always starting, sometimes pausing, never finishing. An unending shuffle forwards: forever more to come, perpetually being born.

In honour of this spirit of restless continuum, the evenings invoked here are a composite of three 'Shrines', all in Lagos and its suburbs: the first opened in Yaba in 1971; the second in the Empire Hotel in Mushin, where it stayed until 1977, when the land was seized by the government; and the third, in People Street, which provided Fela with a permanent home. This is not a tale of a single opening event, but of an institution which managed to make *every night* a first night. An event whose aliveness burnt so fierce, it somehow still lives.

THE ARRIVAL OF ABÀMÌ EDÁ

The evening would commence with improvisational chaos, and continue in that spirit. Schedules were scrambled, and time warped into shifting tempos. People gathered in a nearby courtyard, where the equipment for a band was set up. Anyone could sit in behind the drums, or plug in their guitars and play. Musicians warmed up with a jam around a trad-jazz standard like 'Bye Bye Blackbird' or 'My Funny Valentine'. With no announcement and much charisma, Fela Kuti would glide through, dipping in and out of the band, sometimes leading them into a classic, sometimes elaborating a tune haunting his head, locating the music inside himself. Dressed in his trademark skimpy underpants, he would break off to receive guests and journalists like a Speedoed potentate. Lean as a whippet, with skin-taut skull and eyes clouded red from dearth of sleep and excess of marijuana, this slight figure bore natural authority.

As the African night thickened to a treacly blackness, an entourage would mill around the courtyard, blasting their lobes with cannabis. They blended the styling of Mafia henchmen, the earnest aides of a political leader and the groupies of a rock star. Amongst them would be Fela's skimpily dressed twenty-seven wives, painting each other with tattoos and swirls, and warming their bodies up for a marathon night of athletic dancing. At a certain moment, Fela, the *abàmì edá* ('unique being'), would feel his body limber and the stars in alignment, and it was time to go.

He inserts his frame into a lurid jumpsuit stitched with Yoruba symbols, raises his fist in a Black Power salute, gathers his people and begins the short journey, walking in the middle of the surge like a president. His destination, The Shrine, is on the other side of the main Lagos highway. Underlings stream into the road to hold up the cars, causing traffic jams in both directions. Fela, his saxophone around his neck, would sometimes mount a donkey and cross the road clippety-clop, like a biblical figure, stopping the life of modernity, with wives, band and entourage thronged around him. Three times a week, he stopped the city in its tracks. Just to show who bossed the streets.

The Shrine would be jam-packed already, with a support band at work. When Fela arrived, he was joining an energy, already pulsing. With his own contingent, the capacity went from rammed to stuffed. The Shrine had the jerry-built charm of an oversized shebeen. It was almost covered by a corrugated tin roof and surrounded by open sewers. The yard, big enough for a thousand, though regularly stretched to more, was garlanded with the flags of independent African nations. The band lined up on a T-shaped stage, a blue neon outline of Africa behind them. Through the fog of exhaled smoke could be seen wooden platforms draped with fishnets, housing loosely clad dancers performing languorous grinds.

At the gate there would be an eruption of noise. A cluster of kids, students of the new Fela-sophy, escorted the boss towards the stage like a featherweight world champion through Madison Square Garden. They pushed their way through traders hawking goods by candlelight – snacks, drinks, cigarettes and marijuana. A cacophony of catcalls, whistling and chants of *Baba Kuti*, *Fela Baba* and *abàmì* deafened the music. Fela would wait for the previous band to finish, then Baba Ani, the bandleader, appeared as a herald.

Ani hushed the crowd, hurled some backtalk at the hecklers, and then like hawkers the world over gave his man a build-up – 'Introducing to you, the one and only, A-bà-mì E-dá, Fela Anikulapo Kuti'. This was accompanied by a swooping and surging burst of percussion and brass, with guitars screeching, cresting and rough-riding, in no particular order. And then they all as suddenly stopped. Fela was at the mike, pausing, swaying, mischievous eyes scanning the crowd – his crowd – urchins, politicians, poets, prostitutes, activists, bandits and business people. This was his constituency. He knew their hunger for laughter and a night of happy carelessness. After glaring and staring and connecting, all while taking deep draws from a torch-sized joint, he finally speaks.

'Everybody say "Ye-ye"!'

The crowd roars back, and Fela is off, rampaging on a free-form attack on his government: 'Bros and sisters, if you want to know how corrupt this country is, that word *corruption* has lost its meaning here!'

Fela flips his head back in haughty arrogance, barrels out his chest to monster himself, and imitates the oil-rich fatcats who swank their way through the poverty of Lagos: 'Yeah, I'm corrupt, man!'

The crowd roars approval, as Fela tears on, preaching as if to a revivalist Church: 'You see, bros and sisters, I know dem. They are nothing but spirit beings. They are the same motherfuckers who sold Africans into slavery hundreds of years ago. In fact, the same spirit controls America and England now. Everyone is here to play their same role again. I want you all to know that tonight; I call this time the era of *second slavery*. They don't have to come here and take us by force – our leaders sell us up front. Everybody say "Ye-ye".

The audience shouts 'Ye-ye' back at him, studded with exhortations of 'Yab den!' (Stick it to them!).

'Bros and sisters, I'm gonna play you a little music now.'

Fela turns and gives his orchestra a glare they know well. They watch him carefully. He has unlimited authority on stage, like a schoolmaster with satanic connections. He fines his musicians on the spot if they make a mistake. Slowly, he claps the song's tempo to the band, wiggling his thin frame to the rhythm. A guitarist snakes his way through a single-note line, soon joined by some clattering from a *gbedu* drum. Fela lifts his hands over his head and dances the rhythm section in.

Time shifts towards a trance, soon to envelop the crowd. The chirping of the percussion frames an intricate tapestry. Stepping in behind his electric organ, Fela improvises around the beat weaving a noise of tighter and tighter packed density. On a nod and a glare, the horn section blare in, announcing the song's theme. With instrumental solos to come, exhibitions of dancing and more preaching, it will be a full fifteen minutes before Fela even gets to the lyrics. Already the audience are swaying in shared celebration. This magical hybrid of music, mysticism and eroticism is entering its zone. Another night at The Shrine is in motion.

On, on into the night, Fela orchestrates his communal hallucination. On, on, his featherweight frame warps and struts. Lithe and twisting, the air in the room seems to vibrate with him. He pumps a saxophone till it wails, and pounds an electric organ until the high notes rattle the tin roof. The on-rushing beat shakes the walls. No-one crammed into the room, surrendering wholly to the present moment, would remember when it started, or imagine when it would stop. No-one wants it to stop or to start, no-one wants it ever not to be.

THE MUSIC AND ITS MAKING

Jazz and funk, African chanting and classical composition came together in this unstoppable confection – Fela's invention of Afrobeat. His musical education was rich. As a twenty-year-old, in the 1950s, he was sent to London to study medicine. He skipped that course and instead enrolled in the Trinity College of Music to study composition and piano. He rebelled against some of the traditions here, but not all. Asked later who was his favourite musician, he said 'Handel'. It is hard to imagine a more antithetical figure than the bewigged eighteenth-century German porker, but both were genii and both showmen. Fela's aspiration was to make 'African Classical music'.

In London, Fela formed a group, Koola Lobitos, that played highlife jazz, but that was only the beginning. His later travels across America introduced him to the cutting edge of bebop, and gave him new heroes in Charlie Parker and Miles Davis. Behind much of his work was the tornado of energy and innovation that was James Brown, something of a god in West Africa in the 1960s. Afrobeat was an evolution from the cheery Highlife of Ghana, incorporating the deep funk of Brown and the complex polyrhythms of Yoruban music.

On his return from the US, everything changed. The songs got longer and funkier, their content grew from love to social issues, and their language transformed:

> I changed the name of my group from Koola Lobitos to Africa 70. Koola Loobitos meant nothing. It was a stupid name. Africa 70 had a meaning. It was looking to the future, to the coming decade. Then we opened The Shrine. Why Shrine? 'Cause I wanted some place meaningful, of progressive, mindful background with roots.

When the first Shrine opened in 1971, Fela was all but composing his tracks in public. Every week, an audience member would shout a request for a classic, and Kuti would rebuke, 'I used to play that when I was blind, like you now are.' Show nights were about invention. The crowd hungered for fresh material, and so did their prime artist. Each show, new songs were worked through, Fela riffing lyrics out of his political speeches and his current obsessions, and working his band through arrangements live on stage. Masterpieces like 'Lady', 'Go Slow' and 'Water No Get Enemy' emerged from this rough-hewn forum.

For the audience, these songs were the sounding board of their pain and rage. Forged in every new moment, Fela articulated the pain and salvation of his people.

A compulsive performer, Fela's singing voice was far from melodious; it had the Dylanesque rasp of a battered prophet. Its intention was not to seduce but to awake. His face off-stage could be as expressionless as a death mask, on-stage it flared to life with crazed humour. His frail frame carrying brass it seemed ill-equipped to lift, he would blow his trumpet amongst an army of horns, or solo zigzag patterns on a tenor sax. From a family of musicians, he was prodigiously gifted. Once he had a row with his tenor saxophonist Igo Chico. Refusing to allow insubordination, he sacked Chico on the spot. When asked who was to play his solos the next night, Fela said himself. He practised the instrument for seventeen hours straight, and sailed through.

The Shrine soon became just that for the world's musical connoisseurs. Ginger Baker, the jazz and rock drummer of the age, declared this was the only interesting music happening anywhere, and joined the band for a season. As crazed as Fela, their relationship had its tensions. The political rulers Kuti was always aggravating were Baker's companions on the polo pitch. William 'Bootsy' Collins, the bass guitarist in the James Brown Band, became a devotee: 'They're the funkiest cats we ever heard in our life. We were totally wiped out! That was the one trip I wouldn't trade for nothing in the world.' Paul McCartney, in Lagos to record *Band on the Run*, had a touchingly un-neurotic reaction to the sheer quality of the music. He burst into tears of happiness.

THE BUTTOCKS SPECIAL

Music is ancient, but no more ancient than its chicken-and-egg partner, dance. The latter was central to The Shrine's Dionysiac shenanigans. In the centre was Fela, a jittering figure amongst his cavorting troupe, the spirit of Pan tremoring through him, his eyebrows arching with mischief and his backside twerking way ahead of its time. He would leap from stage to floor and back again – in the words of his cousin, the dramatist Wole Soyinka, 'like a brown, scalded cat, whose miaaow was a rustle of riffs eased from a saxophone'.

He would grab a wife/dancer by the hair, pull her forward to the centre of the circle, and give her, all-tattooed and in raffia skirts, centre stage. Shuddering as if possessed, as if she had picked up a current of Bacchanalian electrics from Kuti, she would interpret the complex rhythms. The twists and turns of others swirled around her, as she executed famed routines of athletic eroticism such as 'opening up', in which a dancer spins on one leg while raising high the other and wiggling her derriere, or the 'buttocks special', in which the dancer stands stock-still while twitching only her butt-cheeks in patterns against the beat.

Behind her, fellow wives thrust in and out of engagement with invisible partners across the stage. Fela, the unapologetic pasha, would signal a dancer to stop if she tired; then another would shimmy in to pick up the baton. This was no place for the woke, yet throughout its life The Shrine was seen as a safe space for women, a place they could go without being harassed. Though, since this was the opinion of Fela, and he had twenty-seven wives, it might need to be taken with a pinch of salt. He had no stock with anyone regulating sex:

Sex is a gift of nature. Why do men make laws to check it? One law telling you where to fuck, and another telling you when to fuck.

TWEAKING AUTHORITY'S NOSE

In the dark streets outside the club, soldiers lurk. Nigeria has just emerged from a long civil war. One region, Biafra, has attempted to secede. Millions have died and, though Nigeria emerged victorious, its society has become militarised. Federal soldiers walk the streets, the brutality of the recent violence still coursing through them. The licence they were given to punish the Igbo people still empowers them. They were the winners of the war, and want to be victors still, even when there is no enemy.

Fela pronounces:

Biafra war just finished, you see. Federal soldiers walking round with fuckin' guns and sticks; pushing people around and acting so big-o! They the 'victors', you see! You get me now?

The thorn in their side is this club, and its visionary leader. Fela was born into a politicised middle-class family, with two formidable parents. His father was the head of the National Union of Teachers, and his mother, a pioneering feminist activist, was the first modern African woman to travel to China, where she met Mao Zedong. She was a renowned Pan-African politician, who counted Ghana's founding president, Kwame Nkrumah, amongst her friends.

Fela Kuti loves to tweak the nose of authority. The status of his family, and the size of his following, initially throws a cordon sanitaire around him. But there is only so much nose-tweaking that authority will take. Nigeria is afflicted by the twin traumas of postcolonial toxicity and the fresh confusion brought by massive oil wealth. No sooner have the British removed their influence than they and others are back trying to exploit Nigeria's natural resources. Stable consensual government is not their goal. Brute military dictatorship serves the turn of the new petro-state.

The plight of the labouring millions trapped between a violent government and rapacious multinationals called out a response from Fela. His career could have been as a cheerful Highlife entertainer travelling the world with a happy trumpet, exemplifying the archetype of the long-suffering but buoyant African. He was having none of that. He knew the people of Lagos wanted something angrier and more daring. Smiling compliance was replaced by glaring defiance.

In the course of Fela's career he was arrested, and his home and workplace raided, nearly two hundred times. Almost every time, he was beaten, sometimes within inches of his life. His son Femi was forced to witness his father's punishment: 'They handcuffed his hands to his legs and threw him in the back of a Land Rover, and he was bleeding from head to toe. They beat him so much he remembered his spirit leaving his body. He thought he was dead. When he felt his spirit go back into his body, he never felt so much pain.'

On one early occasion he was taken to the notorious Alagbon Close Jail. There he was hailed as the president of the most brutal of its cells, named Kalakuta, after the Black Hole of Calcutta. On his release, he memorialised the experience in a protest song 'Kalakuta Show'. He also decided to declare the commune he had created an independent state within Nigeria. He named it the Kalakuta Republic.

The idea of creating a place open to every African escaping persecution began taking shape in my mind. A communal compound – one like Africans had been living in for thousands of years – a place open

to everybody. I'd think to myself: 'Ah-ah! What is this city shit-o?
One man, one wife, one house isolated from everybody else in the
neighbourhood? Is an African not even to know his neighbours?'
Man, even the Bible says, 'Know thy neighbour!' So why all this
individualism shit? This 'mine'. That 'yours'. That 'theirs'. What's
that shit? Is it African?

Within the theatre of Fela's life, the founding of a republic was both
an absurdist and a realistic action. His compound was a commune and
a recording studio, but also a new political entity, and he was its leader.
When the armed forces raided, which they did with frequency, they
were invading a sovereign state. The Kalakuta Republic, with its sexual
openness, narcotic freedom and permanent opposition, was a sort of
whacked-out utopia within a wider craziness.

A NERVOUS CHICKEN

Saturday is 'Divination Night', when The Shrine earns its name. In one
corner is a cubicle, housing a set of Fela's personal deities. There are busts
and photos of his pan-African heroes – Nkrumah, Malcolm X, Patrice
Lumumba and, after her death, his ever-adored mother. Alongside these
were icons devoted to Yoruba divinities, including Esu, the trickster and
divine interpreter; Ogun, the god of creativity; and Sango, the god of
thunder. On Divination Night, at a certain point, Kuti will call for silence
to pay homage to ancestors and gods. The resulting ritual, both ancient
and as freshly minted as the music, occupies fifteen minutes of rapturous
seriousness. Fela has appointed himself high priest.

What did the spirit say? It said that the dead people of Africa weren't
being taken care of. And that I was supposed to start teaching
others to care for their dead. It said there is no Africa left. That only
Kalakuta was Africa.

The cubicle is lit in disco colours of red, green and blue. Beyond the icons
are small mounds of earth on which are placed honey, palm-soaked wicks
and shells. Three bottles of Gordon's gin are hidden away in a corner. A
tethered chicken looks on, with justifiable nervousness.

An acolyte starts the ceremony by lighting the wicks, and a rhythm
is beaten out on a metal gong. A bass drum and cymbals accelerate

the beat, rising to a crescendo just as the smoke from the burning wick forms its widest cloud. At that point, Fela emerges with attendants – masked with white chalk powder. Fela crouches, picks up some shells and kola nuts, casts them on a tray, and attempts to divine their meaning. His face moves between happiness and confusion, concern and calm. He tastes the honey with the fingers of his left hand, sprinkles some gin around to keep the gods happy, and then pours the remainder on the lit wicks, which flare up to bathe the high priest in ecstatic light.

Time is up for the chicken. Fela grabs the poor beast and tears its neck open with both hands. He lifts it above his head and opens his mouth wide to receive the dripping blood. His eyes glitter with a strange access; his body is dripping sweat and now sprayed crimson; his teeth and mouth are stained red. He glares emptily into nowhere, floating in a shamanic limbo. His body is trapped between motion and stillness, and invested with a compulsive charisma. He breaks the magic with a shift of his head, muttering imprecations.

Pouring palm wine into a calabash and drinking a little, he slowly returns to the world and back within his own body. His spirit bears his fleshly frame back to the stage, where he is handed a four-inch joint. He sucks on it, as if it will save his life. His face disappears into a cloud of smoke. When it reappears, looking as if he has travelled far away and returned with news, like a visiting prelate from a more beautiful universe, he starts to tell truths.

WHO JAILS SOCIETY?

On, on, the musical parliament of Nigeria puts on its thrice-weekly show. From a distance, the strobing coloured lights tint the haze of dust and fumes which enshroud The Shrine. Just as the horns' wail, the drum's throb and the rhythm guitar's ceaseless tickle echo through the Lagos night. From the streets outside can be heard the crowd's chant-along of political choruses:

A day of reckoning is coming
A day of reckoning is coming'

Friday night is called 'Yabis Night', and this is when Fela talks politics. It is current affairs night.

Who the fuck is Society? Who jails Society when it does horrors to people? Why Society does nothing to help beggars; to provide jobs and keep people from having to steal just to chop? Why don't Society fight against corruption, punish the powerful ..? Fuck society, man. It's unjust! Fuck society, man.

On these nights Fela savages the government for their inefficiency and incompetence, and preaches a new freedom of expression. These Yabis sessions are about raising consciousness. Fela excoriates his upbringing within a British dependency: 'When you are a colonial boy, you don't know anything about your own culture.' And, about the distorted history he was fed: 'I saw that colonial education and upbringing, which America was involved in too, was very badly wild. History starts with Mungo Park *discovering* the Niger!'

The politics were stitched into everything, including the fabric of the music. The transition from Highlife to Afrobeat was an ideological choice. In the course of his journey through the US, Fela fell in love with the Black Power activist Sandra Izsadore. She opened up a world of militancy to him, introducing him to thinkers like Malcolm X and Stokely Carmichael. His eyes were opened to how his sense of reality had been shaped by neocolonial control. Like soul, his music would now be determinedly 'Black and proud'.

'When I was young we weren't even allowed to speak our own languages in school. They called it *vernacular*, as if only English was the real tongue.' His new language was pidgin – the language of the streets – and its compacted simplicity was ideal for his bullet lyrics.

There were gentler attempts to educate. Books and published speeches were sold at The Shrine. After a performance, winding down in the dawn of a new day, students would be received by Fela in professorial mode. He would sit with piles of books, and tell kids, 'You know nothing, go and read this book ...' The Shrine served as a platform for the exchange of ideas. The students would bring their concerns to Fela. The problems they brought would work their way into his songs. There was a dynamic and direct exchange between the worries of the audience and the creation of the artist. They were making form and content together.

The Shrine reinvented the idea of a club, filling that form with new energies, shamanic and spiritual, radical and activist, all within the ceaseless twitching propulsion of Afrobeat.

It is a light year away from stadium rock.

EXORCISM

Fela's adopted middle name was Aníkulápó, which could be translated as 'He who carries death in his pouch', or interpreted as 'He who will choose when is the moment for death to take him'..Fela certainly seemed in possession of a liberal scattering of lives, more than nine cats. The beatings that he, his wives and his companions took from the military were savage and remorseless. The men were flayed with wire, the women raped with bottles. No matter how hard they were knocked down, the more determined they were to get back up again.

In a moment of heartless cruelty set against many others, soldiers threw his mother out of a second-floor window. She died a year later from medical complications. A chunk of Fela's hold on normality went with his mother's passing. But it wasn't the soldiers who finally caught up with him; rather, his own unlicensed appetites. He died from AIDS in 1997, having refused to accept any treatment from Western doctors. His funeral was his last great show, and again he stopped Lagos.

Since then, his music has come and gone in popularity, though a Broadway musical, the enthusiastic patronage of Beyoncé and Jay-Z, and a growing sense of the rare genius of his musicianship, has secured his status. The Shrine lives on as the New Afrika Shrine, run by his son Femi, and is now a Lagos institution, both memorialising the greatness of the past, and pointing forward to new musical futures. It is attended by visiting presidents, musicians and tourists. It is still live every night, though it is doubtful it can ever be as dirtily, as dangerously, as chaotically alive as it was then. It was a brew of political and musical Dionysiac excess that has rarely been matched.

There was an ancient practice of exorcism in China where a priest would attend a supposedly haunted house and bring with him four deranged people (or actors impersonating madness). They would charge around the house, hurling their bodies hither and thither and emitting terrifying shrieks. Whether they were accepting the possession into themselves, or scaring it off by out-madding it, is moot. But the ceremony was effective. Watching Fela and his dancers now – brilliant, creative and possessed – it can seem they were enacting a similar exorcism on behalf of their community. They were taking the pain and violence of their country's colonial history, and its brutalised present, into their bodies, allowing its toxicity to enter their bloodstreams and jitter their spirits, and then finding a way of hurling it back out into the ether through craft and art. They enacted the full sickness, they named it and, for the night at least, they helped it to pass away.

15

A Song Already Sung

A TALE OF ANTON CHEKHOV
AND *THE SEAGULL*

3 AM, 18 OCTOBER 1896, ST PETERSBURG

Anton Pavlovich Chekhov, aged thirty-six, lay in the dark fully clothed, a blanket pulled firmly over his head. His friend Suvorin, in whose flat he was staying, moved for the light switch. Words emerged from within the blanket. 'Don't turn the light on. I beg you.'

Suvorin explained that Chekhov's sister, Masha, was waiting in the drawing room, and the rest of his family out scouring the city for him.

'I don't want to see anyone. I'll say just one thing.'

A brief pause.

'If I ever write anything for the stage again, you can call me a [very rude word].'

No-one had seen Chekhov since moments after the show, when he strode into the office where his director, Evtikhy Karpov, was hiding (never a good sign). With his face frozen into a rictus, and his lips blue, he had whispered, 'The author has failed.' He had then stolen out past the stage door with collar raised. An audience member pointed and said, 'That is the writer!' – to which his witty companion added, 'And a terrible one!' Chekhov disappeared into the freezing streets of

St Petersburg and walked to the Peripheral Canal before working his way back to the centre of town, and sitting alone in shock in Romanov's restaurant. Finally, with friends searching the city, and glancing with fear into the ice-floed Neva, he had sneaked back to his room.

'Where have you been?', Suvorin ventured to ask.

'Walking the streets. Sitting. If I live another seven hundred years, I won't let any theatre have another play.'

Suvorin chose this moment to unburden himself of several insights he had on how to improve the play. This was not wise. Chekhov's response was brusque. Suvorin retreated to the drawing room where Masha was withering under the assault of his wife's small talk. He told her she could call off the search parties: 'You can calm down. Your brother is back, he's lying under a blanket.' Then he tried his ideas for improving the play on her. On some nights, everyone is a critic.

The last thing Chekhov said to Suvorin was: 'I'm taking the first train out of Petersburg. Don't try to stop me.' True to his word, he ghosted out the next morning, leaving notes for the many who had travelled Russia to share in his supposed triumph. One friend accompanied him to the station. Anton was warned that the noon train was a slow goods train, but was not to be stopped. 'All the better. I'll sleep and dream of glory. Tomorrow I'll be at Melikhovo. What bliss! No actors, no directors, no public, no newspapers.' A newsboy came up and tried to sell him a paper. 'I don't read', he told the boy, and then, to his friend, 'See what a kind face he has, yet his hands are full of poison. In every paper a review.'

As the train pulled out, the friend looked into the writer's shifting theatre of a face, and saw bottomless hurt. Chekhov sat for a day and night in an ill-heated train. As a doctor, he knew what this could mean. For a delicate consumptive, who had recently been coughing gobbets of blood into his handkerchief, this was bad medicine.

7 OCTOBER 1896, IN TRANSIT

Chekhov was too wise to fall into as clumsy a trap as hubris, but he was heedless as he headed north eleven days before. 'The thirst for fame' was pulling him to the northern capital, he wrote to a friend. The Alexandrinsky, the theatre which was to premiere *The Seagull*, was and is an auditorium to make the most ascetic soul feel bubbly. A many-tiered jewel in red and gold, it feels like performing in Champagne.

The opening night was to be a benefit performance for a much-loved comedienne called Elizaveta Levkeeva. She was a star, a jolly and buxom figure of warmth, who only had to appear on stage to tickle up a laugh. Chekhov had been seduced by the excitement and glamour attached to her benefit, but should have heard warning bells. The mismatch between his category-smasher of a play, and the music-hall charms of Levkeeva, was unfortunate. It would be like Samuel Beckett sharing a new work with a benefit for Hattie Jacques. Potentially brilliant, but high-risk.

Allowing himself a little self-delight as a hot playwright, Chekhov wrote letters full of shy exuberance to friends and family, inviting them to share in his potential joy. He wanted them to attend the first night, though his eagerness to host was tempered by the knowledge that he had ransacked their lives for his narrative. A perennial problem for all playwrights, this was acute for Chekhov, who mercilessly burgled the affairs, failed marriages, suicides and artistic failures of his social circle for his stories. He was always amazed when they got upset.

Though he had fears for this play, and his past premieres had been patchy, he knew there was something fresh in *The Seagull*. He knew it could break through theatre's dullness of convention; 'Life is a jumble', he explained, 'where the profound exists alongside the trivial, the great with the insignificant, the tragic with the ridiculous. To express this, new forms are needed.'

Chekhov's intoxication was such on arrival in St Petersburg that he failed to attend the first rehearsal of his own play on 9 October. This was a mistake. It was not a happy occasion. The part of Nina, a febrile ingénue of eighteen, had been given to Mariya Savina, a substantial diva of forty-two. She had doubts about her own suitability, and chose to bypass the first rehearsal as well. The director, Karpov, clearly had no understanding of the nature of the play and had cast his mistress, Kolmskaia, in another leading role. Levkeeva, the queen of the benefit, had lobbied for the third leading female part, but the company had rebelled. Since it was her benefit, she attended the read-through, and listened with a sour face. Once it was finished, she let everyone know she was delighted she wasn't in it, since it was so unremittingly glum. 'Never had there been such a shambles in our ant hill', one of the cast wrote.

When Chekhov did show up to rehearsals, he was dismayed. The cast were distinguished but incoherent, carelessly bunged together for a commercial success without thought for the balance of the ensemble or the style of the play. Their acting revealed their lack of understanding and their constant desire to be vivid. The playwright attempted to explain: 'The chief thing, my friends, is that theatricality is unnecessary. Really unnecessary. It is simple. These are all simple, ordinary people.' His advice was unavailing. Once a company have decided they have to be interesting to help a play, the cause is almost lost. The director and actors asked for clues and Chekhov said despairingly, 'Listen to the play, I wrote it all down, it is there.' They were looking elsewhere.

There were only ever going to be nine days of rehearsal, and time became further attenuated after three, when Savina left the show. She had worked out that the twenty-four-year age gap between herself and her character Nina wasn't aiding the cause of realism. The next day she started to feel unemployed and returned, demanding the part of Masha. The company refused amid tumult. When Chekhov attended rehearsals on the sixth day, several of the cast were absent; those present were reading from their script; and the director had caught the fashion for absence, and vacated the room. At the end of the day, as Simon Callow memorably put it, 'the entire point of a director is turning up'. Being there, and pulling everyone else into the same space, is the primary function. When this breaks down, problems multiply.

Outside rehearsals, Chekhov carried on his usual social and romantic whirl. His health was troubling and, one night when dining with Suvorin, he filled up an ice bucket beside their table with handkerchiefs stained crimson. His feelings about rehearsals had darkened his optimism. He was still wasting energy inviting friends and trying to disperse them correctly around the auditorium, splitting up ex-lovers and ex-wives, and present lovers and present wives, and feuding writers. He could not lie to his sister, though, and wrote: 'The play will not be a sensation, it will be dismal. I advise you not to come.' Nothing could stop her.

With two days left, there was a surge of optimism. The new Nina, Vera Komisarzhevskaya, was a talent, and her boldness and clarity helped set a tempo for the others. For a brief moment, hope emerged. But it was the hope that later hurts. When they moved into the theatre, they encountered the sets. These had not been built for *The Seagull*, but instead were stock sets for bourgeois farces. Vera, was fatally undermined by them (for her final monologue she was hidden behind a big table) and also by her costumes (her principal dress had been built for Savin, who was considerably more ample). When the director was criticised by the cast, he walked out again.

The full dress rehearsal on the 16th, with a cast riven and exhausted, was a disaster. Chekhov asked timorously if they could take the show off, but the blind hope of theatrical despair prevailed.

17 OCTOBER 1896, THE ALEXANDRINSKY

Bizarrely, a terrible dress rehearsal often presages a sudden switch-back and a triumphant first show. The fear of falling and crashing can galvanise everyone. The actors give of their best and the audience respond. Electricity feeds electricity and both discover the story anew together. A healthy dose of panic cleanses the mind, and opens out new vistas. Perversely, a strong dress rehearsal can create complacency, and over-relaxation, and show and audience deflate together on their first encounter. But, sometimes, it just doesn't happen. Sometimes a terrible dress rehearsal leads to a worse first night. *The Seagull* in St Petersburg was the worst first night anyone could remember in a Russian theatre.

Anton met his sister off the Moscow train, looking drawn and sullen. Fits of coughing doubled him up as they walked up the platform. Unable to dissimulate in front of his sister, he sputtered out between coughs: 'The actors don't know their parts. They understand nothing. Their acting is horrible. The play will flop. You shouldn't have come.' He parked her at her hotel, went and cut his hair, put on his best new playwright garb, steeled his spirit and presented himself at the theatre.

A first-night audience – any audience, in fact – is always a volatile mix. Casting it, arranging it and managing it is a delicate art. It takes lifetimes of practice and instinct. However well a producer may craft it, there are always myriad factors that can unsettle careful balances and disturb hoped-for patterns. A single toxic presence (and the world is full of them) can wreck an atmosphere, just as a good and warm heart can beguile the air around them. An opening night will always attract more than its fair share of the toxic, so one needs compensating reservoirs of good heart. These are calculations when there is hope for success. For two reasons, *The Seagull* never got close.

First and most disastrous was the mismatch with Levkeeva's benefit night. *The Seagull* was essentially a curtain-raiser for a short farce of sexual merriment, starring Levkeeva, which was to crown the evening; two and a half hours of Chekhov is a long time to wait for the theatrical equivalent of a *Carry On* film. Her fans had come along for a barrel of laughs, and their patience for the flowing eddies of Chekhovian life was limited. This contingent were first surprised and then quickly frustrated. Some misjudged the tone, and howled with laughter when Masha offered Medvedenko a pinch of snuff. Others were aggressive and heckled. When Konstantin laid the symbolic dead seagull at Nina's feet, a moment of carefully orchestrated stage poetry, a wag shouted: 'Why does he carry that dead duck around?' Others lost interest quickly, twisted round in their seats, and started loud conversations with their neighbours. The action of the play soon became inaudible. By the time they got to the play-within-the-play, when the curtain rose on the inner stage and Vera, wrapped in a big rug, began the symbolist monologue 'People, lions, eagles, grouse', she was met with open laughter, loud conversations and hissing.

Masha, Chekhov's sister, remembered: 'From the first moment I sensed the public's indifference and ironic attitude ... I felt cold inside. At the end of Act One, thin applause was drowned by hissing, and offensive remarks ... I sat it out in my box.' There were three acts left to go. Some of the actors had changed tone midstream and tried to jolly it along on the terms the audience wanted. Others lost confidence and disappeared into themselves. Vera Komisarzhevskaya was shattered. White and shaking in the wings, she asked Karpov the director, with tears in her eyes, if she could skip the rest of the show: 'I'm afraid to go on stage ... I can't act ... I'll run from the theatre.' Karpov said something kind and supportive along the lines of 'GET THE FUCK BACK ON', and pushed her back into the bear pit. The play was lost.

Chekhov could maybe have survived the consequences of the mismatch with the audience for Levkeeva's benefit. He could have made a joke of it. What he could not survive was the concerted viciousness of the other contingent, the vulture literati. Once a journalist like them, he had been on an extraordinary ride with his short stories, with Suvorin lavishing endless attention on him in the fashionable *New Times*. He was being spoken of in the same breath as Tolstoy and Turgenev. Those who had once been colleagues were never going to forgive him such success. A couple of years later, he wrote:

> At the time of the first act I was struck by a particular circumstance, namely that those with whom I had always been frank and friendly, with whom I had dined pleasantly, and on whose behalf I had broken lances – all wore a strange expression, terribly strange ... I cannot forget what happened any more than I could forget a punch in the face.

There is a streak of cruelty, dysfunctional cruelty in those who exercise power without responsibility. And when they come together, the scent of prey in their nostrils, there are few sights more life-denying.

Chekhov's friends were gobsmacked by the glee with which his literary confrères went about wrecking his night. One saw a group huddling together, then dispersing to provoke more belligerent behaviour from the Levkeeva fans. The *Theatregoer* magazine wrote a retrospective opinion piece about the ugliness of this behaviour, observing 'a furious malignant joy among certain parts of the audience – especially those judges of the "Scribbling brotherhood". They were out to settle accounts.' The contingent of wing-clippers wandered the theatre's corridors during the three intervals crowing, 'symbolic trash', 'he's written himself out', 'the fall of a talent' and 'why doesn't he stick to his short stories?' These were not *Daily Mail* or *Sun* kind of critics – they couldn't have hurt Chekhov – these were the smooth-faced assassins of the *Guardian* or *Observer*, those he had foolishly believed had some shared commitment to caring for art, life and politics. More fool Chekhov. This was what broke him. It cankered his feelings, and left a scar he never recovered from. He would never again attend a first night.

He didn't make it to the end of this one. At some point in the second act, he rushed backstage. There he found refuge in probably the least suitable place, the dressingroom of the beneficiary, Levkeeva. He sat there for an hour or so with head bowed, a single lock of hair falling over his brow, his pince-nez sitting crookedly on the bridge of his nose. Levkeeva looked at him with bulging eyes, half in pity, half in apology, with no idea what to say. Catatonically still, Chekhov slipped into a dissociated state, and watched uniformed theatre officials and a policeman coming and going, flirting with the actresses. From his detachment he observed how men became officials who were unable to cope with life, just as those who attached themselves to art and the theatre had no alternative but to be officials. The thought struck him, then he stood and bolted.

After he fled into the night, Levkeeva herself came on to perform the old warhorse of a farce. The audience went crazy, interrupting the show with speeches, gifts and kisses. Amid the madness, *The Seagull* entirely disappeared. A few, a very few, were able to discern within the craziness the emergence of something new. Tchaikovsky wrote: 'It is many years since the stage last gave me such pleasure, and the audience gave me such unhappiness, as on Levkeeva's benefit night.'

MELIKHOVO, 1897, AND MAKING LIFE BETTER

When Chekhov wished for Melikhovo, caught in the agonies of rejection, he wished for his spiritual home. A small estate, about eighty miles from Moscow, it featured a diminutive lake and a modest house in a softly magical green wilderness. Essentially a wooden bungalow of about five rooms, with generous windows pouring ever-shifting light into each room, it was fronted by a delightfully pompous porch. Good-humouredly grandiose columns supported tiny crenellations, like a parody of a castle. In *Death of a Salesman*, the one thing that roots Willy Loman to his life is the porch he built. The porch in Melikhovo was the perfect expression of Chekhov's sensibility. It is a bungalow palace, modest and mighty, where small details of life are magnified into a kindly comic absurdity.

Chekhov's plays are not only observation, nor reflection. He knew there was no beauty without seriousness, and that every writer must understand a purpose. Even if life would always defeat it. His life in Melikhovo was an expression of the same. He sank himself into the life of his community with a passion equalled only by his work. He was a doctor and treated his local patients; he established a local post office; he opened a small hospital with his own money and funds he raised; he established a local school; he agitated for a road to be built from the local station to the river. This was not do-gooding, nor was it shouting one's morals to prove one's sanctity – this was a serious commitment to the well-being of others, mostly the poor and weak. They were passions throughout his life. The disparity between them and the sleek assassins of St Petersburg was a bridge too hard for anyone to bear.

In *The Seagull* and elsewhere, Chekhov took the small details of the currents of life and made them sacred. To achieve this, the objective presentation of life would not suffice – a writer of worth must be prepared to observe the chasm between life as it is, and life as it should be. In Melikhovo, on a small scale, he did all he could to improve the life around him: in his plays, he presented life as it flows, beyond the perceptions or judgements of its participants, yet within a frame which is conscious of its beautiful potential and sorrows over its falling away.

Lost in the swirl of the everyday in Melikhovo, somehow Chekhov could retreat to his humble desk, and re-create in his tragicomedies the shimmering veils of life-as-is, and life-as-should-be. Because of his attuned ear for the music of happenstance, he did it with a harmony which always sounds to an audience like a song they have already sung.

MOSCOW, 1898

Not too far away, two men, Nemirovich and Stanislavsky, a producer and an actor-director, were dreaming of making a theatre which could eradicate the faults which had bedevilled *The Seagull* in St Petersburg. Proper rehearsal time, a true ensemble of equal talents, careful use of design elements, and a commitment to truth, were the conditions they dreamt of. After much lobbying and begging, their dream was close to fruition. They had been promised a stage – the Hermitage Theatre – and the money to pay a company of actors about 900 roubles a year. Enough to keep a talented group committed.

The Moscow Arts Theatre could now be born. They needed scripts. Nemirovich was determined that *The Seagull* should be part of their first season. A play called *Czar Fyodor* was to be first. This was exactly the sort of vehicle for spectacle which was meat and drink for Stanislavky's desire to show off. He had gained a reputation for his crowd scenes and this afforded plenty of opportunities to dazzle. He didn't like *The Seagull* at all, asking his producer colleague, 'Are you sure it can be performed? I can't make head or tail of it.' He wasn't too sure about the playwright, either. Their only encounters had been awkward negotiations of status. Their first meeting was at a fancy-dress ball, though sadly it is unrecorded what these two titans of theatrical art were dressed as.

Nemirovich, however, insisted and eventually Stanislavsky conceded that *The Seagull* could have a small coda role as the final play of the first season. The job was to persuade Chekhov to join in. *The Seagull* had recovered some of Chekhov's reputation in provincial theatres, but the playwright was still in a state of shock from the pundit-mugging he had received in the Alexandrinsky. He didn't want to lose another year of happiness. All life was short – his especially so.

Nemirovich wrote a long letter of elaborate praise. Chekhov declined. He wrote another saying he would come and visit. Chekhov declined again, saying he wouldn't pick him up from the station. He wrote a third letter, and there was no reply. Nemirovich decided to take that as acceptance, and proceeded. Chekhov then travelled to Moscow to talk with them both from the 18th to the 20th of June. Something of their youth and idealism brought a reluctant smile to the playwright's heart, and he consented.

Stanislavsky headed to his brother's house on the edge of the steppes and spent a month working out a detailed *mise en scène*. In design notes, he described the scenery, the costumes, the make-up, the posture and the gaits of the actors. He cluttered the stage up with traffic hazards – seats, bushes, trees, tables – all as opportunities for clever business. He laid down the law for the inflection, gestures and pauses of each actor at every moment. His theories about how actors should spontaneously discover the inner truth of their characters' lives were a thing of the future:

I did not care for the feelings of the actor! I sincerely believed it was possible to tell people to live and feel as I liked them to; I wrote down directions for everybody and those directions had to be carried out.

Stanislavsky wanted to squeeze every drop of theatrical magic from the play, and to fill the stage with activity and action. He wanted it to bustle. However, he decided that the dominant mood of *The Seagull* should be one of depression and melancholy, a pre-emptive decision which Chekhov was later to fight. Stanislavsky's addiction to external devices was something he was later to regret, but, right or wrong, there was a passion in his approach which was the antithesis of the haphazard shabbiness of the Alexandrinsky.

On his return to Moscow, Stanislavsky moved into the Hermitage Theatre with Nemirovich. It was a dump – badly built, filthy and cold. Tired old posters peeled on the walls, the curtain was mildewed and moth-eaten, the front-of-house uniforms much the same. The whole place stank of spilt beer and vodka. Its previous life was as a music hall with a pleasure garden attached. In bad weather, everyone had brought their booze into the auditorium. When Stanislavsky tried to knock a nail into his dressingroom wall, he knocked a brick clean out of the wall, and cold wind streamed through. The chimneys had collapsed, so there was no heating. The electricity was bust, so they rehearsed by candlelight.

The new team had little money, but they rolled up their sleeves and set to. They whitewashed the walls, replaced the blousy old curtain with one of plain grey cloth, put linen covers on the seats, and covered the faded carpets with rugs. They cleaned the windows, and carefully placed laurel trees and flowers to cover the creeping damp and peeling paper. A little life and a sense of spring returned.

9 SEPT, 1898, MOSCOW

Chekhov came up to join the company on the first day of rehearsal on 9 September. He wasn't going to repeat the mistakes he had made in St Petersburg. If you are going to have an effect, it has to be early. He also knew that neither his health nor his nerves would allow him to stay too long with the company, and time was precious. The company showed him two acts, and he was surprised by the amount of work and discussion already invested. The actors were unknown, but their enthusiasm was infectious. One of them, Olga Knipper, who was playing Arkadina, caught his eye and tightened his heart a little. She was to be the last love of his life.

The cast were keen to listen to Chekhov rather than look past him. His response was oblique. As Olga described it:

> We were all taken in by the unusually subtle charm of his personality, of his simplicity, his inability to 'teach', or 'show' ... When Anton was asked a question, he replied in an odd way, as if at a tangent, as if in general, and we didn't know how to take his remarks – seriously or in jest.

Chekhov loved their determination to break with the false pathos and declamation of the past, and to find a new way of communicating with their audience.

The proscriptive nature of Stanislavsky's *mise en scène* created tensions with the playwright. He had set down rhythms and mannerisms for each character: Arkadina 'folds her arms behind her back when she is angry or excited'; Sorin's laugh is 'shocking and unexpected'. Exact facial expressions were predetermined in forensic detail, including when each character would 'clean away dribble, blow their noses, wipe away sweat, or clean their teeth and nails with matchsticks'. Chekhov found the pedagogic certainty unappealing, but something about the beady-eyed attention to detail, even if it ran counter to his own desires, stimulated anew his interest in writing for the theatre. Close attention, even if wrong-headed, is better than lazy neglect even if astute.

The actor playing Konstantin, Vsevolod Meyerhold, went on to become one of Russia's great visionary directors. He moved a long way from realism himself, but respected the work of his master, Stanislavsky. He thought him ill-served when described as a purveyor of atmosphere:

> He understood the poetic nerve-centre, the hidden poetry of Chekhov's prose. Up to Stanislavski people had only played the theme in Chekhov and forgot that in his plays the sound of the rain

outside the windows, the early morning light through the shutters, mist on the lake were indissolubly linked with people's actions.

The playwright sat in the stalls as the company thrilled to the life in his play. The actors shared looks, glances, moments, moves, creating a complex lattice of love and desire and neglect, alive to each other's bodies in space. They listened to each other, to words, to phrases, to tones and breaths, and sank happily into this peculiar music of broken language. The playwright – always private, always bruised, always full of deflecting humour – coughed over and over, shrank down into his overcoat, glanced too frequently at black-haired, bright-eyed Olga, tugged at his beard and fiddled with his pince-nez. As happy as he would ever be.

He had to quit Moscow sometime before the opening, though, Nothing would get Chekhov back into a space so piercingly public. He needed to travel to warm Yalta for his health.

Meantime, at the Hermitage, problems emerged. The first Trigorin had been forced out for Stanislavsky to take over. Masha was found to be inadequate and Stanislavsky's wife took on the part. The company's season had begun with a great success with *Tsar Fyodor*, but that had been followed with five flops in a row, and now the future life of the company was endangered. Their original plan had been that the frail little *Seagull* would trail in after other mighty successes. Now the Moscow Arts Theatre's future depended on the play.

The dress rehearsal was terrible to the degree that the playwright's emissary, his ever-faithful sister Masha, decided that the play had to be taken off. Ever concerned for her brother's feeble health, she knew that another disaster like that in St Petersburg, and another such uprising of bile, could finish him off. Even at the distance he was, his lungs and his intestines would be tightening and twisting from the tension. Weeping, she went to Nemirovich and begged him not to proceed. The producer and director were sympathetic, but, with the company in such a desperate state and having committed so much, they had no choice.

And so the production went ahead. On the opening night, 17 December 1898, carriages clogged up the streets outside, so not all of the full house had squeezed in by the time the plain grey curtains rose on Stanislavsky's production. Those curtains would, from this season forward until the present day, be decorated with the image of a seagull with its wings outspread.

17 DECEMBER 1898, HERMITAGE THEATRE

Stanislavsky could only remember a few details from the first act on opening night. The future of his theatre was on the line, as well as the health of the play's author. He had learnt through rehearsal that his initial incomprehension revealed a fault in himself rather than the text. He now knew the play had greatness in it, which would make failure all the more cruel. As he moved around the stage, he noticed a particular smell. From every actor and actress, he sensed the clear odour of valerian drops, a powerful sedative. The Moscow Arts company were all having a ketamine moment. They had much adrenaline to counteract.

As Nina's monologue began, all of the characters sat with their backs to the audience to watch her. Stanislavsky found his leg shaking so uncontrollably he had to grip it with one hand to bring it under control. Laughs had been thin on the ground, but the silence had appeared attentive. But, as the curtain fell on Act I, the silence prolonged. And continued.

Panic gripped the company, who froze into a huddle behind the curtain listening for any sound. It was customary for each act to be completed with a curtain call of sorts, certainly with applause. And this silence was killing. Even booing would be better. The stagehands peeked around the curtain to see what was occurring. One actor whimpered. Another sat on the floor. Knipper held back tears and felt faint. They had failed their beloved Anton and this could kill him. This was the end for their company. Several began walking off to the wings without words. A thousand miles away, Anton Chekhov sat quietly in his modest home by the Black Sea, his head wrestling to stop imagining what was happening in the centre of his nation.

And then ... the most unearthly roar erupted on the other side of the curtain. A noise without precedent. An animal noise of praise and exultation. In surprise, the fly-man yanked up the curtain without it being called. The picture it revealed was a group of scattered actors, several on the way off, some with their backs to the audience. One sat on the floor, grim looks of failure set on their faces. They stood there, frozen in their previous despair and unable to manage a bow. Then they loosened and found some sort of order. There were five curtain calls after the first act alone. In the audience, one spectator said it looked as if it was 'everyone's birthday'. It certainly was for *The Seagull* and the Moscow Arts.

After the third act, no-one left their seats, so eager were they for the play to continue and for the spell not to be broken. At the end, the ovation was endless. In on-stage pandemonium, all the actors wept and kissed. One lay on the floor in hysterics. Spectators came on stage and joined in with the kissing. One critic rushed the stage and stood on a chair and applauded wildly. If it was everyone's birthday in the auditorium, it was Easter Sunday on-stage, for the newly risen playwright and company. Even though the play dissected the despondent and listless mood of a nation and a culture trapped in stasis, everyone felt understood. The Good Lord Chekhov and his wonderful actors had perceived them in their shame and hope. Stanislavsky, unable to contain his joy, broke into a wild dervish dance.

Author! Author!, the crowd shouted wildly. Nemirovich, who had come onstage to join in the fun, apologised for Chekhov's absence and told them that his health kept him over a thousand miles away. *Send a telegram! Send a telegram!*, they chanted. He acquiesced. He sent the message:

PERFORMED THE SEAGULL, SUCCESS COLOSSAL. PLAY SO TOOK
HOLD FROM FIRST ACT THAT SERIES OF TRIUMPHS FOLLOWED.
CURTAIN CALLS ENDLESS ... WE ARE MAD WITH JOY.

While Moscow shouted and screamed, in the quiet of Yalta, a messenger would have approached a door, telegram in hand, and knocked. A gentle man, with a theatre of a face, pince-nez perched on the end of his nose, would have received the telegram with his customary courtesy, and disappeared inside.

His feelings, as ever, kept to himself.

The next day, he replied:

CONVEY TO ALL INFINITE THANKS WITH ALL MY SOUL ...
I GRIEVE THAT I'M NOT WITH YOU. YOUR TELEGRAM
MADE ME WELL AND HAPPY

GOING FORWARD

'*The Seagull* will be our theatre's battleship', declared Nemirovich, and it has defined the Moscow Arts' ambitions and aesthetics through to the present. It was the perfect calling card to the world. Joyously, the work got greater in the short term, though tensions between Chekhov and Stanislavsky never ceased. In fact, when the playwright finally got to see the show, he was a little disappointed, its radioactive energy having fallen away.

But Chekhov and Stanislavsky's respect for each other grew, and it occasioned three more masterpieces: *Uncle Vanya*, *Three Sisters* and the *Cherry Orchard*. In that brief moment, as Nemirovich described it, '*Everything was new, unexpected, enthralling.*' There are two posed pictures of the playwright and the company, sat around an elegant covered table. They are heartwarming in their vividness and lively humour – many greats, Stanislavsky, Knipper, Chekhov, Meyerhold and others, all trapped in two instants of cheeky theatrical joy.

Love grew rapid and large-souled between Chekhov and Knipper. It was never going to be an easy love, since she had to spend nine months of the year in Moscow, and his health could rarely allow him to join her. Their continual correspondence is a testament to how two complex souls can conquer the most difficult situations. There was a blaze of late work from Chekhov – the plays, and stories as well – plus his customary care for others. It was a race against time and he was dead within six years. It was a sunlit last stretch.

When *The Seagull* resumed after its premiere, every performance was full. A friend of Chekhov writes of passing the Hermitage in the middle of the night and seeing the square outside it full of the young – sitting on stools, reading books by lanterns, some dancing, all waiting through the night to be the first in the morning to book tickets. A new sensibility was being born.

The young sweet-spirited Meyerhold wrote to Chekhov frequently asking questions about the theatre and the right interpretation of roles he was playing. Chekhov was a generous correspondent. For acting advice, he always counselled Meyerhold and others to seek out the opposite of the apparent quality of a character. That is where the truth of their behaviour lay. Meyerhold wrote to him once, when Chekhov had expressed caution about coming to Moscow because of the cold:

Come quickly! Don't fear the cold. You must know that the love your many admirers have for you could warm you, not only in Moscow, but even the North Pole.

16

A Very British Glasnost

A TALE OF THE YBA GANG

THE FETE WORSE THAN DEATH

On the morning of Saturday 31 July 1993, fifty trestle tables were set up in Hoxton Square, London. No-one watching was prepared for the derangement to come. Hoxton was a hollowed-out area of the city, where post-war decline had left cavernous and characterful empty spaces, both wide warehouses and kooky shopfronts – a classic draw for artists and musicians, with its low rents and plentiful vacancy. One such new arrival, an art-school graduate and alternative gallerist called Joshua Compston, was determined to make his mark. To that end, he announced 'The Fete Worse Than Death', a psychedelic village fair to take place that sunny Saturday.

Artists, none yet tainted by success, turned up to this art-house street party to release their greatest virtue – a capacity for subversion and daffy fun. Damien Hirst and Angus Fairhurst dressed as trippy clowns and, with an inverted electric drill, spun washing-up bottles filled with paint across sheets of paper. Signed by both artists, these *Spin* paintings were flogged for a princely £1 a shot. For an extra 50p, the two garish clowns would flash their testicles, painted with colourful spots by their make-up artist, Leigh Bowery. Tracey Emin set up a kissing tent, charging 50p for a kiss. Sarah Lucas had an empty stall with a piece of cardboard placed on it reading 'Our thoughts on any matter for 20p'. So, for only £2.20, one could have got some philosophy, a bit of a snog, some creative flashing, and made a sound investment for the future.

There was a pubic hair exchange, too, where one could pluck out and barter one's private foliage. Gary Hume, dressed as a Mexican bandit, sold tequila; and Gavin Turk set up a 'Bash the Rat' stall where a rodent made of old socks would shoot down a plastic drainpipe and, as it emerged, the contestant would try to pulverise it with a baseball bat. This proved harder than anyone imagined. The day wound down with a good old-fashioned English raffle, with the unconventional top prize of a bag of dildos. The fete concluded with the highly traditional screams of those living nearby to turn the music down.

Much of London's alternative art world turned out for the 'Fete'. It was a gleeful demonstration of their support for each other, for working in a collegiate manner, and their voracious appetite for a party. This was the happy moment before anyone worried about what was or wasn't cool, and when they were more concerned by what was bold. In the cracked synergy between the internal life of cities and the movement of artists, this was the significant moment in putting Shoreditch on the map. The area was battered not only by post-war decline but also by the depredations of the early 1990s recession, and Compston dubbed it an 'undiscovered country'. In its freedom and invention and good humour, his fete marked a highpoint of innocence for both area and movement.

Compston had previously set up a gallery nearby in a former factory named Factual Nonsense. Described ambitiously as a 'cultural think tank', he announced to his friends, to snorts of laughter, that this venture could help revolutionise the lives of the working classes. He was only twenty-two when he put his fete together, and it has all the freewheeling craziness of youth. Three years later, alone and broke, Joshua Compston died of an excess of ether. His body, lying in his gallery on Charlotte Road in the area he helped transform, was left undiscovered for four days. His erstwhile friends in the artists' block across the road ignored the light burning in the gallery. But everyone he had alienated in his short and blazing life turned out for his final piece of public performance, his funeral. Gary Hume, Gavin Turk and Fiona Rae painted his coffin in a dazzling William Morris pattern, bottles of claret were stowed away beside him for his journey into the afterlife and, to the steady pulse of a New Orleans jazz band, the art world marched through the East End. It was both formal and maniacal, pitched in some imaginary place between the Kray Twins (who were, in fact, Hoxton-born) and some arts pharaoh.

The spirit of innocence exemplified by the fete didn't last long. First the coffee shops came in, then the bars, then the shi-shi restaurants, and soon after the property developers. It is a story often repeated in modern cities. The fete, meantime, serves as a paradigm for the movement it showcased, the Young British Artists (YBAs): wild fun, boundary-breaking, with horrible hangovers, and always nearby the bitter odour of money.

GHOST AND SELF

For thirty years, from the 1950s through to the 1970s, the US – and more particularly New York – dominated the world of avant-garde art. This was facilitated by inspirational factors – the presence of unique individual artists in De Kooning, Pollock and Rothko, among others – and cynical ones – the eagerness of America to push soft power and abstract expressionism to defeat Soviet social realism. It was an inverted expression of American economic and military dominance. Then, from the 1980s on, Berlin began to swivel heads eastwards, as Anselm Kiefer and Georg Baselitz presented monumental canvases weighed down with slabby paint.

Britain seemed way off the pace, despite some notable resident artists. New artists had to forge a path through the patrician antiquity of an old establishment. Galleries prepared to showcase new artists were minimal; and those prepared to accommodate new ways of presenting art, even less. Installation art, video work, punk games with the status of subject and object were all the rage, but the tweedy network found it hard to deal with them. Comedians were still cracking jokes about the Tate's 1972 purchase of Carl Andre's *Equivelent VIII* (an arrangement of 120 firebricks), twenty years on. To the degree that new art registered at all, it was greeted with a particularly British derision.

Individual works were starting to make an impact on the public's consciousness, however, and some were sufficiently charismatic to silence the scoffers. Rachel Whiteread's *Ghost* (1990), her extraordinary inside-outing of a domestic sitting room, the interior cast in cement, somehow seemed to trap quotidian life in its solidified air. Damien Hirst's *The Physical Impossibility of Death in the Mind of Someone Living* (1991) played on a childhood terror of sharks, rendered other-worldly in their aqueous suspension. Marc Quinn's *Self* (1991), a casting of his head in his own frozen blood, effected a combination pitched somewhere between ancient death mask and unruly sorbet. All of these by their inherent drama forced their way into the media gaze. Looking mortality square in the eye as these artists did in a world haunted by AIDS, and actively seeking out taboos to push through, the works generated an outsider energy. It was that spirit which exploded in happy silliness on the streets of Shoreditch.

For some, this saturnalian anarchy was the purpose – a Day-Glo celebration of the God of Misrule. Others sensed an opportunity.

PROPERTY DEVELOPMENT

Whiteread's *Ghost* grew into *House*, an extraordinary construction which offered an ironic parallel commentary on the effect of the YBAs. She took a Victorian house – 193 Grove Road in East London, which was on the verge of destruction, the last spiking survivor of a wrecked terrace in the shadow of the Thatcherite edifice of Canary Wharf – and filled it with cement around a steel skeleton, then slowly took away the previous surface, brick by brick. The work was unveiled when the house had just six official days left to exist, on 19 October 1993. It stood there as if time had thickened and cast itself, capturing within its amber all of the small noise of this house – the murmurs of births, shopping, small betrayals, cold nights and new shoes. This was a statue not to 'great' men but to the quiet sanctity of domestic life.

House found itself at the centre of a debate about art, and housing and subsidy. Locals were appalled, politicians outraged. On the day that Whiteread won the Turner Prize, the council voted to demolish the work. And indeed, soon after, and to a huge media hoopla, the work was torn down, and London's philistines whooped in triumph. Whiteread's work was a gentle poem in itself, but in its reconstruction of a house, its repurposing of property, and its transformation of the area around it, it was a prime metaphor of all that art was doing.

A hard core of savvy and sophisticated tutors at Goldsmiths, the south London college which most of the YBAs attended, taught their students that making the work on its own wasn't enough, that they had to be sharp and stylish in how they presented it. London at the time, emptied out by post-war, post-industrialisation and recession, was an Aladdin's cave of gallery possibilities. Empty warehouses, broken-down factories, vacated department stores, disused cellars and boarded-up shops all offered a cornucopia of possibilities. Brick and girders, wide latticed windows and steel gates became frames for the new art, with the environment as powerful as the work.

The very first major exhibition for the YBAs – *Freeze* – a three-part exhibition in the summer of 1988, curated by Damien Hirst, still in his second year at Goldsmiths, took place in the vacant Port of London Authority building in Surrey Docks. It was sponsored by property developers Olympia and Young and by the London Dockland Development Corporation, a quintessentially Thatcherite body set up to refashion London's Isle of Dogs. Its iconic work was Mat Collishaw's *Bullet Hole*, a microscopic image of the exit wound of a bullet, a characteristically reductive and nihilistic portrait of flesh.

The supposed disjunct between the content and the event's patrons didn't matter, or more truthfully didn't exist. Its cynicism and its nihilism were pretty much in lockstep with the vanguard capitalists. Property developers were greedy for the presence and work of artists, knowing that an exhibition brought potential clients and an all-embracing 'sexiness' to an area. Artists were more often than not responsible tenants, dressing up the areas they lived and worked in. They would bring running water and basic electrics to derelict areas, and would leave some fancy murals for good measure. Having worked some magic on Docklands, the YBAs created one of their first major venues, Building One, in an old warehouse in Bermondsey, an area which was soon on the upward capitalist move. As one biographer described them, artists were 'the storm-troopers of gentrification', the first wave of people to wash into an area of broken-down industrial units and instill a jazzy life.

Tracey Emin and Sarah Lucas colonised an old shop near Brick Lane, and retitled it *The Shop*. Their first items on sale were cut-up Polaroids of themselves signing the lease for the gallery, adorned with slogans saying *Help, Help* and *Here Come The Bears*. Other items soon filled the space: a Chopper bike, a fishtank with goldfish, framed photographs and all sorts of clutter. The space became a place for people to gather and invent themselves. Whether this was a witty deconstruction of the British shop is moot – like many of their projects, it felt more like a boozy situationist improvisation that no-one knew quite how to stop.

Less freewheeling, and much sharper, was the first White Cube gallery, which opened in the pukka surroundings of 44 Duke Street, St James's in May 1993. Opened by Jay Jopling, the smooth-operating son of a Tory minister, this was a long way from chaotic. It was the operation of huge marketing intelligence on creative energy, with the focused desire to exploit that energy for profit. The speed with which the movement moved from Bermondsey to Mayfair wasn't happenstance; it was the velocity of profit. Britain's economy was fast picking up and, as the eyes of the international art world began to gravitate towards London, and towards this gang of once-scabrous anarchists, investors began to speculate in the two commodities they had helped to elevate: property and art.

At the junction of these various crossroads – financial, political and artistic – was the Saatchi Gallery. Opened by Charles Saatchi, one of the two advertising brothers who had helped get Margaret Thatcher to power and keep her there, this was by a country mile the most influential gallery for the new art. Founded in 30,000 square feet of an old paint factory in affluent St John's Wood, the gallery began as a place to celebrate the wildest of the new American art. Here, young British artists, before they were YBAs, would come and marvel at the brash commercial confidence of Jeff Koons and others. Here were no qualms about accommodating the difficult or the strange. In one permanent installation entitled *20:50*, by British sculptor Richard Wilson, visitors were asked to walk down an aisle into a room filled waist-high with a reflective black sump oil. There was something awkwardly symbolic about an arch-Thatcherite making successful use of a wrecked industrial space. Equally apt was his enthusiasm for presenting art which was less about making than about refashioning the already made. Craft had gone the same way as industry.

At one decisive moment, Saatchi shifted his sympathies from American art to the home-grown variety. He immediately became a powerful, maybe overpowerful, father figure to the new movement. Just as Paul Durand-Ruel had monopolised the French Impressionists a hundred years before and, through his active marketing of their work in London and New York, had helped transform their fortunes, so Charles Saatchi coalesced a disparate group of individuals into a movement. Voices would drop to a whisper whenever Saatchi attended a student show or a new exhibition – he had the power to make or break a career.

He was an early collector of the new British art, picking up a set of Gary Hume paintings at the first *Freeze* exhibition. Soon after, he acquired Hirst's *A Thousand Years*, in which flies pupate, live, gorge on a cow's head, and die within a glass case – a snip at £4,000. An adman to his fingertips, he recognised the visceral ability of this work to sell itself, to create an aura of magnetism. He also saw that, in the brash blast of a human being that was Damien Hirst, he had found his own Johnny Rotten to synthesise these energies.

GLOSSY MAGAZINES

The money rolled in early and spectacularly. It was all part of the *Gesamtkunstwerk*, the totality of what the project had to offer. Not only the acquisition of cash, but the conspicuous spending. Unapologetic, the YBAs swiftly transformed from people who played with a class-war veneer, to artists who revelled in their Gucci- and Prada-clad luxury. They realised the late capitalist truth that value is about price, and only price, and has little to do with intrinsic merit. The higher the value they put on their own work, the more people queued up to pay for it.

As big cheques were made out to them, they deserted Hoxton, and Bermondsey and the London Docks, and started making public merry in the Groucho Club in Soho. The synthetic grandeur of the Groucho was fast usurping the old seedy charisma of Lucien Freud and Francis Bacon's Soho hangouts like the Colony Room. It was where the phony gangsters of Britfilm, the middle-class louts of Britpop and the wild ones of Britart came together to concoct Cool Britannia.

The image of the artist was shifting, and the public's perception with it. This was no longer the pained or the academic approach, or the impoverished artist struggling on an Arts Council grant – this was a punk relish for possibility. Their icon of lifestyle was the American Jeff Koons, who proclaimed that he preferred flicking through glossy magazines to reading art theory. There was something refreshingly honest and identifiable in this happy hunger for trash. No longer starving in garrets, the group curated swanky new restaurants, and drank in the Chequers Tavern opposite the White Cube, beneath framed photographs of Thatcher. The buzzword of the moment was, cringily, 'sexy' – venues, people, shows, events were judged by their 'sexy' quotient. No-one at the time was 'sexier' than the YBAs. Their presence added a cachet to an opening or a bar or a party, and would attract more money along.

When artists realise that their presence can be monetised, and that they have become a commodity, then a large amount of what gave them that magnetism in the first place vanishes. Money, branding and fame prove the swiftest way to break up the most crucial element of their initial success – their togetherness.

SCENIUS

Whenever I meet anyone in the arts fresh out of school or training, and they ask advice, the first and only thing I say is: 'Find A Gang'. Whether a group attached to a venue, to a political creed, to an aesthetic line, to a perverse way of partying, or some happy intersection of each, it doesn't matter. Whatever the gang, try and find one or, better, several. All the arts thrive on networks, sharing passions, insights, tradecraft and kindness. Your first gang is your first web, which helps you into wider and more complex webs. It is a circuit to test ideas, to find solace for disappointments, and to turbocharge success.

Brian Eno has described the concept of 'Scenius' as a counter to the solipsism of genius. This would be a brilliant concept if its defining word weren't so irredeemably naff. As he describes it, 'Scenius stands for the intelligence and the intuition of a whole cultural scene.' It is about those moments in history when a concatenation of people have come together to share with, steal from, assess and praise each other. The inner gang tolerates the transgressions and the eccentricities of its members. It creates a buffer zone to protect the mavericks. As the curator Norman Rosenthal says, 'It's frightening to make art', and, if the group can offer cover, so much the better. It is also the first means of broadcasting the newness of whatever is being made. However sophisticated the technology, the first medium is friends.

Manet could only be Manet with all his allies flâneur-ing across Paris beside him; Michelangelo's heights were easier to negotiate given that Leonardo, Botticelli and Raphael were sharing the same air; Lorraine Hansberry, Arthur Miller and Tennessee Williams were building on the same movement. At certain moments, hungry artists in step with the zeitgeist they are stumbling to articulate, come together as an ecosystem rather than an egosystem. The moment never lasts – it is soon commoditised, exploited and dissipated but, while it works, it enables each member to reach further.

Togetherness was the defining characteristic of the YBAs. While it lasted, they hunted as a pack. There was nothing like the same structure in New York or Berlin. The Young Brits hung out in the same spots, kept each other afloat financially, and made legends out of each other with their anecdotes. They became myths to each other, so, when they wanted to project the same stature beyond, their foundations were the more robust. The galleries which presented these works were social spaces, where DJs spun records and people danced rather than shuffled; a trip to the loos was like opening an advent calendar in terms of trying to guess what or how many might fall out of a cubicle; and everyone clinked their sponsored beer bottles and felt cool.

There was an element of Little Englanders clinging together in some of this allegiance. When they exhibited together in Cologne or Venice or New York, there was a strong element of a visiting football tribe in their group loyalty and their prankish aggression to others. Later, in the more solitary future that beckoned, when the network had dissolved, they looked less like legends, and their claims to that status sounded as tinny as the old battle stories of football hooligans.

In the middle of the wider social space sat metaphorically the smaller social spaces of Tracey Emin's primary works: her tent entitled *Everyone I Have Ever Slept With 1963–1995*, and her bed, called bluntly *My Bed*. Within the tent were the appliquéd names of over a hundred people Emin had shared a mattress with – boyfriends, relations and old pals.

Her chaotic, debris-strewn bed showed evidence of the same profligacy of combination. What was remarkable in her work was her ability to combine the thrill of the encounter, whether sexual or romantic or tender, with the loneliness which walked beside the hangover.

Throughout the 1990s, the YBAs looked like a group of madcaps plastered to the walls of one of those old fairground centrifugal rotor rides, screaming with pleasure at the danger of it all and the happiness of sharing the scream. Then, one by one, they spun out on their own trajectories, to crash landings of success or failure. But ,whichever, alone.

SENSATION

Norman Rosenthal, the ebullient curator of the *Sensation: Young British Artists from the Saatchi Collection* exhibition in 1997 makes two key assessments of its nature. First, it wasn't a breakthrough, it was a coronation. The YBAs had already been on the scene for almost a decade, they had already hit the front pages, and shifted the culture. Their appearance wasn't news: it was the depth of its impact that surprised. The Impressionists arrived at the Salon des Refusés in 1863, but they weren't a fully fledged movement until the dedicated Impressionism exhibition of 1874. Similarly, the YBAs had had to wait, and this was their defining moment. Second, the significance of the exhibition wasn't in the what, it was the where. They had arrived at the Royal Academy, the bastion of the establishment, in their beautiful grand building on Piccadilly. The inexorable move from the edge to the centre was complete. They had come a long way from Hoxton and Surrey Docks.

The *Sensation* exhibition, curiously, came about by accident. Another more classical fandango on Egyptian art had fallen through. Charles Saatchi had previously suggested to Norman Rosenthal that he would like to bring together his collected works at the Royal Academy. With a hole to fill quickly, Rosenthal took him up on it. The appropriate committee consented, and over four days a selection committee of Rosenthal, Saatchi, Hirst and Goldsmiths tutor (and artist) Michael Craig-Martin, put together the programme. They went for the greatest hits of the last ten years, picking out the images which had landed publicly with the loudest splash. If Saatchi didn't own them at that point, he bought them, picking up Emin's *Tent* and Collishaw's *Bullet Hole* to make sure he had the ultimate poker hand of shock and horror. It is not clear whether the criterion was art, or effect, or whether effect had become art and vice versa.

The show was announced in March, and at a press conference all of the images were shown, including Marcus Harvey's portrait of the child-killer Myra Hindley, composed of hundreds of children's handprints. Several months later, at a quiet moment in the news cycle, Rosenthal was summoned back from a summer holiday to deal with a press storm provoked by the Hindley image. Whatever the ethics of the work, they weren't of concern to the papers who were making the fuss. They just wanted to sell papers, and loved a fuss. The public joined in. A special Royal Academy committee was formed to assess whether these works could be properly classified as art. Rosenthal escorted the members to various studios to discuss the work with the artists, who all scrubbed up posh and talked aesthetics. (Almost all of them are now Academy members.) The committee decided that the images were legitimate.

The controversy didn't go away, however, as the nation shifted into a newly explicit emotional register. Already brought to giddy heights by the landslide election victory for New Labour, which brought more hope than the country had known since England won the World Cup in 1966, the convergence of Britpop, Britfilm and Britart now made London the creative hub of the world. It seemed that 1997 was the year a decade had been waiting for, a fact celebrated in a dizzy *Vanity Fair* issue given over to huzzahs for London and 'Cool Britannia'.

In the midst of all this unaccustomed euphoria for a naturally repressed nation, on a Saturday night in Paris, a car was chased by hungry paparazzi into a tunnel, and Princess Diana and her lover didn't come out alive. After the shock, this event opened up a wound in the United Kingdom's psyche. The euphoria of early summer turned into the national keening of late summer. We were living in a new country, with a kitschily beating heart. Floating over this tide of emotion came the image of Myra Hindley; indeed, when Norman Rosenthal showed it to his Spanish father-in-law, he actually thought it was Princess Diana. Various pathologies were merging in a country fashioning itself anew.

On the day of Princess Diana's funeral, one of the media events of the century, one man was not glued to the television. Charles Saatchi, who you might have assumed would be fascinated by such modern iconography, was not curious. While the rest of the staff were distracted, he wandered alone around the Royal Academy, checking the hangings of his paintings and the positioning of his sculptures. While the rest of the country wept and emoted, this lonely high lord of the synthetic age padded softly around the nation's premier gallery, observing the Chapman Brothers' protruding penises and Sarah Lucas's *Two Fried Eggs and a Kebab*. Obsessive and private, this lonely vigil must have served as some sort of apotheosis.

Whether he suspected what many others did, that ultimately this exhibition was little more than an advertisement for itself, can only be conjectured. Maybe he did and that delighted him. *Sensation* was the ideal title for the rawness and confrontation of the work on show, a punch of high-concentrate attack. Saatchi and the artists were in step, bringing fresh oxygen to a nation waking from a long sleep. This wasn't art that worried about posterity, it was art that jumped the pulse. The question wasn't 'Will it last a hundred years?' but simply 'Does it make today more exciting?'

The Hindley image went on stirring the pot, and its concurrence with Diana's dark long-fringed charisma sharpened the pain. The still living mother of one of Hindley's victims raised justifiable concerns, and many agreed. The fact that children had been used to produce the canvas accentuated the outrage. Demonstrators smashed the windows at Burlington House, the home of the Royal Academy, and hurled eggs and blue and red ink at the work. The image was restored and set behind a Perspex screen guarded by security men.

Such controversy is a fundamental part of the adman's game, and the Harvey painting was given a central position, intended to inflame rather than dampen down such feelings. Given that, and the many other controversies over the years, the show took London by storm. It was a huge success with the public, attracting over 300,000 visitors during its run. The papers ran constant thinkpieces and cartoons and jokey pieces on it. It drew the eye more than any contemporary exhibition had for decades. As Norman Rosenthal says, 'It wasn't a breakthrough for the artists, it was a breakthrough for the public.' It gave them a taste for the sharp flavours of modern art, and took away their shame and embarrassment about visiting these cathedrals of culture.

Another bastion of old snobbery had been overturned by the Thatcherite reordering. The audience were storming the Winter Palace with the same cheer and chutzpah as the artists. Undoubtedly the humour of much of this work, not least Sarah Lucas's *Two Fried Eggs and a Kebab*, opened it up to a wider audience. The humour was provocative, but also worked to loosen the audience up, to unwind its sense of propriety and to access the emotions still quick and volatile after the great Diana outpouring. It felt like a bit of very British *glasnost* – openness with some salty slap and tickle. It is arguable that Tate Modern – which opened three years later – would have achieved its immediate success without the populism of *Sensation*. The sense of freedom, entitlement and curiosity it gave to such a large audience cannot be gainsaid.

The opening of *Sensation* was a classic 'everyone-was-there' night, with curators, collectors, artists and dealers all gathered to applaud an audacious coup. Yet, amid the colonnades and arches and cool marble floors of Burlington House, something evanesced. The anarchy had been replaced by elegance, the ragged invention by style. Slender lines of people dressed in slimming black and holding tall champagne flutes replaced the pantomimic bulges and psychedelic colours and beer cans of Shoreditch. The British establishment had performed its time-honoured trick of co-opting the outsider and making them fall swooningly for its superior stylings. A spirit of party fuelled by Ecstasy and aliveness, a necessary reaction to the miserable puritanism of the 1980s, had been subsumed into the dread deadness of posh and cool. The crazed party had been turned into class, rebellion into money.

Later that night, when in days gone by everyone would have tumbled into the nearest smelly pub, the after-party repaired to the Metropolitan Hotel, where they got steadily smashed. As a blood-orange sunrise spread over Hyde Park, they looked out of the windows of their suite, and felt like masters of the universe. Then there was a thud from the middle of their group. Tracey Emin had fainted and fallen flat on her face. As Sam Taylor-Wood hauled her up, a queasy feeling passed through the group, a shiver of something passing, and potentially passed.

They reeled out into the dawn, and away from each other.

COUNTERBLAST

Amongst all of the conceptual noise, the media-tickling gestures and the distracting sensation, there was a lot of serious and beautiful art amongst the YBAs. The elephant dung attached to Chris Ofili's rich swirls of colour and Byzantine patterning distracts from the beauty it accompanies. Gary Hume's playful abstractions; Jenny Saville's clinical fleshiness; and Ron Mueck's poppy hyperrealism: all provoke and stun in different ways. The greatest achievement of the YBAs was the breadth of its umbrella under which many contrary energies could work and compete. There was something for everyone. A successful grouping, as this proved, should be more market-place than corporation.

Within that breadth, it is hard to point to any themes that draw them together without it proving reductive. There is an element of 'skip art' drawn out of its original poverty of resource, where whatever you found – whether old tabloid spreads, rotting vegetables, medicine cases or computer keyboards – could be refashioned. The ordinary was taken and, curated in a new perspective, given a fresh reality. Kitsch took on a new resonance in classic settings. This was not a technical achievement in art-making so much as a tonic reinvention of what art was.

The spiritual achievement was in demonstrating two complementary sides of the oldest coin. First, this work squared up cold and hard to mortality. Emerging from the AIDS crisis, here was a generation who, having expected to have a long wait to confront mortality, had suddenly had it shoved in their face. Mat Collishaw's *Bullet Hole*; Damien Hirst's rotting corpses; Marc Quinn's *Head*; Rachel Whiteread's ghost edifices – all eschewed art's traditional delicacy about death and brought it right into the room. The skull was no longer beneath the skin.

The other side of the coin was the opposite of all this – an exhilarating relish for being alive. The clinging to every second of its sweet savour, the cold-sea full-body-alive sensation which accompanies a knowledge of mortality. The great muse of the group, the drag act/living work of art that was Leigh Bowery, himself a young victim of AIDS, once executed a complicated bit of performance, that included him speaking a riff on the old Pepsi commercial to some heavy techno. It ran:

Boot-licking, piss-drinking, finger-frigging, tit-tweaking, love-biting,
arse-licking, shit-stabbing, mother-fucking, spunk-loving, ball-busting,

cock-sucking, fist-fucking, lip-smacking, thirst-quenching, cool-living,
ever-giving, useless man.

This all-inclusive, physical hymn to life, almost contemporaneous with Irvine Welsh's hymn in *Trainspotting*, sums up the best of the spirit of YBAs. A virulent, rude, thrilling counterblast to the life-denying miseries of puritanism and academism.

The YBA spirit became lost in an ugly scrabble for status and for fame and for absurd amounts of money, and its capacity for grandiose self-parody stretched the patience long past breaking point. But the initial spirit expressed in the fete, and lost by the time they got to the RA and chinked fluted glasses, remains an irresistible expression of the anaesthetising power of joy. 'Do you know what I most like about life?' Damien Hirst once asked Jay Jopling, and, before he could reply, Hirst blasted out like a trumpet, 'Everything!'

17

Writ on Water

A TALE OF SARAH KANE

The essence of first nights – alongside the art, of course – is the parties. With adrenaline sluicing through all involved, the capacity for post-show delight and derangement is industrial. With theatrical hyperbole, people used to claim the sum of adrenaline coursing through a body on a first night was equivalent to a car crash. We would all nod in agreement, awed at our own endurance, knowing it must be cobblers. Yet the terror before, the focus during, and the surge of relief after, sends the idea of bedtime stretching way across the horizon. The party frocks, the influx of excited attendees, the high flirtiness that flushes the cheeks, and no shortage of alcohol or other narcotics, often dispels bedtime entirely.

Each of the venues I have worked in had a well-burnished reputation for a first night hoolie. It could never be said that the party was more important than the show, but it sometimes ran close. In my first theatre, the Bush, my aide-de-camp at merry mayhem was often the playwright Sarah Kane. She had an enormous appetite for jollies. I always wanted to be the late-night spielmeister, and coordinate the silliness. I never stood a chance with Sarah around. She would give everyone an extra vitality to kick through to dawn. Her favourite amusement was a psychological torture sport called 'The Water Game'. This was all the rage in the 1990s, but would get you arrested in the Age of Compliance.

Sarah worked with us as a literary associate in a loose capacity. She was held close because of her brilliant mind, and because she was top fun. She was a devotee of Jonathan Harvey's success with *Beautiful Thing*. On its first manifestation at the Bush, when it went off like a skyrocket, she joined us for an all-night lock-in. Eight months later, we took it into the Donmar Warehouse. Our partying started there, moved to a fashionable bar, then descended into a subterranean dive of depravity. Sarah and I shared a cab with a couple of others back to Shepherd's Bush at five in the morning. We decided we wanted more from the night and knocked firmly on the door of our local Polish restaurant. Its wonderful chatelaine, Eva, came down in her dressing gown, welcomed us in, and gave us beer, vodka and breakfast. Her husband arrived half an hour later wearing his pyjamas and smoking a pipe. He and Sarah argued passionately about goalkeepers, while the rest of us fell asleep into our scrambled eggs.

Six months later, *Beautiful Thing* moved into the West End, in the bijou Duke of York's. As a group, we weren't suited to the Edwardian elegance of our venue. After another first night, in the beautiful bar upstairs, the party got ragged. It ended with a furious bout of tag-wrestling, with Sarah and I as a team. Everybody else seemed to think it was about touching and posing; Sarah and I took it seriously. It ended with the place wrecked, our producer in tears, and the Bush picking up a bill for repairs. We were neither of us cut out for the commercial theatre.

Only four and a half years later, and Sarah, by then one of England's best-known playwrights, crept into a toilet in a psychiatric hospital just before dawn came in. Having recently tried to end her life with an over-dose, she could not face another cycle of vanished hopes and crushing realities. She hung herself with her shoelaces.

Those that knew her floundered in the wake and watched in confusion as Sarah became the poster girl of modern despair. Within a year or two, she was worshipped by avant-gardistas from Rio to Romania. Shortly before her death, she had been asked to adapt Goethe's novel *The Sorrows of Young Werther*, a book which, when it appeared in 1815, inspired a rash of copycat suicides across Europe. Due to responsible handling of Sarah's legacy and image, thankfully the same didn't happen. What was confounding was that someone who could burn with such brightness could snuff out her light.

A CRITICAL INVENTION

The other central factor of first nights in the modern age, and at the opposite end of the joy spectrum from the parties, are critics. Critics are a relatively recent invention, coming in with periodicals and newspapers. For several millennia, artists got on with pushing art forward in the absence of star ratings. Aeschylus didn't feel the need of a review to help him understand his work; Monteverdi didn't yearn for some snappy overnight coverage. But, with the growth of media, the critic gained a stronger and stranger stranglehold over defining what can or can't, should or shouldn't, does or doesn't.

There was a time, not too long ago, when the critic's ambition was to give the impression of an event, of what it intended and how it was made. An honourable trade, but not one that lasted. That dissolved into higher punditry, where what counted was ferocity of slant. This could be of interest if it came from a place of spiritual or moral passion. It doesn't. Or from a strongly robust sense of taste. Not that, either. It rarely originates from other than tribal power games, and the scared opinions the herd contrive when they huddle together during an event. In Britain, most of our criticism is favouritism to personal friends, a gadfly charting of who's hot and who's not, a grab bag of from-the-moment attitudes and an accumulated collection of grudges. That is not a definition of how to enrich a culture.

Sarah was an avid reader of others' solicited and unsolicited scripts at the Bush. She tore through them hungrily, relishing the humanity and the information within. She was far more generous than mean. One script in particular obsessed her. It was a rendition of the events of the first night of Chekhov's *Seagull* in St Petersburg, the comedy of it, the confusion of intentions, and the horrendous pain. It dealt with the night when the critics advanced their capacity to hunt as a pack, and to hurt as hard as possible. The rest of us thought it rather straightforward, but she loved it, and invited the writer down to talk to him. In the context of what followed, her attachment seems more than coincidence.

25 JANUARY 1995, ROYAL COURT UPSTAIRS, LONDON

The title of Sarah's first play, *Blasted*, lives at each end of Sarah's conflicted nature. It was named after the slang word for being hopelessly drunk: only later did Sarah make the connection with the heath in *King Lear*. Most of the first half of the play is taken up with territorial power games in a bland hotel room, pitched somewhere between Leeds and Nowheresville. A young and vulnerable woman, and a foul-mouthed, middle-aged journalist pursue a tortured and abusive relationship. This may not have been the best template to delight a critical consensus then made up almost entirely of middle-aged men.

The play had floated around London a while before the Royal Court, under Stephen Daldry, picked up the rights. They sat on it for a while, frustrating Sarah before committing to producing it in January 1995. She complained: 'The Court programmed the play into a dead spot. A lot of the people didn't want to do it – they were a bit embarrassed by it so they put it into a spot just after Christmas when no one was going to the theatre and hopefully nobody would notice.' That is only partly true. The moment after Christmas is also a good time to get press coverage, since there is so little going on. Unfortunately for Sarah, the press had very little else to do, and were hungry to make a noise.

The second half of the play, after the Strindbergian circling of the first, explodes into expressionist territory. The war outside, an evocation of the Bosnian conflict, bursts into the hotel. All the atrocities of modern civil warfare – mutilation, humiliation, dehumanisation – invade their minibar world. A soldier roams in, a wall is blown in by an explosion, a baby appears, and various acts of unspeakable horror invade this seemingly secure world. For many, the physical expression of these horrors six feet away from them – rather than the thousand miles that separated London from Sarajevo – was too much. During previews, people started walking out. But not that many. Daldry now remembers: 'I sat there during previews watching an audience that was respectful and quiet. It didn't feel like a bomb going off. The audience were always polite in the Theatre Upstairs – a small congregation in a quiet church.'

Press nights in small spaces like the Royal Court Upstairs in those days were hellishly odd. You could only seat sixty to a hundred people. On a night when there was nothing on elsewhere, you could have forty or fifty critics in. Almost the entire house was made of people who spent every night of the year in each other's company. Sometimes, as a group they all curdle and a peculiar acidic atmosphere enters the air. When you feel it, you know you are in trouble. It is often tied up with humour, or the lack of it. There is a gag early in *Blasted*, when Ian the journalist pompously pronounces, 'I've shat in better places than this.' This got a response during previews. On press night it went for nothing.

Paul Taylor, *The Independent*'s critic, remembered in Sarah's obituary:

> *I was present straight after the first-night performance when two of my colleagues led the charge by deciding to cook up this play as a news item. My informed guess is that: a) neither of them had been profoundly offended by the play, and b) their subsequent behaviour was not motivated by malice, but by an almost childish sense of journalistic fun – they thought that it would be a wheeze to draft the theatre out of the ghetto of the theatre pages and into mainstream public attention.*

This much is confirmed by a conversation Daldry had with the *Daily Mail*'s Jack Tinker. 'Jack said, "This is outrageous! A disgrace! This is nihilistic!". I said, "Oh Jack, come on ...". "No, I'm going to go for it."'. This was the gang on the rampage. Arts and news editors frothed it up into a front page story. The subsidy to the Royal Court was questioned.

Sarah was a twenty-three-year-old woman, only recently out of college. She was vulnerable. No-one should ever be subjected to the gleeful public scorn of a group of powerful men out on a jolly. Nor the accumulated power of the newspapers and platforms behind them. She was resilient enough to cope with it in style, and to rebound with more work of imagination and ferocity. But she was indescribably hurt.

Not having foreseen the trouble, Stephen Daldry had flown to New York before the reviews came out. When he got off the plane, he read them, and decided to fly back. Jack Tinker's noisy headline, 'This Disgusting Feast of Filth', set the tone, and the others piled in alongside, squealing in titillated indignation. Sarah chose to lie low. Stephen fronted up for the Court, and called on the theatre's wider community to help. The senior writers all did, with Edward Bond, Caryl Churchill and Martin Crimp taking up Sarah's cause in public. They wrote to the *Guardian*, declaring that: 'She dares to range beyond personal experience and brings the wars that rage at such a convenient distance from this island, right into its heart.' Most consistent, and most fierce, in her defence was Harold Pinter, who became a good friend to Sarah, and the bear-like shield he placed around her managed to scare many of the jackals away. If not those yapping angrily in her head.

24 FEBRUARY 1821

On the grave of Keats, buried far from home in Rome, is written, 'This grave contains all that was Mortal of a Young English Poet Who on his Death Bed, in the Bitterness of his Heart at the Malicious Power of his Enemies Desired these Words to be engraven on his Tomb Stone: *Here lies One Whose Name was Writ in Water*. The final phrase is Keats's own: the stark anger that courses through the first section may have been supplied by his friends. If they were not the exact words he wanted, we know from Shelley, his editor Leigh Hunt, as well as friends, that his death was ushered along by bad reviews, in particular the group savaging he took for *Endymion*. Byron, in *Don Juan*, refers to the same despair when he wrote;

> 'Tis strange the mind, that very fiery particle
> Should let itself be snuffed out by an article.

Tuberculosis is, of course, a more powerful killer than a one-star review, and Keats was always more in control of his destiny than the flying ants who bit at him. He said of *Endymion* and its reception: 'I was never afraid of failure; for I would sooner fail than not be among the greatest.' He was certain of his own status, and his relationship with death was a compulsive dance of almost erotic desire: 'many a time I have been half in love with easeful death'; 'now more than ever seems it rich to die'. In his inner conviction of his quality, and his tunnelled pas-de-deux with death, he and Sarah were walkers on the same footpaths.

On a visit to Keats' grave in 1877, a young Oscar Wilde, ever keen to claim space for himself which should perhaps be left for others, hurled himself on the earth, wept, and declared it 'the holiest place in Rome'. He wrote a sonnet – *The Grave of Keats*:

> Rid of the world's injustice, and his pain,
> He rests at last beneath God's veil of blue:

Taken from life when life and love were new
The youngest of the martyrs here is lain,
Fair as Sebastian, and as early slain ...
... Thy name was writ in water – it shall stand:
And tears like mine will keep thy memory green.

It serves well for Keats, and Oscar himself, and for all the many artists treated as cruelly, including Sarah. None should ever have to be martyrs.

FREEDOM AND RESPONSIBILITY

Watching *Blasted* was a curious experience. The noises off were hysterical and huge, columns of trenchant defence and screaming attack in the papers, furious discussion on the television and frequent questioning of 'whose side are you on?' The play itself was resolutely quiet. Given a scientifically detached production, it felt immediately harmless. 'It was the opposite of a hot show', says Daldry, and heat was very much the callibration of the age. Yet, even in its downbeat way, it wasn't hard to sense tectonic plates shifting, and something disturbing in its cold, hard deadness.

Edward Bond has written about Sarah as having accepted the primary role of a theatrical writer, or any artist, which is not to mirror reality but to shift it. A great playwright makes a new state of being, and the world adjusts to incorporate that into its ever-growing portfolio of realities. Artists are as much prophetic as they are reflective. They hear the way the world is moving, capture that new direction and, in presenting it, help to shape a new destination. We witness this new reality, and include it in our intersubjective perceptions of the world. The theatre can be such a powerful instrument; the effect of a single imagination can be broadly telling. A significant artist shifts the construct of so many; the aggregation of these perceptions becomes a new objective existence. Shakespearean, Pinteresque, Mozartian, a Turner vista, a Van Gogh sunset – these are not just adjectives, they are new realities. Bond included Sarah in that company.

Whether Sarah was moral or not became part of the debate which raged. The Court and her defenders called her 'a profoundly moral writer' as a means of defence. Sarah argued back that the frame of her play was amoral, and there was no comfortable patterning for people to squeeze it into. She was eager to push back against the empathetic pigeonhole which looms large for female writers. She had a questioning sensibility which spurned facile sympathies and the idea there was a takeaway moral. And she was no glib shock merchant. When they attempted to coerce her into the same corral of outrageous artists as the YBAs, she reared and kicked. She had a problem with Marcus Harvey's *Myra*: 'I had very mixed feelings about it ... I wouldn't want to upset someone by reference to Myra Hindley or a specific situation. Because you are being cynical; you are using people's pain to justify your own work which I don't think is acceptable ... You are tapping in on a group of people who have lost their kids'.

Her great achievement was in emphasising that life is always moral, even if art does not have to be. *Blasted* appeared towards the end of the Clintonesque End of History complacency, and just at the beginning of the synthetic bright dawn of Blairism. Nobody wanted to know about the world's cruelty with so much maniacal grinning going on. Sarah butted two jarring realities – the West's carefree triumphalism and Bosnia's tribal despair – hard against each other and showed how interconnected they are. How acts of negligent cruelty in the first create a moral pattern reflected more brutally in the second. And how one day the Bosnian reality is destined to catch up with the West.

'Freedom makes a huge requirement of every human being. With freedom comes responsibility', as Eleanor Roosevelt said. The destabilising sense of possibility that followed the end of the Cold War in 1989 was a moment when the West had enormous freedom to make itself anew. It was also the moment when it lost its moral compass. The conflict with Communism had kept us honest. Throughout the Cold War, it was incumbent on the West to show it could provide a more just and more caring society, primarily to stop people looking enviously East. Without that need to show ourselves better than our ideological foe, we tipped sharply towards the opposite. All sense of responsibility for ourselves, for each other and the environment we live in, dissolved in greed, and tribalism, and an insane privileging of the individual. Like the ice caps, our moral sense of obligation to each other continues to melt and tumble.

The vanguard of freedom without responsibility in the West has for a long time been its press. Whether the transparent dishonesty and thuggery of the right-wing press, or the more discreet mendacity and snobbery of the boutique progressive left, our primary opinion-forming crucibles have for thirty years been given over to an unchecked relativism, which has little or no respect for facts or neutrality or balance. Any attempt to point this out, or to go to war with it, whether it is the Leveson Inquiry or Hugh Grant on the attack, has met with a swiping and vindictive violence. Brexit and Trump will be one of the the the last gifts to the Western world of its own media, before it is eaten alive by its own savage grandchildren, in the form of the uncontrolled mayhem spawned by the social media titans, and their anonymous troll stormtroopers.

These are large statements to draw from the opening of a small three-hander, in a seventy-seat theatre, in a fashionable square in west London. The muted and downbeat tone of *Blasted* was deceptive. Its reception, though wrong-headed, revealed that it touched raw nerves. It was another canary in the mine. Or, in Sarah's words:

> *While the corpse of Yugoslavia was rotting on our doorstep, the press chose to get angry, not about the corpse, but about the cultural event that drew attention to it. Of course the press wish to deny that what happened in Central Europe has anything to do with us, of course they don't want us to be aware of the extent of the social sickness we're suffering from – the moment they acknowledge it, the ground opens up to swallow them.*

Sarah's rage for truth was shunted off into the marshalling yard for those labelled disturbed.

HUMANITY, HUMOUR AND FREEDOM

Sarah went on to write a reversioning of a classical myth in *Phaedra's Love*, a panorama of cruelty and bombed-out redemption in *Cleansed*, a tone poem about love and obsession in *Crave* (a play of voices very like an Anna Akhmatova poem), and she left behind her a collection of distilled images of a whirlpooled mind in *4.48 Psychosis*. How do they stand up now? Once the clouds had cleared from the bombardment of shock and awe with which they were received, the plays emerged as balanced and mature. There are strains of violence and cruelty coursing through and, beside those, threads of tenderness and delicacy.

An irrepressible delight in sick humour bubbles up: 'I won't strangle you', a boy offers to his prospective love, as guarantee of his bona fides. And their own commitment to truth: 'I love you. Now', a lover declares in *Cleansed* with an ultimate honesty. The plays were saturated in their own mirthlessness when they were first presented, yet Sarah intended the characters, in spite of the bleakness of their surrounds, to be as various as any of us. Sarah had an unbearable capacity for love – the weight of her passions were too much for her to live with – and she shared that capacity magnanimously with her characters.

If she had a particular gift, which is more noticeable now, it was as a listener. Sarah heard speech with an acid accuracy, with a taste for the accidental ironies within the demotic, in a similar vein to Pinter and Orton. The peculiar mix of the banal and the vainglorious which the vernacular moves between was her domain. But, equally, she heard the world. When most had turned their ears off, she continued to listen hard. She went to libraries, read obscure reports, attended speeches, looked at the corners of the newspaper which our eyes glide over. Everything within her plays may look savage, but it is not the invention of a twisted mind. It was happening as she wrote it, in Bosnia, in Chechnya and in Rwanda. Her sensitivity to all of this may have been labelled hyper; our deafness to it was hyper for her. Her awareness, and our lack of it, may have proved too acute a mismatch to manage.

The digital explosion of the past decade would have both fascinated and terrified her. Her greediness for news and information would have loved the highways, byways and twisted alleyways of the Empire of Virtual Information. Just as the capacity for people to lie blatantly within it, and to form different tribes of cant, would have appalled her. For her, knowledge was a life-giving well, and opinion a shallow puddle. To honour her would be to carry on looking for the facts, and to walk straight past the detractors.

From the parties, I remember one extraordinary capacity of Sarah's. However wild and raggedy and dangerous the occasion might get, she always remained lucid and clear, watchful and bright. While the rest could get maudlin, or mardy, or lairy, she didn't. She got kind. Such freedom can be dangerous, and it takes an exceptional spirit to steer through it. She could. 'Once you have perceived that life is very cruel, the only response is to live with as much humanity, humour and freedom as you can.'

Emptiness shivered through bones for months after her death. The process of her suicide was a compelling obsession. The hiding, the shoes, the laces – how long did they have to be, what force did it need, how long did it take? The 'hows' were the only questions to ask, because the 'why' would never yield easy answers. Now, with wider hindsight, it is possible to remember the bright moments beside the dark. And, looking at her plays again, it is possible to see that, even in the inkiest holes of despair, she found a little redemption, a little grace, some muted music. There is a shuffling, accidental movement towards a distant light. One can only hope the last movement of her life was in the same direction.

A GRECIAN URN

If a new reality from an artist is to have any purchase, it cannot just be fantasy. Nor can it be the cynical manipulation of perspective and facts, which empire builders thrive on. The George W. Bush administration prided itself on its capacity to make up its own reality, and with deadly consequences. An artist's new world has to pass two key quality control tests. The first and greatest is truth. The vision has in some way to be allied to the heart of things, how we are and how the world around us is. It has to be an unfolding of a deeper truth we haven't spotted yet. The second, and the ally of the first, is beauty. As Sarah's antique confrere John Keats wrote, when he himself was twenty-three:

> *Beauty is truth, truth beauty, – that is all*
> *Ye know on earth, and all ye need to know.*

The 'ye's are unfortunate, but the sentiment is just. Sarah's plays – their language, their stage poetry, their relationship dynamics – are ever concerned to be beautiful. Greatly so. It is a painful beauty, to be sure, but every moment is winnowed and measured for a stark elegance. The deeper truth which Sarah discovered, as Keats did with his *Ode on a Grecian Urn* and Wordsworth found at Tintern Abbey, was an underlying beauty. The larger reality is goodness.

18

Levity

A TALE OF OSCAR WILDE AND *EARNEST*

On finishing a roughed-out plot for his new play, Oscar Wilde was feeling playful. His outline concludes ...

> *Everything ends happily.*
> *Result.*
> *Curtain.*
> *Author called.*
> *Cigarette called.*
> *Manager called.*
> *Royalties for a year for author.*
> *Manager credited with writing play.*
> *Author consoles himself for the slander with bags of gold.*
> *Fireworks!*

Though Wilde's relentless affectation can exhaust, and his philosophical twists tire, at the centre of his being was a childish silliness, a happiness as simple as an infant's on sight of a balloon. That, and his surfeit of love, make it hard not to forgive him. Such self-delighted dottiness is on unparalleled parade in the play that resulted from this draft. Levity had never been so necessary in an artist's life. The clouds gathering were dark. As catastrophe approached, Wilde dreamt urgently of a more ideal world, and wanted to share it as a consoling gift.

No work has ever displayed a more gracious lightness of being.

ST VALENTINE'S DAY, 14 FEBRUARY 1895

A snowstorm swirled outside the St James' Theatre on London's King Street, between seven and eight in the evening, as a street-wide tangle of hansom cabs barged past each other to deliver their cargo of glitterati. The drifting snow made the jostle the more confused, and the picture all the more magical. Horses and polished wood scraped past each other, spilling out the wealthy and well thought of. A small crowd had gathered to gawp at the gentry in their gems, and amongst them was a claque of 'Wilde fanatics', waiting to cheer their man in to the opening night of *The Importance of Being Earnest*.

Wilde did not disappoint, pulling up in a carriage and stepping down with the practised deportment of a debutante. His outfit was one of 'elaborate dandyism and a sort of florid sobriety'. He wore a coat with a black velvet collar and a white waistcoat, from which dangled a bunch of seals on a black ribbon watch chain. His white gloves were held lightly in one hand, leaving his green scarab ring visible. As his friend Ada Leverson remembered, 'This costume, which on another man might have appeared perilously like fancy dress, and on his imitators was nothing less, seemed to suit him perfectly; he seemed to have the look of the last gentleman in Europe'..As he stepped into the throng, he sprayed performative wit left and right. This, his fourth opening in recent succession, drew a crowd as much for his talent to amuse as for the play itself. Surrounded by *la crème*, he received their adulation with a 'semi-royal graciousness'.

The facade of dazzling gaiety needed energy to fund its bright wattage. Most of the energy came from terror. Oscar had just returned from a trip to Algeria with gonorrhoea. The effects of the illness, and of its medieval cure, would have been spiking his body with tortures. For several years, he had been leading a dizzyingly executed double life as a devoted husband and father in the public eye, while in secret living out a long and bitter romance with Lord Alfred Douglas, in the course of which both took prodigious pleasure elsewhere. It was a pirouette of publicity and secrecy which took enormous effort to sustain. He knew this tightly woven double helix would soon unthread.

One specific threat lurked in the corners of his paranoia. The Marquis of Queensberry, the father of his lover Lord Alfred Douglas, had threatened to attend the night and ruin it. Tipped off by Queensberry's ex-wife, his ticket for the night had been withdrawn by the business manager of the St James, but the threat remained. As Oscar entertained his captive crowd with poise and pose, he would have looked with a flicker of nervousness over and beyond them, and seen police officers discreetly placed around the building, there to stop a Queensberry disturbance.

Oscar was walking close to the precipice, as he always did. His whole life was foreshadowed by a sense of the skull beneath the skin. Within his glamorous garb would have been secreted the one item he always kept with him, the last personal possession he retained on his deathbed: a locket enclosing a lock of his younger sister's hair. Isola, his lodestar, had died at eight, and taken a fair chunk of Oscar's young heart with her. The sense of doom this inculcated in Oscar, along with other family calamities, was one of the factors which helped him to rebound and fly so high.

On that St Valentine's night, he did not know if he was to be allowed one more magical night.

HIS BRILLIANT CAREER

Wilde's creative life began with an extended prologue of footling about, posing as a Great Man without having achieved anything. Declaring himself the embodiment of the Aesthete, he had not yet worked out what that was. He took a long time to justify his oft-repeated declaration of 'I am here! Everything is now different.' To the question 'How?' his response could only have been, 'Erm … I'm not sure yet. But I am here!' His footling about included lecture tours from San Francisco to Hull, slim volumes of self-published poetry, the editorship of *Woman's World*, and having his photo taken. A lot. He ran the risk of being the archetypal modern celebrity, his notoriety fed by nothing more than his notoriety.

But, when achievement did arrive, it was sudden and overwhelming. It began with the publication of *The Portrait of Dorian Gray*, first serialised in *Lippincotts* magazine in 1890. An actor-manager George Alexander, who had recently taken on the fashionable St James's Theatre, spotted a 'dramatic faculty' in the novel and asked for a play. Wilde had been hawking around two plays of unperformable awfulness for some time, the unfortunately titled *Vera and the Nihilists*, and the *Duchess of Padua*, a calamity in verse. These both flash sparks of uniqueness, but are forced and derivative. He had not found his voice. Alexander said he would prefer a modern-dress society play. It was a nudge in the right direction, and accompanied by £100.

The play which resulted, *Lady Windermere's Fan*, was the first in a burst of four social comedies. Occupying the staid geography of the drawing room and country house, plotted within the straight-jacket confines of melodrama and farce, they transcend their origins to be subversive, perverse, witty and profoundly human. Oscar disparaged his method, saying 'the art of play-writing ... consists of writing a series of epigrams, and then finding characters to fit them. With a tag of incident thrown in'. Studying his notebooks, it is clear he did begin with the music of dialogue and speech, before finding situations to suit. But there is false modesty here. He waited a long time to aggregate a sum of wisdom in the storehouse of his heart, before pouring it into these proscenium framed vessels. The characters are delineated and understood, each with their pride and sadness. Wilde's special ability was to balance several different points of view in one paradoxical sentence. Not for him the hammer-headed tweet, with its nauseating slimness of point of view. Theatre, as he knew, is a constant search, through interrogation and empathy, for more complex moral judgements.

Critics hated the showboating of this language, calling it attention-seeking, impertinent and patronising. It does delight in its own dazzle, but its purpose was sincere. The work was aimed at promoting nuance and doubt, and to make people question judgements rather than revel in them. He described the play's doctrine as 'one of sheer individualism. It is not for anyone to censure what anyone else does ... Everyone should go his own way, to whatever place he chooses, in exactly the way he chooses.' With each play he sets up self-appointed saints against self-acknowledged sinners, and reveals how much more likely one is to find kindness amongst the sinners than the saints.

It would be impertinent to Wilde's complexity to ascribe him a moral purpose, but his plays demonstrate over and over that it is healthier for the psyche to realise that one is in error than to waste energy pointing out how others are; that, once wrong is admitted, there is a world beyond; and that all sins can be redeemed by charity and mercy. It is an irony of depth that an artist who preached those last two virtues so earnestly should have been shown so little of either by the world.

Together with his dramatist's skill, Oscar was a maestro of first nights, a prodigy of premieres. He arranged the house with fastidious care, curating combinations of celebrity, political power and intellectual weight. Lily Langtry would be placed in a prominent box, as would he himself, showing off the latest fashions. 'A score of faultless young dandies' would be scattered about. He sat people carefully, placing the loud beside the quiet, and the blithe beside the nervous. For his first major press night for *Lady Windermere's Fan*, he created a fashion for dazzling buttonholes. He instructed his followers in the 'Uranian' movement (one of several contemporary euphemisms, along with the name 'Earnest', for homosexual societies) to acquire green carnations from a fashionable florist. These flowers had had their stems placed in a solution of blue-green aniline dye. Wilde told his good friend Arthur Forbes Robertson:

> 'I want a good many men to wear them tomorrow. It will annoy the public.'
> 'But why annoy the public?'
> 'It likes to be annoyed. People will stare at it and wonder. They will look round the house and see more and more little specs of mystic green. "This must be some secret symbol", they will say, "what on earth can it mean?".'
> 'And what does it mean?'
> 'Nothing whatsoever, but that is just what nobody will guess!'

At each of the three premieres, Wilde appeared after the final curtain, pushing his way through the plush to stand before the footlights, his carnation brightly green. For his first, he bowed, then disappeared and returned with a cigarette, the ultimate accessory of decadence. He nervously puffed a little, before thanking his collaborators, finishing with: 'I think that you have enjoyed the performance as much as I have. And I am pleased to believe that you like the piece almost as much as I do myself.' Everyone loved the straightforwardness of this flippant self-delight (apart from the critics).

On 5 January 1895, at the Haymarket, Wilde opened his third social comedy, *An Ideal Husband*. Defying the laws of gravity, it was a still greater success than its predecessors. Wilde's curtain comment was 'I have enjoyed myself very much' and even something as inert as that quickly became much repeated. Sitting in the audience in a state of displaced anxiety was the American novelist Henry James. He ground his teeth with envy as the audience went wild for Wilde. He was in hiding from his own first night at the St James, for a play he had written called *Guy Domville*. He thought *An Ideal Husband* would be the perfect distraction. As he rushed back to his own theatre, he comforted himself that, if the audience could get so excited for a load of old rubbish like Wilde's play, his own piece should be a triumph. He was wrong. As he bowed on stage at the curtain call, the audience jeered.

The failure of James's play meant an early closure and the St James's Theatre's manager, George Alexander, was suddenly without a show. He didn't need to think hard to work out who was the hottest playwright in town. Having produced *Lady Windermere*, he had a relationship with Oscar already and knew he had a play in his locker. He also knew that he was flying dangerously close to the wind, and that producing any play of his at that moment would be a risk, though he had no idea just how close to peril Oscar truly was.

WALKING THE TIGHTROPE

To say Wilde came from a troubled family would be an understatement. In addition to the death of his beloved sister Isola, his brother Willie was a brilliant but hapless drunk, who floated through the Stygian depths of drink-sodden post-prandial punditry on Fleet Street. His father, Sir William Wilde, a brilliant Dublin ethnographer and ophthalmologist, was an inveterate shagger and spent his life on the brink of public disgrace. He fathered an illegitimate son who he showed an arm's length love for, and two illegitimate daughters, who suffered a tragic demise. In their early teens they attended a winter's dance in the Irish countryside, both bubbling with excitement at their new and extravagant dresses. Tragically, one danced too near the fire, and her crinoline and hoops caught aflame. The other sister grabbed her and rushed her outside and lay on top of her in the snow to put the flames out. Both died of burns.

Wilde's work is full of examples of extreme self-sacrifice to save others, and it is hard not to trace their provenance back to this desperate story, and the image of two teenage sisters, and dresses and fire and snow.

The appetites of Wilde's father caught up with him when one of his amours accused him of rape, and waged a public campaign. In the resulting libel case, which thrilled Dublin, London and New York with its titillating details, honours were eventually even, but the scandal and exposure ruined Sir William. When Oscar launched his own libel action thirty years later, he was in many ways acting out his parents' story, as if compelled to dance within their pattern. Wilde's mother, Lady Jane, went by the moniker Speranza, a name given to her in response to her part in the Irish Republican movement, which she appended to the verse she wrote in that cause. A tall, fierce and independent woman, she ran extravagant salons in Dublin for everyone, and then in London for many of the expatriate Irish community, including a young W.B. Yeats, and George Bernard Shaw. (Speranza is the god of hope who takes Orpheus down to the underworld and delivers him to the boatman, Charon.) Within Wilde's ornate wit is a fierce emotional intensity. The power station funding this was his family, though his love life, or lives, helped keep it churning.

If Wilde's family was problematic, the family of his lover, Lord Alfred 'Bosie' Douglas, outstripped them. The Douglas clan would have given the House of Atreus a run for their money. The British aristocracy have always claimed the patent on the word 'eccentric' and hidden behind that word behaviour which could more accurately be called 'barking'. Lord Alfred's father, the Marquis of Queensberry, was a monster of malevolence, a rich and powerful volcano of inbred spleen who exploded at anything which crossed his path that he didn't care for. He ruined a play of Lord Tennyson's, *The Promise of May,* by turning up on press night and carrying on an argument with the play's content from the stalls. Much of modernity provoked his ire, but nothing more so than his own children, with whom he waged running battles all his life.

Alongside the eccentricity, the Douglas family exhibited a capacity for feuds, which was well over the border into psychotic. This was often the case amongst the aristocracy, where idleness curdled into toxicity. Oscar came on the wrong end of Bosie's fury on a number of occasions, when he would combust into a state of infantile rage. On one such occasion in a Brighton hotel, as Wilde was completing the text of *Importance*, Bosie attacked him with the force of a potential homicide, and Oscar had to rush to a public space to find sanctuary. At such times, Bosie became 'distorted in mind and body' and 'a thing terrible to look at'. More perilous for Wilde was not being on the end of either son or father's fury, but being caught in the crossfire between them.

Neither knew any mode in their interactions other than attack. In one letter to his son, the Marquis wrote: 'With my own eyes I saw you both in the most loathsome and disgusting relationship as expressed by your manner and expression ... Also I now hear on good authority that his wife is petitioning to divorce him for sodomy ... If I thought the thing was true, I should be quite justified in shooting him at sight.' Bosie sent him back a telegram, 'what a funny little man you are'. This did nothing to calm. His father sent by return, 'If you send me any more such telegrams ... I will give you the thrashing you deserve ... ' Neither had any semblance of self-control, and Oscar no control over them.

Queensberry, who had a need for publicity as insatiable as Oscar's, took to patrolling London's clubs, restaurant and bars, seeking out son and lover, and issuing dire warnings. The blood pressure of the Marquis would not have been lowered by a disastrous recent marriage. It collapsed after a year, with the young woman filing for failure of consummation. Queensberry asserted his virility through the courts, and soon the talk of guns became more pronounced. Queensberry told another son, Percy: 'If I were to shoot this hideous monster in the street, I should be perfectly justified, for he has ruined my so-called son.' Bosie, thrilled by the mounting tension, started carrying a pistol and crowing to his father, 'If I shoot you, or if Wilde shoots you, we should be completely justified. I think if you were dead not many people would miss you.'

Oscar was a sufficiently acute observer of life to know that the people who got injured in the feuds of upper-class families were almost always the outsiders. The posh love their dramas, but it is the bystanders who get left as roadkill. And Wilde had his own Celtic pride. He asked his friend Frank Harris forcefully, 'Why should I cringe to this madman?' To which Harris replied sagely, 'Because he is a madman.'

In an effort to cool things off, once *The Ideal Husband* had opened and *Earnest* was in rehearsal, Oscar and Bosie took themselves off to Algeria. The purpose of the trip was to relax and calm down, though it soon turned into the sort of saturnalian sex tourism which gives the nineteenth century a bad name. Bosie found a young lover and disappeared off with him into the mountains. Oscar was left with the young and timid André Gide, who by chance had checked into the same hotel. Wilde initiated the timid French writer into the methods of acquiring sexual favour. Gide noticed 'a dark anxiety' in Wilde. It was clear he knew disaster was approaching, but was determined to drive all to its conclusion. He said to Gide, 'My friends advise prudence. Prudence! But can I have any? That would be going backwards. I must go as far as possible. Something must happen ... Something else.' Given the familial broil, something else was almost inevitable; given the culture beyond it, entirely so.

SHIVERING ESTABLISHMENT TIMBERS

An Ideal Husband continued with huge success as these tensions played out. A witty farce, with a smattering of Ibsenite marital drama, it touches on the great fear of the day, the fear of being found out. The plot-hinge is financial chicanery, but, within a society founded on hypocrisies, it manipulates everyone's fear of exposure.

Embezzlement, murder and sexual shenanigans all carried on in the shadows behind the carapace of Victorian morality, but nothing excited the imagination of an audience, or shivered the timbers of the establishment, as thoroughly as homosexuality. In 1889, an all-male brothel on Cleveland Street had been raided by the police. The press worked themselves into a furious froth, while many aristocrats rushed for the night train to Paris. One went as far as Peru to escape the potential opprobrium. Soon after, a further raid around the corner in Fitzroy Street arrested eighteen men, and found several of them in 'fantastic female garb'. This pointed towards a growing subculture.

The centre of London, and particularly the area around the theatre district, hosted a burgeoning scene. A hitherto underground movement was daring to outrage, and delighting in doing so. Drag acts on stage, transvestitism off it: there was a growing feeling that 'the love that dared not speak its name' had every right to shout its merry head off. This was changing the public arena at a pace that scared the wits out of conservative England. Nor was it only a subculture. A flourishing number of new journals were advancing the argument in everything from short verses to long essays that it was maybe time for civilisation to grow up, and admit that many preferred their own sex. On the one hand a burgeoning wild scene by night, on the other a growing intellectual and aesthetic movement – Oscar was at the intersection of both.

The hypocrisy went right to the top and, to heighten the tension, it involved the poisonous Douglas family. Bosie's older brother, Francis, was engaged in a long and passionate relationship with Rosebery, the Prime Minister. Before the Marquis set to hounding Oscar, he had chased Rosebery across Europe, and charged around Bad Homburg, where the then Foreign Minister was holidaying, shouting about what he was going to do to the 'Bloody Bugger', and 'Jew Queer'. The local chief of police was deputed to run him out of town.

All of the concomitant tensions proved too much for Francis Douglas. His lifeless body was discovered slumped in a ditch, at the edge of a turnip field in Somerset, one cold morning in October 1894, his twelve-bore shotgun at his side. The establishment put a cover up into operation, claiming rather improbably that it was an accident. Queensberry's rage was given a tragic twist and, with the Prime Minister's name popping up in gossip columns in connection with the incident, it became imperative for the establishment to deal with what they viewed as a growing threat. They resolved to shut down the 'Uranian' movement. They needed a figurehead and a scapegoat. The man who sat at the centre of all these elements looked like the perfect sacrificial lamb.

Oscar knew about the violence of the state, and was aware that however many country house parties he had been to, and however much laughter he had provoked, when push came to shove he was on his own. A sensible choice would have been to run for cover, but that was not his style. A thoughtful choice would have been to behave with decorum, but he refused. *Pecca fortiter* ('sin boldly') was the motto of both Luther and Oscar. He carried on his predatory behaviour. Since it was a predation driven on by a punitive society which revelled in barefaced hypocrisy, it is hard to find an excess of retrospective morality.

The state didn't care so much about the behaviour: what they wanted was to punish it with an act of terror aimed at a whole community. Thus pushing that community back into the shadows. Wilde knew what was happening, surrendered himself to his own fate and became a witness of his own catastrophe. As he rode towards the first night of *Earnest*, there would have been the taste of death in his mouth.

Which made it all the more important that he styled it out.

BISH BASH BOSH

The greatest virtue for any theatre producer is the ability to bounce back from failure. No-one can survive without the ability to dance freely when in a pickle. George Alexander, having watched James's lamentably titled *Guy Domville* sink without trace, had a paid-for company and an empty theatre. His response was point-perfect. Having earlier declined Wilde's *The Importance of Being Earnest*, he now bought it from a rival manager, Charles Wyndham. He retained the actors he had for the James play, and added the pre-eminent grande dame of the day, Rose Leclercq, to play the central character, first called Lady Lancing, then Lady Brancaster and finally, triumphantly, Lady Bracknell.

Against the complaints of the author, he transformed the play from a hefty four acts to a sleek and blissful centripetal three. He obtained a licence from the Lord Chamberlain's Examiner of Plays. He cast himself as Jack Worthing, and elegantly slid that character towards the centre of the play. He ordered for his character a sharp morning suit, with a black-bordered handkerchief, for his show-stealing second act entrance. He conducted furiously intense rehearsals with the company with everyone learning as they went along. From a standing start on 6 January, when the *Domville* reviews came in, he had *Earnest* ready for presentation on 14 February. Six weeks – bish bash bosh.

Rehearsals were never easy with Wilde around, since he had a profound problem with adjusting to the reality that the actors were the most important people in the room. Oscar sucked in too much oxygen to allow others fully to occupy the same space. He loved to fuss over everything, and freely distributed notes on blocking, design, how to say his dialogue, and even on the actors' make-up. His tone would be both Olympian and peremptory – 'Pray give your serious attention to all these points' – which is the quickest way to drive collaborators, involved in an evolutionary process, stark mad.

Wilde lost the love of actors on an earlier production by stating in a newspaper interview that they were 'a set of puppets'. He stated to the *Telegraph* that 'the personality of an actor is often a source of danger in the perfect presentation of a work of art'. This caused what was euphemistically described as 'a good deal of well-deserved banter'. One can well imagine it may have been forceful. Oscar himself described his relations with actors as 'a little strained'. When a different producer, Herbert Beerbohm Tree, was asked on an earlier play whether the play had been rehearsed 'with the assistance of Wilde', he replied 'with the interference of Wilde'. Alexander was forced on several occasions to ask Wilde to leave rehearsals, and once described him in the heat of the wrangle as 'this conceited, arrogant and ungrateful man'.

Alexander had little idea of the extra strain that Wilde was under, and proved to be a good friend in later years, so the heat of rehearsal room tensions can be forgiven. But a fraught process, on top of the wagonload of other pressures, would not have lessened the freight of baggage which Oscar carried into the St James that night.

FIREWORKS

With such a kaleidoscope of pressures bearing down, it was unkind of the weather to join in. Leverson described 14 February as 'a dark sinister winter's night – a black bitter threatening wind blew the drifting snow'. Yet somehow, with the magic of theatrical possibility, once the assembled crowd of chaps with capes and canes and toppers, and ladies in pearls and ball gowns, assembled in the warmth, a giddy sensation of delight enveloped them. 'Outside a frost, inside, the very breath of success; perfumed atmosphere of gaiety, fashion and everlasting popularity. The author of the play was fertile, inventive, brilliant.' Oscar had decreed that the flower of the night was not to be the usual carnation, but to be 'the lily of the valley in honour of an absent friend' (Bosie, still up a mountain in Algeria, and presumably up an Algerian), and everyone was duly wearing them. Eager young dandies crammed lilies into their buttonholes. Just to be perverse, Oscar defied his own decree, and in his buttonhole 'a single green carnation bloomed savagely'. Beaming with euphoria, he glided through the 'rippling, glittering, chattering crowd' spraying witticisms like confetti.

One can only pity the poor curtain-raiser, a short and inoffensive play called *In the Season* by Langdon Mitchell. Many had stayed at dinner an extra twenty minutes in order to miss it. Others casually walked in during it, nattering. The resplendent assembly was full of expectation, and it wasn't for that. As the orchestra of Walter Slaughter finished their interlude music, and the of-the-moment electric lights dimmed, the crowd silenced themselves to a held hush. The curtain rose to the sound of an off-stage piano.

A journeyman actor, F. Kinsey Peile, was cast as Lane, Algernon's deadpan butler. After his first scene he came off, and George Alexander came up to him in the wings and whispered, 'Congratulations! You will always have the pleasure of remembering that you got the first laugh in *The Importance of Being Earnest*.' He himself remembered the play 'was received with roars of merriment from beginning to end'. The grande dame herself, Rose Leclercq, had a cold and was not at her best, but still managed to land her iconic zingers including the triple-syllabled legend, 'A handbag?' The evening galloped along, aided by Alexander's pruning, and manifested Wilde's insistence that a farce 'must be played like a pistol shot'. As if the audience were all under the same intense pressure as Oscar, they back-flipped with the same insouciance into joy, and exemplified the same unbearable lightness of being. Leverson spotted a 'strange almost hysterical joy'.

At the conclusion, the applause was delirious and it grew when Oscar appeared for his bow. There was no speech. When an actor asked Wilde earlier if he was going to say something, he replied, 'I don't think I shall take a call tonight. You see, I took one only last month at the Haymarket, and one feels so much like a German band.' Maybe he did not want to tempt providence. Nor did he know for certain where his tormentor was. Backstage he managed to compliment himself, 'I have taken the drama, the most objective form known to art, and made it as personal a mode of expression as the lyric or the sonnet.' And, to deliver the most delicious back-handed compliment to Alexander, 'My dear Aleck, it was charming, quite charming. And, do you know, from time to time I was reminded of a play I once wrote myself called *The Importance of Being*

Earnest.' Despite his on-stage silence, the noise of the applause and the warmth within it must have been a balm. It never got better than this for him; it was the last moment of triumph in his topsy-turvy life.

The extra policeman outside the theatre turned out to be necessary. No-one had known what Queensberry planned, though they soon discovered. Despite his lack of a ticket, he arrived like thunder and brought with him a heavy-set prizefighter and a 'grotesque bouquet of vegetables'. He was determined to make trouble. The police intercepted him out front, and had the stage door covered as well, when he sneaked round the back. This peculiar and tragic man, so interred in his hatreds that he could see nothing beyond them, had intended to stand up like an Old Testament prophet and denounce Oscar as a sodomite. He was foiled.

Unable to admit defeat, he hovered in the snow outside for the duration of the show, while warmth and laughter and delight glowed from within. In a gesture of some bathos, having hoped to hurl the vegetables at the author on his curtain call, he handed them over to the box office, muttering that they were for Oscar Wilde. As Oscar wrote to Bosie, 'Yes, the Scarlet Marquis made a plot to address the audience ... He prowled about for three hours and then left chattering like a monstrous ape.' It was a battle won, but in its humiliation of this demonic man, mired in his own toxicity, it only inspired a harder war.

A SPIRIT OF FORGIVENESS

'What sort of play are we to expect?'
'It is exquisitely trivial, a delicate bubble of fancy and it has its philosophy'.
'Its philosophy?'
'That we should treat all the trivial things of life very seriously and all the serious things of life with sincere and studied triviality.'

Robert Ross and Oscar Wilde

Oscar knew that the most important sentiments can be delivered in the theatre by silliness as well as gravity, and saved some of his wisest writing for his most nonsensical play. *The Importance of Being Earnest*, as well as being funny and frivolous, has earned a reputation as representing the quintessence of Englishness.

But what sort of Englishness? Beneath the smokescreen of butlers, country houses and cucumber sandwiches, stranger forces swirl. This supposed template of our national character features two polyamorous youths, Algernon and Jack, both leading double lives, with distinct identities in different environments. They meet their match in two strong women, who run rings around them, and whose loyalty to the iron-clad laws of whim is greater even than their own. The whole world is presided over by a goddess of supposed order, Lady Bracknell, whose every pronouncement trumps conventional moral and social thinking. The mainspring of the plot, that a baby was left in a handbag at a railway station, is of a piece with this world's derangement. This is a vision of English life which is only a silk screen away from anarchy.

At the centre is professional masquerader Jack Worthing, who can say with conviction, 'I don't know who I really am.' The set-up is comic and deliciously so, since he was 'born, or at any rate bred, in a handbag'. The ramifications are profound, and touch, lightly, on the nature of human modernity. Jack, being unmoored, is free to construct his own identity as he sees fit: he is in a vacuum, both terrifying and liberating. It scares Lady Bracknell, for whom it seems 'to display a contempt for the ordinary decencies of family life that reminds one of the worst excesses of the French Revolution'. But for Jack it gives him freedom to manoeuvre, sexually and socially. It is only at the end that he discovers his true name, and his Earnest-ness. Just as Oscar had to endure a centrifugal whirl of identity confusion, before he discovered his own sincerity.

Throughout his plays, Wilde writes of living on the precipice – those in public position who flirt with disaster. In *The Importance of Being Earnest*, in a benevolent comic universe, he personalises that precipice to two men living double lives, and, through coincidence and generosity, pulls them back from the brink.

He was, of course, taking a leaf out of old theatrical rule books, and the spirit of British comedy, where peril is resolved in marriage and love. *The Comedy of Errors, Twelfth Night, She Stoops to Conquer, The School for Scandal* – all scatter identity and security in positions of danger, then find a route through to complicated resolutions. Theatre lives on the lessening of tensions, and the lightening of terrors. The very process is about fear beforehand, actors and audience locked in a shared tension, which is then resolved by the surprising joy of performance. It is the resolving simplicity of one group of people telling a story to another group, and in the process washing doubts and guilts away. That spirit of forgiveness in the theatre industry, which only survives on the quality of mercy, would have been a sanctuary to Wilde.

Within that spirit, he wanted to forge a new England, one where the eccentric, the double and the confused, could all feel included. A determined outsider himself, a Protestant amongst Catholics, Anglo-Irish in Ireland, his Republican parents alienated from their own community, he brought all of those exclusions to England. There he added the discovery of his essential sexuality. It is not surprising that in his last play he wanted to create a world where there was peril, but where that peril could be (partially) resolved in comic harmony. The Anglo-Irish gay man served up an image of the perfect England, and England, with its peculiar genius for co-option of the outsider, included this play in its new and enlarged sense of itself.

Wilde bequeathed us a batty comedy, which leaves us night after night in the happy hope that in its offering of comic forgiveness, and the sublime re-meeting of the long separated, we may one day live up to its weightless promise.

MARTYRDOM

Queensberry was a diminished spirit beside the munificent soul of Wilde. He compensated with the size of his hatred. He had other assets: money and connection and class have always mattered more when it comes to public war than tenderness or imagination. As Oscar said in incomprehension as his nemesis pursued his vendetta, 'My whole life is ruined by this man. The tower of ivory is assailed by a foul thing. On the sand my life is spilt.' Hysterical but true. The establishment wanted their victim and they duly crushed the butterfly on their wheel.

During the degrading trials and prosecutions, Oscar was given many chances and much encouragement to escape, but he refused. That side of his personality which had always felt a sense of death beneath the glitter, that felt guilt for his many sins, knew his narrative was more truly fulfilled by punishment than the fugitive life. As his friend Frank Harris commented, 'He felt the life-journey of genius would be incomplete and farcical without the final tragedy; whoever lives for the highest must be crucified.' Harris did not know, nor could Oscar have guessed, the banal and crushing realities of the British penal system. The full horror was yet to come. But somewhere he knew there was a completeness to his life and art, and in *Earnest* he had spent accumulated wealth he could never recoup. He may have been ready for martyrdom.

In his post-prison years floating around Europe, before washing up in fin de siècle Paris, his mind in absinthe-soaked decline, his body wrecked by the pain of imprisonment, and with a great cocktail of Europe's most desolating diseases coursing through him, Wilde had time to think about what followed from triumph. Artists, he believed, can be successful incidentally, but never intentionally:

> *If they are, they remain incomplete. The artist's mission is to live the complete life; success, as an episode (which is all it can be); failure, as the real, the final end ... the higher function of the artist is to make perceived the beauty of failure.*

Such beautiful self-pity would only really be possible for an artist who could remember nights like St Valentine's Day 1895, when a glowing crowd forgot who they were and climbed higher together.

Merlin Holland, Wilde's grandson, told me that recently it became necessary to erect a glass screen around Jacob Epstein's tomb for Wilde in the Père Lachaise cemetery in Paris. The tradition of applying thick rouge to one's lips and then planting a kiss on the tomb was a long and glorious one, but the ceaseless washing off of red-printed smackers was starting to damage the stone. A glass barrier was erected to render the monument lip-proof. But, Merlin told me, people simply started kissing the glass. On sunny days, the shadows of hundreds of ghostly kisses now dance like butterflies over his tomb.

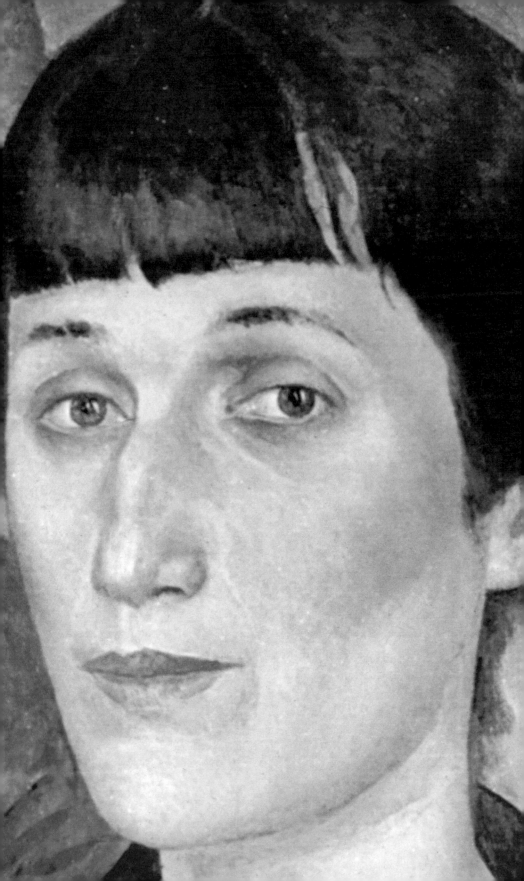

19

Paper and fire

A TALE OF ANNA AKHMATOVA

Anna Akhmatova has many acquaintances. She has no close friends. She is good-natured and does not hesitate to spend her money when she has it. But at heart she is cold and arrogant with a childish egoism. She is helpless when it comes to the practical tasks of everyday life. Mending a stocking poses an insoluble problem for her. Boiling potatoes is an achievement. Despite her great fame, she is very shy.

This is astute and witty. And not inaccurate. It comes from the NKVD character assessment of one of the greatest Russian poets of the twentieth century. One among many such descriptions, it was held in the files of the Lubyanka, the headquarters of the secret police in Stalin's nightmarish state. Stalin himself had been a poet in his Georgian youth, and had taken outsized pride in his few published works. Not without talent, but not with enough, he preserved a special hatred for those who had more. And for a world that was dazzled by the unpardonable genius of others. As a consequence, generations of artists of delicacy and refinement found themselves trapped in a horror novel written by a psychotic child.

At the height of the terror of the mid-1930s, a new prohibition was decreed. It was forbidden to flush books down the toilet. So many intellectuals were trying to dispose of incriminating material, the pipes of Moscow and St Petersburg were getting clogged with paper. It is hard to conjure a clearer image of a defunct society.

Anna Akhmatova lived in the centre of an artistic circle, every one of whom shivered through decades of prolonged terror. They dwelled in decaying flats, wallpaper peeling, smelling dankly of long-boiled everything, waiting in fear of the one-o'clock-in-the-morning rap on the door. It always came. Osip Mandelstam, Akhmatova's close friend and peer as a poet, was carted off for torture, which broke his spirit, then killed him. Vsevolod Meyerhold – Konstantin in the MAT production of *The Seagull* and a director of genius – was taken to the cells at the age of sixty-five and beaten over eight long days with straps and fists. Finally this sweet-spirited and curious man was in such pain he incriminated himself so death would come, and was shot by a firing squad. Vladimir Mayakovsky, the Futurist poet and playwright, who had enthusiastically embraced the new Communist regime, was viciously smeared by the authorities and either committed suicide or was assassinated. The poet Nikolay Gumilyov, Anna's first husband and father of her son, Lev, was arrested for an imagined monarchist conspiracy, and shot in a forest with sixty others in 1923. Nikolay Punin, Anna's long-term lover, and a leading art historian, died in the Gulag of Vorkuta in 1953, after spending the last four years of his life slowly starving in icy barracks, where two hundred prisoners shared a single light bulb.

A handful amongst thousands of others. Each of them, before their murder, would have merited a pithy and precise little character portrait like the one of Akhmatova at the beginning of this chapter. The thought of all these psychological descriptions piling up in secret state files feels like the revenge of the epic Russian novel on its own country of origin.

A LITERARY QUAGMIRE

Anna Akhmatova is a representative of a reactionary literary quagmire devoid of ideas ... one of the standard bearers of a hollow, empty, aristocratic salon poetry which is absolutely foreign to Soviet literature ... The range of her poetry is pitifully limited. This is the poetry of a feral lady from the salons, moving between the boudoir and the prayer stool. It is based on erotic motifs of mourning, melancholy, death, mysticism and isolation ... Half nun, half, whore, or rather both nun and whore, with her petty narrow private life, her trivial experiences, and her religious-mystical eroticism, Akhmatova's poetry is totally foreign to the people.

As well as the knock on the door from the NKVD, this was the second great threat: the public denunciation. A sanctioned takedown of one's ideological position was an act of trolling from which there was rarely a return. These were the words – brilliant rhetoric in themselves – which spewed out of one Andrey Zhdanov, Stalin's 'propagandist-in-chief', in front of the Executive Committee of the Writer's Union in August 1946. It was a moment when Anna believed there might be a thaw in her relations with the authorities, and that a new book might come out after a long silence. The speech refroze the terrain. The book didn't appear, her pension was shut down, and her ration book taken away. It was an attempt to end her working life.

The critical grenade was thrown at a bourgeois woman who had had many opportunities to join friends and peers in fleeing Russia, but decade after decade had refused to budge, ever loyal to her mother country. She had lived a destitute, hand-to-mouth existence since the Revolution of 1917, hefting a battered suitcase, secured with a scrappy belt, from friend's flat to lover's spare room to relation's sofa. She had rarely criticised anyone in public. In response to the above attack, she said: 'I have experienced great fame, I have experienced great disgrace, and I have come to the conclusion that, in essentials, it is all the same.' Beautiful pride and style, and, for men like Zhdanov, unforgivable.

When people get frightened by the worst excesses of the blog commentariat, of newspaper punditry or the line-stepping armies of social media, it is because their natural extension is moral monsters like Zhdanov, and their natural victims are the Akhmatovas. Under the guise of moral purity and ideological commitment, there are always plentiful opportunities for the vicious to scourge the honest. They revel in such historical moments. Such derogation reaches into all lives and can be deadly. In Akhmatova's personal life, it impacted every corner.

The web of her life was more than a mingled yarn, it was a Gordian knot. Her lover Nikolay Punin, whose home she shared for fifteen years, along with his wife and daughter, and her own son, denounced her husband, Gumilyov, three years before his execution:

> With what effort, and only because of the Communist movement, did we leave behind us a year ago the long-standing oppression of the dreary effeminate-licentious bourgeois aesthetic. I have personally felt cheerful and vivacious during this whole year, in part because several poets, Gumilyov for example, stopped writing, or at least stopped being printed or read.

When Lev read this, he was less than pleased that his mother's lover had helped push his father towards the firing squad. Such differences were later dissolved once everyone, old friends and old foes, ended up in the same place, the Gulag.

THE GOOD QUEEN

> She is saucy, egotistical, and plays at being the good queen. She has ceased to live her own life, for she lives only biographically with an eye on the gesture, and the phrase 'for the future'.

This quote – from a friend – is of a piece with many others. In her youth Anna was a bobby-dazzler, seeking out the wild places of the night and carrying on through to the dawn in the bohemian world of pre-revolution St Petersburg. There was much mischief to discover, in a giddy world which knew that the excesses of the Romanovs were swirling Russia towards chaos. Centred around a smoke-filled cafe called the *Stray Dog*, Mayakovsky, Pasternak, Meyerhold, Gumilyov and others spent long nights listening to Futurist poetry and modernist music, watching deconstructed puppetry and arguing through the night about art. 'Polyamory' is an insufficient word to cover the wildness and the frequency of their sexual experiments. Anna, slender and in silk, sat poised and aloof on the edge of these gatherings, until it got seriously Dionysiac, when she would suddenly be discovered in the middle. The damage in broken hearts and suicides was severe, but, with the world tipping over a precipice, the imperative was to keep dancing.

After the Revolution, when many of her class deserted her in the scramble to the West, Anna reassembled her arrogance and her style in a different world. She was often hobbled by illness, but she always kept her clean-cut fringe and hauteur. Though she only had one cap and a light coat for all weathers, and one set of scarlet pyjamas to lounge around whatever home she found, she styled them as if on a Parisian catwalk. Like Ranevskaya in *The Cherry Orchard*, she was compulsively generous when she had no money. She could be as fierce a snob as the worst Bloomsbury grande dame, but was profligate in her help and support for friends of all classes. She would break a man's heart, while remaining close friends with his wife. It was a dizzying whirl, which kept her one step ahead of the authorities. Without ever being able to capture her shifting persona, they were never quite able to condemn her. Her shape-shifting was natural, and a survival mechanism.

When she recited her poetry, whether in the days of decadence or despair, she was transformed, 'standing erect, haughty, and with a fur of some kind on her shoulders'. Her soft, self-mocking smile, a useful line of defence against a world in free fall, disappeared from her face. She was overcome by the feelings in her verse. Then she would be filled with the sense of her own high definition, and those who listened would travel with her.

VERSE BEFORE GOD

She writes verse as if she is standing in front of a man and one should write as if one stands before God.

This was from Alexander Blok, a fellow poet who was refused permission to travel by the Soviet authorities when mortally ill in 1921 and died soon after. From Anna's first collection, she was a popular poet, though rarely in favour with the critics. She was not the only woman poet of her day – Marina Tsvetaeva was a near contemporary and of similar stature – but she suffered the casual dismissal of the men's mob.

She began from within a movement, the acmeists, which was born from a reaction to the symbolists. Where the latter used imagery to grasp at some higher reality, the acmeists attempted to realise individual human experience within this world. The symbolists had a Jungian desire to trace underlying patterns; the acmeists had a Freudian intention to focus down tight on an individual's behaviour. This was not poetry as a priest of the higher mysteries, this was poetry that read the world. What was prized was clarity and sharpness about objects.

Anna was a fierce adherent to her own moment-to-moment truth, and was able to bring this movement into poetic life more richly than any. One moment shall suffice. In her poem 'Song of the Final Meeting', an evocation of the end of an affair, she writes:

> How helplessly chilled was my chest, yet
> My footsteps were nimble and light.
> I unconsciously put on my left hand
> The glove that belonged on my right.
> It seemed the stairs were endless,
> But I knew – there were only three.

The telescoping of the stairs is beautiful and the embarrassed clumsiness with the glove, heartbreaking. Akhmatova had an eye for life, and the accidental tiny moments that tell a story. We are poised in her verse half-way between the epic stillness of the minimal haiku, and the romantic lyricism of the West, a powerful place of equipoise.

SONS AND MOTHERS

> For you, it would have been better if I had died in the camps.

Of all the trashing comments, and there is no shortage, this would have been the most painful for Anna. It came from her son, Lev. The set-up for the central Akhmatova story – the mother who waits for news of her son for a year and a half in a queue of mothers outside a prison's walls – is one that begs a Hollywood beginning and ending. It gets neither.

For most of Lev's childhood, including the time when his father was executed, he was left with his grandmother. Meanwhile, Anna, always amid a whirl of romances, would occasionally turn up, think about taking her son on, and decide against it. When he did come to live with her, it was in the flat of Punin, a man who had denounced his father. He had to sleep in a bed in a cold corridor. When he was away in the camps, his mother's letters were infrequent, a randomness criticised by her son: 'Mama is not writing to me. I imagine I am once again the victim of her psychological games.' Lev never learnt the wisdom of Anna's reluctance to put words on paper. When she started sending short cards, it was the last straw for him. On several of the occasions that he was released from the camps, where Hollywood would have staged a tear-stained clutching embrace of an encounter, Lev simply headed off in a different direction and avoided his mother. She didn't want to see him: he didn't trust her intentions. If there had been any love there, it was sundered and left in bitter tatters by the violence of the state.

Lev was as complex a beast as his mother. Fiercely loyal to the father he never knew, one of his spells in prison was the result of him correcting a teacher who had got a fact wrong about his father's life. Sour of temper before he entered the penal system, he was drawn into a circle of right-wing nationalistic anti-Semites called the 'Black Hundred' while inside. His first lover didn't recognise him on his return from the camps, there were such deep lines circling his eyes and grooved into his forehead. His identity was wrecked by the camps, as it was for many. As Pasternak said of the survivors: 'None of their reactions were like ours – you could not survive if you didn't change your soul.'

There was nothing bogus about what Anna did for her son. She wrote countless letters to anyone in authority she knew; she travelled to and from Moscow to lobby individuals in person; she silenced her own voice; and for long hours and days she stood in a queue of women outside St Petersburg's notorious Kresty Prison bearing food, blankets and clothes to be smuggled in, and begging for information to be smuggled out.

Anna discovered something of her quintessential personality standing in the Kresty courtyard. Often friends tried to force her to take time out, or to sit down, but she carried on standing there. She blistered her feet, she enfeebled her legs, she scrambled her wits, but she carried on. Standing still for endless hours anywhere is painful; for a spirit as listless as Akhmatova's, it was a special sort of torture. But she seems to have found in the blank state of waiting, and in the queue by the hard stone wall, something essential and clear of her self.

In the defining moment of her creative life, a young woman standing behind her leant forward, 'lips blue from the cold, and asked me in a whisper (everyone whispered there), "Can you describe this?" And I said, "I can". Then something like a smile passed fleetingly over what had once been her face.'

THE THEATRE OF MEMORY

Many moments of artistic innovation occur in the space between performers and a crowd. Often it is the dynamic of collective heightened thought, and communal courage, which pushes everyone through to being new together. Often, but not always. Sometimes breakthroughs happen in private spaces.

Lydia Chukovskaya, Anna's great friend, visited her at Punin's shabby flat in St Petersburg. No amount of house pride in 1938 Russia could have combated the exhaustion of living. No-one was keeping up appearances. Clothes lines in the kitchen dripped damp; wallpaper puckered off the walls; floors went long unswept; newspapers were stuck over the windowpanes, and a twisted old shawl hung from the ceiling. Scraps of chaotic elegance studded Anna's room – a carved chair here, a bronze-framed mirror there, some Easter eggs painted by friends on the mantelpiece, a sketch of Anna by Modigliani on the wall. Beside the elegant sat the functional: a bag of tins, and a drawer full of biscuits hoarded for Lev. Anna sat, her legs tucked under her, in an armchair with springs popping out. Her latest of many diseases, Meniere's, meant her sense of balance was shot. Outside, she had to be helped over the road; inside, she was permanently seated.

Beside her was a stove and, in this spot, Anna and her friend Lydia enacted the most potent performance in Russia, and the only one permissible. Anna had been brewing and creating a new cycle of poems, to be called *Requiem*. It was a record of a mother's pain at the loss of her son, of her citizen's heartbreak at the despair of her nation, of her own heart's dismay at the loss of so many lovers and friends, and of her poet's duty to say what she saw. The words of her poetry could not be written, for fear of discovery. They could not be spoken, for fear of being overheard. Anna wrote down the words for a brief life on paper, she and Lydia committed them to their memories in silence, and then Anna burnt the words in the stove. This was the foremost Russian poem of the twentieth century, and its initial life could only exist in the minds of two friends.

Within the great lie of the state, the only place these cold, grey verses could live was in silence round a fire in a locked room. The only amphitheatre for this performance was in the electrical connections of their buzzing silent brains, and the swirling mazurka of mutual understanding in their eyes. The crowd was their synapses whirring. This was a long way from Anna, decked out in the latest Parisian fashions, dazzling with renditions of her hedonistic amours to the *Stray Dog* cafe in 1913. Then, her verse was full of the headlong romantic rush of youth; now, she wrote with the tungsten-hard love of a mother for her endangered son. Somehow, in spite of the destitution around, Anna combed her hair, posed in elegant desolation, and from her poetic imagination summoned up fragments of gold. It was the most private opening performance imaginable.

Was there self-dramatisation to this? Yes in the styling, not a jot in the reasoning. Anna knew that she was being spied on in her home. She had placed a hair in a notebook of her poems when she went out, and it had gone on her return. She will have remembered that Mandelstam spoke his poem, *The Wolf*, a satire on Stalin's predatory intentions on the peasantry, to an audience of no more than ten, including herself. One of the ten informed, and that was the beginning of the end of Mandelstam's life. The state had a fierce gaze that permeated everywhere.

Requiem was a masterpiece that had no life beyond the mind of its creator. Until one friend shared it. Then it became a public work of art, however muted.

Thankfully, two proved enough.

HOW TIRED I AM

After several false dawns, by 1962, Anna was able to commit *Requiem* to paper, and it circulated in samizdat publications at the same time as the transcript of Joseph Brodsky's rigged trial. Both found an audience amongst the young, and those yearning for the new. They would still have to wait a long time for freedom, but Akhmatova's poem was instantly recognised as a classic.

Brodsky was one of a cabal around this old legend in the years before her death. There was no room for her son Lev. Akhmatova's late years were spent surrounded by faded flowers and hidden bottles of vodka and young admirers. She wrote a series of poems for this cabal, including *The Last Rose* for Brodsky:

> *Dear Lord, you see how tired I am*
> *Of dying, resurrrection, life itself.*
> *Take everything away, but let me still*
> *Savour the freshness of this scarlet rose.*

She had indeed died many times over, and been born again too often, for one fragile barque. In a late work, *Poem Without a Hero*, she encounters her past self; in another, we see her staring into a mirror. There is a sense in her old age of sliding in and out of the many different selves she had inhabited – the soignée flapper of the *Stray Dog*, the famous poet, the political dodger, the lover time after time, the survivor of two wars, and finally the softened old Mother Russia, with a bottle of vodka to hand. She lived the truth that a plethora of personalities are the best survival mechanism when you are living within an overpowering and violent lie. In her exhaustion before death, she liked to murmur Yeats' line with its soft iambs, 'When you are old and grey and full of sleep.'

The identity which shone through the others was the one she found in a hard and blank space beside a prison wall. There, she could feel a hundred million 'screaming through her exhausted mouth', and there in vacancy and cold she found herself. In the Second Epilogue of *Requiem*, with her customary grandiosity, she enquires as to where the Russian people might choose to put up a statue for her. It should not be by the sea near her place of birth, nor in the Tsar's garden, but by the wall of the prison she stood beside for three hundred hours, in honour of her and her fellow ghostly attendants:

> *And there, unexpectedly, teardrops will flow*
> *From the eyelids of bronze with the melting snow,*

And prison-yard pigeons will rise to the sky,
As the ships, on the Neva, pass quietly by.

Words which first appeared in silent communion between two friends before being cast into a fire. Not before they had been fastened into the ice-cold store box of the memory.

20

Death Looks at Us

A TALE OF ALFRED HITCHCOCK
AND JANET LEIGH

THE HUCKSTER

The private screening finished with the creative team sitting alongside the Paramount executives, and a heavy silence fell. The jaws of the executives gaped open. They fumbled for words. They did not know how to express the depth of their disapproval. Alfred Hitchcock had recently delivered a run of technicolour spectaculars in the age of widescreen extravaganzas, films of primary colour, high charm and gloss – *Rear Window*, *To Catch a Thief*, *Vertigo*, *North by Northwest*. Now he had delivered this dirty low-budget movie! In black and white! From the tawdry genre of horror! And, worst of all, he had killed off his one star and leading lady a third of the way in!

Had television ruined him? This looked like little more than an extended episode of his series *Alfred Hitchcock Presents*. The one comfort for the execs was that they hadn't paid for it; they had left that madness to Hitchcock himself. But they had to distribute this grubby artefact. They always thought Humpty Dumpty was due a great fall, but this was precipitous. Why? Why was he doing this?

Humpty himself was, as ever, placid and assured. Whether panic stirred inside him, or whatever passions raged, was a matter for him and him alone. His young screenwriter, Joseph Stefano, blanched at the onslaught. He himself thought it 'a truly terrible movie'. Hitchcock looked at him, patted his knee and told him not to worry. The Master knew what he was doing. He was about to put into place one of the most innovative selling campaigns in the history of popular art.

From the very beginning of the creation of any movie, Hitchcock had marketing in mind. For him the whole process was holistic, and he would be thinking of posters and trailers even at the script stage. The audience, and how to titillate and manipulate them, was always at the forefront of his thinking. He had fashioned his persona as the 'roly-poly ringmaster of a macabre circus of horrors'. Now he was going to exploit it. He set in action a publicity campaign of unprecedented hucksterism, and reinvented the marketing wheel. He mailed each cinema exhibitor a twenty-page manual on how the film should be sold and shown. It was stuffed with tricks and gimmicks traditionally associated with a monster movie or a 3D pageant, and never before used by a top Hollywood director.

Hitchcock detailed precisely how the film should be screened:

> *Close your house curtains over the screen after the end-titles, and keep the theater dark for 1/2 minute. During these 30 seconds of Stygian blackness, the suspense of* Psycho *is indelibly engraved in the mind of the audience, later to be discussed among gawping friends and relations. You will then bring up house lights of a greenish hue, and shine spotlights of this ominous hue across the faces of your departing patrons.*

Such detailing, from a cinema titan, of the whys and wherefores of his stunts seduced the exhibitors into compliance. They were all in on the trick, magicians together.

Hitchcock designed an exploitation-flick poster, which played on the horror element, but was careful to frame its two young stars in lurid fashion, with Janet Leigh in white bra and half-slip and John Gavin stripped to the waist. This was not a highbrow operation. He himself was photographed for a spread in *Life* by the same Gordon Parks who captured Lorraine Hansberry's radiant joy on the opening night of

324

A Raisin in the Sun. Parks embeds the portly face of Hitchcock on crumpled paper as if buried within a bed of flowers, while in a fist he squeezes the life from a rose.

In making so much noise, Hitchcock was at odds with his own earlier reticence. From the start he shrouded the project in secrecy. He bought the rights to a novel by Robert Bloch that fictionalised the serial killing of a real-life murderer called Ed Gein. Having paid a lowly $9,000 for the rights, he then spent what he saved on buying as many copies of the book as he could to keep it from the public. On the first day of photography, he forced cast and crew to raise their right hands and promise not to divulge one word of the story. He refused to give the end of the script to the actors until they were about to shoot it. He withheld the release of stills from cinemas, so the audience could not construct a narrative. And, in a time-honoured ploy to create anguish in a certain fraternity, he refused to allow critics to see it in advance. When reporters balked at this, Hitchcock replied, 'I would like the screening at dead of night in a deserted barn. Preferably a barn with owls.'

Once filming had finished, he made a creepy trailer, featuring himself, in trademark suit, soft-treading his way around his own set like a lost child, hinting at what had gone on there: 'In this house, the most dire, horrible events took place. I don't know who's going to buy it now ...' He makes his way through the motel set, stops and turns to us with a lightly ominous tone: 'Ah, the bathroom'. He steps in: 'All tidied up. The bathroom. Oh, they've cleaned all this up now. Big difference. You should have seen the blood ...' In the course of the trailer, Hitchcock declares one of the two primary hooks for the campaign: 'Please don't tell the ending – it's the only one we have.' The screen goes black, and is followed by a voice stating the primary hook, the command that would change film attendance for ever: 'The picture you must see from the beginning or not at all'.

16 JUNE 1960, DEMILLE THEATER, NEW YORK

A hot summer's day, and cinemagoers queue around the block by New York's DeMille Theater, to see *Psycho*. 'Queues around the block' is an expression we would imagine as old as the movies, but to a large extent it was the product of this movie. The queue itself was an event, insisted on by the master of publicity. He had declared in an extensive ad campaign that (in a cinema first) no latecomers would be admitted. The enforcement of this decree has been a contractual prerequisite for all exhibitors. Up to this point, cinema exhibition had been a continuum. Features, double features, information shorts, news features, coming attractions all streamed continuously and the audience interrupted as they wished. Not for *Psycho*. Everyone had to turn up on time.

As the audience shuffled forwards, they were regaled by Hitchcock, his corrupted plummy voice piped through a tannoy. What was said, and its peculiar tone, gives testament to the weird grip the unmoored Englishman had over his American public. 'I've suggested *Psycho* be seen from the beginning. In fact it is more than a suggestion, it is required.' The last word is elongated on its last arcing syllable, 'requuuuiiirreeedd', like a clammy headmaster. 'This queueing up is good for you – it will make you appreciate the seats inside,' he goes on in tones fat with excess and decay. 'The point of all this is to help you enjoy *Psycho* more. You see...' – his voice leaning in conspiratorially, an odd wetness in his tone – '..I like you. And I want you to be happy ... What more can I say?' The same speech in 2020 would get you arrested; fifty years ago, people were happy to follow the instructions.

As the audience come into the foyer, they are met by a cardboard cut-out of Hitchcock himself, one hand gravely pointing at his watch. A note informs: 'The manager of this theater has been instructed, at the risk of his life, not to admit any persons after the picture starts. Any spurious attempt to enter by side doors, fire escapes or ventilating shafts will be met by force.' The extremity of these diktats, in a parody of autocracy, were carried on in further signs, informing the public that no-one got in late, 'Not even the director's brother, not the President of the United States, nor the Queen of England. (God bless her.)' Beside the cut-outs and stern signs, in the larger venues, an off-duty policeman or Pinkerton agent was placed, to make it look as though the law was behind Hitchcock's admonishments.

A profoundly odd infomercial discusses the release. It shows an executive from Paramount in a shabby suit, behind a wooden desk, reading from a script about the nature of this new mode of distribution. His tone is sepulchral, as if he is a nervous Soviet apparatchik organising a show trial. Beside him are lined up four uneasy theatre-owners and distributors. 'The release of *Psycho* has been an enormous success' they mouth stiffly, as if reacting nervously to a gun off camera.

At an early preview screening, Hitchcock attended with his wife Alma. He nervously paced outside in the foyer. He was awaiting the moment, just two-fifths of the way through, when the story's heroine steps into a shower in an out-of-the-way guesthouse, the Bates Motel. As the moment approached, he leant towards the double doors and held his breath. The gasps were followed by what Peter Bogdanovich remembered as 'sustained shrieking', noise so piercing and continuous it blended with Bernard Herrmann's terrifying score and the sound team's calibrated effects of savagery to create a horrendous cacophony. Hitchcock stood still and smiled. *Psycho* was a hit.

His act of guerrilla aggression against the big, rich, Technicolor films was going to work. He had outflanked them with a vehicle light, mobile and terrifying. Everybody could start counting multiple dollars. The question for the Paramount executives remained.

Why was he doing this?

DO YOU KNOW THE WORLD IS A FOUL STY?

Fifteen years earlier, Sidney Bernstein, a young film producer working in the British Ministry of Information, had been set an impossible task. Embedded alongside army units advancing into the heartlands of Germany were young cameramen. As they encountered newly liberated camps, they were capturing footage unlike anything seen before. What went on in these camps had been known by a few, and rumoured by many, but no-one had a clue about the scale or its depravity. When advancing Soviet armies in the East had told of the camps' atrocities, wise heads in the West had put it down to Russian exaggeration. This footage shut the wise up. It was beyond exaggeration, beyond human imagination.

Captured by the cameramen in unshrinking footage, the images had the blank honesty of the innocent eye. Even now, as shown in the documentary *Night Must Fall*, they punch a hole in the soul. For anyone who thinks they have achieved a conscientious level of exposure, these images take one to new realms. They instruct anew how ignorant we can only be of what the life was like.

Desiccated, emaciated bodies are cast aside across plots of land; some single, some in heaps, some lined up like carpets, uncountable piles bull-dozed into pits. Carriers hike dead bodies, besmirched and beshitten, over their shoulders, and swing them into trucks with a deadened func-tionalism. Shrunken and smeared genitalia flap around like a rebuke to clothing. Dysentery, typhoid and all kinds of disease pockmark every surface. Bundles of bones dribble out of the ovens, and within them jigsaws of limbs parody the idea of human dignity. When the camera goes close, scorched bones tangle together like wiring. Old skin slacks, slashed and burnt. Skulls are stoved in or punctured. Eye-sockets robbed of eyes stare back. Widened mouths scream silence.

Alongside these images are some of the soldiers who had been trained as cameramen – men in their early twenties, cigarettes hanging from their mouths, and boxy cameras hoisted on their shoulders. They look and look with the unknowing courage of the young. No-one was trying to argue or arrange; just to give witness. There is no message, simply a determination to record. To wake humanity up to what it is capable of.

Bernstein was authorised in the spring of 1945 by the Allied forces to turn this footage into a film. It was given the mechanical title *German Concentration Camps Factual Survey*. Its task was to capture the mon-strous realities found during the liberation of Bergen-Belsen, Dachau and Auschwitz. He got together the best editors he could find; a distin-guished writer, Richard Crossman, to pen a voiceover; Trevor Howard to speak it; and, to pull the whole thing together, Britain's greatest living director, Alfred Hitchcock.

Hitchcock had long maintained his rage at the innocence of the UK and the US in the face of the growing threat of Fascism. Moments of anger stud his work in the late 1930s and through the war. Joseph Cotten raps out in *Shadow of a Doubt*: 'Do you know the world is a foul sty? Do you know? If you ripped the fronts off houses, you'd find swine.' The director had always suspected that civilisation was made of thinner fabric than anyone suspected. So, when the call came from Bernstein, he sailed over and went down to Pinewood to watch the footage. There is a section in *Night Must Fall* when one of the editors who watched the first footage, John Krish, describes what it was like to see a continuous four hours of the images from Dachau. In negative, where their ghostliness is electrified, and burns the eye. The editor doesn't break down, nor does he falter, as he describes looking into 'the most appalling hell possible'. There is a stiff courage in the completion of his every sentence, which doesn't bear consideration. The images are as crazed as a Hieronymus Bosch painting, and then you remember that there is nothing aesthetic here. These are the relatives of people still alive today. Hitchcock sat alongside these technicians, and watched the footage in silence. He retreated from Pinewood for a week afterwards. For that week, he would not come near the studios.

Once he had regained his balance, he rolled up his sleeves and tried to shape the unshapeable. He thought it vital to make it as convincing as possible, with no suspicion of fakery. He encouraged maintaining the slow deliberateness of long panning shots, which allowed for no editing trickery. He argued the film must show how Germans went along with their lives normally and pleasantly as horror unfolded on their doorsteps. It was important to remind the viewer how capable of denial the human is. He encouraged simple, almost childlike maps, which showed the staggering extent of the camps across the territory the Nazi regime controlled. He swallowed his fear and sat down with the editors and did what he could.

Hitchcock, Bernstein and Crossman were at pains not simply to condemn the German nation; they wanted to make a piece of work which could instruct humanity of what it was capable, and strengthen resolve for it never to happen again. This required clarity and dispassionate diagnosis. What they presented is a world out of joint, a catastrophe of inhumanity, as real as it is incomprehensible. A ubiquitous psychosis, refined by industrial organisation. The neutral blankness of the black-and-white footage shakes more powerfully than hectoring could.

The work was careful and slow, as it had to be. Too slow. The Americans, who had contributed much of the footage, became impatient. They reclaimed their footage, and cut a short from it, which they entitled *Death Mills*. It was overseen by the great German-Jewish director, Billy Wilder. Hitchcock retreated from the project and sailed back to the US, just as the British government got cold feet. Compounding a tale of shame about their willed ignorance of the existence of the camps, the British government decided that an 'atrocity' film was not right for that moment. Facing a war with the newly settled Jewish population in Palestine, they had no

desire to release anything which made a further argument for the existence of Israel. They also were concerned about German apathy, as they
tried to encourage the people to rebuild their nation from the rubble. It
took seventy years for the film to see the dark of day.

It is impossible to say what influences an artist, impossible to say how
long psychological revelations or revolutions take to trigger a response.
It can be the next day, a year hence, ten years, fifty years. Hitchcock was
always happy to talk about his life and his work. In print, in books, on
chat shows, and in documentaries, he was prepared to talk about his
career as a showman and artist, his roly-poly bonhomie spilling out trade
secrets. He never spoke in public of the images he saw in negative in
Pinewood. Not once.

A SHOWER SCENE

*I think the thing that appealed to me and made me decide to do the
picture was the suddenness of the murder in the shower, coming, as
it were, out of the blue. That was about all.*

In a book of conversations with François Truffaut, during which he is
consistently disparaging about the source material for *Psycho* – the novel
by Robert Bloch – this is the only inspiration Hitchcock cites. Everything
about the film is controlled and deliberate, the flat black-and-white
texture, the play with motifs, the spare Bernard Herrmann music, but
Hitchcock knew that the scene in the shower was the centrepiece. He
lavished a large part of his obsessional heart on it.

Marion Crane is having an affair with a soon to be divorced man.
Against her own nature, she purloins a chunk of cash from her estate
agency business and drives through the night to be with her lover. After
one night sleeping in her car, the next she checks into a motel. She chats
briefly with its owner, Norman Bates, over a sandwich and milk, then steps
into a shower. A figure appears beyond her. A deceptively banal filmic
landscape is suddenly launched into a different stratosphere. A regular
rhythm is suddenly junked, and we see 75 different frames in only 45
seconds. In this short burst, Hitchcock elevates film into a new medium.

Seven days was timetabled on a short shoot to do justice to this
sequence, since everyone knew it was the fulcrum of the film. Saul Bass,

a genius of design, was brought in to help storyboard, thus igniting an ongoing controversy over whose achievement it truly was. But Hitchcock was the man who was there. For seven days he kept his focus steady, always arrayed in his customary undertaker's garb – black suit, white shirt and black tie. The atmosphere was intense, broken only by the presence of Marli Renfro, a carefree nudist and the body double of Janet Leigh. Entirely unaffected by the pressure around her, she queued up for coffee and doughnuts, and sat waiting her turn, stark naked.

In the very first scene of the film, we see a shower over Janet Leigh's shoulder, a wink at what is to come. When Norman shows Marion around her rooms, his tentativeness about the word 'bathroom' cranks up the tension. Even before Marion gets into the shower, cinematic conventions are broken. Hitchcock shoots a toilet, and then a toilet being flushed: neither had been portrayed in mainstream film before. Once Marion is under attack, we are in new territory.

In a firestorm of film, we see the curtain flung open and a figure coming at Marion and us with a kitchen knife. The script demands: 'A KNIFE SLASHING AS IF TEARING AT THE VERY SCREEN, AS IF RIPPING INTO THE FILM'. In rapid jump cuts we close in on Marion's face, hollowing out into an open scream. We see the water streaming top right to bottom left, and the knife rushing through it in the opposite direction. We see hands in action, two determined and definite, two flailing and confused: hands blocking, waving, flapping, stretched out like a starfish against the wall, gripping the shower curtain in weakness, and then reaching out towards us for help. The edit is so fast, it jumps ahead before you've caught up with where you are. Bernard Herrmann's strings punctuate the chopping. What rushes past at synaptic speed had to be manufactured with the most fastidious care and artistry. In the midst of all this, we never see the knife pierce flesh, though our imagination does much worse; nor is there a scrap of nudity, so careful was Hitchcock to steer past the censors.

In a penetratingly blank piece of acting, Janet Leigh falls back against the wall of the shower, and slides down it, her hair plastered thickly to the wall, following her down. Her eyes deadened and replete with horror, she reaches out towards us, unavailing. The look, the wet head of a young woman, surrounded by clean-tiled negative space, is as blank as night. It is the look of a human without love or hope. Shocked and exhausted by life. It could be the look of a suicide. She slumps forward, half out of the shower, and her head hits the bathroom floor. The blood swirls in the water, and disappears down the plughole. The plughole is one of a series of rhyming circles: the shower head, the toilet bowl, her screaming mouth, as Hitchcock leads us down through a series of shrinking rings. Finally, we come in very tight on the most fundamental of all circles to cinema, the eye. The camera goes in tight on her pupil and iris, gyrates slowly as if looking at a swirling supernova, and then pulls out away from pupil, eye and face as she spirals down to her end. The camera tracks back across the floor of the bathroom and, just as it does, there is the barest twitch of her pupil, like a dying animal. We are looking at death; death is looking back at us.

Janet Leigh's gaze is one of many in the course of the film. As she climbs into the shower, Norman removes a painting to look through a peephole in the wall of the bathroom. (The painting he removes is *Susanna and the Elders*, a tale of voyeurism itself, once famously painted by Artemisia Gentileschi.) We look through the aperture with Norman, a thin aperture like a camera's. We are complicit. As they share a sandwich earlier, Marion is transfixed by the dead-eyed stare of the stuffed birds that surround her. On her journey, she is interrogated by the eyeless stare of faceless authority in the form of a highway cop who hides his thoughts behind reflective sunglasses. When we meet Mother, she looks out at us from eyeless cavity sockets. At the end, in one of cinema's most unnerving connections, Norman looks up at us from deep within his own psychosis, and swears he wouldn't harm a fly. But Janet Leigh's gaze as Marion pierces the furthest – it goes through you and beyond.

There are many reasons why the creation of *Psycho* may owe a debt to what Hitchcock witnessed in Pinewood. It is hard to discount the nature of Marion's dehumanising journey towards the motel, as she is intimidated by figures of authority and slowly slips out of her own environment. Norman's obsessive clean-up after the event, his denial of who he is and dissociation from himself, seems to chime with the nature of the camps. Hitchcock was always at pains to push away seriousness or gravity. He called the whole film a prank. But it is hard to separate the repetitive way in which the unappeasable fact of death stares at you from the camps' footage, from the frequency with which it stares at us – hard – from the heart of this film.

BREAKING THE COVENANT

The critics took their revenge for being shut out, as they always will. But the public went crazy for it. Hitchcock's hold over them was still watertight. State police were called in to untangle gridlock at drive-in cinemas. One long queue at the Woods Theater in Chicago threatened to riot as they stood in the pouring rain. The manager rang Paramount to complain they were going to tear the cinema apart. Hitchcock got on the line and commanded, 'Buy them umbrellas.' They did.

Once inside, people went berserk. There was multiple fainting, hysterical folk running up and down the aisles, outraged walkouts and organised boycotts. One young child sneaked in and watched four or five shows in a row, rushing round before each screening to shriek, 'Just wait till you see this'..(One wonders who he grew up to be.) And the numbers were huge – from Boston, the manager cabled, 'Three faintings at Paramount Theater and expect many more among trades when weeks' figure published.' *Psycho* had a mainline into a dark place in the American psyche. During the shower sequence, people grabbed at each other and screamed like abandoned children. After it was over, group paralysis set in. As the film theorist William Pechter described the audience: 'it had the solidarity of a convention assembled on the common understanding of some unspoken entente terrible; it was, in the fullest sense, an audience; not the random gathering of discrete individuals attendant at most plays and movies.'

The film spoke to a world on the brink of change. The other major films of 1959 included *Some Like It Hot*, *Anatomy of a Murder* and *Suddenly Last Summer*, all in different ways nudging their audience into more adult material. Birth control was just around the corner, along with psychedelic drugs. As was a world ready to attack what it deemed intolerable with acts of violence, whether motivated by ideological difference, racial rage, racial injustice, a desire for political change or psychosis. *Psycho* made murder an acceptable form of entertainment. Nothing had portrayed it in such relentless isolation before. Previous horror movies of the 1950s had largely been about alien invasions or science gone wrong. They were fantasies about what could not happen to you. *Psycho* was about making everyone feel unsafe, even in the shower.

Guillermo del Toro has spoken of the central narrative surprise of the film, and the reason why Hitchcock insisted with such intensity on people being present at the beginning. In a brutal and chaotic overturning of all expectations, he was prepared to murder his star, Janet Leigh, a third of the way through the story. Not since Hermione was wiped out of *The Winter's Tale* before the interval had a heroine left a story so early. It was done in the most savage three minutes of cinema committed to film up to that point. In that moment, in not just exiting his star, but slaughtering her, Del Toro says that Hitchcock 'broke the covenant between film-maker and audience – he invented modern cinema'. Nothing in narrative structures was certain any more. Unlike Hermione, Janet Leigh would not return at the end. A film had now portrayed the world as Hitchcock had been shown it in a cutting room in 1945, a world ever vulnerable to man's causeless inhumanity to man.

THIS BLOODY PIECE OF CRAP

Hitchcock went to any and every length to disclaim the importance of his films, and his own stature as an artist. He was a technician first and foremost, interested in pure film, and terrified of being thought so pompous as to bear a message. Or, as he put it, 'I'm more interested in the technique of storytelling by means of film, rather than in what the film contains'. He told Truffaut: '*Psycho* is a film that was made with quite a sense of amusement on my part. To me, it's a fun picture ... It's rather like taking the audience through the haunted house at the fairground.' He told his regular cameraman: 'Here's this bloody piece of crap, and the money doesn't stop coming in.'

This supposed lack of seriousness came under serious assault from the French critics of *Cahiers du Cinéma* – Truffaut, Resnais, Chabrol – who went on to become the Gallic new wave. They adored Hitchcock and dug into his old opus and made it magnum. They were as determined to place the auteur crown on his head as he was to tilt it at a jaunty angle. Their flattery, together with the huge sales and international hullabaloo that followed in *Psycho*'s wake, unbalanced Hitchcock. Arguably he never regained his aplomb. The clockwork within him was delicately assembled, and the response to this film unsettled it. After his next film, *The Birds*, which extends the chaos of *Psycho*'s violence to the natural world, he went adrift and lost his touch. There is a self-consciousness which grows out of acknowledged greatness, which is a worse enemy than struggle.

Psycho did indeed make an extraordinary amount of money and, because of his own early investment, much of that flowed back to the director. It is calculated that he earned $14 million from the film, an astronomical sum. The cynical pleasure he took in making money from a cold-hearted portrait of psychosis is in some ways morally appropriate. Mercenary coldness is perhaps a truer response to atrocity than sentimental redemption. His delight in the financial rewards was compromised by him missing out on the prize he wanted most, the Best Director Oscar. That went to Billy Wilder.

Beneath his obscuring persona, Hitchcock was an artist of terror, the world's and his own. His acute understanding of the fragility of human life was only exacerbated by what he saw at Pinewood. In *Psycho*, he delivered a long-delayed response. He left an indelible image. Janet Leigh sunken down, her wet head plastered against the white wall. Negative space everywhere. Destroyed, cold, satisfied, and an outsider to life. As implacable as death.

21

Belonging

A TALE OF THE GLOBE
(AND MANY CEREMONIES)

'I hope the shows are good.'
'What?'
'I hope the shows are good.'
'Oh. Christ. Yes! I'd forgotten about that.'

We were to launch, the next day, a six-week festival of thirty-six plays at London's Globe Theatre. Each week, six new groups – national theatres, distinguished companies, revered artists – would arrive from the four corners of the earth, and present a Shakespeare play in their own language. Some of the companies were presenting pre-existing shows, but most had chosen to craft new productions. One country, the (new) South Sudan, had created a national theatre company for the event. It all presented a maelstrom of logistical organisation: whether we could get the actors there, how to freight their small allowance of set and costumes, how to dodge political bullets, and how to pull in an audience, shaped our every waking moment. Whether the shows were good seemed less pressing.

We had been so entrenched in technical contingencies, we had taken our eye off this ball. Now, as my producer Tom Bird was suggesting, it suddenly mattered above all else.

Shakespeare's Globe was unique in many respects, not least in that it lived outside both the commercial and subsidised theatre families. This allowed freedom to imagine. When you came up with a mad idea, people were eager to join in. Which meant things happened. Across the time I was lucky enough to work there, we built a new indoor theatre, an outreach touring company and an online VOD platform. We filmed most of the canon, toured *Hamlet* to every country in the world, and held this international festival – *Globe to Globe*. Alongside all the regular ongoing productions. This seemed normal.

Having come up with the idea as a response to an invitation to take part in the Cultural Olympiad of 2012, the Globe's first task was to find the companies. Tom and I set off across the planet. We watched shows in tiny studios, grand prosceniums, rehearsal rooms and amphitheatres. We toasted Shakespeare through the night in chic cafes and dank shebeens. In Beijing, I had to stay upright through a ferocious drink-off with the president of the National Theatre, as vats of rice wine emptied. In Moscow, I argued fiercely with the director of the Vakhtangov about the necessity of pausing in Shakespeare, until – in one of his own long pauses – I noticed he had gone to sleep. In Tbilisi, I arrived shortly after the Russian army had quit the country, and realised how having the tanks of an adjacent country bearing down on your families gives you a particular insight into Shakespeare. We made our choices based on whether people could play the Globe, whether they had the theatrical muscles, and whether we fell in love with them. It was a festival led, as with all things Globe, by the heart.

The jigsaw-puzzle pleasure of fitting plays to cultures followed. In each we endeavoured to make tough choices. So, for the Hebrew company, *The Merchant of Venice*; for the three Balkan companies, the *Henry VI* trilogy, those masterpieces about civil war; for the Palestinians, *Richard II*; and, for Deafinitely, a company working in sign language, Shakespeare's most verbally ostentatious play, *Love's Labour's Lost*. Having sorted this out, the hard job began. Getting the companies to London. With a team of four people. Somehow they managed not to drown in flight-booking, hotel-negotiating, form-filling, sponsor-chasing, visa-applying, set-design, budget-juggling, ego-appeasing, fear-negating and hope-strengthening.

Just when we thought we had more than enough going on, a political issue would explode in our face. The Greeks refused to share festival space with the Macedonians. The Chinese Mandarin contingent wondered why we needed a Cantonese contingent. People wondered how we could countenance a show from Zimbabwe (two brilliantly inventive Black actors climbing from a suitcase and performing *Two Gentlemen of Verona* in Shona). The Armenian genocide intruded its way into the rehearsal room of the show from Turkey. The Afghani production was bombed out of its home rehearsal space by insurgents. And the attempt to have both an Israeli and a Palestinian company appear at the same festival created a world of trouble. We were branded as fascists by left and right. The bigots on the right questioned why we were involving all these foreigners in Shakespeare, and the boutique progressives wondered why we weren't following their rigid rules of exclusion.

Crossing fingers and toes, we got to the eve of our festival, and asked ourselves that most important question, *Would the shows be any good?* And in the same last minute, eve of launch chat, another urgent need arose: 'Fuck! We need a ceremony!' 'A what?' 'A ceremony. Something every company does together.'

VENUS AND ADONIS, 23 APRIL 2012

The opening day dawned unreal with terror, so there was little room for the vanity of nerves. We shuffled in, looked sheepishly at the box-office figures, which were suddenly rather healthy, then went out to join the first company for our newly devised ceremony. It was the end of each company's on-stage rehearsal, and an hour before they went on for their first show. It became a daily event for the next six weeks.

'This is an ancient ceremony,' I said to accusing looks from colleagues, who knew we had cobbled it together the night before. 'It is an offering to Dionysus, the god of theatre and wine.' I then provided the instructions. Two members from each new company were given a bottle of booze each, sent stage right and stage left, and instructed on a countdown to charge downstage and then across the front towards each other, liberally pouring their hooch from the stage into the yard. The liquor chosen was as culturally specific to each company as we could source in the local off-licences. Everyone cheered wildly. It was wasteful, silly and magical.

'This is a modern ceremony,' Tom would say, introducing the second half of our ritual. We asked the youngest member of each company to come to the front of the stage, lean out, and release two helium balloons tied together – one with our company name, one with theirs – as a sign of shared adventure. As the shiny pink balloons bobbled their way through the wide 'O' of our roof, then caught the wind and soared away across London, everyone cheered their lungs out, caught up in the childish delight. Each day, we performed these two quick and scruffy and joyful rites.

Later we travelled the world to witness other festivals which had grown from friendships forged at *Globe to Globe*, and watched other companies perform the same rite. An element of ceremony has been forever woven into public art. We make stuff, and the act of making is intertwined with our relationships to the seen and the unseen world. We fashion things to describe those worlds, to celebrate them and to add to them. That act of creation stirs a jittery pot, full of fears: fears of what we connect with when we make, and fears of the powers of the objects made. Childish superstitions all, but a greyer world without them.

What began from ritual now needs ritual to keep it steady. However demystified and rational we may have become, we still need to give a nod to something greater. These gestures can be private, like touching wood or undergoing routines before performing. Or they can be collective, when a group chant or hold hands or lower their heads. These observances are not a way of winning luck, but an act of humility to go alongside one of creation. They are a way of aligning oneself, of finding just proportion to time and place, and of paying due respect.

That first ritual completed, we found our way into the yard of the Globe and waited for the first show to begin. With props and panic and politics swirling in our heads, we still had no idea whether the festival would work. In our minds we may have been privately anticipating disaster, though without the courage to admit it. Then at two o'clock on a sunny Saturday afternoon, thirty-odd actors and singers from the South African company Isango walked steadily in arrow formation to the front of the stage, stood serene and gracious for a still moment and opened their mouths. The sheer unexpected beauty of what poured out left the audience slack-jawed and heart-happy. Led at the point of the arrow by the regal Pauline Malefane, one of the founders of the company, they took the moment, breathed it into themselves, then defined the shape of what the festival could and should be. Just as we had hoped, the artists had taken over.

What followed for an hour and a half was a glory. The company already had a name for taking classics of the Western canon and reimagining them in a distinctive South African township style. Their *Magic Flute* and *La Bohème* had stunned the world. Now they applied their unique style to Shakespeare's erotic poem of hunting for blood and sex, and of a goddess's relentless pursuit of a proud young man. Seven women from the company, led by Pauline, played different manifestations of Venus, all entrapping one slight and sprightly Adonis. The company reinvented the idea of lyric theatre, blending dance, song, movement and gesture with township wit.

The music was composed by Mandisi Dyantyis, another Isango stalwart, and employed only the simplest instruments – drums, marimbas, whistles and a kudu horn, an early form of the dread vuvuzela. And, in keeping with the Globe, it relied above all on the human voice, which was employed for *Venus and Adonis* in every way from elegiac keening in elaborate harmonics to pop ballad to Zulu warrior chant. The Shakespeare poem is far from a jolly celebration of love and sex – it views festive life as an energy born from opposition to death – and, in this staging, Death was displayed with a tough ferocity that terrified the audience. Katlego Mmusi rampaged on to the stage as a bald, white-painted, scythe-armed skeleton with a lolling tongue of blood-red. This was Death as an active and greedy enemy, as portrayed in the poem. The languages used flitted freely through IsiZulu, IsiXhose, Sesotho, Setswana, English and Afrikaans. It was one of the most authentically Shakespearean entities we ever presented on our stage. The energy, wit and charisma held a full house spellbound, happy and heart in mouth. At its end, the audience roared.

TROILUS AND CRESSIDA – MAORI-STYLE

We took great pleasure in the brilliance of the show, and great relief. We were pleased the ceremony had been devised, and had the desired effect. What we didn't know was that, just as we had needed to invent a ceremony for others, so we needed others to make a ceremony for us. This too was taken out of our hands, by people invoking more ancient gods than Dionysus. Immediately after *Venus and Adonis*, the gift was served up by the company who had travelled furthest to be there.

Our old friend, Rawiri Paratene, is a great actor and an elder of the Maori tribe. From the moment we conceived the festival, we wanted him and his community to be involved. Rawiri is a blast of laughter and energy and cheek, but, a couple of days before, he had sent a sombre email. He asked us to assemble a group of our Globe community, the elders as he called them, on the stage to greet his company. He had proscribed a few simple things to occur, though none of us were prepared for what happened. Gathered on the stage, we waited for a given moment, when the doors were pulled open. Outside was a company of twenty-five Maori, gathered together scrum-tight, a thick block of humanity, babies and grandparents amongst them. All were trembling visibly, their bodies shaking and their eyes flickering here and there. I invited them to come in to the space, and, when they all felt comfortable, they shuffled as a group into the theatre, led by a young actor, his baby over his shoulder, keening an unearthly cry. Still shaking and still alert, they looked like they were entering an alien village and braced for violence. Exceptionally wary to the spirits of the place, they were ready to attack or flee.

I had been asked to make a speech of welcome on behalf of the ghosts of the Globe. I still wake up in the middle of the night cringing with embarrassment at the things I said that afternoon and their synthetic inauthenticity. But the address proved sufficient for them to climb onto the stage at my further invitation. Still braced for violence, in silence they arranged themselves in three ranks, and we corresponded, facing them. On an instant, as one, they erupted into a haka, the Maori war dance. I had witnessed these on television at rugby matches, but the feeling of facing one down, and on an intimate stage, is unearthly. Breath and blood, the heart and the head, all the biology we forget, suddenly becomes actual and crucial within one's body in response to the rawness of the haka's physicality. With eyes popping, and every muscle in their bodies definite in purpose and deadly in power, and with the group elevating each other above the individual to a different realm, it is hard on witnessing it simply to stand one's ground.

At its conclusion, their elder, a formidable man with a bald and conical head, launched into the most possessed rant I have ever witnessed, a large chunk of it inches away from my face. Red-faced, eyes bulging and skin tingling, it was impossible to know how to respond beyond a level stare. I had no idea what he was saying, but felt like I was getting the most almighty telling-off for all my sins. He then went to the centre of the room, let out an unearthly yell, and, on a breath, said: 'Well, that's enough of that bollocks. Great to see ya.' Then with laughter, and cheek, they came to us; we all put our foreheads to theirs, and rubbed noses in greeting. The Maori, as we are now seeing in the ascendancy of Taika Waititi, have an amazing capacity to take what matters seriously and find themselves ridiculous at the same time. They have a large-souled humour.

We weren't sure what they had said; I'm still not. We knew the blessing they brought from the other side of the world was a gift we didn't know we needed, until, with some theatricality, it was given. They were following a proscribed pattern of their own, bound together with ritualised actions and modes of behaviour. In each moment their engagement was so compelling we entered wholly into their reality. Just as in a play.

Those of us still capable of neurosis (most of us) worried that this splendid beginning might be a chimera to be followed by a crash landing. We were concerned the first show may have set the bar a little high. Such doubts were dispersed when the Maori company, NgaKau Toa, swept onto the stage with their bruised masculinity, and their visceral tribal take on *Troilus and Cressida*. Their bodies were almost naked, their buttocks painted with swirling green Pacific patterning, their eyes popping and their feet stamping so hard, it was as if they were trying to pound their way through the earth back to New Zealand.

For Rawiri, having grown up in a school system which banned the use of his own language, and having pursued a lifetime of activism to resurrect Maori speaking, this was a moment of huge significance. The rest of the company shared his passion. To return to London, the capital of their original oppressor, and to lay claim to London's poet in his own theatrical space, in their words, and to do so with supple command and witty authority, was a measure of deliverance.

A further ceremony, and another surprise one, took the still young festival to new heights. The show ended, the audience went wild, and the curtain call erupted into the articulate yell of another haka from the company. The blood was thrilled afresh, and then the audience had a fright. At the back of the yard, where 600 people stand for every show, about sixty New Zealanders, many of them Maori, had discreetly positioned themselves in several lines. As the actors finished their haka, this section of the audience suddenly shrieked back at the stage, threw their coats and jackets to the floor, and hunkered down, pounding out a combative rhythm on the yard floor. At first the audience were terrified, thinking there was about to be an almighty rumble, then thrilled. This was a haka-off, a to-and-fro of battle cries. Two groups of mammoth Maori rehearsing an old war rite in Southwark. No-one had expected it: no-one could have dreamt of anything better.

Standing up in the upper gallery, I had a bird's eye view of the whole event, the stage, the shout-back and the audience in between and all around. At the conclusion everyone went crazy with the delirium of the event, unsure how to decipher it beyond gawping at each other and saying 'Wow!' I watched the babbling audience filtering out of the theatre and saw one group left alone in the middle. It was the hearing-impaired company, Deafinitely, as excited as anyone by what they had seen, signing their insights and excitement to each other, in silent exuberance.

GREAT BLISS IT WAS TO BE PART OF IT

The thirty-four shows that followed were each vividly different, each true to its own culture and traditions. Fear of failure soon gave way to disbelief that the standard could pertain and to simple enjoyment at being alive and there. Happily, the companies wanted to come and play raw, human and dirty. There was no room for concepts, no mediation, no filter – just the plays, those remarkable, eternal human documents, told from the lit eyes of the actors to the lit eyes of the audience.

If the shows were an achievement, so too were the audiences. There was a hard core of fanatics who came to every show – Shakespearean completists who helped to bond the event together. But many others came who had never been to the Globe, or any theatre, before, and they filled the house with their own personality and style. One night we would be in Moscow, the next Athens, the next Mumbai, as London's communities came out to claim their own. We saw five generations of a Bengali family taking over an entire bay; the yard filling with swirls of a proudly unfurled Palestinian flag; the hearing-impaired audience waving their hands in celebration; a group of Albanian children holding an impromptu birthday party in the yard; and the South Sudanese community invading the stage at the end of their show and refusing to leave – the curtain call becoming a party. Every afternoon and every evening, in the rain and the sun, these audiences laid claim to these stories, to their own culture and language, and to each other. A congregation of collaboration and goodwill, they lifted each show to heights it could not have imagined.

It feels poignant now – after Brexit and Trump – to recall an environment when people combined in such benevolent, purposeful and intellectually curious ways. Likewise for the *Hamlet* tour which followed two years later, when the Globe's own company travelled to every country in the world. Such enquiring internationalism seems a thing of the past. We did it so that others in different nations could do it differently and better. As they have since. Even if the idea gets buried in the sand, someone may uncover it in the future, dust it down and improve on it.

Before the performance of *Cymbeline* in Juba Arabic by the newly formed South Sudan company, their director, Joseph Abuk, said a few words. He spoke of the difficulties of his nation gaining independence – of the importance to them of Shakespeare through that struggle, and how *Cymbeline*, with its wonder-filled lesson of forgiveness and reconciliation, spoke powerfully to them. His words were carved out with a light gravity, and finally he thanked us for inviting him to this 'festival of happiness, and of togetherness, and of human ...' – he searched for the word – '... belonging'.

The event was lifted throughout by that generosity and that sense of belonging. Great bliss it was to be part of it. Neither would have fallen into place had an accidental ceremony on our part, and an intended one on the part of our Maori guests, not helped to align it with whichever odd powers or energies smile or frown at these events.

22

History in the Making

A TALE OF BEYONCÉ

14 APRIL 2018, INDIO, CALIFORNIA

The desert air had cooled, but a hot breath of vertiginous anticipation vortexed up towards the stars from the crowd, tens of thousands, packed in tight together. Their bodies held each other upright, their adrenaline pooled to create a communal high so uplifting it seemed they might levitate into the California night sky as one big human balloon. Many had come to worship – their knowledge of the lyrics, its meanings, the details of biography, and the history behind every minuscule previous choice, close to idolatry. Any church would be delighted to have such devoted followers: any rabbi would be proud to be so learned on the Torah.

After an emphatic clattering drum roll, the first of many, and as the stage filled with a bedazzling army of dancers, musicians and singers, the super-screens relayed the propulsive tracking shot of a camera speeding down a catwalk. Fiercely fit dancers wearing Sphinx leotards spun out of the way of the hurtling eye, as if endangered by its headlong progress. After the final one had fallen by the wayside, the camera's destination was revealed. The back of an imperious figure, her shimmering cape emblazoned with the silhouette of the predecessor she worships, Queen Nefertiti from a 3,500-year-old Egypt. She turns with a regal swish, and

347

there she is, a glittering pulse of silver, wearing her ancestral avatar's headdress: Empress Beyoncé.

As the true believers would tell you, when lecturing each other on the meaning behind every decision, context is everything, and here context was queen. Beyoncé, with her brand of hyperliterate hip-hop and pop, was to be the first Black woman to headline at Coachella, traditionally one of the whitest festivals in the US. This was the storming of the Bastille: an unapologetic representative of Black culture, raised in the belly of the south, swanking her way into the traditional preserve of white rockers. The stakes were high. The audience knew it, and as she appeared they hurled psychic goodwill towards her. Even on the West Coast, where being needlessly cool and disaffected is a way of life, they were all merrily losing their shit together.

Drinking in the noise and the adulation flung in her direction, this slight figure in life now stands mighty as an oak of bling. She walks back towards the camera with a sneer of cold command, her legs sashaying past each other. The camera retreats in lowly obeisance. The crowd goes further insane. This is not an entrance: it is a coronation or, more accurately, a deification. They came for a messiah, and they got one. It is a spectacular act of self-aggrandisement, and somehow, by sheer willpower, hard work and native genius, she looks set to pull it off.

Baudelaire called for Manet and his contemporaries to make gods and goddesses from the figures of everyday life. Leonardo and Michelangelo asserted the importance of the artist against the power of secular and religious figures. Lorraine Hansberry had encouraged her generation of Black artists to take a big step forward. Fela Kuti had claimed a status equal to the politicians of his country. Thespis had stepped out from the chorus of singers and separated the individual from the tribe. Whatever the aspiration of these figures – whether individuation, or freedom, or advance – what Beyoncé is doing here is on a new scale. She has gone all-in. This is not the faux-humble stumble forward with an acoustic torch song: this is the full-blast power play of domination. This is Artist-as-Pharaoh, with a smattering of the semi-divine, and it leaves kings and queens looking a bit small-time.

A bank of lights rise to reveal a double pyramid, and soon enough Queen Beyoncé is back at the top of the pyramid, now dressed as the

Platonic ideal of the girl from the hood, in hoodie and Levi cut-offs, her top bearing a crest of Black Power insignia, including Nefertiti. The show is about to begin, the climacteric of the career of a mature woman, whose long journey has moved to this point. She is poised to deliver a once-in-a-generation performance. Ahead of her lies two hours of hyperactive singing and pneumatic dancing, in a Barnum barnstormer blending art, history, heart and politics.

If she can pull it off.

TWINS

Beyoncé headlining at Coachella had been announced for the year before and had stirred up the predictable level of controversy, with a certain white rock contingent uneasy about their playground being occupied by kids who knew how to have more fun. It is always hard to take public space away from the entitled and the sullen. When she had announced she was unable to perform, there was a level of told-you-so schadenfreude from that contingent. Her reason, that she was unexpectedly pregnant, and was due to give birth to twins, brought out a level of high-school misogyny: 'Typical woman – rushing off and having babies.'

The pregnancy was difficult and, in the final trimester, she developed pre-eclampsia and toxaemia. These conditions increase the fragility of the pregnancy and consume what little energy is left from carrying the baby. When one of the twin's hearts stopped beating, she had to undergo an emergency C-section. Having a single baby in normal conditions is an achievement that can inspire little but awe. Managing that after illnesses that drain the body of its usual vital force maximise that awe. The construction of a child has always struck me as the equivalent of the construction of a cathedral inside a body – as spacious, as gracious, and packed with as much variety and complexity. Two at the same time defies metaphor. It is a source of astonishment that mothers are capable of anything more than sitting up for years afterwards.

In the documentary *Homecoming*, which recounts the making and performance of her Coachella show, Beyoncé reveals that she thought the toll taken on her body by twins would be irreversible: 'There were days that I thought I'd never be the same. My strength and endurance would never be the same.' But she was determined to disprove the doubters, and to stake her claim in history. Having spent nine months making two human lives, only a few months afterwards she started a similar gestation period for her gargantuan show.

She had to shed the weight she had gathered, and put herself on an extreme diet of no carbs, no sugar, no dairy, no meat, no fish, no alcohol. She had to rebuild her body from cut and wasted muscles. And she had to rehearse the dancing at the heart of the show for four months of intense physical effort. The choreography is a compulsive, propulsive blend of the pneumatic, the festive and the graceful, and it is relentless. To dance a conga at a party a year after giving birth is an achievement. Beyoncé's resurrection is superhuman. It defies usual human gravity. But this show had to be everything. She wanted to put her 'twenty-two-year career into my two-hour performance'.

Beyond the physical achievement – though it's hard to get beyond that – there was the mental one. 'A lot of the choreography is not technical, it's about feeling. And that's hard when you don't feel like yourself. It took me a while to feel confident enough to give it my own personality.' It was hard to connect to old material, and to reclaim it for her body, after an experience which had rewritten body and spirit. The title 'Homecoming' referred to her return to the home of the stage, the material and the audience. And, more than anything, a return to the home of herself.

Or a new self, augmented by the experience of childbirth. In defiance of the old cultural norms of concealing and hiding a new mother, burying them away and leaving their old self occluded in memories, Beyoncé burst forward, bringing the emotional largesse and spiritual magnanimity which follows making new life, and passing the joy of it on as a gift.

REHEARSAL RESURRECTION

When traditional rockers play Coachella, they often rely on little more than their back catalogue, and their unshakable conviction of their own charisma. A lack of effort is inalienably attached to their conception of their own potency. Making an effort would be letting the side down, like a group of churlish boys being disdainful towards the first in their group who goes over to talk to the girls. Turning up with their guitar, standing still in front of a microphone and intoning, is as much as they believe is necessary. Beyoncé set out to invert all that. She was going to put on a show.

An extravaganza of design, costume, lighting and music – a huge army of band, orchestra, singers, dancers and performers would come together to overwhelm the crowd. This was a major operation that required extended logistical support. Three sound stages were taken for six months: one for music, one for dancing and one for the creatives. The show was scripted in fine detail before they undertook rehearsals. The casting was meticulous, going out in search of those with the technical ability, and with the individual flair to shine. The costumes, worked out with the Balmain creative director, Olivier Rousteing, were thought through in intensive detail, so that the iconography they represented was in step with what the show intended to say.

And one person was in complete control of it all:

I respect things that take work. I respect things that are built from the ground up. I'm super specific about every detail. I personally selected each dancer, every light, the material on the steps, the height of the pyramid. Every patch was hand-sewn. Every tiny detail had an intention.

The show's company rehearsed and rehearsed, and rehearsed. Gradually, Beyoncé's body and her music realigned, though only after intense and continual effort. The film of her driving her body harder and harder gives witness to the virtues of graft. At the beginning she is sweaty and exhausted and off the pace, the bewildered follower of her colleagues. Over time, her body gets to grip with her desires and starts to fall in sync, and she levels up with the troupe. As the opening approaches, she starts to assume the authority of the leader. We see her taking notes – and tough notes – from collaborators, and the transformation of self which rigorous rehearsals necessitate. As she says, 'You gotta be humble, you gotta be willing to look awkward and you've got to study.'

The dedication is brutal and exemplary, and all the while Beyoncé is making what time she can to be a mother to two young babies. An army of assistants helps, of course. It is not the same as bringing up children alone in a council estate, as many begrudgers have pointed out. But it would be fun to see those begrudgers trying to achieve the same dance routines. The ambition was unprecedented and the work behind it had to be equally so. 'We did a lot of things that were very unconventional for a festival show. It takes a village and I think we all worked to our limit'.

On one issue, Beyoncé was very clear: 'I will never, never push myself that far again.'

NO SWAGGERERS HERE

In Shakespeare's *Henry IV*, Mistress Quickly panics at the prospect of the invasion of ancient Pistol into her inn, the Boar's Head. 'We'll have no swaggerers here,' she intones repetitively at the prospect of this hooligan. 'No swaggerers.' It is a wonderfully comic parody of the petit-bourgeois terror of personalities outsized and extravagant. I wonder what she would have made of Beyoncé. From the top, she announces she is going to get her swag on, and she well and truly does. *Homecoming* is probably the most flamboyant display of swaggering ever executed.

The epic scale has a comic edge, of course, but not so much as to undermine its intention to overwhelm. The pyramid, as with the Nefertiti referencing, is both a nod to the African heritage and, to be blunt, awesome. Several times, the apex is used for a new manifestation of the Bey-deity, with flames and spotlights and smoke eruptions underscoring the momentousness. Beyoncé opens with her first solo hit 'Crazy in Love' from 2003, which for many of the young millennials in her audience was the beginning to the soundtrack of their lives. It opens with the swagtastic line, *History in the making*. This doesn't feel like a claim, but more an assertion of fact.

A vast and vigorous brass section powers through this number and many of the rest. Much of the material is culled from her masterpiece album, *Lemonade*, but there are tracks from across her career. The accent throughout on the brass links these disparate parts into a new sound – part jazz, part college band, part sass, part pomp. It gives the whole show a new consistency, with lashings of hot sauce. The brass also supports the grandiosity. Queens and angels have always enjoyed arriving to a fanfare.

Halfway through the show, performing 'Drunk in Love', Beyoncé is isolated from her army, and ascends to the sky lifted by a giant steel arm, which looks like a stairway to heaven. The audience stare up at their idol as if she has slipped the restrictions of mortality and is in touch with celestial spirits. Many seem to be having a spiritual experience themselves. Gloriously, the song couldn't be less suitable for such epiphanies, detailing the joys of sex with hard-core detail. The disjunct, between the framing – Beyoncé's cherubic locks flowing out behind her like a Botticelli angel – and the content – grinding, rubbing and graining – couldn't be more mad, or effective.

The unapologetic swaggering would be a dead and arrogant act if Beyoncé wasn't able to take the audience with her. Which, of course, she can. She has charisma by the bucketload, and even in her most extreme pomp her glare momentarily twitches into the tiniest grin or smirk. Laurence Olivier plays a similar game in his film of *Henry V*. Right at the beginning, he places the briefest smirk, which is then buried for the rest of the film. It is the smallest reminder of the Prince Hal who became the King Henry, and a reminder to the audience that, for all the extreme seriousness, they are not to underestimate him. Beyoncé, too, can pull off extreme grandeur, with the hint that humour lurks within.

She is framed to look immense for the stadium screens and for the film which followed. The camera is frequently beneath her, and the film is a testament to bulbous, globular and curvaceous flesh. In a deliberate push towards inclusivity, many of her dancers and musicians have a wide range of body shapes, and they are happy and proud to give them a good old shake. 'I wanted everyone to feel thankful for their curves, their sass, their honesty – thankful for their freedom.' It is hard to perform your own coronation, and to take so many people with you, in a state of fluid ecstasy. Beyoncé manages it with liberal swagger.

BIG TELLING-OFF

Handel's Italian opera seasons in London were exercises in showmanship with mountains moving and dragons breathing fire. Within all the hullabaloo he placed delicate melodies which trigger the heart. A similar game is played in Coachella, where the imperial thunder is interrupted by oases of privacy.

With the stakes so high, and the scale so monumental, it is astonishing how calm and loose its commander-in-chief is, when she wants to kick back. When her sister joins her towards the end, for an outbreak of competitive vogueing, they look precisely like two young girls playing in their bedroom, and dreaming of being exactly where they are. When her former band, Destiny's Child, flank her, it is as if they have come over to join the party. What they deliver is tightly drilled, but always in a spirit of generosity and gift, not with the deadening hand of neurotic control. When the drums erupt, there is a distinct party mood, which keeps the grandiosity at bay.

This sensibility was nurtured in rehearsal and carried through into performance. She wanted the experience to be 'Thankful for the beauty that comes with a painful history and rejoice in the pain. Rejoice in the imperfections and the wrongs that are so damn right. It was no rules and we were able to create a free, safe space where none of us were marginalised.' It is an inclusive and celebratory space which is opened out to the audience. When, in one dance number, the cymbals whirr and gyre with quick-wristed frenzy at the front of the stage, they catch and flare the light. It is as if we are back in Akhetaten, and Nefertiti's worshippers are holding up metal sheets to catch and share the light from their god, Aten.

At the centre of the emotional content of the show, as with the album *Lemonade*, is an incident of such intense privacy it feels intrusive to share it. The heart of the story is an infidelity, the feelings of betrayal and loss and rage that followed, the near collapse of the relationship, and its eventual redemption. The fact that it coincides almost precisely with what was known of the marriage of Beyoncé and her equally legendary husband Jay-Z, doesn't require Sherlock Holmes to make a biographical reading. It also makes *Lemonade* and *Homecoming* one of the biggest public telling-offs ever delivered to a husband.

This is the *Hamlet* trick of inverting something intensely private into the broadest possible arena, while retaining its earnestness. Hamlet says 'Now I am alone,' then tells three thousand tightly packed people in the play's first Globe performance about the dregs and the lees of his existence; Beyoncé breaks free from the imperial register and opens her soul in revealing the most painful and humiliating matter the heart can know. The larger part of her reaction inclines to rage. The fury is in the lyrics, the stomping movement, the four-square stance and the deadpan glare. The rebuke to the errant husband opens out and extrapolates to a hunger for independence and a wholly explicit sexual control. This looks like a revenge taken on all those who deceive and exploit, and implies that today's cheated wife is tomorrow's world leader.

Throughout the rehearsals, Jay-Z is a low-key and supportive presence. He sits beside his wife as she delivers tough notes to her team, and looks awestruck by the strength of her leadership. 'OK, guys,' he mutters as he slips out of one rehearsal, acknowledging his diminished status in this environment. In the performance he comes on to share one song. Their rapport and ease together is transparent as they mouth each other's words while the other is singing. Once done, Jay-Z slips away as if he knows it is not his show. It is a charming act of modesty and a deliberate transference of power.

The matter of the show – rage and pain – is the furnace which smelts the metal, to hold the edifice upright.

BRINGING THE CULTURE

Both the live *Homecoming* performance and the subsequent film are saturated with resonances from Black history. Quotes from Maya Angelou, Toni Morrison, Nina Simone, Alice Walker, and other icons, are interspersed throughout. The voice of Malcolm X rings out sternly at the end: 'The most neglected person in America is the Black woman.' There is gratitude from Beyoncé to Coachella for inviting her, but also a rebuke for being the first: 'aint that bouta bitch'.

The concept for *Homecoming* was based around the cultural traditions of the Historically Black College and University (HBCU) experience. Greek sororities, majorettes and marching bands invoke that world. The letters 'BAK' sparkle across the front of her hoodie, a tribute to the Divine Nine, the umbrella organisation of African-American fraternities and sororities. Beyoncé did not attend college herself, skyrocketing into a pop-star life at a young age, but her father was an alumnus of Fisk College, and she spent much of her childhood rehearsing at Texas Southern University, an HBCU in Houston. She describes her vision behind the show:

> *Instead of me pulling out my flower crown, it was more important that I brought our culture to Coachella.*

Symbolism from the Black Lives Matter movement, and from the 1960s Black Panther movement, surfaces over and over. Beyoncé has always been unashamed to make a point, even in enemy territory. At the 2013 Super Bowl, in the presence of tens of thousands of jocks in the stadium and millions more on television, she dressed her dancers in black leather and berets, and had them proudly echo the Panthers in raising clenched fists into the air.

Greater than the rage is the achieving. This display of entitlement, and defying traditional categories to excel in whatever she wished, is the most eloquent way of pushing back against the limits imposed on African-American possibility. Being a singer and controlled is now no longer enough. Being one's own manager doesn't suffice. A fulfilled artist is now her own mogul, her own curator, and her own lifestyle designer. She runs and creates her own reality, and in the process shifts that of all who watch in awe.

> *I wanted to be a powerhouse and have my own empire and show other women when you get to this point in your career, you don't have to share your money and your success – you do it yourself.*

This is the final exemplum of the command of the matriarch of the Younger family in Lorraine Hansberry's play: 'Push on out and do something bigger.'

ULTIMATE

There is something ultimate about *Homecoming*. In its unapologetic grandeur it feels like the end of one of history's curves of ambition. In its scale, its naked greed for pleasure – both sexual and consumerist – and in its outsized summation of a life and career, it feels ultimate. Certainly, it is hard to imagine anything as triumphalist happening again for a long time from the perspective of a world shrunken by Covid-19.

Being the best – at drinking Cristal, grinding, collecting cash, controlling one's world – has always been close to the heart of hip-hop and rap. It is achievement as revenge, and the historical reasoning is compelling. Exceptionalism is a cause in itself. Everything about *Homecoming*, including the extraordinary recovery from childbirth only a year before, is designed to flout normal human expectations.

The meaning of the show is not only held in the content of the songs, nor solely in the frequent political referencing. It is in the dreamlike spectacle of a woman defying gravity. The pleasure, and the alarm, is in watching a human being, like Icarus, flying up towards the sun.

Encounters and Connections

AN AFTERWORD

All of us have treasured encounters with art, moments that somehow answer many of our questions, feed our hungers. Everyone can remember occasions when the scattering shrapnel of history, and the swirling atoms of personal confusion, meet a piece of work which somehow helps such chaos to dance for a while. Events that seem to occur in some hole in time, in which mysteries are briefly and tantalisingly illuminated.

One such that I witnessed was Anoushka Shankar, the sitar virtuoso, playing her own score for the Indian classic film *Shiraz*, a silent black-and-white classic from 1928, whose subject was the creation of the Taj Mahal. I tried afterwards to burble something clever about what I had just seen. My companion for the evening, the director Kathy Burke, was blunter: 'Fuck all that, it was just the best of everything.'

The evening incarnated three openings, three seismic moments, and managed to give the impression you were present at each. The first was the subject of the film, the creation of the Taj Mahal, that marble dream built from love and grief for a dead wife. In 1607 – just as *L'Orfeo* was ringing in ears in Mantua and Okuni was stepping lightly in Kyoto – the young Shah Jahan fell in love with Arjumand, a young bead-seller in a market. In 1631, after a long marriage as loving and public as that of Nefertiti and Akhenaten, Arjumand died delivering their fourteenth child, her husband beside her. Stricken with grief, he dived into a depth of mourning unmatched since Orpheus. Unable to find his way to the underworld, he resolved to memorialise his wife with the greatest monument to love the world had seen.

An unprecedented gathering of architectural influences blending Muslim, Persian, Hindu and Mongol traditions, the Taj Mahal required 20,000 workers putting in a twenty-year shift to shape the surrounding countryside, to build its surrounds and sculpt the jewel at its centre. The result is a miracle of mathematics, geometry, gardening, watercoursing, the human and the sacred. A dazzling technicolour celebration of the world's pigments, it choreographed into a frozen dance marble from Makrana, turquoise from Tibet, sapphire from Sri Lanka, carnelian from Arabia, jade from China, jasper from the Punjab, and rich blue lapis lazuli, that metamorphic rock, from Afghanistan. The different colours were able to match and enrich the milky white of the morning and the saffron blush of the evening. As Tagore described it, 'a teardrop on the cheek of eternity.'

On seeing the completed building for the first time, the Shah wept. Later deposed from power and imprisoned, he died in bed, looking at a mirror placed so it might reflect his love-struck dream of a building. Its ability to float in a shimmering haze at dawn or in moonlight still casts a spell. The film summons the magic of its first unveiling, a unique vision of earth and heaven in harmony.

The second seeming opening was the film, an international cooperation whose creators truly justify the title movie moguls. *Shiraz: A Romance of India* first opened in 1928, showcasing armies of acting talent and film craft, and introducing on an epic scale the potential of Indian film. A German director, Franz Osten, and some British technicians, were put to work by the Indian producer and star, Himanshu Rai, who dreamt of telling Indian stories to global audiences. He succeeded, founding the legendary company Bombay Talkies. Rai was able to persuade a collection of maharajas - the rulers of Jaipur, Udaipur and Mysore - to throw open the gates of their palaces as locations, and to help furnish the film with extravagant jewellery and costumes. They emptied their zoos to help provide the 1,000 horses, 300 camels and seven elephants which enliven the film. One of the latter acts as a potential executioner in a Hitchcockian suspense sequence, his foot poised to crush the leading man's skull in an act of punishment remitted at the last minute. The maharajas contributed 50,000 extras to fill out monster battle scenes, to enact unending caravans through deserts, and to people vast tableaux of religious ceremony and prayer. The film is not set in seventeenth-century India – it takes you there.

A fresh take on the creation of the Taj Mahal, its invented backstory tells of the enduring passion of a natural artist and architect, falling in love with the heroine as a youth, when she is kidnapped and brought into the world of the Shah. He follows her there but is refused admittance. Rejected, punished and tortured, he grows old and blind as a beggar. After the death of his beloved he is redeemed by designing the Taj in her honour in a state of visionary ecstasy.

A romantic melodrama of sumptuous scale, the film could be ridiculous, were it not for the compositional brilliance with which its outsize imagery is framed, and exquisite acting. It includes some of the most enchantingly honest child actors caught on film until Satyajit Ray's *Pather Panchali* thirty years later. All the cast play emotional scenes with a tender unfussy truth which would have delighted Elia Kazan. Throughout, alongside the size and noise, the film flushes out a host of moments of ripe stillness, as brimful of life as an unpunctured peach. It shone afresh in a beautifully restored new print.

The third element in the trinity was the new score composed by Anoushka Shankar, and played live by her and her group. Satyajit Ray had praised *Shiraz* for its 'decided penchant for realism'. Ray's own early achievements in cinema were enabled by the scores of Anoushka's father, Ravi. For the three *Apu* films, all composed when Ravi's life was something of a whirl, he would turn up, watch the film once, then improvise, live and plangent, to his second viewing. And there was the score. That garage-band rawness, only accessible to those with the highest skill, is the perfect accompaniment to the roughhouse realism of Ray's early films. Anoushka was aware of the inheritance when she was asked to score this film from an earlier age; 'It was hard for me, because as a novice, there wasn't an expert shaping the process. I felt a lot of pressure to do justice to the film with no-one telling me what they'd intended.'

Her score became an extended experiment in time. For the premiere, at the Barbican in London in 2017, she led an octet working in two different musical languages: two Indian percussionists, Anoushka herself on the sitar, an Indian flautist, an Indian violinist, a clarinetist, a pianist and a cellist. The score was made purely for the last three, playing Western instruments; for the classical Indian musicians, a hundred pages of notes was not going to serve. For them, Anoushka's team created audio cues and Indian notation to play and learn by ear: 'They would have little prompts in their ears to say *in four bars play raga-this for four bars*.' Two entirely different time schemes were allowed to coexist with inventive freedom. A task of equal difficulty was for the Indian musicians to restrain their need to improvise within the rigour of staying true to images locked in sequence. 'Part of the joy of their music is playing games with time – stretching time, concentrating it and concertina-ing it. Film with its emphasis on precision at each moment could be claustrophobic. It's two hours of having to stay focused to the millisecond, keeping up with something that doesn't stretch or slow with us, but we have to keep alongside.'

An already complex chronological jigsaw puzzle was rendered far more difficult, when Anoushka discovered that the print she had been working on for months was set at the wrong speed. It was seventeen minutes shorter than the fully restored print they were going to show. 'I just thought it was the quality of the cinema that people looked that tiny bit sped up,' she remembered. 'I had to redo the whole thing just three weeks before; I nearly had a heart attack, I nearly lost the plot.' Remarkably (and the lesson of this book should hopefully have proved it possible), from such a calamity an extraordinary triumph emerged. With Anoushka sitting, like her father, at the centre of the circus, still and poised to begin, and then ferociously virtuosic when necessary, the marriage of Western and Eastern music, of improvised freedom and rigorous restriction, afforded a rich musical experience which partnered the film perfectly, and lived happily in its own splendour.

Here we were, a couple of thousand of us, in a London concert hall, drawn back to the very beginnings of our public art, back to the earliest cave rituals, pictures on a wall, the light flickering from a projector rather than from a fire, music stoking the heart and soul, telling and hearing a story that holds us in its grasp and tells us new truths about worlds seen and unseen. The technology may have developed; the show remained the same.

The evening was special for its brightness and its reach. It serves as a conclusion here because it helps to illuminate many of the mysteries I have explored within these tales. Taking significant cultural moments, bright points from time and space, it layered them on top of each other, as Stravinsky loved piling his hard rural rhythms atop each other to forge something new.

Unashamedly beautiful in all incarnations, as building, film and glorious music, the evening delighted in its own dazzle. Beauty alone can be meretricious, but, without proportion and harmony and truth, art is a poor lot. Life well arranged on stage, notes well arranged in music, matter well arranged in art, all help take us to a place where we can float a little in a well-arranged universe, and then when we settle back down we discover we too are a little rearranged. Oscar apostrophised beauty – perhaps a little too much – but even the Sex Pistols would have been lost without it.

I loved it for the rigour of its craft. Anoushka sits at the end of a chain of teaching. She learnt the sitar from her father, Ravi, who learnt it from his guru, Baba, and on through centuries of knowledge passed from teacher to student. This is no easy handing on of a set of skills; this is endless hours spent learning to be the best in the presence of brutal masters. Baba used to tie his own hair, and that of his students, to a beam which crossed his roof, so that, however hard and long the practice, they couldn't nod off. Like Michelangelo with his Carrara marble, Nijinsky punishing his corps with endless rehearsal, Monteverdi banging out his madrigals, or Hitchcock with his seven long days set aside to achieve forty-five seconds of film, these people knew that access to the highest goals doesn't come without broken fingernails.

The event was properly international, curious and hungry for the influence and inspiration of others, without losing sight of its own distinctness. The Taj Mahal was the most extraordinary act of combining, gathering seemingly irreconcilable faiths and aesthetics into a piece of perfection. The film *Shiraz* brought Western technical know-how to make a story totally Indian, on a scale and with a poetry that would have been beyond the rest of the world. Anoushka brought together two different classical traditions working from different time schemes, and managed to get them to dance together with a printless step. The artists encountered here have all revelled in the fresh consciousness delivered by work from different cultures. Manet loved the Japonisme, much of which emerged from the *ukiyo* tradition so closely allied to kabuki. Xiao Lu was responding to a slew of conceptual ideas which invaded China from across the globe. Ravi Shankar's career was built on acts of transnational communication. As the Hong Kong director Tang Shu-wing once said to me, 'I love differences. It is only through them we discover our similarities.'

Shiraz, in this new incarnation, also started fresh conversations across time, feeding on the past, reconnecting all together in the now, and sending new connections towards the future. These bright points in our cultural history often come from the least likely places, yet all feed off each other's brightness. Fela Kuti worshipped Handel above all other musicians. Beyoncé reveres Fela and Nefertiti and Lorraine Hansberry. Hansberry hymned the virtues of Michelangelo and Arthur Miller. Miller learnt from Williams. Williams revered Wilde. Wilde worshipped at Michelangelo's *David*. All are chakra points, alongside many others, in our cultural history, a series of events impossible to chart on a line, or a two-dimensional map. Something outlandish like Einstein's space-time cylinder would be all that could serve. They are points on a nervous system wiring the body of time, songlines through our troubled history, all coexistent.

Each new event adds complexity to that network. Each adds a perspective, and by doing so expands the possibilities of how to imagine the future. The collision of multiplying perspectives –whether it is the many souls creating the Taj Mahal, the thousands of people forging the film *Shiraz*, and Anoushka providing the perfect music all colliding together, or the many other collisions that take place in this book – all ignite prodigious possibilities. In that very prodigality there is hope. All create space for the artists and for us the viewers to perceive, amongst the infinite of other viewpoints, a brief impression of the sacred which walks beside all great art. When we are lucky we catch a glimpse of 'something far more deeply interfused', as Wordsworth phrased it. Even through the grey mist thrown up by our anger and sin, we spy a little of the wonder and the goodness that lies beyond.

Each tale effects some quantum of change. They needed to then, and still do. The future is best transformed by reconfiguring the way we imagine it. As Brecht told us, 'Art is not a mirror to reflect the world but a hammer with which to shape it.' They may do so dazzlingly, wowing one and all, and transforming perceptions in the instant. *Psycho*, the *David* and the *Messiah* all arrived with blasts of trumpets. They may fail in their own here and now, and have to wait for the tides of history, slowed by cynicism and idleness, to reveal them anew. Nefertiti, Anna Akhmatova and Okuni travelled harder roads. But, even if it takes millennia, failures are not necessarily failures. Any push towards brightness is a move in the right direction.

In our ceaseless clumsy fumble for understanding, these are events that have helped to bring us closer to ourselves, and each other. One of the ways we best safeguard our future is observing and noting such moments of freedom and of goodness from our past. And creating new ones in the present, to gift to the future.

Early in the process of composing this book, I was invited by an old colleague to one of a series of events he runs in a beautiful but neglected church, in the out-of-the-way London neighbourhood of Walthamstow. Something of a gentle saint, and a distinguished player of the double bass himself, when not playing with top orchestras, he has spent much of his life travelling the country playing for free in shopping centres and pubs. For years he has persuaded, by the simple example of his goodness, world-class colleagues to play at his Wednesday evenings in Walthamstow. He pays a modest fee; he takes nothing for himself. They play to seventy or eighty elderly folk, spread out across pews, clutching their frayed coats around them in the cold, and listening with a misty-eyed intensity.

I had just listened to the great Trevor Pinnock casting a spell over the scattering of grey and white hairs with his harpsichord, the spareness of its clean notes asserting a thrilling authority over the echoey space. As I was leaving, I praised one particular Bach piece to my friend.

'Hold on,' he said and rushed off into the night. Moments later, he returned clutching a CD. 'Here, I had that piece in the car. You can have it.'

'I really can't.'

'Of course you can – what is life but to share things?'

*

End Matter

PHOTOGRAPHS
INFORMAL BIBLIOGRAPHY
ACKNOWLEDGEMENTS

Photographs

PUSH ON OUT AND DO SOMETHING BIGGER

18 Lorraine Hansberry poses for a portrait in her New York City apartment at 337 Bleecker Street (where she had written *A Raisin in the Sun*). *David Attie/ Getty Images*

GIANT

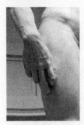

38 Michelangelo's *David* (sculpted 1501-04), in its current home in the Galleria dell'Accademia, Florence. *Wikimedia Commons*

I, AN ACTOR

54 Dionysus with two maenads – detail of Attic red-figure krater by the painter of the Niobids, 460 BC. *Museo Archeologico, Ferrara, DeAgostini/ Getty Images*

THE EYE OF THE STORM

66 Ravi Shankar with his friend, George Harrison, at the time of the Concert for Bangladesh. *Michael Ochs Archives/Getty Images*

ASTONISH ME!

82 Igor Stravinsky's *Rite of Spring* production at the Théâtre des Champs-Élysées, Paris, 1913. *Charles Gerschel/ Alamy Images*

BOWLS OF LIGHT

102 Excavator Ludwig Borchardt (left) brought Nefertiti to Berlin after her discovery in 1912. © *Staatliche Museen zu Berlin, bpk-Bildagentur*

JUMPING ROCKS

114 Twelfth page of *Kunijo Kabuki Ekotoba* (illustrated manuscript of Kuni's kabuki) showing Izumo no Okuni, the founder of kabuki theatre, on stage. The manuscript dates from the Edo period, Keich era (1596–1615). *Wikimedia Commons*

KILLING US SOFTLY

128 Frontispiece of the score of Monteverdi's *L'Orfeo*, published in Venice in 1609 by Ricciardo Amadino. *UtCon Collection/Alamy Stock Photo*

BEFORE

144 Alfred Jarry, *Deux Aspects de la marionnette originale d'Ubu Roi*. Premiered at the Théâtre de l'Œuvre, 10 December 1896. *Wikimedia Commons*

THE FEMALE GAZE

160 Édouard Manet's portrait of Victorine Meurent (c.1862), now in the Museum of Fine Arts, Boston. *Francis G. Mayer/ Getty Images*

AN ACT OF VIOLENCE

178 The artist Xiao Lu's *Panel No. 6* (15 Shots Series), 2003. Image from *www.liveaction.se*

SOMETIMES – THERE'S GOD – SO QUICKLY

194 Elia Kazan ('Gadg'), on set in the 1950s. *United Archives GmbH/Alamy Stock Photo*

AN IDEA OF HEAVEN

216 English opera singer Susannah Maria Cibber, in an engraving by John Faber the Younger after Thomas Hudson (1746). *Wikimedia Commons*

A DAY OF RECKONING

232 Fela Anikulapo Kuti on stage in 1982. *AF archive. Alamy Stock Photo*

A SONG ALREADY SUNG

246 Anton Chekhov with actors of the Moscow Art Theatre in 1899. Chekhov is on the left, staring at the camera through his glasses. *Lebrecht Music & Arts/Alamy Images*

A VERY BRITISH GLASNOST

264 Damien Hirst (left) and Angus Fairhurst dressed as clowns at their spin-painting stall, A Fete Worse Than Death, Hoxton, London, July 1993. *Guy Moberly/Alamy Stock Photo*

WRIT ON WATER

280 Sarah Kane, September 1998. *Marianne Thiele/ Ullstein bild via Getty Images*

LEVITY

292 Scene from first production of *The Importance of Being Earnest*, 20 March 1895, featuring Alan Aynesworth (Algy, left) and George Alexander (Jack). Originally published in *The Sketch*. *Wikimedia Commons*

PAPER AND FIRE

310 Kuzma Petrov-Vodkin's portrait of the writer Anna Akhmatova in the Tretyakov Gallery, Moscow. *Photo12/ Universal Images Group via Getty Images*

DEATH LOOKS AT US

322 Alfred Hitchcock and Janet Leigh on the set of *Psycho*, directed by Alfred Hitchcock. *Sunset Boulevard/Corbis via Getty Images*

BELONGING

336 An on-stage haka is performed by New Zealand's Ngakau Toa company on 23 April 2012, at the launch of the *Globe to Globe* international Shakespeare theatre festival *Yui Mok/PA Images/Alamy Images*

HISTORY IN THE MAKING

346 Beyoncé Knowles performs on stage during the 2018 Coachella Valley Music And Arts Festival on 21 April, 2018 in Indio, California. *Kevin Mazur/Getty Images for Coachella*

ENCOUNTERS AND CONNECTIONS

358 Still from the Franz Osten film, *Shiraz: A Romance of India*, featuring Enakshi Rama Rau as the heroine, Selima. *Juno Films*

Informal bibliography

These tales are impure history, blending the fine work of more scrupulous historians, some proper grown-up research, some scampering through the branches and digging in the roots of the internet, an accumulated weight of personal experience, and the benefits of long conversations with experts. I have enjoyed films alongside documentaries, and novels beside sober studies, believing that imaginative responses are often as stimulating as factual ones. It was a pleasure to fall into the work of these artists and the worlds they lived in and I hope this book prompts others to go travelling in the same places. They will find masses of great material awaits.

For almost every chapter, there was a single book, or a couple, which opened the door to the world I was writing about and helped steer me through. I am indebted to all of these books, as well as others.

The compilation of Lorraine Hansberry's writings, *Young Gifted and Black*, is a good primer for her and also for living a life. *Looking for Lorraine* by Imani Perry is a personal revealing of her importance and a great telling of her story. Philip Rose's inimitably titled *You Can't Do That On Broadway* filled in the backstage gaps.

From Marble to Flesh by A. Victor Coonin is an elegant summary of the creation of David; *Michelangelo: His Epic Life* by Martin Gayford is an insightful steer through a huge subject; the *Poems and Letters of Michelangelo* are worth dwelling on; Vasari's *Lives* continues to be a model.

Ravi Shankar's life has been recently and expertly told in *Indian Sun* by Oliver Craske. Howard Worth's documentary *Raga: A Journey Into the Soul of India* tells an incredible story of global ambition and devotional craft.

There is a wealth of great writing on *The Rite of Spring*, including a brilliant essay by James Wolcott and a revelatory television film written by the late great Kevin Elyot, *Riot at the Rite*. Richard Buckle's biography, *Nijinsky*, was a treasure stumbled on in an old book store.

Egyptology is a fabulously rumour-filled and gossipy world to fall into and I was indebted to Nick Drake's imaginative reconstruction of that world in *Nefertiti: The Book of the Dead*, alongside other detailed studies.

There is a lot of surmise around Okuni, much of it led by the Japanese scholar Sawako Ariyoshi, whose stunning magical-realist novel, *Kabuki Dancer*, received none of the attention it deserves.

For *L'Orfeo*, as for the *Messiah* and for the *Rite*, I was grateful to *First Nights: Five Musical Premieres* by Thomas Forrest Kelly, a feast of musicological detail.

The Sex Pistols first night in Manchester has already entered the realms of myth, and *I Swear I Was There* by David Nolan is a great work for unpicking the bigger fibs from the lesser.

There are several entertaining novels about Meurent, Manet and the Impressionists, alongside one classic, *The Masterpiece* by Zola. There is also a brilliant piece of art history and storytelling to be enjoyed in *The Judgement of Paris* by Ross King.

Xiao Lu's is a story far too little told, so we are lucky that we have her own passionate telling, *Dialogue*. I can't recommend it highly enough as the testament of an artist.

Anything by John Lahr is immediately canonical, and his biography of Tennessee Williams, *Mad Pilgrimage of the Flesh*, is a classic. This, alongside his writings about Arthur Miller in various books, have long been an inspiration. I also enjoyed Elia Kazan's monumental autobiography, *Kazan*, and Richard Schickel's *Elia Kazan: A Biography*.

The Messiah in Dublin is exhaustively documented, but nowhere better than in *Hallelujah* by Jonathan Bardon, a work of revelatory local detail and particular gems.

Handel's great fan Fela Kuti is memorialised in many media, but the most authentic voice I found was in *Fela: This Bitch of a Life* by Carlos Moore, which includes many of the musician's own compelling words.

I've been reading Chekhov biographies all my life, and Donald Rayfield's *Anton Chekhov: A Life* remains the most reliable and enjoyable. *My Life In Art* by Konstantin Stanislavsky is always good for a laugh, if only in considering the amount of headaches it occasioned for young actors.

There is a plethora of Internet information around the YBAs, and *Lucky Kunst* by Gregor Muir is a richly funny sifting of all the stories.

As with Chekhov, I find a Wilde biography hard to resist, most recently returning to the books of Neil Bartlett, Matthew Sturgis, Philip Hoare and Neil McKenna. Fresh perspectives recently from Emer O'Sullivan in *The Fall of the House of Wilde* and Eleanor Fitzsimons in *Wilde's Women* have enriched the landscape. Every first night deserves a study as detailed and caring as that found in Joseph Donohue's reconstructive critical edition of the text of the first production of *Earnest*, a treasure which the author was kind enough to send to me.

Routes in to Anna Akhmatova include some stunning films as well as her poetry, but the best told is *Anna of All The Russias* by Elaine Feinstein.

The screenwriter Stephen Rebello has huge knowledge and passion for his subject in *Alfred Hitchcock and the Making of Psycho*. The other guiding spirit of this chapter is the terrifying documentary *Night Will Fall*, directed by André Singer, which handles its nightmare material with astonishing humanity.

The true book about Beyoncé waits to be written.

Acknowledgements

On the grown-up research front, I have to thank the distinguished classicists Lucy Jackson and Armand D'Angour for giving me a steer through the world of Thespis and Orpheus. Bridgett Pride at the Schomburg Centre in New York opened some fascinating boxes of Lorraine Hansberry material, and was kind enough to scan them mid-lockdown. Kai-Chuan Chapman and Alexandra Ault showed me some of the British Library jewels. And Adam Waterton in the Royal Academy Archives pushed me helpfully in various directions. Many thanks for help with various translations to Isaac Hui, Cherie Abeyawardene, and Colin and Sandy Cheung.

I am grateful for long conversations on specific subjects to Anoushka Shankar, Stephen Daldry, Norman Rosenthal, Trevor Pinnock and Nick Drake. It was a particular thrill to converse with Xiao Lu in Beijing, and I am grateful for her long written responses. At the beginning of the process, I enjoyed a trip to Dublin, where I met up with Anthony Roche, Chris Morash, Frank MacGuinness and Mairead Delaney in the Abbey Archive. At the time I thought I would be writing about O'Casey and Synge and Brian Friel's *Translations*. Then I discovered that Chris Morash had got there first, and unimprovably, in his *History of the Irish Theatre*. However 'by indirections we find directions out', and these conversations helped my thinking for the whole book.

The book was first commissioned by Helen Conford, and generously inherited by Andrew Franklin, at Profile. It has been a privilege and a pleasure to be edited by Mark Ellingham, whose capacity to give a book a good shake has been constantly invigorating. His choice of beautiful photos reflects his enormous passion for the aesthetics of a book. Further thanks to Nikky Twyman for skilful proofreading, and to Henry Iles and Peter Dyer for helping to make the book a thing of elegance. Everyone I have met and worked with thus far at Profile – Mark, Niamh Murray and Anna-Marie Fitzgerald – has proved a delight, and I look forward to further engagement. Along the way, and when orphaned, I was lucky enough to be adopted by the agent Natasha Fairweather, which feels rather like being picked up by a Rolls Royce when hitchhiking.

My thanks to Marcus Coles for allowing me room away from other projects while writing this book. The book's writing began in Torun in Poland while enjoying the hospitality of Tim and Hanke O'Grady, and at other moments I was made welcome by Gordon Snell in Dublin, Quentin and Rowena Seddon in Somerset, Isabella Tree and Charlie Burrell in Sussex, and Patrick and June Dromgoole in Ayrshire. My thanks for their generosity and support.

Over the length of the project I have been blessed with some supportive and critical reading from Patrick and Jessica Dromgoole, Patrick Walsh, John Light, John Dove, Eric Schlosser and Malu Ansaldo. Particular thanks to Dinah Wood for regular scrutiny.

My initial research team during lockdown numbered two daughters, Siofra and Grainne. Together with the third, Cara, they have been my constant companions throughout the writing of this book and through years which they have made blessed and blissful. Even if the seas are choppy, their capacity to forge forward, both as brilliant individuals and keeping the raft of family tightly lashed together, quite simply takes my breath away. This book is for them.